THE ROUTLEDGE DIASPORA
STUDIES READER

The Routledge Diaspora Studies Reader provides a comprehensive resource for students and scholars working in this vital interdisciplinary field. The book traces the emergence and development of diaspora studies as a field of scholarship, presenting key critical essays alongside more recent criticism that explores new directions. It also includes seminal essays that have been selected specifically for this collection, as well as one brand new paper. The volume presents:

- introductions to each section that situate each work within its historical, disciplinary, and theoretical contexts;
- essays grouped by key subject areas including religion, nation, citizenship, home and belonging, visual culture, and digital diasporas;
- writings by major figures including Robin Cohen, Homi K. Bhabha, Avtar Brah, Pnina Werbner, Floya Anthias, James Clifford, Paul Gilroy, and Salman Rushdie.

The Routledge Diaspora Studies Reader is a field-defining volume that presents an illuminating guide for established scholars and also those new to diaspora.

Klaus Stierstorfer is Chair of British Studies at the University of Muenster, Germany.

Janet Wilson is Professor of English and Postcolonial Studies and Director of Research in the School of the Arts at the University of Northampton, UK.

ROUTLEDGE LITERATURE READERS

Also available in this series:

The Routledge Reader in Caribbean Literature

The History of Reading

Literature and Globalization: A Reader

World Literature: A Reader

Literature and the Bible: A Reader

Ecocriticism: The Essential Reader

Science Fiction and Cultural Theory: A Reader

The Routledge Auto|Biography Studies Reader

For further information on this series visit: www.routledge.com/books/series/RLR

THE ROUTLEDGE DIASPORA STUDIES READER

Edited by Klaus Stierstorfer and Janet Wilson

LONDON AND NEW YORK

First published 2018
by Routledge
2 Park Square, Milton Park, Abingdon, Oxon OX14 4RN

and by Routledge
711 Third Avenue, New York, NY 10017

Routledge is an imprint of the Taylor & Francis Group, an informa business

British Library Cataloguing-in-Publication Data
A catalogue record for this book is available from the British Library

Library of Congress Cataloging-in-Publication Data
Names: Wilson, Janet, 1948- editor. | Stierstorfer, Klaus, editor.
Title: The Routledge diaspora studies reader / [edited by] Janet Wilson
and Klaus Stierstorfer.
Other titles: Diaspora studies reader
Description: Milton Park, Abingdon, Oxon; New York, NY: Routledge,
2017. | Series: Routledge literature readers | Includes bibliographical
references.
Identifiers: LCCN 2017006090 | ISBN 9781138783195 (hardback: alk.
paper) | ISBN 9781138783201 (pbk.: alk. paper)
Subjects: LCSH: Emigration and immigration. | Immigrants–Social
conditions. | Ethnology. | Human geography. | Transnationalism. |
Acculturation. | Cultural pluralism.
Classification: LCC JV6013.5.R68 2017 | DDC 304.8–dc23
LC record available at https://lccn.loc.gov/2017006090

ISBN: 978-1-138-78319-5 (hbk)
ISBN: 978-1-138-78320-1 (pbk)

Typeset in Bembo
by Sunrise Setting Ltd., Brixham, UK

CONTENTS

Digital diasporas

PERMISSIONS

1   Safran, William. 'Diasporas in Modern Societies: Myths of Homeland and Return.' *Diaspora: A Journal of Transnational Studies* 1:1 (1991), 83–99. Reproduced with permission of William Safran.

2   Clifford, James. 'Diasporas.' *Cultural Anthropology* 9:3 (1994), 302–38. Reproduced with permission of American Anthropological Association.

3   Cohen, Robin. 'Four Phases of Diaspora Studies' from Robin Cohen (ed.). *Global Diasporas: An Introduction.* London: Routledge, 2008, 1–19. Reproduced with permission of Routledge.

4   Vertovec, Steven. 'Religion and Diaspora' from Peter Antes, Armin W. Geertz, Randi R. Warne (eds). *New Approaches to the Study of Religion. Vol. 2: Textual, Comparative, Sociological, and Cognitive Approaches.* Berlin: Walter de Gruyter, 2004, 275–304. Reproduced with permission of Walter de Gruyter.

5   Baumann, Martin. 'Conceptualizing Diaspora. The Preservation of Religious Identity in Foreign Parts, Exemplified by Hindu Communities Outside India.' *Temenos* 31 (1995), 19–23. Reproduced with permission of *Temenos*.

6   Bhabha, Homi K. 'DissemiNation' from *The Location of Culture*. London and New York: Routledge, 1994, 291–322. Reproduced with permission of Routledge.

7   Brubaker, Rogers. 'The "Diaspora" Diaspora.' *Ethnic and Racial Studies* 28:1 (2005), 1–19. Reproduced with permission of Rogers Brubaker.

8   Gilroy, Paul. 'The Black Atlantic as a Counterculture of Modernity' from *The Black Atlantic: Modernity and Double Consciousness*. Cambridge, MA: Harvard University Press, 1993, 1–40. Reproduced with permission of Paul Gilroy.

9   Cho, Lily. 'Diasporic Citizenship: Contradictions and Responsibilities for Canadian Literature' from Smaro Kamboureli and Roy Miki (eds). *Trans.Can.Lit: Resuscitating the Study of Canadian Literature*. Ontario: Wilfrid Laurier University Press, 2007, 93–109. Reproduced with permission of Wilfrid Laurier University Press.

10   Soysal, Yasemin Nuhoglu. 'Citizenship and Identity: Living in Diaspora in Post-war Europe?' *Ethnic and Racial Studies* 23:1 (2000), 1–15. Reproduced with permission of Taylor and Francis.

11   Fleischmann, Aloys N.M. and Nancy van Styvendale. 'Introduction' to *Narratives of Citizenship: Indigenous Diaspora People Unsettle the Nation-state*. Edmonton: University of Alberta Press, 2011, xi–xlv. Reproduced with permission of the University of Alberta Press.

12 Gamlen, Alan. 'Why Engage Diasporas?' Working Paper 08-63. COMPAS. University of Oxford, 2008, https://www.compas.ox.ac.uk/media/WP-2008-063-Gamlen_Why_Engage_Diasporas.pdf. Reproduced with permission of Alan Gamlen.

13 Brinkerhoff, Jennifer M. 'Migration, Information Technology and International Policy' from A. Alonso and P. J. Oiarzabal (eds). *Diasporas in the New Media Age: Identity, Politics and Community*. Reny: University of Nevada Press, 2010, 39–48. Reproduced with permission of the University of Nevada Press.

14 Skeldon, Ronald. 'International Migration as a Tool in Development Policy: A Passing Phase?' *Population and Development Review* 34:1 (March 2008), 1–18. Reproduced with permission of John Wiley and Sons Ltd, and Blackwell Publishing Ltd.

15 Cho, Lily. 'The Turn to Diaspora,' *Topia* 17 (2007), 11–30. Reproduced with permission of *TOPIA: Canadian Journal of Cultural Studies*.

16 Anand, Dibyesh. 'Diasporic Subjectivity as an Ethical Position.' *South Asian Diaspora* 1:2 (2009), 103–11. Reproduced with permission of Taylor and Francis.

17 Davis, Colin. 'Diasporic Subjectivities.' *French Cultural Studies* 17 (2006), 335–48. Reproduced with permission of Sage Publications Ltd.

18 Rutherford, Jonathan. 'The Third Space: Interview with Homi Bhabha' from Jonathan Rutherford (ed.). *Identity: Community, Culture, Difference*. London: Lawrence & Wishart, 207–21. Reproduced with permission of Homi Bhabha.

19 Anthias, Floya. 'New Hybridities, Old Concepts: The Limits of "Culture".' *Ethnic and Racial Studies* 24:4 (2001), 619–41. Reproduced with permission of Taylor and Francis.

20 Hutnyk, John. 'Hybridity.' *Ethnic and Racial Studies* 28:1 (2005), 79–102. Reproduced with permission of Taylor and Francis.

21 Werbner, Pnina. 'The Limits of Cultural Hybridity: On Ritual Monsters, Poetic Licence and Contested Postcolonial Purifications.' *The Journal of the Royal Anthropological Institute* 7:1 (2001), 133–52. Reproduced with permission of John Wiley & Sons Ltd.

22 Anthias, Floya. 'Evaluating "Diaspora": Beyond Ethnicity?' *Sociology* 32 (1998), 557–80. Reproduced with permission of Sage Publications Ltd.

23 Gopinath, Gayatri. 'Impossible Desires: An Introduction' from Gayatri Gopinath, *Impossible Desires*, 2005, 1–28 © 2005, Duke University Press. All rights reserved. Republished by permission of the copyright holder.

24 Wesling, Meg. 'Why Queer Diaspora?' *Feminist Review* 90 (2008), 30–47. Reproduced with permission of the *Feminist Review* and Palgrave Macmillan.

25 Goyal, Yogita. *Romance, Diaspora and Black Atlantic Literature*. Cambridge: Cambridge University Press, 2010, 7–16. Reproduced with permission of Cambridge University Press.

26 Lee, Yoon Sun. 'The Postcolonial Novel and Diaspora', from Ato Quayson (ed.). *The Cambridge Companion to the Postcolonial Novel*, 2016, 116–32. © Cambridge University Press 2016, reproduced with permission.

27 Mercer, Kobena. 'Diaspora Culture and the Dialogic Imagination' from Mbye Cham and Claire Andrade-Watkins (eds). *Blackframes: Critical Perspectives on Independent Black Cinema*, 1988, 50–61. © 1988, Massachusetts Institute of Technology. Reproduced with permission of MIT Press.

28 Naficy, Hamid. 'An Accented Cinema: Exilic and Diasporic Filmmaking.' © 2001 Princeton University Press. Reprinted by permission of Princeton University Press.

29 Lim, Song Hwee. 'Speaking in Tongues: Ang Lee, Accented Cinema, Hollywood' from Lúcia Nagib, Chris Perriam and Rajinder Dudrah (eds). *Theorizing World Cinema*. London: I. B. Tauris & Co., 2012, 129–42. Reproduced with permission of I. B. Tauris.

30   Rushdie, Salman. 'Imaginary Homelands' from Salman Rushdie (ed.). *Imaginary Homelands: Essays and Criticism 1981–1991*. London: Granta, 1991, 9–21. Reproduced with permission of Granta.

31   Mummery, Jane. 'Being Not-At-Home: A Conceptual Discussion' from Cynthia Vanden Driesen and Ralph Crane (eds). *Diaspora: The Australasian Experience*. New Delhi: Prestige, 2006, 27–43. Reproduced with permission of Prestige.

32   Brah, Avtar. *Cartographies of Diaspora: Contesting Identities*. London: Routledge, 1996, 190–5. Reproduced with permission of Routledge.

33   Cohen, Robin. 'Solid, Ductile and Liquid: Changing Notions of Homeland and Home in Diaspora Studies' from Eliezer Ben-Rafael and Yitzhak Sternberg (eds). *Transnationalism: Diasporas and the Advent of a New (Dis)order*, Leiden: Brill, 2009. Reproduced with permission of Brill.

34   Alonso, Andoni and Petro J. Oiarzabal. 'The Immigrant Worlds' Digital Harbors: An Introduction' from A. Alonso and P. J. Oiarzabal (eds). *Diasporas in the New Media Age. Identity, Politics and Community*. Reny: University of Nevada Press, 2010, 1–19. Reproduced with permission of University of Nevada Press.

35   Parham, Angel Adams. 'Internet, Place, and Public Sphere in Diaspora Communities.' *Diaspora: A Journal of Transnational Studies* 14:2/3 (2005), 349–80. Reproduced with permission of Angel Adams Parham.

36   Bernal, Victoria. *Nation as Network: Diaspora, Cyberspace, and Citizenship*. Chicago and London: University of Chicago Press, 2014, 8–11. Reproduced with permission of University of Chicago Press.

Disclaimer

The publishers have made every effort to contact the copyright holders of the essays reprinted in *The Routledge Diaspora Studies Reader* and to obtain permission to publish these essays. This has not been possible in every case, however, and we would welcome any correspondence from those individuals/companies whom we have been unable to contact. Any omissions brought to our attention will be remedied in future editions.

GENERAL INTRODUCTION

Klaus Stierstorfer and Janet Wilson

Global movements: Migration, diaspora, transnationalism

It is now almost axiomatic to state that the early twenty-first century is an age of globalization. In fact the global movement of people, capital, products, cultures, information and ideologies has increased exponentially since 2000;[1] and the acceleration in the rate of migration, intensified by economic instabilities following the global financial crisis of 2008 and ongoing political upheavals in the Middle East since 2011, is predicted to continue (Nail 2015, 1, 239). These developments have been matched by an equally steep rise of research interest in the field. Research efforts have been increased in the wider area of migration studies in both its historical and contemporary dimensions, as the plethora of recent publications testify (see, e.g. Cresswell 2006; Collier 2013; Kenny 2013; Bartram, Poros and Monforte 2014; Sassen 2014; Nail 2015; Maley 2016; Tinti and Reitano 2016). At the same time, studies of specific aspects and consequences of migration have also gained in importance. Here, diaspora studies forms a particularly promising field, not only because diasporas have become ever more prominent in politics and culture world-wide, but also because the concept of diaspora straddles the divide, so to speak, between studies of people on the move and the changes that happen locally in traditionally 'settled' contexts as a result of migration movements. Although diaspora studies is not a new discipline and emerges from the last quarter of the twentieth century, the renewed topicality of the field calls for both an assessment of what has been achieved so far, and of what the future of diaspora studies might look like. The texts reprinted in this Routledge *Reader* will help students, and all who want to gain a grounding in the field, to find their bearings, even if it can offer neither complete historical coverage of what diaspora studies has been so far, nor an exploratory or speculative advance into what it may become in the future. It does, however, try to provide recent 'classics' in diaspora scholarship along with a good complement of selected texts that exemplify the numerous perspectives from which diasporas can be perceived and thus help readers reflect on the place of diaspora studies in today's humanities and social science research environments.

As to specific disciplinary approaches, in the last 25 years vigorous debates, revised theoretical paradigms and changing models of movement and resettlement under the impact of globalization have marked the flourishing of the multiple and interlinked social science and humanities approaches that comprise this inter- and transdisciplinary area. Development of the field devoted to this phenomenon is notable for a preoccupation with the terminology used to define and explain types of movement, whether these be contained or expanding, whether caused by economic failures, unemployment or aspirations for a better future, or whether as transnational movements associated with trade, finance or business they function as spheres of power and influence. The identities of those who move are also categorized: for example, transnational migrants, political refugees, asylum seekers, illegal immigrants, dispersed economic migrants, nomads, sojourners, tourists and exiles.

The number of international migrants worldwide reached 244 million in 2015 according to the United Nations (UN) Sustainable Development Home Page (n.d.; see Brah, Chapter 23, this volume) and in 2017 of that number, 65.6 million are refugees.[2] The current crisis in Europe – political exiles seeking asylum from Syria and Iraq, refugees from northern Africa, and many other homeless people displaced by war, poverty, political conflict or discrimination – involves various forms of movement, only some of which may lead to the forming of diasporas. In the face of an increasingly dense web of state regulation and diminishing opportunities for migration through official channels, illegal migrants take their chances and willingly risk their lives in the hope of finding a better life in a new society. The search for political asylum and a new start in more affluent western European countries illustrates the increasing desperation of the world's poor and disadvantaged (Brubaker 2005, 9). Many of these stateless groups remain caught between one culture and another, confined to transit camps, detention centres or refugee zones, often situated near or on national borders as in the recently-dismantled 'Jungle' transit camp in Calais or on offshore islands such as Nwaru and Manus, detention centres for asylum seekers to Australia. These camps are seen as new juridico-political units, influencing the way society is organized (Agamben 1997, 113–114). For long-term refugees, especially those whose formative years are spent in such limbo settings, being suspended in transit is now considered a way of life, a normative form of constructing an identity, and a different way of being in the world (Agier 2011).

Despite the uncertain and changing status of these groups, which makes categorization problematic, they are potential sources of diasporas: they will either coalesce into new communities or integrate into already existing diaspora groups in host nations (Brah, Chapter 23, this volume; Sokefield 2006, cited by Cohen 2008, 13).[3] This may take several decades if political asylum is sought after, although in cases of economic migration such as the Turks in Germany or the Poles in the UK, the settlement process is usually faster. Within the many flows of migratory journeys, factors such as the numbers of migrants at any one time, the role of politics and culture in the mobilization process or conditions of labour and the local economy, can make a difference in helping transform a category of underprivileged migrants into a fully-fledged diaspora, providing them with greater visibility and some status.

Such hazardous movements, and provisional arrangements for the asylum seeker, refugee or political exile before any settlement can take place, may be contrasted with the mobilizations of the Irish, Jewish or Indian diasporas, which rely on the more prosperous status and brokerage of co-ethnic elites of established diaspora communities in the new hostlands. These movements carry some assurance of entitlement of citizenship and belonging through the facilitation of sponsorship from the collective identity in solidarity – already established groups such as international corporations or non-governmental organizations (NGOs) with influence, financial independence and vocational control.[4] In addition, in the widening gap of economic inequality between the disenfranchised, impoverished victims of war and civil upheaval, and the more affluent beneficiaries of globalization, are the 'scattered diasporas' of multiply-displaced people who share transnational bonds of mobility: overseas contract workers, casual labourers and female domestic servants, often trapped and exploited in situations of temporary employment (Parry 2002, 72).

This snapshot of the variable, often harsh conditions experienced by migrants describes current population movements that are often summarized by an unspecific use of 'diaspora' as an umbrella rubric, frequently including related concepts such as transnationals, refugees, asylum seekers, expatriates, exiles, contract workers and so on. Such lexical eclecticism and expansion of terms referring to migration due to many new contexts of movement (e.g. Syrians fleeing civil war, refugees from Northern Africa, Mexicans crossing into the US and East-European peoples moving to the UK) show the risk of the label diaspora being applied as a generic one indiscriminately, to the point of losing distinctiveness and hence usefulness as a descriptive tool in research (Brubaker, Chapter 7, this volume; Braziel and Mannur 2003, 3). Although diasporas originate as a dispersion or a migration, not all dispersals can be defined as diasporas, if the term is to be used in its more specific focus (Quayson and Daswani 2013, 3). That is, diaspora movements which lead to the formation of new communities in the host nation with the aspiration to a more secure future differ in this sense from those of transmigrants, transnationals or exiles – who do not necessarily consolidate into a diaspora.

Diaspora subjects who have relocated usually maintain symbolic ties to the homeland, displaying a cultural pattern of longing, nostalgia and identity, sometimes dominated by the expectation of a return – real or imagined; they also benefit from the presence of political or cultural facilitators or brokers who promote that relationship, often with a utopian nationalism associated with the notion of home in diaspora. With a shared sense of belonging to a 'nation in exile, dispersed throughout the world' (Bruneau 2010, 49) they work towards the consolidation of a translocal cultural identity, inflected by relations with communities of their co-ethnics and co-diasporans. Through trans-state diasporic networks as well as local networks within host nations, diasporas function 'as a hinge between different spaces and different geographical scales' (Bruneau 2010, 48). Like the related term 'transnationalism', they are reconfiguring modernity's social and political structures in the transnational social sphere of migration. With national and regional borders rendered increasingly permeable, social space fractures into new configurations and groupings ex-centric to the nation state, which is no longer considered to be the principal analytical category of the global sphere or of its interrelations (Werbner 2013, 109). This interconnectivity is increasingly facilitated by the digital netscapes of the new information and communication technology in which the internet has become the central frame for networking (Kissau and Hunger 2010, 246). Yet the transborder communities that emerge from the spaces of transmigration and transnationalism, whose subjects circulate within a transnational region like the European Union (EU), differ from long-term diasporas. They do not relocate within the host nation to form coherent communities, or organize long-term co-ethnic networks, but have parallel lives in one or more nation-states (Bruneau 2010, 49; Sheffer 2006, 127). Indeed, the presence of such mobile, circulating communities within western nations that have come to be designated as havens for multicultural cosmopolitan citizens, has produced a backlash against such transnational globalizing trends, as recent political decisions in the UK (for Brexit) and the US (the recent presidential election of Donald Trump) and local manifestations of nationalist xenophobic sentiment, evident in the growth of populist, anti-elite or outsider political formations, testify.

Diaspora studies

The disciplinary label of diaspora studies gained widespread currency in the 1990s alongside cognate areas such as transcultural studies, transnational migration studies or globalization studies, as part of a 'paradigm shift' triggered by deconstructionist and poststructuralist theories that foreground the fluidity and hybridity of transnational formations (Glick-Schiller 2003, 121, cited in Sheffer 2006, 124).[5] As an area of research, diaspora studies acquired more coherence, as well as a predominantly interdisciplinary character after the American Armenian scholar Khachig Tölölyan founded *Diaspora: A Journal of Transnational Studies* in 1991; it rapidly grew into a forum for debate and the consolidation of research initiatives and perspectives. The expansion of the field from its beginnings in the social and political sciences, in which diaspora was used as a descriptive and typological tool for understanding migration and settlement in the global era (Cohen 2008, 5; Anthias 2001, 631), and its developing intersections with disciplines such as area studies, cultural theory, postcolonial studies, film studies and queer theory, is reflected in the multi-sectional structure of this *Reader* as well as in the diversity of perspectives offered by the articles chosen for inclusion. The genealogy and disciplinary complexity of diaspora studies are comprehensively mapped by sociologist Robin Cohen (2008) in the second edition of his *Global Diasporas*. Cohen's overview of the field's expansion in keeping with the increase in migration, transnationalism and globalization since the early 1990s identifies four phases. Acknowledging the diverse theoretical approaches, disciplinary frameworks and categories of analysis that have emerged at the intersection of diverse disciplines within social sciences and the humanities, he identifies the most recent phase as one of consolidation, and advocates the reaffirmation of the diaspora idea in terms of its 'core elements, common features and ideal types' (Cohen, Chapter 3, this volume).

Readers, companions, special issues of journals (see, e.g. Thayil 2006), overviews (see, e.g. Mishra 2006) and studies of particular diasporas (on the Indian diaspora see, e.g. Brown 2006; Mishra 2007; Oonk 2007; Raghuram, Sahoo, Maharaj and Sangha 2008; Koshy and Radhakrishnan 2008; Rai and Reeves 2009; Dwivedi 2014; Gamez-Fernandez and Dwivedi, 2015; Mehta 2015) play a part in the explosion of diaspora studies spearheaded by the founding of the journal *Diaspora*; these, however, are now unable to do justice to the proliferating approaches that have added to diaspora's complexity as a concept. In between the two editions of Cohen's *Global Diasporas* appeared the pioneering *Theorizing Diaspora: A Reader*, edited by Jana Evans Braziel and Anita Mannur (2003). Like Cohen, the editors recommend a balance between theorizing diaspora in order to open up critical spaces for further research, and acknowledging the historical and cultural specificity of various diasporic movements. They steer between the dominant disciplinary models – the historical, empirical approach of social science research, and the cultural studies, social constructivist approach dominant in the 1990s, which challenged the prevailing view that attachment to the homeland and nostalgia for return were key to the diasporic experience – and they focus instead on the community of relocation in the hostland.[6] Braziel and Mannur point to a 'nomadic turn', reflecting the fact that nomadism is one of the many forms that diasporas have taken throughout history, rather than a 'postmodern turn from history'.[7] Drawing on the literal and metaphoric meanings of the term diaspora, they argue that in diaspora 'specific historical moments are embodied and – as diaspora itself suggests – are scattered and regrouped into new points of becoming' (2003, 3). *Theorizing Diaspora* was followed by the second edition of the *Postcolonial Studies Reader* (Ashcroft, Griffiths and Tiffin 2006), which expands the first edition (published in 1994) with new sections including a selection of seven articles on diaspora. The editors point out that during the intervening decade diaspora had become increasingly relevant to postcolonial studies. They elaborate that the Janus-like dualism of the split diasporic subject who looks back to the cultural identity and heritage of the homeland and forward to the new society of relocation, drawing upon both perspectives in identity construction, can be linked to the doubled and hybrid discourse of postcolonialism (425). But while theories of nation, social marginality and cultural hybridity, made familiar through the work of postcolonial theorists like Homi Bhabha, Stuart Hall and Paul Gilroy, have been applied to the material conditions of diasporic communities, the relationship between diaspora studies and postcolonial studies is a shifting one. The two overlap through their common engagement with the marginalization and cultural specificity of minority groups. Experiences of diaspora and exile occur more often and more widely than those of colonization, however, as the semantically capacious and wide-ranging term 'diaspora' suggests. While the postcolonial field has thus developed a diverse set of practices and theoretical tools to deal with a range of phenomena relating to historical and contemporary conditions of political domination and subservience, extending far beyond its original moment of disciplinary formulation, it cannot on its own now either accommodate or account for the diverse examples and conditions of diaspora under globalization.

The new conditions of global movement in the present century inform the selection of articles in *A Companion to Diaspora and Transnationalism*, edited by Ato Quayson and Girish Daswani (2013), which focus on diaspora and transnationalism. Claiming that diasporas 'transcend nations, areas and regions', the editors argue that both diaspora and its cognate term transnationalism are core concepts by which to understand movements of people and goods in today's globalized world (6). Indeed, diaspora and transnationalism seem to displace some of the key concerns of postcolonial studies with identity, resistance and decolonization, or at least to reconfigure these, as for example, in Islamic resistance to the west.

By contrast to the *Readers* and their limited representation of articles that mark key concepts and debates about diaspora, and the *Companion*, which studies diaspora exclusively in relation to transnationalism, aiming to disentangle these two concepts, the Routledge *Diaspora Studies Reader* presents a spectrum of articles on topics and issues drawn from a diverse range of disciplines within the humanities, social sciences and cultural studies: it includes articles which build on established theoretical formulations and disciplinary formations as in the sections on cultural identity and hybridity, queer studies and intersectionality, as well as others which represent recent developments, through emerging or under-represented topics such as subjectivity, citizenship, international policy and diaspora, and digital diasporas.

Diaspora, migration, transnational: Disciplinary intersections and differences

Diaspora studies as a field of enquiry has appeared at the intersection of several distinct disciplinary interests both in the social sciences and the humanities, all of which have at their heart the concept of migration and its different manifestations across centuries. Diaspora emerges here as a specific understanding of this larger social movement, as it is always construed in relation to its cardinal points of reference: the hostland and homeland. However, given its overlap with several other scholarly fields, questions of terminology and conceptualization have occupied much of the early debate on how to properly define the object of diaspora studies.

Diaspora studies partly overlaps with migration and refugee studies, social and human geography, globalization studies and postcolonial studies, and for this reason has often been either elided by or included within these areas of research. Yet the themes and acts of migration and exile are recurrent in all cultures and societies from their very beginnings and this gives diaspora studies continued relevance and resonance within the disciplinary frameworks of postcolonial or migration studies with which it is most often associated. The persistence and growth of diaspora communities as diaspora expands into one of the most prominent forms of global migration, has enabled diaspora studies to develop in ways that are distinct from these cognate disciplines and to form its own boundaries of enquiry and terms of scholarly engagement. Although the varied approaches and disparate discourses hint at the contradictions and ideological differences inherent in the evolution of this heterogeneous, cross-disciplinary field, diaspora studies shows growing coherence and consolidation with new areas of investigation developing, critiquing and expanding earlier arguments and debates.[8]

Notably, by contrast to other disciplines that seek to examine different movements and societies in relation to migration, the nation and globalization, the central focus of diaspora studies is on the connections between homeland and hostland generated by mobile subjects, including the perspectives of long-term residents both at home and abroad. Diaspora is about home and belonging, cultural connectivity, hybridity and diversity, settlement and location. The different structures of belonging experienced by hybrid, migratory communities have been dominated by the foundational geographical model of the Jewish and Armenian diasporas, which foregrounds the points of origin and return, and associates home with 'roots, soil and kinship' (Huyssen 2003, 151). Among the 'victim' diasporas of cataclysm and trauma, where exile may be forced and return to the homeland denied, the classic cases are the Jews after the Babylonian captivity in 586 BC, the African diaspora created by the slave trade, the Armenians following the Turkish genocide of 1915, the Irish migration following the potato famine in 1845–52, and the Palestinian diaspora after the British withdrawal in 1948 (Cohen 2008, 2–4). One can contrast these prototypical diasporas which emphasize nostalgia and loss with the more recent conceptual framework that takes as its central reference point the society of relocation and the strategies of making a new home within it. Here the idea of home is detached from its association with territory and broadened to include the affective response to dispersion. As Avtar Brah (1996) points out, this approach to living in diaspora is built on a 'homing desire', the wish to construct a home, by contrast to the 'desire for a homeland' (180, 192–3).

Overlapping with this latter model of diaspora are the heightened circuits of transnational, transglobal mobility and those forms of the deterritorialized nation that are marked by social networks, information technologies, digital netscapes and affordable air travel (Laguerre 2009, 197). Such circulations of movement identified with cross-border communities and multi-locational, mobile identities, undercut the binaries of models framed by the bounded entity of the nation state: of dispersal from the homeland and/or relocation in a hostland. They emphasize the proliferation of migrant identities and collectivities across national borders, and of interlinked, translocal, co-diaspora communities which are both 'multi local' and 'polycentric' (Tölölyan 2007, 651). As Quayson and Daswani point out, these go well beyond the usual imagining of modern nation states which is linked to the concept of the migrant; for the transmigrant may have affiliation to more than one nation and develop ties of loyalty and experience nostalgia for two or more locations simultaneously (2013, 5–6).

Research in social science and humanities disciplines has begun to identify a body of recurring themes and preoccupations that can be recognized as part of a diaspora consciousness: transnationalism, subjectivity, paradigms in the visual and performing arts and literature identifiable as distinct generic and aesthetic forms, new modes of citizenship that supersede national boundaries. Diaspora focuses on the unequal power relations between different groups, ethnicities and nationalities who are uprooted by migration, and marginalized and/or displaced by various kinds of gender, ethnic, religious difference. The article, 'Multiple axes of power: Articulations of diaspora and intersectionality', specially written for this *Reader* by Avtar Brah (Chapter 23, this volume), shows their changing relationship to the traditional centres of power and institutional authority. The discipline's flexibility of interpretation along the lines of difference, for example, has encouraged recognition of the parallels between the social and national exclusions resulting from migration that are associated with diaspora, and the sexual difference and non-heteronormativity that define queerness. The semantically defining properties of the term diaspora, of scattering, splitting and spreading of seeds, links diaspora as a form of dispersion to the queer subject's state of being ex-centric to the social norms of gender, family and kinship.

This alignment can be summarized as a shared sense of being 'unhomed', and indeed it has been extended to applying diaspora as a framework in the context of transglobal adoption, requiring a realigning of family relations, described as 'queer kinship' (Eng 2003, 301). In a dynamic interdisciplinary conjunction, diaspora studies thus becomes aligned with queer theory, through the theorization of the concept of a 'queer diaspora' that functions under the terms of contemporary globalization, transnationalism and other mobilizations that involve 'unwriting the nation' (George 1996, 83).

Yet the unevenly powered global networks and netscapes of the social media, as well as the new forms of connectivity, suggest some redefining or interrogation of persistent racial hierarchies and power inequalities as currently understood within diaspora studies. The challenge to the framework of marginality that often defines minority diaspora communities – that is, of low-skilled and economically disadvantaged workers – comes from highly skilled 'privileged migrants' or 'mobile professionals', often called 'expatriates'. These circulating transnationals who might have a home in more than one country are the contemporary globalized counterparts to the entrepreneurs of the commercial networks and trade diasporas that in the eighteenth and nineteenth centuries emanated from China, Lebanon and India (Cohen 2008, 83). In globalizing cities like Dubai and Shanghai, they have become locally integrated entrepreneurs, achieved cultural and economic dominance, and often act as political or cultural brokers for co-diasporics in order to consolidate local and global networks (Fechter and Walsh 2012, 10, 18).

Diaspora studies over the last 25 years has expanded to embrace the different axes of home and modes of belonging; studies of national and international policy-making (long distance, migration); it has taken note of the changing relations of the nation state and diaspora communities in relation to the homeland, and facilitated transnational concepts of citizenship; while the new media, digitalization of information and other technological advances have contributed to the respatialization of marginal minority groups in new and shifting constructions of co-diasporas, globally scattered but linked communities that affirm each other and share bonds of loyalty and affect.

Definitions and approaches to diaspora

Diaspora has its etymological origins in the Greek verb *diaspeirein*, comprising the elements *dia-*, 'through, across', and *-speirein*, 'to sow or scatter'. It originally appeared in Deuteronomy 28.25, which in the King James Bible is translated as 'thou [. . .] shall be removed into all the kingdoms of the earth', and in the Septuagint, the Greek translation of the Hebrew, as 'thou shalt be a diaspora in all kingdoms of the earth'. From the beginning, then, it was a term used to refer to the dispersion of the Jews after the Babylonian exile, a state that has overtones of punishment. It also refers to dissemination and scattering, with implications of communities dislocated from their place of origin through migration or exile, and relocated in one or more states, nations or territories. Metaphorically there are hints of fertility in the scattering of seeds, and an etymological and conceptual link between diaspora and dissemination (Davis 2006, 338). This has remained the concept's most significant definition, but recent uses have widened and expanded its meaning, as interdisciplinary research which defines mobile populations in the current era of globalization links diaspora subjects with other kindred terms such as exiles, transnationals, refugees and asylum seekers. What is included in discourses of diaspora often depends on the ideological perspective or dominant disciplinary affiliations of the writer; for example, whether referring to longing for home and homeland, the remaking of home or the deterritorialization of home, to transnational movements of capital, products and information, as well as people or to relocation and readjustment in the host society. Most theorizations of diaspora are based on a particular understanding of what constitutes the centre of power and its margins, whether these be formulated in economic, racial or gendered terms. One of the strengths of the discipline in its current symbolic incarnation is the way it transcends all such border constructions and includes virtually any group (such as privileged elites and transnationals alongside low-skilled, blue collar workers or labourers) within some kind of diasporic experience. This inclusiveness may also be seen as a limitation (Brubaker, Chapter 7, this volume), and in response to such criticism and caveats, it is worth recalling the core constituency, traceable to the term's Greek and Hebrew etymologies: of migrating, travelling populations or geographically dispersed groups of any kind.

The present *Reader* seeks to represent all the major strains of diaspora studies today, from its roots in anthropology, migration studies and human geography, to the inclusion of new paradigms emerging from sociology, cultural studies, communication technology and humanities research in literary studies and visual culture. The *longue durée* of the Jewish and Armenian expulsions, highlighting the seminal concept of a distant homeland and the nostalgia of return, is traceable to the paradigmatic case of diaspora as found in Jewish and Hebrew mythology and belief. Its pragmatic and empirical orientation around history and practice is represented by the articles included in Part I of this *Reader*. By contrast, the sociological, cultural-studies approach draws on more abstract concepts of diasporic spaces and defines a particular diaspora consciousness or subjectivity, as in the two articles by Avtar Brah, who argues that diasporas are centres of power struggles, and the first of two by Lily Cho, who sees citizenship as a category or practice. Yet another interpretation of the field sees the humanities and social sciences approaches as complementary categories of diaspora that explain diaspora as both a social phenomenon and a subjective experience. In this configuration the work of Avtar Brah is grouped with that of sociologists Robin Cohen and Stephane Dufoix (2008) in providing social typologies of diaspora, while critics like Paul Gilroy (1993), James Clifford (1997) and Marianne Hirsch (2012; Hirsch and Miller 2011) engage with the 'affective economies of dispersal' (Quayson and Daswani 2013, 8). Their broad cultural-studies approach includes the transient feelings of desire, nostalgia and loss, and familiarizing practices of subjects who live outside the homeland, evident in memorabilia and particularized indicators of origins and cultural heritage, such as calendars, photographs, music and cuisine, all expressive of the double consciousness of living in one place and retaining strong emotional attachment to the home of origin (Quayson and Daswani 2013, 7–8).

Other approaches stem from different views of expulsion and dislocation from some kind of centre (expanding the semantic associations of dissemination and dispersal), implying a degree of transgression or contradiction of social norms as well as geographical boundaries (as with the concept of a queer diaspora), and the distinction between how diasporas present themselves (the emic or participant's view) and how they are transformed into an object of study (the etic or observer's view) (Cohen 2008, 5; Tölölyan 2007; Quayson and Daswani 2013, 7).

The structure of the *Diaspora Studies Reader*

The overall structure of the Routledge *Diaspora Studies Reader* considers the multiplicity of definitions and approaches sketched earlier, and organizes the five parts – or 'metaframes' – according to particular theoretical or disciplinary emphases. Within each part, the distinct sections draw together various thematic threads shared across the articles included in them. One of the key objectives of the volume, which informs its organizing principle, is that of simultaneously highlighting the rootedness of diaspora studies in many already established fields, even while celebrating its porousness and ability to borrow from and blend with other disciplines.

Part I: Origins

This first section of the *Reader* highlights the cardinal points of origin and definition of diaspora in Biblical, Jewish and Hebrew studies, and reflects the institutional and historical origins and usages of the term before the 1990s resurgence of diaspora studies. The articles included discuss the archetypes of diaspora against which modern forms can be measured, and the concept of 'victim diasporas'– communities that, at the outset, like the paradigmatic Jewish and Armenian diasporas, may lack the agency to determine their own destinies. Here is the strongest and most conservative insistence on understanding diasporas as social and cultural formations motivated by a possible return to an (idealized) homeland, by contrast to contemporary ethnonational diasporas, which remain involved in the affairs of the original homeland as well as those of the hostland where co-diasporics reside, and which are more inclined than most diasporas to become involved in criminal or terrorist activities (Sheffer 2006, 129).

Part II: Geopolitics

This section, like the first, brings into play social science and historical approaches to the study of diaspora, and notably to their definition in relation to geographical and geomorphic categories – land masses, regions, continents and interlinking oceans – and political allegiances. It illustrates that these create exclusions through disenfranchisement, but lend a semblance of coherence across national borders and collectively help define the structures of world power. This section also emphasizes the overlap between diaspora and various kinds of religious identity and worship across eastern and western cultures, prioritizing the crucial links between religious intolerance and discrimination, and cultural scattering and dissemination.

The articles in this section point to how much new understandings of diaspora remain grounded in concepts that can be traced to the seminal Jewish and Armenian diasporas, as the discourse around diaspora has developed and been reconfigured through related concepts like transnationalism, deterritorialization, exile, the transglobal and so on, terms that have entered the language in response to the new global movements of the late 20th and early 21st centuries.

The very term 'geopolitics' feeds into the contemporary phenomenon of globalization and the ongoing tension between the nation state and its diasporas: this includes new forms of exclusion through mechanisms such as global checkpoints, reinforced borders, new identities and populist, anti-elite political parties focused on sovereignty and homeland, indigenous forms of belonging, and re-evaluations of citizenship including new aspirations. Embedded in this section is the acknowledgement that diaspora and migration are tightly woven into the texture of each nation state; that alternative communities exist which are distinct but nonetheless share belonging; that diasporas have their own jurisdictions of power, existing as levers of national governments and agents of development (Appiah 2016).

Part III: Identities

The term defining this metaframe belongs to cultural studies, and its use shows that diaspora intersects with this field as much as it does with social sciences and religious studies. Research since the 1990s has moved away from issues of nation, national frameworks or categories of analysis in tension with diaspora, towards a new emphasis on the subjectivity of being displaced (diaspora is often being used as a metaphor, a figure of hybridity in cultural studies). The study of the types of consciousness that develop around dislocation and resettlement in the host nation comes with this shift of focus to culture and cultural identity in the pioneering works of black writers like Stuart Hall, Homi Bhabha and Paul Gilroy. Hybridity in these conditions comes about not as a result but as a precondition of all cultural life: this and other terms also familiar from postcolonial studies such as double consciousness, interrogate some of the homogenous notions of the nation state as well as of apparently monolithic diasporic communities.

Part IV: Cultural production

Diaspora studies, like postcolonial studies, moves into the realm of arts, visual culture, performance, literature and other types of artistic production where the effect of diaspora is found in the disruption of traditional art forms, including genres, narrative and media formats. Overlapping with the postcolonial is the focus on the imaginary, beginning with the imaginary homeland, as represented in Salman Rushdie's (1991) seminal article (see *Reader*, Chapter 31), and adapted by Vijay Mishra (1996, 2007) in his study of the Indian diaspora; while Ato Quayson (2013), in stressing the affective economy of diaspora, claims that textual genres and media, as in the production of images of homeland for displaced communities, as well as arguments about the politics of representation in hybrid, multicultural societies, are significant responses to the spatial and temporal dislocations of movement (147). Cultural production associated with diaspora shows that art not only reflects but creates and performs diasporic experiences. Furthermore, international festivals and exhibitions, together with prizes and awards like the Turner Prize for Art and the Man Booker Prize for Fiction, show that the artistic forms that stem from diaspora cultures can acquire fame and prominence on national and international levels. Diaspora cultural production differentiates itself from the mainstream, with a distinctive aesthetics that features a cross-cultural dynamic, and foregrounds the role of language through insistence on its hybridity and pluralism. But, as great art usually does, it can also transcend the conditions of its production and the borders of its location to acquire greater representativeness, enter the mainstream, and in time compel a reconfiguration of the canon.

Part V: Community

Home and belonging are quintessential concepts in diaspora, and the area in which diaspora studies has made its most seminal contributions. In addressing this very contentious aspect of the field, diaspora studies has produced the most vibrant contributions to the notions of home through a range of philosophical, sociological and artistic approaches. These issues have anchored the entire debate around twentieth-century philosophical thought and have been enhanced by the rise of the internet as a new form of interconnectedness, promoting the immediacy of networking, and introducing new notions of citizenship and belonging. The *Reader* concludes with the consideration of the internet as a new metaphor of home, joining up the world, creating new forms of nostalgia, a point of focus for states of being at home and homelessness.

Research context and acknowledgements

The Routledge *Diaspora Studies Reader* has its origins in international research collaborations between the Universities of Muenster, Germany and Northampton, UK; a Transatlantic Exchange/European Partnership with the Universities of York and Fraser Valley in Canada from 2009–12, and then from 2012–15 an EU–funded Marie Skłodowska Curie project, the Initial Training Network (ITN) called Diasporic Constructions of Home and Belonging (CoHaB).[9] During this time, diaspora studies has been part of our syllabus, research exchange networks and individual research initiatives. In this context the editors wish to record their gratitude to

Dr Annika Merk, former lecturer in English at Muenster University and one of the research coordinators for the ITN project who refined the concept of this *Reader*, and provided substantial input in its preliminary research; to Dr Chris Ringrose (Monash University) for his invaluable assistance after Dr Merk left the project; to Dr Cristina Sandru for her comments on the introductions; and to Dr Larissa Allwork, the CoHaB research coordinator at the University of Northampton. The project was stimulated by the enthusiasm and diligence of the Fellows on the CoHaB network, and we gratefully acknowledge their input over four years. Finally, we remain indebted to the CoHaB International Advisory Group for their intellectual inspiration and guidance: Homi Bhabha, Avtar Brah, Ceri Peach and Khachig Tölölyan.

Notes

1 According to the UN Sustainable Development Home Page (n.d.), there has been, since 2000, a 41% increase in the number of international migrants.
2 The figures for refugees, i.e. forcibly displaced people worldwide, comes from the UN High Commissioner for Refugees (n.d.).
3 As not all migrations will cohere into communities, and as community is one of the principle definitions of a diaspora, the term diaspora cannot be used of temporary sojourns.
4 Cohen (2008) stresses that these bonds of loyalty between co-ethnics in other countries might compete with a duty of 'co-responsibility', as not all mobile subjects wish to be associated with lower-class ethnics abroad (7). This is, in fact, one of the reasons why diasporas take so long to form and consolidate.
5 The Modern Language Association of America (MLA) bibliography lists at least 104 entries on diaspora up to the 1980s and then 150 entries in that decade alone.
6 The seminal statement comes from Safran 1991, 83–99; cf Brah 1996. Social constructivism argues that knowledge is produced in the discourses which construct the objects we take to be the 'things' of the world; and such discourses are part of relations of power or everyday relations of communication (Burkitt 1999, 67–71).
7 Nomadism is one of the categories of migration adopted by Thomas Nail (2015).
8 For example, Cohen (2008) comments that social constructivist scholars privileged the 'emic over the etic', ignoring the history and evolution of the concept of diaspora (9); the opposing view might be represented by El Tayeb (2011), critiquing the backward-looking character of exclusive identification with the culture of origin (52–3).
9 As well as the universities of Muenster and Northampton, this partnership included the universities of Mumbai, Stockholm, Oxford and the School of Oriental and African Studies, London; see www.itn-cohab.eu.

References

Agamben, Giorgio. 1997. 'The Camp as Nomos of the Modern.' Trans. by Daniel Heller-Roazen. In *Violence, Identity and Self-Determination*, edited by Hent de Vries and Samuel Weber, 106–118. Stanford: Stanford University Press.

Agier, Michel. 2011. *Managing the Undesirable: Refugee Camps and Humanitarian Government*. Cambridge: Polity Press.

Anthias, Floya. 2001. 'New Hybridities, Old Concepts: The Limits of "Culture".' *Ethnic and Racial Studies* 24 (4): 619–641.

Appiah, Kwame Anthony. 2016. 'Country.' *Mistaken Identities: The 2016 BBC Reith Lectures*. Lecture 2. Available at: www.bbc.co.uk/programmes/b00729d9.

Ashcroft, Bill, Gareth Griffiths, and Helen Tiffin. 2006. 'Diaspora.' In *The Post-Colonial Studies Reader*, 2nd ed., edited by Bill Ashcroft, Gareth Griffiths, and Helen Tiffin, 425–427. London: Routledge.

Bartram, David, Maritsa V. Poros, and Pierre Monforte. 2014. *Key Concepts in Migration*. London: Sage.

Brah, Avtar. 1996. *Cartographies of Diaspora: Contesting Identities*. London: Routledge.

Braziel, Jana Evans, and Anita Mannur. 2003. 'Nation, Migration, Globalization: Points of Contention in Diaspora Studies.' In *Theorizing Diaspora*, edited by Jana Evans Braziel and Anita Mannur, 1–22. Oxford: Blackwell.

Brown, Judith M. 2006. *Global South Asians: Introducing the Modern Diaspora*. Cambridge: Cambridge University Press.

Brubaker, Rogers. 2005. 'The "Diaspora" Diaspora.' *Ethnic and Racial Studies* 28 (1): 1–19.

Bruneau, Michel. 2010. 'Diasporas, Transnational Spaces and Communities.' In *Diaspora and Transnationalism: Concepts, Theories and Methods*, edited by Rainer Bauböck, and Thomas Faist, 35–49. Amsterdam: Amsterdam University Press.

Burkitt, Ian. 1999. *Bodies of Thought: Embodiment, Identity & Modernity*. London: Sage.

Clifford, J. 1997. *Routes: Travel and Translation in the Late Twentieth Century*. Cambridge, MA: Harvard University Press.

Cohen, Robin. 2008. *Global Diasporas: An Introduction*, 2nd ed. London: Routledge.

Collier, Paul. 2013. *Exodus: How Migration is Changing Our World*. Oxford: Oxford University Press.

Cresswell, Tim. 2006. *On the Move: Mobility in the Modern Western World*. Abingdon and New York: Routledge.

Davis, Colin. 2006. 'Diasporic Subjectivities.' *French Cultural Studies* 17 (3): 335–348.

Dufoix, Stephane. 2008. *Diasporas*. Trans. by William Rodamor. Berkeley, CA: University of California, Los Angeles Press.

Dwivedi, Om Prakash. 2014. *Tracing the New Indian Diaspora*. Amsterdam & New York: Rodopi.

El Tayeb, Fatima. 2011. *European Others: Queering Ethnicity in Postnational Europe*. Minneapolis, MN: University of Minnesota Press.

Eng, David L. 2003. 'Transnational Adoption and Queer Diasporas.' In *The Routledge Queer Studies Reader*, edited by Donald E. Hall and Annamarie Jagose with Andrea Bebell and Susan Potter, 301–323. London and New York: Routledge.

Fechter, Anne-Meike, and Katie Walsh. 2012. 'Examining "Expatriate" Continuities: Postcolonial Approaches to Mobile Professionals.' In *The New Expatriates: Postcolonial Approaches to Mobile Professionals*, edited by Anne-Meike Fechter and Katie Walsh, 9–22. London and New York: Routledge.

Gamez-Fernandez, Cristina M., and Veena Dwivedi, eds. 2015. *Shaping Indian Diaspora: Literary Representations and Bollywood Consumption Away from the Desi*. Lanham, MD: Lexington Books.

George, Rosemary Marangoly. 1996. *The Politics of Home: Postcolonial Relocations and Twentieth-Century Fiction*. Cambridge: Cambridge University Press.

Gilroy, P. 1993. *The Black Atlantic: Modernity and Double Consciousness*. Cambridge, MA: Harvard University Press.

Glick-Schiller, Nina. 2003. 'The Centrality of Ethnography in the Study of Transnational Migration.' In *Anthropology Engages the New Immigrants*, edited by Nancy Foner, 99–128. Santa Fe, NM: School of American Research Press.

Hirsch, Marianne. 2012. *Family Frames: Photographs, Narrative and Postmemory*. Cambridge, MA: Harvard University Press.

Hirsch, Marianne, and Nancy K. Miller, eds. 2011. *Rites of Return: Diaspora Poetics and the Politics of Memory*. New York, NY: Columbia University Press.

Huyssen, Andreas. 2003. 'Diaspora and Nation: Migration into our Pasts.' *New German Critique* 88: 147–164.

Kenny, Kevin. 2013. *Diaspora: A Very Short Introduction*. Oxford: Oxford University Press.

Kissau, Kathrin, and Uwe Hunger. 2010. 'The Internet as a Means of Studying Transnationalism and Diaspora.' In *Diaspora and Transnationalism: Concepts, Theories and Methods*, edited by Rainer Bauböck and Thomas Faist, 245–265. Amsterdam: Amsterdam University Press.

Koshy, Susan, and Rajagopalan Radhakrishnan. 2008. *Transnational South Asians: The Making of a Neo–Diaspora*. New Delhi: Oxford University Press.

Laguerre, Michel S. 2009. 'The Transglobal Network Nation: Diaspora, Homeland and Hostland.' In *Transnationalism: Diasporas and the Advent of a New (Dis)order*, edited by Eliezer Ben-Rafael and Yitzhak Sternberg, 195–210. Leiden and Boston: Brill.

Maley, William. 2016. *What is a Refugee?* London: C. Hurst & Co. Ltd.

Mehta, Sandhya Rao, ed. 2015. *Exploring Gender in the Literature of the Indian Diaspora*. Newcastle upon Tyne: Cambridge Scholars Publishing.

Mishra, Sudesh. 2006. *Diaspora Criticism*. Edinburgh: Edinburgh University Press.

Mishra, Vijay. 1996. 'The Diasporic Imaginary: Theorising the Indian Diaspora.' *Textual Practice* 10 (3): 189–237.

Mishra, Vijay. 2007. *The Literature of the Indian Diaspora: Theorizing the Diasporic Imaginary*. London: Routledge.

Nail, Thomas. 2015. *The Figure of the Migrant*. Stanford, CA: Stanford University Press.

Oonk, Gijsbert, ed. 2007. *Global Indian Diasporas: Exploring Trajectories of Migration and Theory*. Amsterdam: Amsterdam University Press.

Parry, Benita. 2002. 'Directions and Dead Ends in Postcolonial Studies.' In *Relocating Postcolonialism*, edited by David Theo Goldberg and Ato Quayson, 66–81. Oxford: Blackwell.

Quayson, Ato. 2013. 'Postcolonialism and the Diasporic Imaginary.' In *A Companion to Diaspora and Transnationalism*, edited by Ato Quayson and Girish Daswani, 139–159. Chichester: Wiley-Blackwell.

Quayson, Ato, and Girish Daswani. 2013. 'Introduction: Diaspora and Transnationalism: Scapes, Scales and Scopes.' In *A Companion to Diaspora and Transnationalism*, edited by Ato Quayson and Girish Daswani, 1–26. Oxford: Wiley Blackwell.

Raghuram, Parvati, Ajaya Mumar Sahoo, Brij Maharaj, and Dave Sangha, eds. 2008. *Tracing an Indian Diaspora: Contexts, Memories, Representations*. London: Sage.

Rai, Rajesh, and Peter Reeves, eds. 2009. *The South Asian Diaspora: Transnational Networks an Changing Identities*. London & New York: Routledge.

Rushdie, Salman. 1991. 'Imaginary Homelands.' In *Imaginary Homelands: Essays and Criticism, 1981–1991*, by Salman Rushdie, 9–21. London: Granta.

Safran, William. 1991. 'Diasporas in Modern Societies; Myths of Homeland and Return.' *Diaspora: A Journal of Transnational Studies* 1 (1): 83–99.

Sassen, Saskia. 2014. *Expulsions: Brutality and Complexity in the Global Economy*. Cambridge, MA: Belknap Press of Harvard University Press.

Sheffer, Gabriel. 2006. 'Transnational and Ethnonational Diasporism.' *Diaspora: A Journal of Transnational Studies* 15 (1): 121–145.

Sokefield, Martin. 2006. 'Mobilizing in Transnational Space: A Social Movement Approach to the Formation of Diaspora.' *Global Networks* 6 (3): 265–284.

Thayil, Jeet, ed. 2006. *Divided Time: India and the End of Diaspora*. Special issue of *Journal of Postcolonial Studies* 42 (2).

Tinti, Peter, and Tuesday Reitano. 2016. *Migrant, Refugee, Smuggler, Saviour*. London: C. Hurst and Co. Ltd.

Tölölyan, Khachig. 2007. 'The Contemporary Discourse of Diaspora Studies.' *Comparative Studies of South Asia, Africa and the Middle East* 27 (3): 647–655.

United Nations High Commissioner for Refugees (n.d.) Available at: www.unhcr.org/figures-at-a-glance. html.

United Nations Sustainable Development Home Page (n.d.) Available at: www.un.org/sustainabledevelopment/sustainable-development-goals/.

Werbner, Pnina. 2013. 'Migration and Transnational Studies: Between Simultaneity and Rupture.' In *A Companion to Diaspora and Transnationalism*, edited by Ato Quayson and Girish Daswani, 105–124. Oxford: Wiley Blackwell.

PART I

Origins

TERMS AND CONCEPTIONS

Introduction

The term diaspora, and the constellation of terms that surrounds it and interconnects with it,[1] have been subject to a complex series of redefinitions – not only because the concept itself has an extremely long history, but because the history of modernity, and in particular of the twentieth and twenty-first centuries, means that almost every significant historical moment has been linked to the movement of populations across borders, and the consequent reconstitution of national populations and national identities. As James Clifford says in an article included in this section, 'in the late twentieth century, all or most communities have diasporic dimensions (moments, tactics, practices, articulations) [although] some are more diasporic than others'. For these reasons, and because of the constantly changing picture of human settlement, assimilation and resistance, the phenomenon of diaspora has affected every element of political and cultural life. Bringing these changes under a common conception of 'people living outside the homeland', while self-evident in one sense, is clearly fraught with difficulties, as the fundamental differences between, for example, the Jewish and the African diasporas make apparent. Moreover, as Thomas Nail (2015) says in *The Figure of the Migrant*:

> the history of migration is not a linear or progressive history of distinct 'ages'. Rather, it is a history of coexisting and overlapping social forces of expulsion. The same techniques of territorial, political, juridical, and economic expulsion of the migrants that have emerged and repeated themselves in history are still at work today.
>
> (6)

The influential journal *Diaspora: A Journal of Transnational Studies*, edited by Khachig Tölölyan at Wesleyan University, was established in 1991,[2] its title a challenge to social and political scientists to explore the term 'diaspora', and its boundaries, inclusions and exclusions. At the start of his article published in that inaugural issue, 'Diasporas in modern societies: Myths of homeland and return', the social/political scientist William Safran claimed that 'in most scholarly discussions of ethnic communities, immigrants, and aliens, and in most treatments of relationships between minorities and majorities, little if any attention has been devoted to diasporas'. He notes, however, that usage of 'diaspora' had already begun to move away from reference solely to Jewish exile and dispersion towards it being a generic term used in a variety of other contexts. Safran lists the many disparate groups that can be filed under this heading, from Cubans and Mexicans in the

United States to Corsicans in Marseilles. Safran's article is seminal in that it conveys the most influential aspect of thinking about diaspora up to that time. Safran turns to beliefs drawn from Jewish thinking and traceable to Exodus, in focusing his definition of a diaspora around the concept of 'return to the homeland'. His expanded definition enumerates a number of features: dispersal from an original centre; a collective memory, vision or myth about the homeland; a sense of not being fully accepted by the host society; a desire to return to an original homeland; commitment to the maintenance or restoration of that homeland; and a continued personal or vicarious relation to that homeland. Safran's discussion of 'the homeland myth' similarly takes as its starting point the Jewish experience of exile – though it also draws sophisticated parallels between this and other diasporas in terms of diaspora/host and nation/homeland relationships. The article also proposes a far-reaching set of potential research questions, which were to inform subsequent thinking on diaspora. Even in 1991, Safran clearly considered that the term was in danger of being used too indiscriminately and without sufficient attention to its historical origins. His founding definitions have, however, proved controversial in that they appeared too narrow to accommodate present-day population flows and migratory patterns, and have since been challenged by other writers such as Rouse (1991), Brubaker (2004) and Ashcroft (2010). Nevertheless, Safran's is the text to turn to for a starting point in considering contemporary conceptions of diaspora.

James Clifford's anthropological research informs his article 'Diasporas'. Clifford stresses that diaspora is 'a traveling term' (the play on the semantic and geographical meanings of the word 'traveling' is significant), the definition of which has to be made against the background of 'changing global conditions'. He draws on the work of Safran, and he interrogates his core question of return to the homeland, and his reading of the nature of 'homeland' in a Jewish context – finding complicating features, for example, in the medieval Jewish Mediterranean. Clifford's emphasis is more on what Roger Rouse (1991) had called 'transnational migrant circuits' and on the model proposed by Paul Gilroy (1993) in his seminal study *The Black Atlantic* (see Part II, Chapter 8).

Diasporas need to be 'defined against the norms of nation states' (though diasporas need not always be antinationalist, and may have national aspirations of their own): 'indeed, claims of a primary link with "the homeland" usually must override conflicting rights and the history of others in the land', as in the case of the Jewish state of Israel. Clifford is one of the first to propose that diaspora should also be seen against 'indigenous and especially autochthonous, claims to travel in terms of tribal peoples', as the aspirations of migrants and of indigenous or first peoples may be antagonistic. He thus raises the question of how far dispersed 'tribal peoples' may also claim diasporic identities (see the section on 'Citizenship and the transglobal' in Part II).

Clifford could be said to discuss diasporas in terms of what they are not, by examining and defining the boundaries between them and other types of minority communities – testing the term, for example, against the related but distinct notion of 'immigrant communities', and exploring the ways in which a diaspora consciousness is constituted both negatively (by experiences of discrimination and exclusion) and positively (through identification with world historical cultural/political forces, such as 'Africa' or 'China'). He raises the question of the gendered nature of diasporic experience, and how such experience can encourage coalitions between different groups, and he also acknowledges Kobena Mercer's 'rigorously anti-essentialist' argument: namely, that diasporic communities are fundamentally ambivalent, since they 'grapple with the entanglement of subversion and the law, of invention and constraint – the complicity of distopia (sic) and utopia' (Clifford 1994, 319). (See Kobena Mercer's essay in Part IV, Chapter 28.)

Robin Cohen, revising and expanding his 1997 book *Global Diasporas* in 2008, reflects on the impact of the new research and scholarship that had occurred since 1991, in his assessment of the ongoing developments and debates in the field. Cohen identifies four phases in diaspora studies themselves: first, attention to the prototypical category of victim diasporas, whose history includes a cataclysmic event; later, a more 'metaphoric designation' examining all minority groups who have been displaced from their homeland without necessarily having experienced trauma (including labour and trade diasporas); then social constructivist critiques from the mid 1990s – a phase influenced by postmodern and poststructuralist thought, which moves diasporas away from the ideas of homeland and return and 'ethnic/religious community' and sees them as more fluid and hybrid. Finally, he suggests the need for a consolidation of these earlier and current concepts, some of which have emptied the term of its original meanings, in order to undertake a cautious return to ideas of homeland and belonging in the renewed search for 'core elements, common features and ideal types'.

Cohen draws on the work of Safran, and in fact includes a number of Safran's defining categories in his set of 'common features of diasporas'. This useful schema adds four more characteristics/aspects to Safran's typology:

1   groups who disperse for colonial or voluntary reasons (labour, trade and imperial diasporas);
2   recognition of the positive virtues of retaining a diasporic identity;
3   mobilising a multi-nodal collective identity in solidarity with co-ethnic members in other countries;
4   deterritorialised diasporas which can describe transnational bonds of mobility – i.e. multiply-displaced people, religious communities and cyberspace.

The picture emerging from these three articles is that of a sophisticated and sustained reassessment of the idea of diaspora, and of the politics surrounding its definition. They should be seen in the light of Avtar Brah's (1996) arguments about 'living diasporically' in *Cartographies of Diaspora*, which introduces a model different from Safran and Cohen's, based on the idea that diasporas are relocated communities (with a longing for the homeland that becomes materialised as a project of reconstruction in the hostland), rather than Clifford's travelling cultures, or Safran's homeland-oriented exiles.

Notes

1   James Clifford, in the article included in this volume, describes 'terms such as border, travel, creolization, transculturation, hybridity, and diaspora (as well as the looser diasporic)' as 'jostling and conversing' with 'diaspora'. Transnationalism, hybridity, globalization, postcolonial, minority and other related terms also feature in the process of definition and discrimination.
2   Khachig Tölölyan and Robin Cohen discuss Tölölyan's Armenian background, the genesis of *Diaspora*, and definitions of diaspora in a relaxed conversation recorded in Oxford in 2011. Tölölyan refers there to diaspora's usefulness as 'a term to think with'. See: https://vimeo.com/25020401.

References

Ashcroft, Bill, 2010. 'Globalization, Transnation and Utopia.' In *Locating Transnational Ideals*, ed. Walter Goebel and Saskia Schabio, 13–29. London: Routledge.

Brah, Avtar. 1996. *Cartographies of Diaspora: Contesting Identities.* London: Routledge.

Brubaker, Rogers. 2004. *Ethnicity without Groups.* Cambridge, MA: Harvard University Press.

Clifford, James. 1994. 'Diasporas.' *Cultural Anthropology* 9 (3): 302–338.

Gilroy, Paul. 1993. *The Black Atlantic: Double Consciousness and Modernity.* Cambridge, MA: Harvard University Press.

Nail, Thomas. 2015. *The Figure of the Migrant.* Stanford, CA: Stanford University Press.

Rouse, Roger. 1991. 'Mexican Migration and the Social Space of Postmodernism.' *Diaspora* 1 (1): 8–23.

1

DIASPORAS IN MODERN SOCIETIES

Myths of homeland and return

William Safran

1. Minorities, aliens, and diasporas: The conceptual problem

In most scholarly discussions of ethnic communities, immigrants, and aliens, and in most treatments of relationships between minorities and majorities, little if any attention has been devoted to diasporas. In the most widely read books on nationalism and ethnonationalism,[1] the phenomenon is not considered worthy of discussion, let alone index entries. This omission is not surprising, for through the ages, *the Diaspora* had a very specific meaning: the exile of the Jews from their historic homeland and their dispersion throughout many lands, signifying as well the oppression and moral degradation implied by that dispersion. But a unique phenomenon is not very useful for social scientists attempting to make generalizations. Today, "diaspora" and, more specifically, "diaspora community" seem increasingly to be used as metaphoric designations for several categories of people—expatriates, expellees, political refugees, alien residents, immigrants, and ethnic and racial minorities *tout court*—in much the same way that "ghetto" has come to designate all kinds of crowded, constricted, and disprivileged urban environments, and "holocaust" has come to be applied to all kinds of mass murder.

Basing their studies on a fairly broad working definition of diaspora such as that of Walker Connor, "that segment of a people living outside the homeland" (1986, 16), scholars have applied the term to Cubans and Mexicans in the United States, Pakistanis in Britain, Maghrebis in France, Turks in Germany, Chinese communities in Southeast Asia, Greek and Polish minorities, Palestinian Arabs, blacks in North America and the Caribbean, Indians and Armenians in various countries, Corsicans in Marseilles, and even Flemish-speaking Belgians living in communal enclaves in Wallonia. Lest the term lose all meaning, I suggest that Connor's definition be extended and that the concept of diaspora be applied to expatriate minority communities whose members share several of the following characteristics: 1) they, or their ancestors, have been dispersed from a specific original "center" to two or more "peripheral," or foreign, regions; 2) they retain a collective memory, vision, or myth about their original homeland—its physical location, history, and achievements; 3) they believe that they are not—and perhaps cannot be— fully accepted by their host society and therefore feel partly alienated and insulated from it; 4) they regard their ancestral homeland as their true, ideal home and as the place to which they or their descendants would (or should) eventually return—when conditions are appropriate; 5) they believe that they should, collectively, be committed to the maintenance or restoration of their original homeland and to its safety and prosperity; and 6) they continue to relate, personally or vicariously, to that homeland in one way or another, and their ethnocommunal consciousness and solidarity are importantly defined by the existence of such a relationship. In terms of that definition, we may legitimately speak of the Armenian, Maghrebi, Turkish, Palestinian, Cuban, Greek, and perhaps Chinese diasporas at present and of the Polish diaspora of the past, although none of them fully conforms to the "ideal type" of the Jewish Diaspora.

[. . .]

2. The operative aspect of the homeland myth: A triangular relationship

In an old Jewish joke from an Eastern European shtetl, the husband asks his wife: "What will happen to the million zloty I invested in the business if the Messiah comes, and we have to leave everything behind?" And the wife answers: "With God's help, the Messiah will not come so soon."

A cartoon appeared in Le Monde several years ago, showing an old man who says: "I have never lost hope of returning to my homeland some day. However, I no longer remember where I came from."

Some diasporas persist—and their members do not go "home"—because there is no homeland to which to return; because, although a homeland may exist, it is not a welcoming place with which they can identify politically, ideologically, or socially; or because it would be too inconvenient and disruptive, if not traumatic, to leave the diaspora. In the meantime, the myth of return serves to solidify ethnic consciousness and solidarity when religion can no longer do so, when the cohesiveness of the local community is loosened, and when the family is threatened with disintegration.

For many strictly religious Jews of Eastern Europe, the homeland myth was devoid of practical consequence, not only because until the nineteenth century the Holy Land was not open to mass resettlement but, more important, because any physical return before the advent of the Messiah would be considered anathema. For many secular (Yiddish-speaking) Jews of Eastern Europe the homeland myth was displaced by a striving for communal autonomy *within* the diaspora. By contrast, among American Jews who were neither religious nor Yiddish-speaking the homeland myth was not a powerful force because they lived in a settler country that defined membership in the political community in functional rather than organic terms. The myth took on real meaning to many American Jews after World War II—in part because it helped them to assuage their feelings of guilt for not having done enough to save their brethren in the European diaspora. At the same time, American Jews defined their diaspora in theologically "neutral" terms, that is, as a purely physical dispersion (*golah*), in opposition to much of the Israeli political leadership, which continued to think of diaspora in terms of its traditional associations with moral degradation, insecurity, and persecution (*galut*).

There are Jews—including religiously observant ones—who argue that with the establishment of Israel the diaspora in the purely theological sense has been brought to an end, although the physical (and voluntary) dispersion of Jews may be continuing (see Cohen 1979, 184ff). There are others, however, who believe that, in a sociopsychological sense, the diaspora has not ended, because the state of Israel is itself in a "diaspora" condition globally to the extent that it is treated as a pariah state by international organizations and regarded as not even "belonging" to the region in which it is located. This may be a questionable metaphorical use of the term; it does, however, serve to fortify the sympathies of the physical diaspora for the homeland community.

While the homeland myth exists, however, it is exploited for a variety of political and social purposes by the diaspora, the homeland, and the host society. This "triangular relationship"— alluded to by Sheffer but not subjected to a comparative analysis (1986, 1–15)—has interesting implications for majority–minority relations and has political consequences that may be both advantageous and disadvantageous for the diaspora.

Members of diaspora communities are by turns mistreated by the host country as "strangers within the gates" or welcomed or exploited for the sake of the domestic and diplomatic interests of the host country. Internal social unity has on some occasions *required* that minorities be kept as diasporas. Thus the persistence of the Jewish diaspora was for generations a convenient and even necessary element of Christian theology, the "wandering Jew" provided daily proof of the superiority of the Christian faith, on which Western societies were based. This was the obverse of the Jews' own *post hoc* theological rationalization for their diaspora condition: the belief (reaffirmed by the devout in their daily prayers) that they had been exiled from their land as a collective punishment for their sins (which, in the eyes of the Jews, did *not* include deicide). The members of the Armenian diaspora have been spared a general demonization; the slave, and later free, members of the black diaspora may have been stigmatized according to certain biblical interpretations and, in more modern times, according to pseudo-scientific genetic criteria; and the Palestinians are often stigmatized collectively as terrorists par excellence. However, the members of these diasporas have not castigated themselves in the same manner as have the Jews. On the contrary, their diaspora conditions have been attributed to the sins of others: the cruelties of the Ottoman Turks, the greed of American colonists, and the duplicity of the British, the Americans, and the Zionists. Conversely, there are Christian fundamentalists who have theological motivations for putting an end to the Jewish diaspora: the conviction that the Jews' return to the Holy Land would expedite the Second Coming of Christ.

Sometimes the interest of internal unity requires that minority group relations with a (potential or actual) homeland be disrupted—in effect, that the diaspora character of a minority be ended. This approach was reflected in France during the era of the Revolution and Napoleon, when the "Jewish nation" was transformed into a mere religious cult. It was also reflected in the Soviet Union in the 1920s when the authorities began to use the Cyrillic alphabet for the Turkish languages spoken within their country, in order to differentiate them (and their speakers) from the language spoken in Turkey, for which Kemal had just introduced the Latin script (see Lewis 1972, 217ff); again after World War II when the Cyrillic alphabet was used for the language spoken in the Moldavian Soviet Republic, in order to distinguish its speakers from the Romanians west of the Prut river; and when the use of Hebrew was banned and words of Hebrew origin in Yiddish were spelled phonetically so that the connection of the language with Zionism would be obscured.

Sometimes the host country finds it useful to emphasize and strengthen diaspora sentiments. This was done in France during the 1920s and 1930s when the Ministry of Public Instruction ordained that the children of Polish workers be instructed in the Polish language; in Germany in the 1930s, when (for purposes of scapegoating) the Nazis denaturalized Jewish citizens, thereby transforming most of them into Zionists; in the United States during the 1950s, when politicians stressed the diaspora aspect of Latvian and other immigrants from the "captive nations," in order to delegitimate the postwar incorporation of Baltic lands into the Soviet Union, and during the 1960s, when the Cuban immigrants' homeland sentiments were fanned for the purpose of recruiting them for the fight against Castro; by Arab governments since the 1960s, when they helped foster a diaspora consciousness among Palestinian Arabs in order to mobilize them against Israel;[2] and by German authorities at present, when they emphasize the provisional character of the Turkish workers' residence in order to increase the latter's incentive to return to their homeland.

Occasionally, a minority's interest in its homeland is stimulated for the sake of the promotion of a foreign-policy goal and ignored later when the direction of foreign policy has altered. This occurred when the United States at the end of World War I made grandiose promises to Armenians in the United States of an independent Armenia in eastern Anatolia—in order to weaken the Ottoman Empire, only to lose interest after the war as a result of a growing rapprochement with Turkey (Lang and Walker 1981, 2). It occurred also during World War II, when the British encouraged the formation of a Polish brigade to fight for a free Poland, only to sacrifice that aim in the interest of a postwar accommodation with the Soviet Union.

Diaspora sentiments may be manipulated by the government of the host country in order to influence the behavior of the homeland. United States government officials attempted on several occasions (especially during the presidency of Jimmy Carter) to have American Jews exert pressure on Israel; and during the post-World War II period, the Soviet Union cultivated the fear among Turks that it would someday use Armenian claims to eastern Anatolia as a lever for further Russian expansion at the expense of Turkey (Matossian 1968, 194–5).

Conversely, a "homeland" government may exploit diaspora sentiments for its purposes. Early in the twentieth century, Sun Yat-sen solicited support among overseas Chinese in his efforts at overthrowing the Ch'ing dynasty; later, the Nazis manipulated the Sudeten Germans and the *Volks-deutsche* in other parts of Eastern Europe to promote German territorial expansion and tried (without success) to have German Americans exert pressure on the United States government to stay out of World War II. The Greek government has attempted to use the Greek diaspora in the United States to lobby against Turkey; the Israeli government has used American Jewish leaders as interlocutors for the promotion of pro-Israeli policies; and France under de Gaulle attempted to use the francophone "diaspora" in Quebec to promote French cultural influence (and, incidentally, to annoy the "Anglo-Saxons"). Some factions of the PLO, representing (*inter alia*) one diaspora, the Palestinian, have tried to enlist the support of a second diaspora, the Armenian, against the homeland of a third diaspora, the Jewish. Finally, diasporas have expressed their sentiments spontaneously, in the form of general political support and remittances that are sent to Algeria, Greece, Israel, Mexico, and other homelands.

While the homelands are grateful for that support, they view the diaspora with a certain disdain for having been enticed by the fleshpots of capitalism and for retaining a vulgarized ethnic culture. This is among the reasons why homelands do not necessarily want to welcome their diasporas back from abroad. Returnees, particularly from host countries that are more advanced than the homeland, might unsettle its political, social, and economic equilibrium; returning Maghrebis, Mexicans, and Turks might be too ambitious and too demanding politically; blacks too Americanized; and Armenians too capitalist. Palestinian Arabs returning to Jordan from abroad might pose a threat to the throne (and life) of King Hussein. Even Israel (despite the Law of Return) is somewhat ambivalent about a massive influx of Soviet or American Jews—the former, because of the problem of integrating them professionally, and the latter, because they are too "Anglo-Saxon."

The homeland myth plays a role in the political behavior of diasporas and is reflected both in voting and in interdiaspora relations. In France, Mahgrebi–Jewish relations are complicated by the Arab–Israeli conflict; in the United States, black support of the Arab cause has translated itself into hostility toward Jews (though, to be sure, that hostility has multiple determinants); and in both countries diaspora Armenians, despite their capitalist outlook, have been positively inclined to the Soviet Union (for harboring the only Armenian political entity) (see Szaz 1983). In France, many Jews have voted for the Socialist party because of its more favorable attitude toward Israel, and one may assume that if in the future there is Maghrebi bloc voting it would benefit the Gaullist party for the opposite reason. In Britain, many Pakistanis voted for the Conservative party because of Mrs. Thatcher's anti-Soviet attitudes; and in the United States, Cubans, ethnics of East European origin, and (increasingly) Jews have voted for the Republican party because of its reputation for a tougher stand against Communism. Sometimes, the interest of the diaspora in the domestic affairs of the homeland takes the form of direct political interference, as, for example, the interference of the leaders of the Lubavitch Hasidic sect in Brooklyn in the politics of Israeli coalition formation.

In sum, both diaspora consciousness and the exploitation of the homeland myth by the homeland itself are reflected not so much in instrumental as in expressive behavior. It is a defense mechanism against slights committed by the host country against the minority, but it does not—and is not intended to—lead its members to prepare for the actual departure for the homeland. The "return" of most diasporas (much like the Second Coming or the next world) can thus been seen as a largely eschatological concept: it is used to make life more tolerable by holding out a utopia—or *eutopia*—that stands in contrast to the perceived *dystopia* in which actual life is lived.

The problem of diaspora/host country/homeland relationships—and, indeed, the very definition of diaspora—goes beyond the purely ethnic, genetic, and emotional. Devout Roman Catholics who live in largely Protestant countries may see themselves as living in a religious diaspora and look to Rome as their spiritual homeland. Catalans of Perpignan, who may be patriotic French citizens, may regard Barcelona as their cultural and linguistic homeland; and the German-speaking Swiss may locate the Germanic cultural center somewhere in Germany and view themselves as living in a "dispersed" or peripheral *Kulturgebiet*. For French and Italian Stalinists, the "hieratic" homeland was, for many years, Moscow, and they may have seen themselves as living in an ideological diaspora. For multinational corporations—and their executives—the economic diaspora may be constantly changing, and the homeland may be functionally defined: *ubi lucrum, ibi patria*. The complex and flexible positioning of ethnic diasporas between host countries and homelands thus constitutes a prototype for various sets of coordinates that social units and individuals use for defining, centering, and (if necessary) "delocalizing" their activities and identities, and that social scientists may use in analyzing the relationship between "insiders" and "outsiders" and between state and society.

Notes

1 For example, see Cobban (1969); Shafer (1955); Smith (1971); Rothschild (1981); and Enloe (1973).
2 According to Zuheir Mohsen, head of the Saiqa faction of the PLO, "There are no differences between Jordanians, Palestinians, Syrians, and Lebanese . . . It is only for political reasons that we carefully underline our Palestinian identity." Saiqa is backed by the Syrian government.

References

Cobban, Alfred. 1969. *The Nation State and National Self-Determination*. New York: Crowell.
Cohen, Arthur A. 1979. *The Natural and the Supernatural Jew*. 2nd rev. ed. New York: Behrman.
Connor, Walker. 1986. "The Impact of Homelands Upon Diasporas." *Modern Diasporas in International Politics*. Ed. Gabriel Sheffer. New York: St Martin's, 16–46.
Enloe, Cynthia. 1973. *Ethnic Conflict and Political Development*. Boston: Little.
Lang, David Marshall, and Christopher Walker. 1981. *The Armenians*. Rept. 32, 5th ed. Minority Rights Group: London.
Lewis, E. G. 1972. *Multilingualism in the Soviet Union*. The Hague: Mouton.
Matossian, Mary Kilburn. 1968. "Communist Rule and the Changing Armenian Cultural Pattern." *Ethnic Minorities in the Soviet Union*. Ed. Erich Goldhagen. New York: Praeger, 185–97.
Rothschild, Joseph. 1981. *Ethnopolitics*. New York: Columbia UP.
Shafer, Boyd C. 1955. *Nationalism: Myth and Reality*. New York: Harcourt.
Sheffer, Gabriel, ed. 1986. *Modem Diasporas in International Politics*. New York: St. Martin's.
Smith, Anthony D. 1971. *Theories of Nationalism*. New York: Harper.
Szaz, Z. Michael. 1983. "Armenian Terrorists and the East-West Conflict." *Journal of Social, Political, and Economic Studies* 8: 387–94.

2

DIASPORAS

James Clifford

Diaspora's borders

A different approach would be to specify the discursive field diacritically. Rather than locating essential features, we might focus on diaspora's borders, on what it defines itself against. And, we might ask, what articulations of identity are currently being replaced by diaspora claims? It is important to stress that the relational positioning at issue here is not a process of absolute othering, but rather of entangled tension. Diasporas are caught up with and defined against (1) the norms of nation-states and (2) indigenous, and especially autochthonous, claims by "tribal" peoples.

The nation-state, as common territory and time, is traversed and, to varying degrees, subverted by diasporic attachments. Diasporic populations do not come from elsewhere in the same way that "immigrants" do. In assimilationist national ideologies such as those of the United States, immigrants may experience loss and nostalgia, but only en route to a whole new home in a new place. Such narratives are designed to integrate immigrants, not people in diasporas. Whether the national narrative is one of common origins or of gathered populations, it cannot assimilate groups that maintain important allegiances and practical connections to a homeland or a dispersed community located elsewhere. Peoples whose sense of identity is centrally defined by collective histories of displacement and violent loss cannot be "cured" by merging into a new national community. This is especially true when they are the victims of ongoing, structural prejudice. Positive articulations of diaspora identity reach outside the normative territory and temporality (myth/history) of the nation-state.[1]

But are diaspora cultures consistently antinationalist? What about their own national aspirations? Resistance to assimilation can take the form of reclaiming another nation that has been lost, elsewhere in space and time, but powerful as a political formation here and now. There are, of course, antinationalist nationalisms, and I do not want to suggest that diasporic cultural politics are somehow innocent of nationalist aims or chauvinist agendas. Indeed, some of the most violent articulations of purity and racial exclusivism come from diaspora populations. But such discourses are usually weapons of the (relatively) weak. It is important to distinguish nationalist critical longing and nostalgic or eschatological visions, from actual nation building—with the help of armies, schools, police, and mass media. Nation and nation-state are not identical.[2] A certain prescriptive antinationalism, now intensely focused by the Bosnian horror, need not blind us to differences between dominant and subaltern claims. Diasporas have rarely founded nation-states:

Israel is the prime example. And such "homecomings" are, by definition, the negation of diaspora.

Whatever their ideologies of purity, diasporic cultural forms can never, in practice, be exclusively nationalist. They are deployed in transnational networks built from multiple attachments, and they encode practices of accommodation with, as well as resistance to, host countries and their norms. Diaspora is different from travel (though it works through travel practices) in that it is not temporary. It involves dwelling, maintaining communities, having collective homes away from home (and in this it is different from exile, with its frequently individualistic focus). Diaspora discourse articulates, or bends together, both roots *and* routes to construct what Gilroy describes as alternate public spheres (1987), forms of community consciousness and solidarity that maintain identifications outside the national time/space in order to live inside, with a difference. Diaspora cultures are not separatist, though they may have separatist or irredentist moments. The history of Jewish diaspora communities shows selective accommodation with the political, cultural, commercial, and everyday life forms of "host" societies. And the black diaspora culture currently being articulated in postcolonial Britain is concerned to struggle for different ways to be "British"—ways to stay and be different, to be British *and something else* complexly related to Africa and the Americas, to shared histories of enslavement, racist subordination, cultural survival, hybridization, resistance, and political rebellion. Thus the term *diaspora* is a signifier, not simply of transnationality and movement, but of political struggles to define the local, as distinctive community, in historical contexts of displacement. The simultaneous strategies of community maintenance and interaction combine the discourses and skills of what Vijay Mishra has termed *diasporas of exclusivism* and *diasporas of the border* (1994).

The specific cosmopolitanisms articulated by diaspora discourses are in constitutive tension with nation-state/assimilationist ideologies. They are also in tension with indigenous, and especially autochthonous, claims. These challenge the hegemony of modern nation-states in a different way. Tribal or "Fourth World" assertions of sovereignty and "first nationhood" do not feature histories of travel and settlement, though these may be part of the indigenous historical experience. They stress continuity of habitation, aboriginality, and often a "natural" connection to the land. Diaspora cultures, constituted by displacement, may resist such appeals on political principle—as in anti-Zionist Jewish writing, or in black injunctions to "stand" and "chant down Babylon." And they may be structured around a tension between return and deferral: "religion of the land"/"religion of the book" in Jewish tradition; or "roots"/"cut 'n' mix" aesthetics in black vernacular cultures.

Diaspora exists in practical, and at times principled, tension with nativist identity formations. The essay by Daniel and Jonathan Boyarín that I will discuss below makes a diasporist critique of autochthonous ("natural") but not indigenous ("historical") formulations. When claims to "natural" or "original" identity with the land are joined to an irredentist project and the coercive power of an exclusivist state, the results can be profoundly ambivalent and violent, as in the Jewish state of Israel. Indeed, claims of a primary link with "the homeland" usually must override conflicting rights and the history of others in the land. Even ancient homelands have seldom been pure or discrete. Moreover, what are the historical and/or indigenous rights of *relative* newcomers—fourth-generation Indians in Fiji, or even Mexicans in the southwestern United States since the sixteenth century? How long does it take to become "indigenous"? Lines too strictly drawn between "original" inhabitants (who often themselves replaced prior populations) and subsequent immigrants risk ahistoricism. With all these qualifications, however, it is clear that the claims to political legitimacy made by peoples who have inhabited a territory since before recorded history and those who arrived by steamboat or airplane will be founded on very different principles.

11

Diasporist and autochthonist histories, the aspirations of migrants and natives, do come into direct political antagonism; the clearest current example is Fiji. But when, as is often the case, both function as "minority" claims against a hegemonic/assimilationist state, the antagonism may be muted. Indeed there are significant areas of overlap. "Tribal" predicaments, in certain historical circumstances, are diasporic. For example, inasmuch as diasporas are dispersed networks of peoples who share common historical experiences of dispossession, displacement, adaptation, and so forth, the kinds of transnational alliances currently being forged by Fourth-World peoples contain diasporic elements. United by similar claims to "firstness" on the land and by common histories of decimation and marginality, these alliances often deploy diasporist visions of return to an original place—a land commonly articulated in visions of nature, divinity, mother earth, and the ancestors.

Dispersed tribal peoples, those who have been dispossessed of their lands or who must leave reduced reserves to find work, may claim *diasporic* identities. Inasmuch as their distinctive sense of themselves is oriented toward a lost or alienated home defined as aboriginal (and thus "outside" the surrounding nation-state), we can speak of a diasporic dimension of contemporary tribal life. Indeed, recognition of this dimension has been important in disputes about tribal membership. The category tribe, which was developed in U.S. law to distinguish settled Indians from roving, dangerous "bands," places a premium on localism and rootedness. Tribes with too many members living away from the homeland may have difficulty asserting their political/cultural status. This was the case for the Mashpee who, in 1978, failed to establish continuous "tribal" identity in court (Clifford 1988:277–346).

Thus, when it becomes important to assert the existence of a dispersed people, the language of diaspora comes into play, as a moment or dimension of tribal life.[3] All communities, even the most locally rooted, maintain structured travel circuits, linking members "at home" and "away." Under changing conditions of mass communication, globalization, post- and neocolonialism, these circuits are selectively restructured and rerouted according to *internal and external* dynamics. Within the diverse array of contemporary diasporic cultural forms, tribal displacements and networks are distinctive. For in claiming both autochthony and a specific, transregional world-liness, new tribal forms bypass an opposition between rootedness and displacement—an opposition underlying many visions of modernization seen as the inevitable destruction of autochthonous attachments by global forces. Tribal groups have, of course, never been simply "local": they have always been rooted and routed in particular landscapes, regional and inter-regional networks.[4] What may be distinctively *modern*, however, is the relentless assault on indigenous sovereignty by colonial powers, transnational capital, and emerging nation-states. If tribal groups survive, it is now frequently in artificially reduced and displaced conditions, with segments of their populations living in cities away from the land, temporarily or even perma-nently. In these conditions, the older forms of tribal cosmopolitanism (practices of travel, spiritual quest, trade, exploration, warfare, labor migrancy, visiting, and political alliance) are sup-plemented by more properly diasporic forms (practices of long-term dwelling away from home). The permanence of this dwelling, the frequency of returns or visits to homelands, and the degree of estrangement between urban and landed populations vary considerably. But the specificity of tribal diasporas, increasingly crucial *dimensions* of collective life, lies in the relative proximity and frequency of connection with land-based communities claiming autochthonous status.

I have been using the term *tribal* loosely to designate peoples who claim natural or *first-nation* sovereignty. They occupy the autochthonous end of a spectrum of indigenous attachments: peoples who deeply "belong" in a place by dint of continuous occupancy over an extended period. (Precisely how long it takes to *become* indigenous is always a political question.) Tribal cultures are not diasporas; their sense of rootedness in the land is precisely what diasporic peoples have lost. And yet, as we have seen, the tribal-diasporic opposition is not absolute. Like *diaspora's* other defining border with hegemonic nationalism, the opposition is a zone of relational contrast, including similarity and entangled difference. In the late twentieth century, all or most communities have diasporic dimensions (moments, tactics, practices, articulations). Some are more diasporic than others. I have suggested that it is not possible to define diaspora sharply, either by recourse to essential features or to privative oppositions. But it is possible to perceive a loosely coherent, adaptive constellation of responses to dwelling-in-displacement. The currency of these responses is inescapable.

The currency of diaspora discourses

The language of diaspora is increasingly invoked by displaced peoples who feel (maintain, revive, invent) a connection with a prior home. This sense of connection must be strong enough to resist erasure through the normalizing processes of forgetting, assimilating, and distancing. Many minority groups that have not previously identified in this way are now reclaiming diasporic origins and affiliations. What is the currency, the value and the contemporaneity, of diaspora discourse?

Association with another nation, region, continent, or world-historical force (such as Islam) gives added weight to claims against an oppressive national hegemony. Like tribal assertions of sovereignty, diasporic identifications reach beyond mere ethnic status within the composite, liberal state. The phrase *diasporic community* conveys a stronger sense of difference than, say, *ethnic neighborhood* did in the language of pluralist nationalism. This strong difference, this sense of being a "people" with historical roots and destinies outside the time/space of the host nation, is not separatist. (Rather, separatist desires are just one of its moments.) Whatever their eschatological longings, diaspora communities are "not-here" to stay. Diaspora cultures thus mediate, in a lived tension, the experiences of separation and entanglement, of living here and remembering/ desiring another place. If we think of displaced populations in almost any large city, the transnational urban swirl recently analyzed by Ulf Hannerz (1992), the role for mediating cultures of this kind will be apparent.

Diasporic language appears to be replacing, or at least supplementing, minority discourse.[5] Transnational connections break the binary relation of *minority* communities with *majority* societies—a dependency that structures projects of both assimilation and resistance. And it gives a strengthened spatial/historical content to older mediating concepts such as W. E. B. Du Bois's *double consciousness*. Moreover, diasporas are not exactly immigrant communities. The latter could be seen as temporary, a site where the canonical three generations struggled through a hard transition to ethnic American status. But the "immigrant" process never worked very well for Africans, enslaved or free, in the New World. And the so-called new immigrations of non-European peoples of color similarly disrupt linear assimilation narratives (see especially Schiller et al. 1992).[6] While there is a range of acceptance and alienation associated with ethnic and class variations, the masses of these new arrivals are kept in subordinate positions by established structures of racial exclusion. Moreover, their immigration often has a less all-or-nothing quality, given transport and communications technologies that facilitate multi-locale communities. (On the role of television, see Naficy 1991.) Large sections of New York City, it is sometimes said, are "parts of the Caribbean," and vice versa (Sutton and Chaney 1987). Diasporist discourses reflect the sense of being part of an ongoing transnational network that includes the homeland, not as something simply left behind, but as a place of attachment in a contrapuntal modernity.[7]

Diaspora consciousness is thus constituted both negatively and positively. It is constituted negatively by experiences of discrimination and exclusion. The barriers facing racialized sojourners are often reinforced by socioeconomic constraints, particularly—in North America—the development of a post-Fordist, nonunion, low-wage sector offering very limited opportunities for advancement. This regime *of flexible accumulation* requires massive transnational flows of capital and labor—depending on, and producing, diasporic populations. Casualization of labor and the revival of outwork production have increased the proportion of women in the workforce, many of them recent immigrants to industrial centers (Cohen 1987; Harvey 1989; Mitter 1986; Potts 1990; Sassen-Koob 1982). These developments have produced an increasingly familiar mobility "hourglass"—masses of exploited labor at the bottom and a very narrow passage to a large, relatively affluent middle and upper class (Rouse 1991:13). New immigrants confronting this situation, like the Aguilillans in Redwood City, may establish transregional identities, maintained through travel and telephone circuits, that do not stake everything on an increasingly risky future in a single nation. It is worth adding that a negative experience of racial and economic marginalization can also lead to new coalitions: one thinks of Maghrebi diasporic consciousness uniting Algerians, Moroccans, and Tunisians living in France, where a common history of colonial and neocolonial exploitation contributes to new solidarities. And the moment in 1970s Britain when the exclusionist term *black* was appropriated to form antiracial alliances between immigrant South Asians, Afro-Caribbeans, and Africans provides another example of a negative articulation of diaspora networks.

Diaspora consciousness is produced positively through identification with world historical cultural/political forces, such as "Africa" or "China." The process may not be as much about being African or Chinese, as about being American or British, or wherever one has settled, differently. It is also about feeling global. Islam, like Judaism in a predominantly Christian culture, can offer a sense of attachment elsewhere, to a different temporality and vision, a discrepant modernity. [D]iasporic consciousness "makes the best of a bad situation." Experiences of loss, marginality, and exile (differentially cushioned by class) are often reinforced by systematic exploitation and blocked advancement. This constitutive suffering coexists with the skills of survival: strength in adaptive distinction, discrepant cosmopolitanism, and stubborn visions of renewal. Diaspora consciousness lives loss and hope as a defining tension.

Notes

1 The distinction between immigrant and diasporic experiences, heightened for definitional clarity in this paragraph, should not be overdrawn. There are diasporic moments in classic assimilationist histories, early and late, as new arrivals maintain and later generations recover links to a homeland. Diasporic populations regularly "lose" members to the dominant culture.

2 In Jewish anti-Zionism, see, for example, the work of "diaspora nationalist" Simon Dubnow, whose secular vision of "autonomism" projected a cultural/historical/spiritual "national" identity beyond the territorial/political (1931, 1958). In an (un)orthodox vein, Jonathan and Daniel Boyarin argue that a rigorous eschatology of "return" at the end of historical time can produce a radical critique of Zionist literalism (1993).

3 In *The Western Abenakis of Vermont, 1600–1800: War, Migration, and the Survival of an Indian People*, historian Colin Galloway argues that Abenaki survival as a people was accomplished through "diaspora" (1990). The mobile family band, not the settled village, was the basic unit of group life. In response to conquest, many Abenaki bands moved, to Canada and all over the Northeast United States, while some stuck it out in Vermont. When so many villages disappeared, it *seemed* to outsiders that the group had been fatally decimated. In Galloway's perspective, diasporic communities such as Mashpee—where displaced members of several Cape Cod communities came together—seem less aberrant.

4 Recent interest in the oxymoronic figure of the *traveling native* complicates and historicizes, though it does not eliminate, the tension between tribal and diasporic claims to legitimacy. I am drawing here on the

insightful work of Teresia Teaiwa (1993). She evokes a long history of Pacific Islander travels (linked to contemporary practices):

> This mobility can be traced along ancient routes of exchange like the *kula* ring which linked the east peninsula of mainland New Guinea with the Trobriand Islands and Louisiade Archipelago; the epic voyages between Hawai'i, Tahiti, and Actearca/New Zealand; the consistent migration and exchange within the Fiji-Tonga-Samoa triangle; and the exchange of navigational knowledge among Carolinian and Mariana Islanders. These, of course, are just a few of the circuits within which Pacific Islanders represented/performed their identities as both dynamic and specific—ways they thought about difference through connection.
>
> *[Teaiwa 1993:12]*

5 In the U.S. academy, "minority" discourse has been theorized as a resistance practice (e.g., JanMohamed and Lloyd 1990). It is often institutionalized in programs defined by ethnicity/race. Diasporic transnationalism complicates and sometimes threatens this structure, particularly when "minorities" have defined themselves in ethnically absolutist, or nationalist, ways. In Britain, the tension betwen minority and diaspora articulations of identity takes place in a different context: "minority discourse" has been largely an official discourse.

6 The distinction between old and new, European and non-European immigrants, while critical, should not be overdrawn. Immigrants from Ireland and central, southern, and eastern Europe have been racialized. And anti-Semitism remains an often-latent, sometimes-explicit force. But generally speaking, European immigrants have, with time, come to participate as ethnic "whites" in multicultural America. The same cannot be said, overall, of populations of color—although region of origin, shade of skin, culture, and class may attenuate racist exclusion.

7 Edward Said has used the term *contrapuntal* to characterize one of the positive aspects of conditions of exile:

> Seeing "the entire world as a foreign land" makes possible originality of vision. Most people are principally aware of one culture, one setting, one home; exiles are aware of at least two, and this plurality of vision gives rise to an awareness of simultaneous dimensions, an awareness that—to borrow a phrase from music—is contrapuntal. . . . For an exile, habits of life, expression or activity in the new environment inevitably occur against the memory of these things in another environment. Thus both the new and the old environments are vivid, actual, occurring together contrapuntally.
>
> *[Said 1984:171–172; see also Said 1990:48–50]*

These reflections on exile apply to experiences of diaspora, but with the difference that the more individualistic, existential focus of the former is tempered by networks of community, collective practices of displaced dwelling, in the latter.

References

Boyarin, Daniel, and Jonathan Boyarin 1993 Diaspora: Generational Ground of Jewish Identity. *Critical Inquiry* 19(4):693–725.

Clifford, James 1988 *The Predicament of Culture*. Cambridge: Harvard University Press.

Cohen, Robin 1987 *The New Helots: Migrants in the International Division of Labour*. Aldershot, England: Gower.

Dubnow, Simon 1931 Diaspora. In *Encyclopedia of the Social Sciences*. pp. 126–130. New York: Macmillan.

——— 1958 *Nationalism and History: Essays in Old and New Judaism*. Philadelphia: Jewish Publication Society of America.

Galloway, Colin 1990 *The Western Abenakis of Vermont, 1600–1800: War, Migration, and the Survival of an Indian People*. Norman: University of Oklahoma Press.

Gilroy, Paul 1987 *There Ain't No Black in the Union Jack: The Cultural Politics of Race and Nation*. London: Hutchinson.

Hannerz, Ulf 1992 *Cultural Complexity: Studies in the Social Organization of Meaning*. New York: Columbia University Press.

Harvey, David 1989 *The Condition of Postmodernity: An Inquiry into the Origins of Cultural Change*. Oxford: Blackwell.

JanMohamed, Abdul, and David Lloyd, eds. 1990 *The Nature and Context of Minority Discourse*. New York: Oxford University Press.

Mishra, Vijay 1994 "The Familiar Temporariness" (V.S. Naipaul): Theorizing the Literature of the Indian Diaspora. Paper presented at the Center for Cultural Studies, University of California, Santa Cruz, February 2.

Mitter, Swasti 1986 *Common Fate, Common Bond: Women in the Global Economy*. London: Pluto Press.

Naficy, Hamid 1991 Exile Discourse and Televisual Fetishization. *Quarterly Review of Film and Video* 13(1–3):85–116.

Potts, Lydia 1990 *The World Labour Market: A History of Migration*. London: Zed Books.

Rouse, Roger 1991 Mexican Migration and the Social Space of Postmodernism. *Diaspora* 1(1):8–23.

Said, Edward 1984 Reflections of Exile. *Granta* 13:159–172.

——— 1990 Third World Intellectuals and Metropolitan Culture. *Raritan* 9(3):27–50.

Sassen-Koob, Saskia 1982 Recomposition and Peripherialization at the Core. *Contemporary Marxism* 5: 88–100.

Schiller, Nina Glick, Linda Basch, and Cristina Blanc-Szanton, eds. 1992 Towards a Transnational Perspective on Migration: Race, Class, Ethnicity, and Nationalism Reconsidered. *New York Academy of Sciences*, 645. New York: New York Academy of Sciences.

Sutton, Constance, and Elsa Chaney, eds. 1987 *Caribbean Life in New York City: Sociocultural Dimensions*. New York: Center for Migration Studies.

Teaiwa, Teresia 1993 Between Traveler and Native: The Traveling Native as Performative/Informative Figure. Paper presented at the University of California Humanities Research Institute, Minority Discourse II Conference, Santa Cruz, June.

3

FOUR PHASES OF DIASPORA STUDIES

Robin Cohen

Arguably, diaspora studies have gone through four phases, which I specify below, then explore in greater detail:

- First, the classical use of the term, usually capitalized as Diaspora and used only in the singular, was mainly confined to the study of the Jewish experience. The Greek diaspora made an off-stage appearance. Excluding some earlier casual references, from the 1960s and 1970s the classical meaning was systematically extended, becoming more common as a description of the dispersion of Africans, Armenians and the Irish. With the Jews, these peoples conceived their scattering as arising from a cataclysmic event that had traumatized the group as a whole, thereby creating the central historical experience of victimhood at the hands of a cruel oppressor. Retrospectively and without complete consensus, the Palestinians were later added to this group.
- In the second phase, in the 1980s and onwards, as Safran notably argued, diaspora was deployed as 'a metaphoric designation' to describe *different categories* of people – 'expatriates, expellees, political refugees, alien residents, immigrants and ethnic and racial minorities *tout court*'.[1] Moreover, a point again made by Safran, the term now designated a vast array of *different peoples* who either applied the term to themselves or had the label conferred upon them. Given their number (certainly now over one hundred), their historical experiences, collective narratives and differing relationships to homelands and hostlands, they were bound to be a more varied cluster of diasporas than the groups designated in phase one.[2]
- The third phase, from the mid-1990s, was marked by social constructionist critiques of 'second phase' theorists who, despite their recognition of the proliferation of groups newly designated as diasporas and the evolution of new ways of studying them, were still seen as holding back the full force of the concept.[3] Influenced by postmodernist readings, social constructionists sought to decompose two of the major building blocks previously delimiting and demarcating the diasporic idea, namely 'homeland' and 'ethnic/religious community'. In the postmodern world, it was further argued, identities have become deterritorialized and constructed and deconstructed in a flexible and situational way; accordingly, concepts of diaspora had to be radically reordered in response to this complexity.
- By the turn of the century, the current phase of consolidation set in. The social constructionist critiques were partially accommodated, but were seen as in danger of emptying the

notion of diaspora of much of its analytical and descriptive power. While the increased complexity and deterritonalization of identities are valid phenomena and constitutive of a small minority of diasporas (generally those that had been doubly or multiply displaced over time), ideas of home and often the stronger inflection of homeland remain powerful discourses and ones which, if anything, have been more strongly asserted in key examples (see Chapter 7). The phase of consolidation is marked by a modified reaffirmation of the diasporic idea, including its core elements, common features and ideal types. [. . .]

Conclusion: The tools to delineate a diaspora

There is little doubt that the reason why the term diaspora has become so contested is that it has become so popular. Friends, enemies and sceptics at least concur on that. For Soysal, the term has become 'venerated', for Anthias it has become a 'mantra', for Chariandy it is 'fashionable' and 'highly-favoured', for Sökefeld the term is 'hip' and 'in'. One scholar, Donald Akenson, is so annoyed at its popularity that he complains that 'diaspora' has become a 'massive linguistic weed'.[4]

One possible way of dealing with this escalation is to allow self-declaration (the emic view) to prevail. In such a hands-off approach, any group can be a diaspora if it wishes to and a wide range of meanings can be applied to the term. Who are we to object? Another strategy is to follow the tactic adopted by the ancient Greek, Procrustes, who offered hospitality in his iron bed to passers-by. So that they would fit the bed precisely, he stretched short people and cut off the limbs of long people. By analogy, we could espouse an utterly rigid set of criteria to which all newer diaspora claimants would have to conform before we would allow them to lie on our conceptual bed. Rejecting these two strategies, I propose instead to deploy the four tools of social science mentioned earlier (emic/etic claims, the time dimension, common features and ideal types) to help us find a middle path in delineating a diaspora.

Let us start with the emic/etic relationship. Here I can be blunt. Not everyone is a diaspora because they say they are. Social structures, historical experiences, prior conceptual understandings, and the opinions of other social actors (among other factors) also influence whether we can legitimately label a particular group a diaspora. Understanding a social actor's viewpoint is important, but it is not the end of the argument. We would be on stronger ground, however, if we were to argue that diasporas can be formed and mobilized in certain circumstances. The mould (the opportunity structure) will constrain the extent to which this is possible. The clay (the history and experience of the group in question) will act like sedimented silicate, providing the necessary and basic chemical compound. And the potters (the active political, social and cultural leaders of the putative diaspora) will have to organize effective institutions to create and shape diasporic sentiments and galvanize them to a common purpose.

Our second social scientific tool is the rather convenient wisdom of hindsight, the passage of time. This was first strongly emphasized by Maricnstras, who argued that 'time has to pass' before we can know that any community that has migrated 'is really a diaspora'.[5] In other words, one does not announce the formation of the diaspora the moment the representatives of a people first alight from a boat or aircraft at Ellis Island, London Heathrow or Chatrapati Shivaji (Bombay). Many members of a particular ethnic group may intend to and be able to merge into the crowd, lose their prior identity and achieve individualized forms of social mobility. (The changing of ethnically identifiable names by new immigrants signals this intention.) Other groups may intermarry with locals, adopt or blend with their religions and other social practices (creolize) and thereby slowly disappear as a separable ethnic group. A strong or renewed tie to the past or a block to assimilation in the present and future must exist to permit a diasporic consciousness to emerge, while the active fraction of the incipient diasporic must have time to mobilize the group concerned.

My third tool is to produce a consolidated list of the 'common features' of a diaspora, drawing on the classical tradition, on Safran's desiderata, his revised list and my own views (Table 3.1).[6] And here comes the first of my two health warnings. I deliberately use the expression *common* features to signify that not every diaspora will exhibit every feature listed, nor will they be present to the same degree over time and in all settings. These are the main strands that go into the making of a diasporic rope (see Chapter 9). The number of strands present and the more tightly coiled they are will provide the descriptive tool needed to delineate any one diaspora.

I turn now to my fourth and final tool to aid in the delineation of a diaspora, the use of Weberian 'ideal types'. By using a qualifying adjective – victim, labour, imperial, trade and deterritorialized – I have evolved a simple means of typologizing and classifying various diasporas, not by ignoring what they share in common, but by highlighting their most important charac-teristics (Table 3.2). In subsequent chapters of this book I explore these types in detail. But here comes the second, and sterner, health warning. Students who are unfamiliar with Weber's method are understandably annoyed at the adjective 'ideal', thinking that if the group they are examining does not conform, it is less than ideal, imperfect, or even inferior in relation to some gold standard. This is definitely not the case. 'Ideal' is meant to contrast with 'real'. Weber uses a deliberately exaggerated abstraction, which is useful for analytical and comparative purposes. It is normal, general, indeed *expected,* that real diasporas will differ from their prototypical ideal types. The scholar gains purchase on the phenomenon by acknowledging and evaluating the extent of real-life deviation from the ideal type.[7]

The above ways of delineating a diaspora should also enable students to understand the dia-sporic phenomenon in the round, though there are other aspects of diaspora that have not yet been covered. As I explain in the concluding two chapters, the new themes in diaspora studies

Table 3.1 Common features of diaspora

1	Dispersal from an original homeland, often traumatically, to two or more foreign regions;
2	alternatively or additionally, the expansion from a homeland in search of work, in pursuit of trade or to further colonial ambitions;
3	a collective memory and myth about the homeland, including its location, history, suffering and achievements;
4	an idealization of the real or imagined ancestral home and a collective commitment to its maintenance, restoration, safety and prosperity, even to its creation;
5	the frequent development of a return movement to the homeland that gains collective approbation even if many in the group are satisfied with only a vicarious relationship or intermittent visits to the homeland;
6	a strong ethnic group consciousness sustained over a long time and based on a sense of distinctiveness, a common history, the transmission of a common cultural and religious heritage and the belief in a common fate;
7	a troubled relationship with host societies, suggesting a lack of acceptance or the possibility that another calamity might befall the group;
8	a sense of empathy and co-responsibility with co-ethnic members in other countries of settlement even where home has become more vestigial; and
9	the possibility of a distinctive, creative, enriching life in host countries with a tolerance for pluralism.

Table 3.2 Ideal types of diaspora, examples and notes

Main types of diaspora	Main examples in this book	Also mentioned and notes
VICTIM	Jews, Africans, Armenians	Also discussed: Irish and Palestinians. Many contemporary refugee groups are incipient victim diasporas but time has to pass to see whether they return to their homelands, assimilate in their hostlands, creolize or mobilize as a diaspora.
LABOUR	Indentured Indians	Also discussed: Chinese and Japanese; Turks, Italians, North Africans. Many others could be included. Another synonymous expression is 'proletarian diaspora'.
IMPERIAL	British	Also discussed: Russians, colonial powers other than Britain. Other synonymous expressions are 'settler' or 'colonial' diasporas.
TRADE	Lebanese, Chinese	Also discussed: Venetians, business and professional Indians, Chinese, Japanese. Note also the auxiliary elements discussed in Chapter 5.
DETERRITORIALIZED	Caribbean peoples, Sindbis, Parsis	Also discussed: Roma, Muslims and other religious diasporas. The expressions 'hybrid', 'cultural' and 'post-colonial' also are linked to the idea of deterritorialization without being synonymous.

include looking at their changing role in international politics (particularly in the wake of 9/11) and seeing them as a means of facilitating the development of their home areas. Regrettably, I have insufficient space to cover literature, the visual and performing arts and some other areas of the humanities on which diaspora studies have made a dramatic impact in recent years.

In closing this chapter it might be worth explaining why the concept of diaspora is so attractive to so many groups. I advance the thought that in the face of the insecurity, risk and adversity characteristic of our global age, many social groups want to reach in and to reach out, to be simultaneously ethnic and transnational, local and cosmopolitan, to have a comfort zone and a questing impulse. We must thus consider not only whether the concept of diaspora has been appropriately used or improperly abused, *but also* what function it is serving to the many groups that have adopted it. For better or for worse, the ancient Greeks launched this conceptual vessel, and some may want to repel all recent boarders. However, many unexpected passengers are embarking whether we like it or not. Scholars of diaspora need to recognize the potency and ubiquity of the term, and to be open and flexible to new experiences and uses, without neglecting the constraints that the history, meaning and evolution of the term impose. As a casual internet search will show, the sceptics have conspicuously failed to blunt the popularity, rude good health and continuing heuristic value of the concept of diaspora.

Notes

1 William Safran 'Diasporas in modern societies: myths of homeland and return', *Diaspora*, 1 (1), 1991, p. 83.

2 I have used the expression 'social constructionist' to signify a mode of reasoning, closely associated with postmodernism, which suggests that reality is determined by social interaction (or intersubjectivity), rather than by objectivity (the acceptance of a natural or material world) or by subjectivity (a world determined by individual perceptions). The perspective tends to favour voluntarism and collective human agency over structure, history and habituation.

3 See the various case studies in Khalid Koser (ed.) *New African diasporas*, London: Routledge, 2003.

4 Floya Anthias, 'Evaluating "diaspora": beyond ethnicity', *Sociology*, 32 (3), 1998, p. 557. See also Akenson cited in Vic Satzewich *The Ukrainian diaspora*, London: Routledge, 2002, p. 14; David Chariandy, 'Postcolonial diasporas', *Postcolonial Text*, 2 (1), 2006. http://postcolonial.org/index.php/pct/article/view/440/159 (online journal with no page numbers) and Yasemin Nuhoglu Soysal, 'Citizenship and identity: living in diasporas in post-war Europe?', *Ethnic and Racial Studies*, 23 (1), 2000, pp. 1–15.

5 Richard Marienstras 'On the notion of diaspora', in Gérard Chaliand (ed.) *Minority peoples in the age of nation-states*, London: Pluto Press, 1989, p. 25. See also Rogers Brubaker 'The "diaspora" diaspora', *Ethnic and Racial Studies*, 28 (1), 2005, p. 7.

6 See William Safran, 'The Jewish Diaspora in a Comparative and Theoretical Perspective', *Israel Studies*, 10 (1), 2005, p. 37 for a similar list, which I admire and from which I have drawn. The differences between us, which were more marked in the past, are not fundamental, but are largely matters of nuance.

7 A number of reference books will explain this. See, for example, the entry under Weber in Adam Kuper and Jessica Kuper (eds) *The social science encyclopaedia*, London: Routledge, 1999, pp. 906–910.

RELIGION AND DIASPORA

Introduction

What is religion? What is diaspora? Such fundamental and sweeping questions can be answered by very short introductions on the one hand, and by libraries of profound thought spanning centuries of reflection and dispute on the other. Neither is intended or envisioned with the texts in this section of the *Diaspora Studies Reader*, but the claim is upheld that the nexus of religion and diaspora is foundational to diaspora studies at large, with the implication that the statement possibly works vice versa as well. Here, the Jewish religion stands at the origin of the entire concept of diaspora, as, at least in the early Greek versions of the Bible, this is where 'diaspora' first appears to designate the relationship between a religious 'homeland' and dispersed religious groups living in far-off lands. Here, the diasporic tradition goes back in Biblical history to the so-called Babylonian Exile or Captivity, and has remained in continuous use after the loss of that homeland with the destruction of the Temple in Jerusalem in 70 AD and beyond the formation of the modern state of Israel in 1948. It seems obvious that neither Jewish religious practice or theology nor Jewish culture and cultural history would have been the same without this engrained diasporic experience. Similarly, diasporic concepts have been central to Christian theology and history, starting with St. Paul's view of all Christians living in diaspora in this world before they return to their true home in the heavenly Jerusalem (Gal. 4:26 and Phil. 3:20), and including Paul's own situation/identity as a Jew of the Hellenistic diaspora and the formation of Christian diasporic communities around the Mediterranean. As Christianity split up into various churches and denominations, the idea of diaspora stuck, so that nowadays 'denominational diaspora' refers to Christians living in areas where their denominational orientation is a minority, i.e. Catholics in Scandinavia or Protestants in parts of southern Germany and Austria; and the specifics of a 'double diaspora' express the experience of being in a minority situation as Christians within a generally secularized society and, within that minority, further forming a small denominational minority.

In the various branches of Islam, similar importance can be attributed to the Muslim diaspora, beginning with the concept that dispersion is already underway with the distance separating most Muslim communities from the holy sites in Mecca and Medina. This topographic experience of separation has given rise to a wealth of Muslim diasporic configurations, spanning the globe and informing Islamic history. Hinduism, as a further example, again binds together many diasporic groups around the world with their imagined homeland in India. In recent history, these diasporic religious practices in particular seek to synchronize with authoritative Hindu centres in India, but have their own dynamics and impact on Hinduism at large (Vertovec 2000, 162).

Thus, today's major world religions all appear to have a formative diasporic element of one kind or another in their theologies and belief systems as well as in their cultural histories. At the same time, many diasporic group identities are based on a shared faith or religion, which can be seen as the other side of the same coin. In fact, both Baumann and Vertovec in their articles reprinted in this section, address religion in the context of their respective explorations of the very 'meanings' or 'conceptualizations' of diaspora. Baumann's text is reprinted here as a classic study exploring the Jewish-Christian roots of the diaspora concept, but then abstracting from this paradigm so that it becomes applicable to other religious contexts as well. Having arrived in the first part of his article in formulating such a distillation of the meaning of diaspora, he then goes on to explore how it can be transferred to other religious contexts and other diasporas. He takes the Hindu diaspora as his example, illustrating how religious practices and belief systems have been both preserved and transformed among Indian communities dispersed and shaped in the wake of British colonialism, notably by the indentured worker system, and then later migration move-ments after India's independence in 1947. The different diasporic communities which emerged are shaped by their context which Baumann sees as mainly configured by four factors which consist of 'the nature of the migration process' and the 'ways of settlement', the 'nature of the migrant group', the situation in the host country and 'the situation and subsequent developments in the emigrants' home country'. Beyond this valuable differentiation, Baumann nevertheless is able to identify the common trait that the religious heritage remains a prime location for identity formation even among the younger generation of Indian diasporics, even if the kind of religious identity in the diasporic group is reformulated and reinterpreted, as Baumann exemplifies by an examination of the Hindu temples built in the diaspora.

Vertovec directly takes up Baumann's emphasis on the importance of religion in diaspora studies and his article essentially constitutes an elaborate justification of this claim. He substantiates this with three theses that structure his argument, pointing out the relevance of the insight to be gained from religious transformations in diasporas for the transformation of religions in general; addressing the potential impact of religious developments in the diasporas on those in the homeland, and exploring the impact produced by the (co-) presence of a multitude of diasporas today. Vertovec is particularly helpful in highlighting obfuscations in terminology by clarifying distinctions between the concept of diaspora on the one hand and 'religion', 'minority' or 'transnationalism' on the other. He elaborates this differentiation by exploring, in the following sections of his article, 'patterns of change surrounding migration and minority status', 'sur-rounding diaspora', 'surrounding transnationalism' and, finally, 'patterns of global religious change', the last of which takes up the former three and illustrates how diasporas, as well as the other factors described, have a share in and can help to elucidate global changes in religion.

Both Baumann and Vertovec assert religion as a core constituent of the diasporic concept in general, at the same time expressing their surprise at the neglect of the religious dimension in diaspora research. Although these two texts appeared in 1995 and 2000 respectively and have contributed to promote the study of religion and diaspora, and although some further work has been done (e.g. Kokot, Tölölyan and Alfonso 2004),[1] the observation remains valid that religion deserves a more central place in diaspora studies as a foundational concept in the field than it currently holds. New, challenging perspectives on this area of research are of course opened up under the impression of spreading religious fundamentalism and its (sometimes too facile) association with terrorism in recent history, where (in this case) Muslim diasporic groups within Western societies have come to be suspected of functioning as hotbeds, or at least hiding places, for terrorists with religious or pseudo-religious motivation. Much further research is called for in this area, but the two texts provided here form a reliable basis to start from.

Note

1 In his Reith Lectures (Lecture 4: Creed), Anthony Kwame Appiah (2016) addressed the importance of religion for (diasporic) identity formations.

References

Appiah, Anthony Kwame. 2016. *Mistaken Identities: The Reith Lectures 2016*. Available at: www.bbc.co.uk/programmes/b07z43ds, accessed 16 December 2016.
Kokot, Waltraud, Khachig Tölölyan, and Carolin Alfonso, eds. 2004. *Diaspora, Identity and Religion: New Directions in Theory and Research*. London and New York: Routledge.
Vertovec, Steven. 2000. *The Hindu Diaspora. Comparative Patterns*. London and New York: Routledge.

4

RELIGION AND DIASPORA

Steven Vertovec

Surprisingly, religion has been the focus of relatively little attention within this growing field [of diaspora studies]. The following article surveys a range of recent literature in order: (a) to outline some of the understandings of "diaspora" that have developed over the past ten years or so, (b) to argue that current "diaspora" concepts often suffer from conflation with "migration", "minority" and "transnationalism", and that each of these areas of study involve distinct — albeit related — dynamics of religious transformation, and (c) to indicate some patterns of religious change in connection with each of these concepts. [. . .]

Most writings on diaspora today have, in fact, "marginalized the factor of religion and relegated it to second place in favour of ethnicity and nationality" (Baumann 1998: 95).

Why study religion and diaspora?

As a response to the above question, Ninian Smart (1999) offers three basic reasons why it is important to study the connection between religion and diaspora (or, we might further suggest, why it is important to study the religious aspects of diasporic experience). Firstly, the study of diasporas and their modes of adaptation can give us insights into general patterns of religious transformation. Secondly, diasporas may themselves affect the development of religion in the homeland: the wealth, education and exposure to foreign influences transferred from diaspora may have significant effects on organization, practice and even belief. Finally, because of the great incidence of diasporas in the modern world, "multiethnicity is now commonplace" (Smart 1999: 421). These three facets are addressed in more detail under various headings below.

In appreciating the transformative potentials of religion in diaspora, we must first recognize that this is nothing new. Jonathan Z. Smith (1978) notes that almost every religion in Late Antiquity occurred in both a homeland and in diasporic centres (see, for instance, van der Toorn 1998, Dirven 1998). In homelands during this period, religions developed inextricably with local loyalties and ambitions, including as part of resistance to foreign domination.

> Each native tradition also had diasporic centers which exhibited marked change during the Late Antique period. There was a noticeable lessening of concern on the part of those in the diaspora from the destiny and fortunes of the native land and a relative

severing of the archaic ties between religion and the land. Certain cult centers remained sites of pilgrimage or sentimental attachment, but the old beliefs in national deities and the inextricable relationship of the deity to particular places was weakened.

(Smith 1978: xii)

In probing the meanings of religion, diaspora and change, we must also consider the implications of what we might call religious travel. James Clifford (1992) has written of "traveling cultures", suggesting how the meanings and relationships of dwelling-and-travelling displace conventional notions of culture and place (as well as challenge the ability of conventional methods of ethnography for representing cultures on the move). Since ancient times, religious travel has included pilgrimage, proselytization and the movement of students and scholars as well as exiles and migrants. Dale F. Eickelman and James Piscatori (1990a, b) have underlined the importance of such travel on the development of Islam. They consider travel foremost as a journey of the mind, including an imaginary connection with many sacred centres that has a significant impact on notions of religious belonging over distance, collective identity with those elsewhere, and ritual practice that is both universal and localized. Obviously these ideas have relevance for the understanding of diasporic dynamics.

In thinking about travelling religion, however, Ninian Smart (1999) raises a caveat through the example of Hinduism. He asks us to consider:

themes such as caste, yoga, *bhakti* [devotion], pilgrimage, temple rituals, austerity (*tapasya*), wandering holy men, instruction in the scriptural traditions, regional variation, pundits, a strong sense of purity and impurity, household rituals, veneration of the cow, the practice of astrology, belief in reincarnation, the importance of acquiring merit, etc. These themes, which are woven together into the complicated fabric of Hinduism in India, do not all travel equally easily to new environments.

(Smart 1999: 424)

Regarding categories and definitions, Robin Cohen (1997) questions whether religions can or should be described as "diasporas" alongside the dispersed ethnic groups which conventionally comprise the term. For Cohen, religions generally do not constitute diasporas in and of themselves. He describes religions at best as posing phenomena "cognate" to diasporas. This is largely because religions often span more than one ethnic group and, in the case of faiths that have come to be widely spread around the globe, religions normally do not seek to return to, or to recreate, a homeland. From Cohen's (1997: 189) perspective, while religions do not constitute diasporas themselves, they "can provide additional cement to bind a diasporic consciousness."

Judaism and Sikhism are the obvious exceptions, as Cohen recognizes. Dispersed members of these two traditions do represent diasporas since they are considered to comprise discrete ethnic groups, albeit especially marked by their religion, among whom many do indeed hold strong views about their conceived homelands. To these two, we should add groups like Ismailis, Alevis, Bahais, and Rastafarians whose respective religious distinctiveness usually tends to set them apart as ethnic groups. I have argued elsewhere (Vertovec 2000), too, that it is possible to talk of a "Hindu diaspora" especially because, no matter where in the world they live, most Hindus tend to sacralize India and therefore have a special kind of relationship to a spiritual homeland.

Other scholars are quicker to work with notions of "diaspora religion" (such as Smart 1999). John Hinnells (1997a: 686) defines diaspora religion as "the religion of any people who have a sense of living away from the land of the religion, or away from 'the old country'"; he even extends the term to cover situations in which a religion represents "a minority phenomenon" (Hinnells 1997a: 686). Gerrie ter Haar (1998) connects religion and diaspora through the assumption that migration means diaspora, migrants practice religion, and therefore diaspora implicates religion.

However, this is where conceptual waters begin to get muddy. Firstly, we begin to obfuscate the relationships of religion and diaspora, not to mention diaspora itself, if we regard it as involving any kind of migration or dispersal. It broadens the term far too much to talk – as many scholars do – about the "Muslim diaspora", "Catholic diaspora", "Methodist diaspora" and so forth. These are of course world traditions that span many ethnic groups and nationalities that have been spread by many other means than migration and displacement. Hinnells (1997a) himself flags up one problem with his own definition: are Muslims in Pakistan part of a diaspora religion because Islam is derived from and broadly centred on Mecca?

Secondly, to equate migration and subsequent minority status with diaspora also unnecessarily lumps together related yet arguably distinct conditions. "[O]ne does not announce the formation of the diaspora the moment the representatives of a people first get off the boat at Ellis island (or wherever)" Cohen (1997: 24) quips. The same holds for patterns of "transnationalism", a concept that also tends to be wrongly used interchangeably with diaspora. Migration and minority status, diaspora and transnationalism are intuitively linked, of course (Vertovec and Cohen 1999). But linked does not mean synonymous. Each of these abstract categories can be seen to comprise specific processes of socio-religious transformation.

Here, I argue that religious and other socio-cultural dynamics develop distinctively within the realms of (a) migration and minority status (of course a dual category that, given space to discuss, needs much unpacking as well), (b) diaspora, and (c) transnationalism. I consider migration to involve the transference and reconstitution of cultural patterns and social relations in a new setting, one that usually involves the migrants as minorities becoming set apart by "race," language, cultural traditions and religion. I refer to diaspora here especially as an imagined connection between a post-migration (including refugee) population and a place of origin and with people of similar cultural origins elsewhere. [By "imagined" I do not mean such connections might not be actual. Rather, by this I emphasize the often strong sentiments and mental pictures according to which members of diasporas organize themselves and undertake their cultural practices. This recalls Richard Marienstras' (1989: 120) definition of a diaspora as a group based on "a degree of national, or cultural, or linguistic awareness" of "a relationship, territorially discontinuous, with a group settled 'elsewhere'."] By transnationalism I refer to the actual, ongoing exchanges of information, money and resources – as well as regular travel and communication – that members of a diaspora may undertake with others in the homeland or elsewhere within the globalized ethnic community. Diasporas arise from some form of migration, but not all migration involves diasporic consciousness; all transnational communities comprise diasporas, but not all diasporas develop transnationalism. [. . .]

We should not assume that religious pluralism only refers to the co-presence of different faiths. Migrants – like travellers – newly often come across, for the first time, members and practices of distinct traditions within their own religion. As Eickelman and Piscatori (1990a: xv) point out, "the encounter with the Muslim 'Other' has been at least as important for self-definition as the confrontation with the European 'Other'. . . . The ironic counterpart to travel broadening one's consciousness of the spiritual unity of the umma is that travel may define frontiers between Muslims and thus narrow their horizons."

The self-consciousness of migrant minorities due to a condition of pluralism relates to, and may in certain ways overlap with, the identity dynamics associated with the condition of diaspora.

Patterns of change surrounding diaspora

As Shaye and Frerichs (1993) emphasized above, matters of cultural and religious adaptation-yet-continuity are foremost on the agendas of most diasporic groups. "[W]hat we have to grasp is a diasporic duality of continuity and change," suggests Martin Sökefeld (2000: 23), while we remain cognizant that "The rhetoric of continuity obscures that [sic] actors constantly re-constitute and re-invent (or refuse to re-constitute) in diverse manners what is imagined as simply continuing." [We must appreciate, too, that parallel forms of change may well be happening in the homeland as well, stimulated either from the diaspora or by non-diasporic factors altogether.] The "diasporic duality of continuity and change" is evident in a number of socio-religious domains.

Identity and community. "[R]eligious identities," writes R. Stephen Warner (1998: 3), "often (but not always) mean more to [individuals] away from home, in their diaspora, than they did before, and those identities undergo more or less modification as the years pass." One reason this occurs, he suggests, is because "The religious institutions they build, adapt, remodel and adopt become worlds unto themselves, 'congregations', where new relations among the members of the community – among men and women, parents and children, recent arrivals and those settled – are forged" (Warner 1998: 3). One example of this is to be found among Cubans in the United States who make pilgrimage to a purpose-built shrine in Miami. There, "through transtemporal and translocative symbols at the shrine, the diaspora imaginatively constructs its collective identity and transports itself to the Cuba of memory and desire" (Tweed 1997: 10).

"Identities change over time," Eickelman and Piscatori (1990b: 17) emphasize. Moreover, diasporic identification involves complexities and permutations: some people "continue to regard their land of birth as 'home', while others come to identify primarily with their land of settlement [Karpat 1990]. Others, such as Turkish workers in Germany [Mandel 1990], or indeed such intellectuals as Salman Rushdie (1988), may feel at home in neither place, at ease in neither their land of settlement nor their land of origin. There may also be multiple, co-existing identities" (Eickelman and Piscatori 1990b: 17).

Ritual practice. Complexities and permutations also often characterize processes of modifying or "streamlining" religious practices in diaspora (Hinnells 1997b). By way of illustration, in some places outside India basic Hindu ritual procedures have become truncated (as in Malaysia; Hutheesing 1983), refashioned (in Britain; Michaelson 1987), or eclectically performed (in East Africa; Bharati 1976); in others, much of the style or corpus of rites has been virtually "invented" in conjunction with social change in the community (evident in Trinidad; Vertovec 1992), and in still other places, basic rites have been mutually "negotiated" so as to provide a kind of socio-religious bridge between migrants from regionally distinct traditions (in England, Knott 1986; in Scotland Nye 1995; and in the USA, Lessinger 1995). In most places, many rites have been popularized in order to appeal to young, diaspora-born Hindus even to the chagrin of conservative elders: in Malaysia, for instance, Hindu leaders have complained that the inclusion of India-produced music has wrought the "disco-ization" of Hindu ritual (Willford 1998)!

"Re-spatialization". Jonathan Z. Smith described how, in the ancient world of the Mediterranean and Near East,

> For the native religionist, homeplace, the place to which one belongs, was *the* central religious category. One's self-definition, one's reality was the place into which one had been born – understood as both geographical and social place. To the new immigrant in the diaspora, nostalgia for homeplace and cultic substitutes for the old, sacred center were central religious values. . . . Diasporic religion, in contrast to native, locative

religion, was utopian in the strictest sense of the word, a religion of "nowhere", of transcendence.

(1978: xiv, emphasis in original)

Barbara Metcalf (1996) seems to recapitulate Smith through her interest in religious/diasporic "spaces" that are non-locative. "[I]t is ritual and sanctioned practice that is prior and that creates 'Muslim space'," Metcalf (1996: 3) proposes, "which thus does not require any juridically claimed territory or formally consecrated or architecturally specific space." She extends the spatial metaphor through reference to the "social space" of networks and identities created in new contexts away from homelands, the "cultural space" that emerges as Muslims interact, and "physical space" of residence and community buildings founded in new settings. Together, these spaces comprise the "imagined maps of diaspora Muslims" (Metcalf 1996: 18).

Pnina Werbner (1996) echoes Metcalf's "imagined maps" by suggesting that Muslims in diaspora connect via a "global sacred geography." This is created anew through the ritual sacralization of space in diasporic settings – a process, Werbner describes among Pakistani Sufis in Britain, which inherently conjoins sites both at home in Pakistan and in Manchester, UK. Similarly for Senegalese Sufis (Mourides) in diaspora, their holy city of Touba is metaphorically "recreated in the routine activities of the migrants and through recurrent parallels of the migrants' lives with that of the founder of the order, Cheikh Amadu Bamba" (Carter 1997: 55).

Diasporic transformation also involves a changing sense of religious time as well as space. As Werner Schiffauer (1988: 150) recalls among Turkish Muslims in Germany:

> The specifically peasant experience of an oscillation of one's social world between states of religious community and society is no longer present. During sacred times, society no longer changes into a religious community but, rather, one leaves the society and enters the religious community – if possible, we must add, since the opposition between secular and sacred times is now determined by the more fundamental notions of the working day and leisure.

Religion /culture. The reconfigured distinctions of sacred and secular space and time that occur in diaspora are matched by the sharpening of distinctions between religion and culture. To illustrate what is meant here: David Pocock (1976) observed that in one branch (the Bochasanwasi Shri Akshar Purushottam Sanstha) of the Hindu Swaminarayan movement there has emerged a tendency to consider certain aspects of Gujarati culture (including family structure, language, diet, marriage networks, and the position of women) as quasi-religious phenomena – that is, as behavioural and ideological facets contributing to the fulfillment of *dharma*. The subsequent problem Pocock discerned for the Sanstha is that of "dis-embedding a set of beliefs and practices – a 'religion' from a 'culture' which would then be defined as 'secular'" (1976: 362). This is a critical yet common dilemma for Hindus throughout the diaspora (and, some observe, in India itself). It entails moves toward a self-conscious "rationalization of the distinction religion/ culture" (Pocock 1976: 357) despite the everywhere-asserted dictum that "Hinduism is a way of life."

Processes of self-consciously distinguishing elements of religion/culture are bound to have differing results in various domains (in temples, in religious or cultural associations, in homes, in the workplace). In each case among Hindus in diaspora, such processes inherently involve both some kind of adaptation to religiously and culturally plural environments and the generation or heightening of distinct "ethnic" sentiments.

Martin Sökefeld (2000: 10) considers relevant developments among Alevis in diaspora:

> One could speak of an Alevi revival in Germany (and in Turkey) since 1989, but this revival was not a simple renewal of Alevism as it had been practiced until a few decades ago in Turkey. Instead, it implicated a serious transformation of Alevism and its rituals which can be glossed over as "folklorization": Although originally "religious" rituals were practiced, Alevism was re-constituted mainly as a secular culture.
>
> (Sökefeld 2000: 10)

The secularization of Alevism occurred, not least, due to the role of hardcore, anti-religious Marxists within the Alevi community in Germany. A further process of "desacralization" has occurred, Sökefeld notes, through the core Alevi collective ritual (*cem*) being turned into a public ritual solely to affirm identity based on symbolic cultural difference (from other Turks and Sunni Muslims)

In a similar way, both Madawi Al-Rasheed (1998) and Erica McClure (2000) detail ways in which members of the Assyrian diaspora sharply contend whether religion or ethnicity (or language) forms the basis of community identity.

Many young South Asian Muslim women interviewed by Kim Knott and Sadja Khokher (1993) are also conceptually establishing a firm distinction between "religion" and "culture" – a distinction between what, for their parents (particularly prior to migration), were largely indistinguishable realms. Further, they are rejecting their parents' conformity to ethnic traditions that the parents consider as emblematic of religiosity (such as manner of dress) while wholly embracing a Muslim identity in and of itself. Among these young women, Knott and Khokher explain, there is a "self-conscious exploration of the religion which was not relevant to the first generation" (1993: 596). [. . .]

Patterns of global religious change

Migration and minority status, diaspora and transnationalism each relate to different, but overlapping, grounds upon which religious transformations take place. The social scientific task of comprehending and analyzing these trends calls for a high degree of clarity as to which of these realms we are addressing at any time. Fuzziness and conflation of categories will cause us to chase our theoretical tails.

With special reference to South Asian religions, for instance, useful methodological frameworks for comparative study of the factors conditioning change among religious communities through migration, diaspora and transnationalism and are suggested by authors such as Jayawardena (1968, 1980), Clarke, Peach and Vertovec (1990), Knott (1991), Ballard 1994, Hinnells (1997b), and Vertovec (2000). They emphasize the need to take into mutual account pre-migration factors (including economic patterns, social structure and status relations), modes of migration, atmospheres and frameworks of reception and settlement, and trajectories of adaptation.

Inquiry into patterns of religious change surrounding this set of categories – migration and minority status, diaspora and transnationalism – will shine significant light on yet broader processes affecting religion in the world today. The final list of themes and short examples, below, suggest some of these.

Awareness of global religious identities. Smart (1999) points to the fact that, due in large part to migration, diasporas and transnationalism, there are now world organizations for every major religious tradition and subtradition located in most parts of the world. "Such a consciousness of belonging to a world community has grown considerably in very recent times," Smart (1999: 423) writes. "Consequently, the divergences between diaspora and home communities are diminishing." Even for relatively remote groups, transnational narratives "construct and negotiate the relationships between multiple identities" by tying individuals and communities into larger common constituencies (Robbins 1998: 123). [. . .]

Universalization v. localization. Ira Lapidus (2001) describes how there has always been inherent tension between Islamic universals and the experience of specific traditions being rooted in particular cultural contexts. Much of Islamic history has seen an "oscillation" between the two. Similar tensions are found in every world religion, and processes surrounding migration, diaspora and transnationalism continue to exercise or exacerbate them. [. . .]

What is essential in a religious tradition? As we have already seen above, the conscious disaggregation of "religion" from "culture" is sometimes prompted among people in diaspora. Raymond Williams (1984: 191) comments,

> The critical assumption here is that there are some aspects associated with past religious practice that are fundamental and essential to the continuation of the religion and others that are cultural accoutrements that are not so fundamental. Thus, the process of searching for an adaptive strategy becomes the attempt to distinguish what is essential in the religion and what is not.

Jacques Waardenburg (1988) points to the growing trend (especially among young people?) for discarding national or regional traditions and focusing upon the Qur'an and Sunna in order to distinguish what is truly Islamic – that is, normative – from what is secondary. The felt need to make this distinction is often what prompts young people in diaspora situations to join so-called "fundamentalist" movements (Schiffauer 1999).

Politico-religious activity. Religious-cum-political groups and networks that are dispersed across the borders of nation-states – or indeed, scattered globally – have in recent times developed their agendas in arguably new and distinct ways. The adoption of diverse modes of communication (including electronic and computer-mediated forms), the changing nature and manipulation of resources (channelling people, funds and information to and from a number of localities), and the maintenance of various kinds of relationships in relation to encompassing social and political contexts (including ties with people in the homeland / settlement land / and elsewhere in the world) are among the factors characterizing many politico-religious movements as diasporic or transnational. [. . .]

Reorienting devotion. Smith's (1978: xiv) account of religion of Late Antiquity posits that

> Rather than a god who dwelt in his temple or would regularly manifest himself in a cult house, the diaspora evolved complicated techniques for achieving visions, epiphanies or heavenly journeys. That is to say, they evolved modes of access to the deity which transcended any particular place.

Such modes represented fundamental shifts in belief or religious orientation. [. . .]

Compartmentalization. In assessing developments affecting religions and diasporas, Hinnells (1997b) stresses the impact of contemporary Western notions of religion on transplanted non-Western faiths. Such notions include secularization, liberal notions of inter-faith dialogue, and a broad tendency to treat religion as just another "compartment" of life. Hence it may come as no surprise that for many Hindus in Britain, Hinduism now "has the status of a 'compartment', or one of a number of aspects of life.

"Some are beginning to think of Hinduism as many people do Christianity, something to be remembered during large festivals and at births, marriages and deaths" (Knott 1986: 46).

This kind of religious shift should not be limited to non-Western traditions, however. As Susan Pattie (1997: 214) discovered, "For Armenians today, especially those in London, the sphere of religion is becoming increasingly isolated and definable as a distinct category of experience." Peggy Levitt (1998) relatedly suggests that Dominicans in diaspora have developed a more formal and utilitarian relationship to their church than do their counterparts in the Dominican Republic.

The problem with the past. Pattie (1997: 231) describes the "double bind" characterizing the situation of the Armenian Apostolic Church among Armenians in diaspora:

> On the one hand, its role as a national institution, imbued with visual, linguistic, and musical traditions, forges deep psychological links with the past. Looking at their diaspora situation, Armenians in Cyprus and London place great value on this continuing, seemingly unchanging aspect of the Church. Yet at the same time the old presentation is not always understood and, worse, not even experienced, as attendance and participation dwindle with each new generation.

In the Armenian example, it would seem the past is of lessening interest to newer generations. On the other hand, "Now that modern communication and travel technology brings dispersed peoples together more than ever, the usual assumption that attachment to the homeland will decline significantly after the first generation, and even more after the second, seems less self-evident" (Tweed 1997: 140). But of course – like with notions of presumed diasporic "continuity" discussed above – the idea of "attachment" to a homeland and a past signals what will most likely be a highly transformed mode and meaning of relationship.

Trajectories. A final theme of change involves the possible trajectories of collective identities and of local/regional or sectarian traditions in contexts of diaspora and transnationalism.

Possibilities for trajectories of identity are represented by Jacques Waardenburg's (1988) proposed set of "options" for Muslims in Europe (cf. Vertovec and Peach 1997, Vertovec and Rogers 1998). These can be summarized as (a) the secular option – discarding Muslim identity altogether; (b) the cooperative option – playing upon Muslim identity in the process of pursuing common goals with other groups; (c) the cultural option – maintaining particular social and cultural practices without much religious sentiment; (d) the religious option – emphasizing wholly scriptural modes of religious affiliation at the expense of cultural aspects (an option described by some as "fundamentalist"); (e) the ethnic-religious option – perpetuating a specific national or regional form of Islam (e.g. Moroccan); (f) the behavioural option – expressing Islamic tenets through moral or ritual behaviour only; and (g) the ideological option – identifying with or opposing the "official" Islam of a particular home country.

The possible trajectories of specific sub-traditions, I have suggested (Vertovec 2000), come down to the following: (1) remaining intact, as represented by processes of community "fission" described earlier; (2) homogenizing parochial forms through lowest common denominators of belief and practice (as developed within Hinduism in the Caribbean; van der Veer and Vertovec 1991, Vertovec 1992, 1994); (3) promoting a kind of ecumenism, in which a number of forms co-exist under a kind of umbrella organization (Williams 1988); (4) universalizing a specific form (such as the Hinduism of the VHP) by claiming it to be all-encompassing; and (5) cosmopolitanism, whereby the possibility of multiple, successive forms is celebrated (cf. Williams 1998).

Conclusion

The possible trajectories of identity and tradition in diaspora – like most of the themes of change suggested throughout this article – are not mutually exclusive. They are taking place simultaneously worldwide, and often within the same diaspora.

By isolating, as discrete categories, conditions surrounding migration and minority status, diaspora and transnationalism, we can gain more concise insights into processes and patterns of religious change. These tell us as much about a specific group's experience as they do about general characteristics of religious transformation on a broader level of abstraction. While in most ways the rush to study diaspora is certainly welcomed – as it challenges us to reconsider fundamental concepts such as identity and community, culture, continuity and change – it should not lead us to obfuscate the very categories we wish to clarify.

References

Al-Rasheed, Madawi (1998) *Iraqi Assyrian Christians in London: The Construction of Ethnicity*. Lewiston, NY: Edwin Mellen Press.

Ballard, Roger (1994) Introduction: The emergence of Desh Pardesh. In R. Ballard (ed.), *Desh Pardesh: The South Asian Presence in Britain*, 1–34. London: C. Hurst.

Baumann, Martin (1998) Sustaining "Little Indias": Hindu diasporas in Europe. In G. ter Haar (ed.), *Strangers and Sojourners: Religious Communities in the Diaspora*, 95–132. Leuven: Peeters.

Bharati, Agehandanda (1976) Ritualistic tolerance and ideological rigour: The paradigm of the expatriate Hindus in East Africa. *Contributions to Indian Sociology* 10: 317–39.

Carter, Donald M. (1997) *States of Grace: Senegalese in Italy and the New European Immigration*. Minneapolis: University of Minnesota Press.

Clarke, Colin, Ceri Peach and Steven Vertovec (1990) Introduction: themes in the study of the South Asian diaspora. In C. Clarke, C. Peach and S. Vertovec (eds), *South Asians Overseas: Migration and Ethnicity*, 1–29. Cambridge: Cambridge University Press.

Clifford, James (1992) Traveling cultures. In L. Grossberg, C. Nelson and P.A. Treichler (eds), *Cultural Studies*, 96–116. New York: Routledge.

Cohen, Robin (1997) *Global Diasporas: An Introduction*. London: UCL Press.

Dirven, Lucinda (1998) The Palmyrene diaspora in East and West: A Syrian community in the diaspora in the Roman period. In G. ter Haar (ed.), *Strangers and Sojourners: Religious Communities in the Diaspora*, 59–75. Leuven: Peeters.

Eickelman, Dale F. and James Piscatori (1990a) Preface. In D.F. Eickelman and J. Piscatori (eds), *Muslim Travellers: Pilgrimage: Migration and the Religious Imagination*, xii–xxii. London: Routledge.

—— (1990b) Social theory in the study of Muslim societies. In D.F. Eickelman and J. Piscatori (eds), *Muslim Travellers: Pilgrimage: Migration and the Religious Imagination*, 3–25. London: Routledge.

Hinnells, John R. (1997a) The study of diaspora religion. In J.R. Hinnells (ed.), *A New Handbook of Living Religions*, 682–90. Oxford: Blackwell.

—— (1997b) Comparative reflections on South Asian religion in international migration. In J.R. Hinnells (ed.), *A New Handbook of Living Religions*, 819–47. Oxford: Blackwell.

Hutheesing, M.O.L.K. (1983) The Thiratee Kalyanam ceremony among South Indian Hindu communities of Malaysia. *Eastern Anthropologist* 36: 131–47.

Jayawardena, Chandra (1968) Migration and social change: A survey of Indian communities overseas. *Geographical Review* 58: 426–49.

—— (1980) Culture and ethnicity in Guyana and Fiji. *Man* (N.S.) 15: 430–50.

Karpat, Kemal H. (1990) The *hijra* from Russia and the Balkans: the process of self-definition in the late Ottoman state. In D.F. Eickelman and J. Piscatori (eds), *Muslim Travellers: Pilgrimage: Migration and the Religious Imagination*, 131–52. London: Routledge.

Knott, Kim (1986) *Hinduism in Leeds: A Study of Religious Practice in the Indian Hindu Community and Hindu-Related Groups*. Leeds: Community Religions Project, University of Leeds.

—— (1991) Bound to Change? The religions of South Asians in Britain. In S. Vertovec (ed.), *Aspects of the South Asian Diaspora*, 86–111. New Delhi: Oxford University Press.

Knott, Kim and Sadja Khokher (1993) Religious and ethnic identity among young Muslim women in Bradford. *New Community* 19: 593–610.

Lapidus, Ira M. (2001) Between universalism and particularism: The historical bases of Muslim communal, national and global identities. *Global Networks* 1(1): 37–55.

Lessinger, Joanna (1995) *From the Ganges to the Hudson: Indian Immigrants in New York City*. Boston: Allyn & Bacon.

Levitt, Peggy (1998) Local-level global religion: The case of U.S.–Dominican migration. *Journal for the Scientific Study of Religion* 37(1): 74–89.

Mandel, Ruth (1990) Shifting centres and emergent identities: Turkey and Germany in the lives of Turkish *Gastarbeiter*. In D.F. Eickelman and J. Piscatori (eds), *Muslim Travellers: Pilgrimage: Migration and the Religious Imagination*, 153–71. London: Routledge.

Marienstras, Richard (1989) On the notion of diaspora. In G. Chaliand (ed.), *Minority Peoples in the Age of Nation-States*, 119–25. London: Pluto.

McClure, Erica (2000) Language, literacy and the construction of ethnic identity on the internet: The case of Assyrians in diaspora. Paper presented at the Conference on "Writing Diasporas – Transnational Imagination", University of Wales Swansea.

Metcalf, Barbara (1996) Introduction: Sacred words, sanctioned practice, new communities. In B. Metcalf (ed.), *Making Muslim Space in North America and Europe*, 1–27. Berkeley: University of California Press.

Michaelson, Maureen (1987) Domestic Hinduism in a Gujarati trading caste. In R. Burghart (ed.), *Hinduism in Great Britain*, 32–49. London: Tavistock.

Nye, Malory (1995) *A Place for Our Gods: The Construction of an Edinburgh Hindu Temple Community*. Richmond: Curzon.

Pattie, Susan P. (1997) *Faith in History: Armenians Rebuilding Community*. Washington D.C.: Smithsonian Institution Press.

Pocock, David F. (1976) Preservation of the religious life: Hindu immigrants in England. *Contributions to Indian Sociology* 10: 341–65.

Robbins, Joel (1998) On reading "world news": Apocalyptic narrative, negative nationalism and transnational Christianity in a Papua New Guinea society. *Social Analysis* 42(2): 103–30.

Rushdie, Salman (1988) *The Satanic Verses*. New York: Viking.

Schiffauer, Werner (1988) Migration and religiousness. In T. Gerholm and Y.G. Lithman (eds), *The New Islamic Presence in Europe*, 146–58. London: Mansell.

———— (1999) Islamism in the diaspora: The fascination of political Islam among second generation German Turks. *ESRC Transnational Communities Programme Working Paper* WPTC-99-06, www.transcomm.ox. ac.uk.

Shaye, J.D. Cohen and Ernst S. Frerichs (1993) Preface. In J.D.C. Shaye and E.S. Frerichs (eds), *Diasporas in Antiquity*, i–iii. Atlanta, GA: Scholars Press.

Smart, Ninian (1999) The importance of diasporas. In S. Vertovec and R. Cohen (eds), *Migration, Diasporas and Transnationalism*, 420–9. Aldershot: Edward Elgar.

Smith, Jonathan Z. (1978) *Map is Not Territory: Studies in the History of Religions*. Leiden: E.J. Brill.

Sökefeld, Martin (2000) Religion or culture? Concepts of identity in the Alevi diaspora. Paper presented at Conference on "Locality, Identity, Diaspora", University of Hamburg.

ter Haar, Gerrie (1998) Strangers and sojourners: An introduction. In G. ter Haar (ed.), *Strangers and Sojourners: Religious Communities in the Diaspora*, 1–11. Leuven: Peeters.

Tweed, Thomas A. (1997) *Our Lady of the Exile: Diasporic Religion at a Cuban Catholic Shrine in Miami*. New York: Oxford University Press.

van der Toorn, Karel (1998) Near Eastern communities in the diaspora before 587 BCE. In G. ter Haar (ed.), *Strangers and Sojourners: Religious Communities in the Diaspora*, 77–94. Leuven: Peeters.

van der Veer, Peter and Steven Vertovec (1991) Brahmanism abroad: On Caribbean Hinduism as an ethnic religion. *Ethnology* 30: 149–66.

Vertovec, Steven (1992) *Hindu Trinidad: Religion, Ethnicity and Socio-Economic Change*. Basingstoke: Macmillan.

———— (1994) "Official" and "popular" Hinduism in the Caribbean: Historical and contemporary trends in Surinam, Trinidad and Guyana. *Contributions to Indian Sociology* 28(1): 123–47.

———— (2000) *The Hindu Diaspora: Comparative Patterns*. London: Routledge.

Vertovec, Steven and Ceri Peach (1997) Introduction: Islam in Europe and the politics of religion and community. In S. Vertovec and C. Peach (eds), *Islam in Europe: The Politics of Religion and Community*, 3–47. Basingstoke: Macmillan.

Vertovec, Steven and Alisdair Rogers (1998) Introduction. In S. Vertovec and A. Rogers (eds), *Muslim European Youth: Re-producing Religion, Ethnicity and Culture*, 1–24. Aldershot: Avebury.

Vertovec, Steven and Robin Cohen (1999) Introduction. In S. Vertovec and R. Cohen (eds), *Migration, Diasporas and Transnationalism*, xiii–xxviii. Cheltenham: Edward Elgar.

Waardenburg, Jacques (1988) The institutionalization of Islam in the Netherlands. In T. Gerholm and Y.G. Lithman (eds), *The New Islamic Presence in Europe*, 8–31. London: Mansell.

Warner, R. Stephen (1998) Immigration and religious communities in the United States. In R.S. Warner and J.G. Wittner (eds), *Gatherings in Diaspora: Religious Communities and the New Immigration*, 3–34. Philadelphia: Temple University Press.

Werbner, Pnina (1996) Stamping the Earth in the name of Allah: Zikr and the sacralizing of space among British Muslims. *Cultural Anthropology* 11(3): 309–38.

Willford, A. (1998) Within and beyond the state: Ritual and the assertion of Tamil-Hindu identities in Malaysia. Paper presented at the conference on "Globalization from Below," Duke University.

Williams, Raymond B. (1984) *A New Face of Hinduism: The Swaminarayan Religion*. Cambridge: Cambridge University Press.

——— (1988) *Religions of Immigrants from India and Pakistan: New Threads in the American Tapestry*. Cambridge: Cambridge University Press.

——— (1998) Training religious specialists for a transnational Hinduism: A Swaminarayan sadhu training center. *Journal of the American Academy of Religion* 66: 841–62.

5

CONCEPTUALIZING DIASPORA

The preservation of religious identity in foreign parts, exemplified by Hindu communities outside India

Martin Baumann

This article attempts to treat the phenomena and concept of "diaspora" in a systematic and comparative way: Although social and political sciences have been using the term abundantly for the past decade or so, a theoretical conceptualization is lacking. In addition, reference to the term's origin within a religious context is rarely found in these discourses. Likewise, within the field of the academic Study of Religions (*Religionswissenschaft*), the notion is most often used only within the study of Judaism and Christianity. The paper will argue that it is well worth endeavouring to detach the notion from its Judeo-Christian setting and to employ "diaspora" as a general, i.e. theoretical concept. It should be applicable to various religious traditions. [. . .]

Surveying social and political scientific literature it becomes obvious that the "factor of religion", to my mind indissolubly linked to the concept, has become relegated to second place in favour of ethnicity and ethnic adherence.

Thus, this paper in its first part attempts to define the term "diaspora" and to regain the importance of the "religious factor". The second part will illustrate, by example of Hindu communities outside India, certain structures and dimensions of diaspora situations. The conclusion will indicate some systematic and methodological implications involved in the study of diasporas.

Part I: Conceptualizing "diaspora"

The notion "diaspora" is embedded within Jewish history. In the *Septuaginta*, the Greek translation of the Hebrew Scripts, the word *"diaspora"* appears twelve times. As a curious linguistic fact, the Greek word has no direct equivalent in the Hebrew Bible[1]. The usage of the term takes on at least three different meanings, pertaining to the Jews living outside Palestine: First, it relates to the course of becoming scattered and the situation of being dispersed among peoples of non-Jewish faith; second, the term denotes the community of those living under these conditions in foreign parts; and, third, the word refers to the place or geographic space in which these dispersed Jews lived (Rothenberg 1965: 372; Krüger 1994: 98–99).

To complicate matters of definition, the self-interpretation of living in the diaspora changed over time. The Old Testament prophets Jeremiah (17:1–4) and Ezekiel (12: 15) thought of the diaspora as the judgement of God for "the unbelief of the Jewish people". In the course of time, life in Babylonian and Egyptian Exile became interpreted less as a punishment but rather as a strategic dispersion aiming to unfold missionary activities among non-Jewish peoples (Isaiah 60, Haggai 2: 7, Sacharía 8: 20–23). The New Testament took on both interpretations, placing an emphasis on the missionary propagation of the Gospels (Acts of the Apostles 8: 4 and 11: 19; 1. Peter 1: l).

As a matter of fact, in both the Old and the New Testament the term "diaspora" is very tightly related to theological and soteriological concepts. In the Old Testament, diaspora is interpreted as a special kind of punishment, divinely imposed on Israel for its sin (one interpretation). In the New Testament a different understanding comes to the foreground. According to Paul, the Christians' home is not on earth, but rather in the heavenly domain, where the glorified Lord Jesus already is (Gal 4: 26; Phil 3: 20). Consequently, Christians should regard their existence on earth, in analogy to that of the sojourning people of God in the old covenant, to be a wandering and an alien one. Considering themselves as pilgrims on a home-bound journey, i.e. towards the final assembly in the heavenly city (Jerusalem), the Christian existence in the world is in itself of a diasporic nature. During their sojourn in the world, Christians as the scattered, albeit newly chosen people are given the religious obligation to preach the Gospel among their non-Christian neighbours. In brief, the *heilsgeschichtliche* ("interpretation of history stressing God's saving grace") diaspora-concept offered to the early Christian church a legitimation of its own and set its relationship with non-Christian society. It provided a rationalisation both for its distress and its task and promise (Schnackenburg 1971; Arowele 1977; Sänger 1982).

Taking these *religious* connotations, one rightfully has to question whether it is possible to apply the concept to non-Jewish and non-Christian religions at all. This is a consideration one has to bear in mind while attempting to establish the term as a theoretical one. The theological meaning and interpretation appear to mark a clear boundary with regard to the general application of the concept.

In order to establish the term as a general concept, one has to bracket out its theological meanings. Emphasis has to be placed on the notion's structural and functional characteristics. [. . .]

Abstracting key characteristics from this and further situations of Jewish and Christian diaspora, a working definition in all its provisional state will be given. Thus, a *diaspora is made up of a religious, often ethnic group which lives as a minority outside its land of origin. The immigrant minority has a religious orientation different to that of the members of the host society.* As a hypothesis it shall be deduced that in this context the preservation and perpetuation of one's religious identity becomes a core issue. To this end, cultural and material links are maintained with the country of origin, irrespective of living permanently in foreign parts. [. . .]

The next part will outline some aspects of the preservation and transformation of a religious tradition in a diaspora situation. The theoretical issues will be illustrated by example of Hindu communities outside India. Emphasis will be laid on processes of institutionalisation and identity maintenance.

Part II: Preservation and transformation in Hindu diasporas

Apart from settlements in Southeast Asia (esp. Bali), Hindus have been living outside India for about 150 years. During British colonialism, Indian workers were recruited for plantation and construction work in Africa and the Caribbean. The indentured worker system, by Tinker characterized as "a new system of slavery" (Tinker 1974), operated from 1834 to 1917; Indians were brought to British colonies such as Mauritius, British Guiana, Trinidad, Natal in South Africa, East Africa and the Fiji islands. Among the Hindus, indentured workers were recruited from all castes, and even Brahmans, for various reasons, signed the contract. In the colonies, however, most of the restrictions pertaining to caste exclusiveness lost importance or even vanished.

The second main period of Hindu emigration covered the decades following the Second World War and India's independence (1947). During the 1950s and early 1960s, large numbers of skilled and semi-skilled labourers moved to Britain. Since the mid-1960s Hindus have been allowed to settle in Australia, Canada and the United States. Since the 1970s, furthermore, Indians have crossed the Arabian Sea to work in the Arab States. During this period, chain migration was the dominant pattern of settling in the new country. As a consequence, a multitude of different Hindu diaspora situations have emerged. [. . .]

As observable among many migrant groups, not until living away from one's home country is the religious adherence consciously valued as significant. In a way, the religious affiliation moves from the latent to the manifest (Abramson 1979: 6).

Contrary to the assumptions of many social scientists, the young generation has not given up its parents' religious heritage in favour of modern individualism. Although, to a certain extent, cultural features such as, marriage patterns, diet, dress and skill in the home language have changed and often diminished[2], reference to the home country's religion has remained. In particular, confronted by racial and societal discrimination, religion is employed to reinforce one's cultural peculiarity and identity (Ballard 1994: 160, 270). The growing awareness of one's religious and cultural distinctiveness has led to a "setting up of boundaries that mark off the limits between the ethnic minority and the host society itself" (Taylor 1991: 208). In order to maintain one's identity, boundaries are pointed out, marked, if necessary accentuated[3].

The identity of the diaspora community is subjected to change and formation. "Identity" should not be conceived of as a static entity, but rather as a dynamic temporal process. Its key notion is not so much "identity-sameness as discerned continuity" (Hayes 1986: vii). In foreign parts, the preservation of this "discerned continuity" in particular becomes obvious. It arises as a problem that needs to be treated. Means have to be taken to counteract the constant threat of dispersal. In this regard, the Jewish and Christian history of religion already pointed to the peril of dissolution, to "the temptation of weekly assimilation" (Kruska 1956–61: 931) and the loss of one's identity. As such, the transplantation of a religious tradition and its preservation in a diaspora situation always entail the reinterpretation and reformulation of its religious identity.

Conclusion

[. . .]

Taking diaspora situations, various typologies can be set up on a systematic level. First, there is the opposite of *dispersal* or *perpetuation* of the religious tradition in the foreign parts. Between these contrastive poles various gradings are discernable, i.e. developments of decline on the one hand and processes of revival on the other. For example, both phases of decline and revival are observable among the 150-year-old Hindu diaspora community in Trinidad (Vertovec 1991b: 80–83; Vertovec 1992a: 117–127).

Another contrastive set of types may be constructed with regard to the ways and means the religious tradition is perpetuated. Is it done in close alignment to the home tradition, allowing very rare changes and innovations? Or is it done in various strategies of adaptation with regard to the socio-cultural situation of the host society? Here, diaspora situations are of particular importance, as they encompass modes of conservative "retraditionalisation" (Knott 1994: 237, King 1987: 132) as well as possibilities to select, emphasise and reinterpret religious rituals and concepts. Thus, one might label a transplanted religious tradition as *flexible* or *inflexible* in its attitude to adapting and to allowing for new forms and contents (Baumann 1994: 36).

Another typology may focus on processes of fusion versus fission. Fusion and/or fission in a diaspora occur on an organisational level, for example the construction of a common or of a regional and sectarian-based place for worship. Fusion and fission also take place with regard to the homogenisation or the fragmentation of doctrinal and conceptual reinterpretation. It remains to be seen whether the size and number of the immigrant group is decisive to take on either fusion or fission, or whether the duration of settlement and thus generational shifts may be of casual importance[4].

Notes

1 Arowele 1977: 5. Raphael Patai, as the only author I could trace so far, states that "in the entire Bible there are only two passages in which a Hebrew noun's form corresponding in meaning to Diaspora appears, and even one of these is doubtful." The forms are *n'futzot* (in Isaiah 11:12} and *t'fuzot* {in Jeremiah 25: 34), meaning "to disperse" or "to scatter", see Patai 1971: 24.
2 See, for example, the studies of Pocock 1976: Anderson and Frideres 1981: 105–126, Fitzgerald 1989.
3 For this point, see Mol 1976; Mol 1978; Mol 1986; Lewins 1978; Dashefsky 1979; Seiwert 1986; Knott 1988: 122; Williams 1988: 278.
4 For the point of "fusion or fission" among immigrant groups and communities, see Dahya 1974; Humphrey 1987: 240–244; Barot 1991: 195; Taylor 1991: 207; Doumanis 1992; Vertovec 1992c: 17.

References

Abramson, Harold J. 1979 Migrants and Cultural Diversity: On Ethnicity and Religion in Society. *Social Compas* 26: 5–29.
Anderson, Alan B. and James S. Frideres 1981 *Ethnicity in Canada. Theoretical Perspectives.* Toronto: Butterworths.
Arowele, Aiyenakun P. J. 1977 Diaspora-Concept in the New Testament. Studies on the Idea of Christian Sojourn, Pilgrimage and Dispersion according to the New Testament. [unpublished Ph.D. Thesis, Wurzburg University.]
Ballard, Roger (ed.) 1994 *Desh Pardesh. The South Asian Presence in Britain.* London: Hurst & Company.
Barot, Rohit 1991 Migration, Change and Indian Religions in Britain. In: W. A. R. Shadid and P. S. van Koningsveld (eds.), *The Integration of Islam and Hinduism in Western Europe*; pp. 188–200. Kampen: Kok Pharos Publishing House.
Baumann, Martin 1994 The Transplantation of Buddhism to Germany – Processive Modes and Strategies of Adaptation. *Method & Theory in the Study of Religion* 6: 35–61.
Dahya, Badr 1974 The Nature of Pakistani Ethnicity in Industrial Cities in Britain. In: Abner Cohen (ed.), *Urban Ethnicity*; pp. 77–118. London: Tavistock.
Dashefsky, Arnold 1979 And the Search Goes on: The Meaning of Religio-Ethnic Identity and Identification. *Sociological Analysis* 33: 239–245.
Doumanis, Nicholas 1992 Eastern Orthodoxy and Migrant Conflict: The Greek Church Schism in Australia, 1959–74. *Journal of Religious History* 17: 60–76.
Fitzgerald, Thomas K. 1989 Coconuts and Kiwis: Identity and Change among Second-Generation Cook Islanders in New Zealand. *Ethnic-Groups* 7: 259–281.
Hayes, Victor C. (ed.) 1986 *Identity Issues and World Religions. Selected Proceedings of the Fifteenth Congress of the International Association for the History of Religions.* Bedford Park: University Relations Unit.
Humphrey, Michael 1987 Community, Mosque and Ethnic Politics. *Australian and New Zealand Journal of Sociology* 23: 233–245.
King, Ursula 1987 Religionen ethnischer Minderheiten in England. Bericht über ein Forschungsprojekt der Universitat Leeds. In: Michael Pye and Renate Stegerhoff (eds.), *Religion in fremder Kultur. Religion als Minderheit in Europa und Asien*; pp. 123–133. Saarbrücken-Scheidt: Dadder.
Knott, Kim 1988 Strategies for Survival among South Asian Religions in Britain: Parallel Developments, Conflict and Cooperation. In: Chuo Academic Research Institute (ed.), *Conflict and Cooperation between Contemporary Religious Groups*; pp. 95–128. Tokyo.
———— 1994 *Hinduism in Leeds: A Study of Religious Practice in the Indian Hindu Community and in Hindu-Related Groups.* Leeds: University of Leeds.
Krüger, René 1994 Das biblische Paradigma der Diaspora. Die solidarische und missionarische Gemeinschaft der Gläubigen. *Die evangelische Diaspora* 63: 87–109.

Kruska, Harald 1956–61 Diaspora. In: Heinz Brunotte and Otto Welier (eds.), *Evangelisches Kirchenlexikon. Kirchlich-theologisches Handwörterbuch*; 4. vols.; pp. 930–934. Göttingen: Vandenhoeck & Ruprecht.

Lewins, Frank W. 1978 Religion and Ethnic Identity. In: Hans Mol (ed.), *Identity and Religion. International, Cross-Cultural Approaches*; pp. 19–38. London: SAGE.

Mol, Hans 1976 *Identity and the Sacred. A Sketch for a New Social-Scientific Theory of Religion*. Agincourt: Book Society of Canada.

———— 1986 Religion and Identity. A Dialectical Interpretation of Religious Phenomena. In: Hayes, Victor C. (ed.), *Identity Issues and World Religions. Selected Proceedings of the Fifteenth Congress of the International Association for the History of Religions*; pp. 64–79. Bedford Park: University Relations Unit.

Mol, Hans (ed.) 1978 *Identity and Religion. International, Cross-Cultural Approaches*. London: SAGE.

Patai, Raphael 1971 *Tents of Jacob. The Diaspora, Yesterday and Today*. Englewood Cliffs: Prentice-Hall.

Pocock, D. F. 1976 Preservation of the Religious Life: Hindu Immigrants in England. A Swami Narayan Sect in London. *Contributions to Indian Sociology*, N.s., 10, 2: 341–365.

Rothenberg, F. S. 1965 Diaspora, Zerstreuung. In: Lothar Coenen, Erich Beyreuther and Hans Bietenhard (eds.), *Theologisches Begriffslexikon zum Neuen Testament*; pp. 372–373. R. Brockhaus Verlag.

Sänger, Dieter 1982 Überlegungen zum Stichwort 'Diaspora' im Neuen Testament. *Die evangelische Diaspora* 52: 76–88.

Schnackenburg, Rudolf 1971 *Schriften zum Neuen Testament. Exegese in Fortschritt und Wandel*. München: Kösel.

Seiwert, Hubert 1986 What Constitutes the Identity of a Religion. In: Hayes, Victor C. (ed.), *Identity Issues and World Religions. Selected Proceedings of the Fifteenth Congress of the International Association for the History of Religions*; pp. 1–7. Bedford Park: University Relations Unit.

Taylor, Donald 1991 The Role of Religion and the Emancipation of an Ethnic Minority. In: W. A. R. Shadid and P. S. van Koningsveld (eds.), *The Integration of Islam and Hinduism in Western Europe*; pp. 201–212. Kampen: Kok Pharos Publishing House.

Tinker, Hugh 1974 *A New System of Slavery. The Export of Indian Labour Overseas, 1830–1920*. London: Oxford University Press.

Vertovec, Steven 1991b Inventing Religious Tradition: *Yagnas* and Hindu Renewal in Trinidad. In: Armin W. Geertz and Jeppe Sinding Jensen (eds.), *Religion, Tradition and Renewal*; pp. 79–97. Esbjerg: Aarhus University Press.

———— 1992a *Hindu Trinidad. Religion, Ethnicity and Socio-Economic Change*. London: Macmillan.

———— 1992c On the Reproduction and Representation of 'Hinduism' in Britain, paper presented at *the day workshop "Culture, Identity and Politics: Ethnic Minorities in Britain"*, Oxford 9.5.1992. [unpubl. ms.]

Williams, Raymond Brady 1988 *Religions of Immigrants from India and Pakistan: New Threats in the American Tapestry*. Cambridge: Cambridge University Press.

PART II

Geopolitics

NATION AND DIASPORA

Introduction

Ernest Renan first posed the question 'What is a nation?' ([1888] 1990) in 1888 and this has hardly been settled with a single answer any more today than when he first asked it then. Renan invoked a spiritual principle based on a combination of past sacrifice and present-day solidarity, with a kind of moral conscience acting as a binding force; but he argued that, like any other geopolitical construction, nations could have a beginning and an end. In commenting that they would eventually be replaced by a European confederation, he anticipated the loose transnational conglomeration of nation states and transmigratory flows that now constitute the European Union (EU). In the latter half of the twentieth century, as the high tide of nation formation, which had been reached after decolonisation and the two world wars, began to ebb, the political ideal of the nation as an exclusionary political formation has undergone numerous changes. The main ideas underpinning nationalist ideology, based on an understanding of the 'nation' as an organic *Volk* and founded on various myths of cultural purity and continuity, have been called into question and often discredited (Young [1995] 2002).[1] The argument from migration studies about 'methodological nationalism', that the nation-state was the most appropriate framework for studying society, was challenged by researchers in globalisation and transnational studies; post-colonial and cultural studies theorists pointed to the multiplicity of voices, layered temporal dimensions, and fertile interaction within and beyond the space of the nation from the dispersed groups of the diaspora.

The relationship between what Benedict Anderson (1983) calls the 'imagined community' of the nation to the diaspora groups within and beyond its borders has been a contentious yet productive site of analysis in diaspora studies. Since the mid-1990s, critics including Avtar Brah (1996), Vijay Mishra (1996) and Bryan Cheyette (2013) have questioned conceptions of diaspora such as William Safran's (see Chapter 1, this volume), which focus exclusively on the teleology of 'return' to the original homeland.[2] Much scholarship since then has turned to the study of the practices that people use to make themselves feel 'at home' in the host nation. This refocusing of diaspora-as-movement onto diaspora-as-settlement and occupancy has accompanied revised conceptions of the nation-state that stress new cultural formations, redefined hybrid identities and cultural syncretism. The ongoing tensions between nation and diaspora as each is defined against its other (see Cohen, Chapter 3; Brubaker, Chapter 7; this volume) have contributed vitally to the evolution of contemporary understandings of diaspora as used in discourses concerning global migration.[3] Where the nation-state is esteemed as the preeminent institution of modernity, diaspora is stigmatised as an unruly and destabilising force, functioning to disrupt its norms; where diasporas are celebrated, in the words of Khachig Tölölyan (1996), as 'the exemplary communities of the transnational moment' (31), they displace the earlier conception of the nation state as a more convenient model for examining today's mobile and displaced populations (see also Cohen 2008, 15).

Transnationalism is another term that rose to prominence in the 1990s to describe the concepts of nation, identity and migration under the conditions of globalisation. But while diasporas consist of tightly bonded, coextensive communities and solidarities between the places of origin and arrival (Soysal, Chapter 10, this volume), studies of transnationalism frame the relationship with the homeland more ambivalently, focusing on how migrants 'build transnational social fields that cut across geographic, cultural and political borders' (Quayson and Daswani 2013, 12), or on relations between multiple diasporic sites of 'the transglobal network nation' (Laguerre 2009, 197). Quayson and Daswani point out that transnational communities supersede diasporas in scale because they emerge 'from elective modes of identification involving class, sexuality and even professional interest' rather than from diasporic cultural and ethnic forms of identification (2013, 4): for example, interfaith practices of religious groups that cross national boundaries, gay communities seeking recognition of their rights for marriage, Human Rights groups or the proponents of global capitalism. Yet there are affinities with diasporas, especially concerning the affective consequences of displacement, because ties of belonging and loss might develop for transnational subjects in relation to both host and homeland nations simultaneously.

The three articles in this section can be read as critiques of the nation as a stable, bounded entity in its relation to diaspora, and they exemplify the shift in diaspora studies by the mid-1990s away from the exclusive emphasis on the paradigmatic concept of exile and return associated with the Jewish and Armenian diasporas. Both Bhabha and Gilroy read the term diaspora metaphorically, associating it with the 'third' or middle space (Bhabha) and with the 'middle passage' (Gilroy) rather than the binary points of geographical origin and return. Rogers Brubaker provides a critique of the contradictory positions and disciplinary frames represented in the debates about diaspora in the 1990s and warns of the risks of emptying the term of its cultural and historical specificity. Other critics have also voiced this view (see Braziel and Mannur 2003, 6–7).

Following Benedict Anderson's metaphor of the nation as an 'imaginary community' (1983), Homi Bhabha in 'DissemiNation', sees the nation's 'cultural construction [. . .] as a form of social and textual affiliation'. By examining the fusion of narration within nations – in an attempt to make space for other narratives besides the dominant ones – he exposes the stable identity and linear temporality associated with national form. He celebrates the in-betweenness of minority cultures that disrupts the temporality of the nation by embracing the contentious performative space – arguing that in representing that which cannot be incorporated, and highlighting multiple markers of cultural difference, their unruly presence is a source of energy and potential change.

Bhabha's essay title 'DissemiNation' punningly alludes to the features of dispersion and scattering that define the movements of populations from nation into exile, and that focus his critique of the modernist idea of the state. Paul Gilroy's (1993) conceptualisation of the diaspora of the Black Atlantic in his seminal study *The Black Atlantic: Modernity and Double Consciousness* offers another critique of modernity as represented by the nation-state and its implication in systems of colonialism and slavery. In defining the Black Atlantic as a 'rhizomorphic, fractal structure of the transcultural international formation' (4), Gilroy implies the limits and irrelevance of the nation state and establishes a distance from the tangled binary of nation and diaspora that emerged from earlier models. In his geopolitical reconfiguration, the transnational place of crossings and transitions emerges as an alternative to territorial locations: the contact zone of the 'middle passage', with its limited identifications of temporality or territory, is one of cultural production, transnational movement and mobility, yet also of 'belonging': those who make such crossings identify themselves as a community even though this is a mobile rather than a grounded one.

Rogers Brubaker, by contrast, responding in 2005 to this now fully-fledged transdisciplinary research field (Kläger and Stierstorfer 2015, 1), points to the need for new perspectives on the models offered by the different schools: the diaspora scholars with their attachment to roots and territory, and the 'social constructivist' critics, concerned with routes, and homes away from home in the space of displacement where belonging can be negotiated (Cohen 2008, 12). Brubaker warns against allowing such oppositional structures to harden into fixed positions that might essentialise the terms diaspora and nation state: 'diaspora' is at risk of enacting its own meaning of scattering, and becoming a '"diaspora" diaspora', with its meaning dispersed 'in semantic, conceptual and disciplinary space'. Brubaker's redefinition intersects with new interpretations of citizenship and cultural production which draw upon transnational frameworks. He sees diaspora not as a descriptive category, but instead as a 'category of practice', one that does not so much '*describe* the world as seek to *remake* it' (italics in original); more radically, rather than being entities or groups, diasporas are like a narrative, an 'idiom, stance, and claim' by which to develop practices of identity and belonging.

In today's world of globally interconnected frameworks, the nation continues to be a dominant category through which practices of sovereignty and citizenship are addressed. In the multiple contexts of its functionality, it continues to loom large in the everyday lives of its citizens and residents who are connected transnationally to different countries or regions through transitional movements of peoples, whether they are members of multiply-located groups and networks of communication or not (Quayson and Daswani 2013, 15). The recent resurgence in many European countries and the USA of a divisive right-wing nationalism promoting sovereignty, economic protectionism and 'authentic origins' points to a revaluation of what seemed to be outdated concepts of fixed belonging, ethnic or indigenous community and nationhood as a backlash against contemporary transnational movements. This retreat from the global liberal order (of which Brexit and the results of the recent US elections are likely to be the most impactful), proclaimed after 1989 as heralding 'the end of history', is being forged through various democratic practices like political campaigns, referenda and elections. It suggests that transnationalism and its cognate ideas of cosmopolitan citizenship and belonging are increasingly being questioned by large masses of people within precisely those nation states whose borders have become more permeable to migrations and diasporic formations. Even as the nation state continues to be reframed as inherently more mobile, and – as people continue to flow back and forth across national borders – subject to the negotiations of class, ethnicity and citizenship, the spectre of isolationism, of retreating behind 'closed walls' and keeping the 'Other' out is looming increasingly large.

Notes

1 Young ([1995] 2002) argues that the organic paradigm grew alongside those of hybridity and splitting (4).
2 According to Sudesh Mishra (2006, 83), studies by these and other critics – a number of them published in 1996 – introduced the 'lateral' turn in diaspora studies.
3 Floya Anthias (1998, cited in Cohen 2008, 10), claims that diaspora scholars ignore the social mobilisation of transethnic groups; while Soysal (Chapter 10, this volume) argues that emphasis on the nation limits the usefulness of diasporas in considering global migration.

References

Anderson, Benedict. 1983. *Imagined Communities*. London: New Left Books.
Anthias, Floya. 1998. 'Evaluating Diaspora: Beyond "Ethnicity".' *Sociology* 32 (3): 557–580.

Brah, Avtar. 1996. *Cartographies of Diaspora: Contesting Identities*. London: Routledge.

Braziel, Jana Evans, and Anita Mannur. 2003. 'Nation, Migration, Globalization: Points of Contention in Diaspora Studies.' In *Theorizing Diaspora: A Reader*, edited by Jana Evans Braziel and Anita Mannur, 1–22. Oxford: Blackwell.

Cheyette, Bryan. 2013. *Diasporas of the Mind: Jewish and Postcolonial Writing and the Nightmare of History*. New Haven, CT: Yale University Press.

Cohen, Robin. 2008. *Global Diasporas: An Introduction*, 2nd ed. London and New York: Routledge.

Gilroy, Paul. 1993. *The Black Atlantic: Modernity and Double Consciousness*. Cambridge, MA: Harvard University Press.

Kläger, Florian, and Klaus Stierstorfer. 2015. 'Introduction.' In *Diasporic Constructions of Home and Belonging*, edited by Florian Kläger and Klaus Stierstorfer, 1–7. Berlin and Boston: De Gruyter.

Laguerre, Michel D. 2009. 'The Transglobal Network Nation: Diaspora, Homeland, and Hostland.' In *Transnationalism: Diasporas and the Advent of a New (Dis)Order*, edited by Eliezer Ben-Rafael, and Yitzhak Sternberg, 195–210. Leiden and Boston: Brill.

Mishra, Sudesh. 2006. *Diaspora Criticism*. Edinburgh: Edinburgh University Press.

Mishra, Vijay. 1996. 'The Diasporic Imaginary: Theorising the Indian Diaspora.' *Textual Practice* 10 (3): 189–237.

Quayson, Ato, and Girish Daswani. 2013. 'Introduction: Diaspora and Transnationalism: Scapes, Scales, and Scopes.' In *A Companion to Diaspora and Transnationalism*, edited by Ato Quayson and Girish Daswani, 1–26. Oxford: Wiley-Blackwell.

Renan, Ernest. [1888] 1990. 'What is a Nation?' In *Nation and Narration*, edited by Homi K. Bhabha, 8–22. Abingdon: Routledge.

Tölölyan, Khachig. 1996. 'Rethinking Diaspora(s): Stateless Power in the Transnational Moment.' *Diaspora* 5 (1): 3–36.

Young, Robert J.C. [1995] 2002. *Colonial Desire: Hybridity in Theory, Culture and Race*. London: Routledge.

6

DISSEMINATION

Homi K. Bhabha

The entitlement of the nation is its metaphor: *Amor Patria; Fatherland; Pig Earth; Mother-tongue; Matigari; Middlemarch; Midnight's Children; One Hundred Years of Solitude; War and Peace; I Promessi Sposi; Kanthapura; Moby-Dick; The Magic Mountain; Things Fall Apart.*

There must be a tribe of interpreters of such metaphors – the translators of the dissemination of texts and discourses across cultures – who can perform what Said describes as the act of secular interpretation.

> To take account of this horizontal, secular space of the crowded spectacle of the modern nation . . . implies that no single explanation sending one back immediately to a single origin is adequate. And just as there are no simple dynastic answers, there are no simple discrete formations or social processes.[1]

If, in our travelling theory, we are alive to the *metaphoricity* of the peoples of imagined communities – migrant or metropolitan – then we shall find that the space of the modern nation-people is never simply horizontal. Their metaphoric movement requires a kind of 'doubleness' in writing; a temporality of representation that moves between cultural formations and social processes without a centred causal logic. And such cultural movements disperse the homogeneous, visual time of the horizontal society. The secular language of interpretation needs to go beyond the horizontal critical gaze if we are to give 'the non-sequential energy of lived historical memory and subjectivity' its appropriate narrative authority. We need another time of writing that will be able to inscribe the ambivalent and chiasmatic intersections [. . .]

How does one write the nation's modernity as the event of the everyday and the advent of the epochal? The language of national belonging comes laden with atavistic apologues, which has led Benedict Anderson to ask: 'But why do nations celebrate their hoariness, not their astonishing youth?'[2] The nation's claim to modernity, as an autonomous or sovereign form of optical rationality, is particularly questionable if, with Partha Chatterjee, we adopt the postcolonial perspective:

> Nationalism . . . seeks to represent itself in the image of the Enlightenment and fails to do so. For Enlightenment itself, to assert its sovereignty as the universal ideal, needs its

Other; if it could ever actualise itself in the real world as the truly universal, it would in fact destroy itself.[3]

Such ideological ambivalence nicely supports Gellner's paradoxical point that the historical necessity of the idea of the nation conflicts with the contingent and arbitrary signs and symbols that signify the affective life of the national culture. The nation may exemplify modern social cohesion but

> Nationalism is not what it seems, and *above all not what it seems to itself*. . . . The cultural shreds and patches used by nationalism are often arbitrary historical inventions. Any old shred would have served as well. But in no way does it follow that the principle of nationalism . . . is itself in the least contingent and accidental.[4]
>
> (My emphasis)

[. . .]

Both gentleman and slave, with different cultural means and to very different historical ends, demonstrate that forces of social authority and subversion or subalternity may emerge in displaced, even decentred strategies of signification. This does not prevent these positions from being effective in a political sense, although it does suggest that positions of authority may themselves be part of a process of ambivalent identification. Indeed the exercise of power may be both politically effective and psychically *affective* because the discursive liminality through which it is signified may provide greater scope for strategic manoeuvre and negotiation.

It is precisely in reading between these borderlines of the nation-space that we can see how the concept of the 'people' emerges within a range of discourses as a double narrative movement. The people are not simply historical events or parts of a patriotic body politic. They are also a complex rhetorical strategy of social reference: their claim to be representative provokes a crisis within the process of signification and discursive address. We then have a contested conceptual territory where the nation's people must be thought in double-time; the people are the historical 'objects' of a nationalist pedagogy, giving the discourse an authority that is based on the pre-given or constituted historical origin in the past; the people are also the 'subjects' of a process of signification that must erase any prior or originary presence of the nation-people to demonstrate the prodigious, living principles of the people as contemporaneity: as that sign of the present through which national life is redeemed and iterated as a reproductive process.

The scraps, patches and rags of daily life must be repeatedly turned into the signs of a coherent national culture, while the very act of the narrative performance interpellates a growing circle of national subjects. In the production of the nation as narration there is a split between the continuist, accumulative temporality of the pedagogical, and the repetitious, recursive strategy of the performative. It is through this process of splitting that the conceptual ambivalence of modern society becomes the site of writing the nation.

[. . .]

Cultural difference

Cultural difference must not be understood as the free play of polarities and pluralities in the homogeneous empty time of the national community. The jarring of meanings and values generated in the process of cultural interpretation is an effect of the perplexity of living in the liminal spaces of national society that I have tried to trace. Cultural difference, as a form of intervention, participates in a logic of supplementary subversion similar to the strategies of minority discourse. The question of cultural difference faces us with a disposition of knowledges or a distribution of practices that exist beside each other, abseits designating a form of social contradiction or antagonism that has to be negotiated rather than sublated. The difference between disjunctive sites and representations of social life have to be articulated without surmounting the incommensurable meanings and judgements that are produced within the process of transcultural negotiation.

The analytic of cultural difference intervenes to transform the scenario of articulation – not simply to disclose the rationale of political discrimination. It changes the position of enunciation and the relations of address within it; not only what is said but where it is said; not simply the logic of articulation but the topic of enunciation. The aim of cultural difference is to rearticulate the sum of knowledge from the perspective of the signifying position of the minority that resists totalization – the repetition that will not return as the same, the minus-in-origin that results in political and discursive strategies where adding to does not add up but serves to disturb the calculation of power and knowledge, producing other spaces of subaltern signification. The subject of the discourse of cultural difference is dialogical or transferential in the style of psychoanalysis. It is constituted through the locus of the Other which suggests both that the object of identification is ambivalent, and, more significantly, that the agency of identification is never pure or holistic but always constituted in a process of substitution, displacement or projection.

Cultural difference does not simply represent the contention between oppositional contents or antagonistic traditions of cultural value. Cultural difference introduces into the process of cultural judgement and interpretation that sudden shock of the successive, non-synchronic time of signification, or the interruption of the supplementary question that I elaborated above. The very possibility of cultural contestation, the ability to shift the ground of knowledges, or to engage in the 'war of position', marks the establishment of new forms of meaning, and strategies of identification. Designations of cultural difference interpellate forms of identity which, because of their continual implication in other symbolic systems, are always 'incomplete' or open to cultural translation. The uncanny structure of cultural difference is close to Lévi-Strauss's understanding of 'the unconscious as providing the common and specific character of social facts . . . not because it harbours our most secret selves but because . . . it enables us to coincide with forms of activity which are both *at once ours and other*' (my emphasis).[5]

It is not adequate simply to become aware of the semiotic systems that produce the signs of culture and their dissemination. Much more significantly, we are faced with the challenge of reading, into the present of a specific cultural performance, the traces of all those diverse disciplinary discourses and institutions of knowledge that constitute the condition and contexts of culture. As I have been arguing throughout this chapter, such a critical process requires a cultural temporality that is both disjunctive and capable of articulating, in Lévi-Strauss's words, 'forms of activity which are both at once ours and other'.

I use the word 'traces' to suggest a particular kind of interdisciplinary discursive transformation that the analytic of cultural difference demands. To enter into the interdisciplinarity of cultural texts means that we cannot contextualize the emergent cultural form by locating it in terms of some pre-given discursive casuality or origin. We must always keep open a supplementary space for the articulation of cultural knowledges that are adjacent and adjunct but not necessarily accumulative, teleological or dialectical. The 'difference' of cultural knowledge that 'adds to' but does not 'add up' is the enemy of the implicit generalization of knowledge or the implicit homogenization of experience, which Claude Lefort defines as the major strategies of containment and closure in modern bourgeois ideology.

Interdisciplinarity is the acknowledgement of the emergent sign of cultural difference produced in the ambivalent movement between the pedagogical and performative address. It is never simply the harmonious addition of contents or contexts that augment the positivity of a pre-given disciplinary or symbolic presence. In the restless drive for cultural translation, hybrid sites of meaning open up a cleavage in the language of culture which suggests that the similitude of the symbol as it plays across cultural sites must not obscure the fact that repetition of the sign is, in each specific social practice, both different and differential. This disjunctive play of symbol and sign makes interdisciplinarity an instance of the borderline moment of translation that Walter Benjamin describes as the 'foreignness of languages'.[6] The 'foreignness' of language is the nucleus of the untranslatable that goes beyond the transferral of subject matter between cultural texts or practices. The transfer of meaning can never be total between systems of meaning, or within them, for 'the language of translation envelops its content like a royal robe with ample folds . . . [it] signifies a more exalted language than its own and thus remains unsuited to its content, overpowering and alien'.[7]

Too often it is the slippage of signification that is celebrated in the articulation of difference, at the expense of this disturbing process of the overpowering of content by the signifier. The erasure of content in the invisible but insistent structure of linguistic difference does not lead us to some general, formal acknowledgement of the function of the sign. The ill-fitting robe of language alienates content in the sense that it deprives it of an immediate access to a stable or holistic reference 'outside' itself. It suggests that social significations are themselves being constituted in the very act of enunciation, in the disjunctive, non-equivalent split of *énoncé* and *enonciation*, thereby undermining the division of social meaning into an inside and outside. Content becomes the alienating mise-en-scène that reveals the signifying structure of linguistic difference: a process never seen for itself, but only glimpsed in the gap or the gaping of Benjamin's royal robe, or in the brush between the similitude of the symbol and the difference of the sign.

Benjamin's argument can be elaborated for a theory of cultural difference. It is only by engaging with what he calls the 'purer linguistic air' – the sign as anterior to any site of meaning – that the reality-effect of content can be overpowered which then makes all cultural languages 'foreign' to themselves. And it is from this foreign perspective that it becomes possible to inscribe the specific locality of cultural systems – their incommensurable differences – and through that apprehension of difference, to perform the act of cultural translation. In the act of translation the 'given' content becomes alien and estranged; and that, in its turn, leaves the language of translation *Aufgabe*, always confronted by its double, the untranslatable – alien and foreign.

Notes

1 Edward Said, 'Opponents, audiences, constituencies and community', in H. Foster (ed.) *Postmodern Culture* (London: Pluto, 1983), p. 145.
2 Benedict Anderson, 'Narrating the nation', *The Times Literary Supplement*, June 13, 1986, p. 659.
3 Partha Chatterjee, *Nationalist Thought and the Colonial World: A Derivative Discourse* (London: Zed, 1986), p. 17.
4 Ernest Gellner, *Nations and Nationalism* (Oxford: Basil Blackwell, 1983), p. 56.
5 Claude Lévi-Strauss, *Introduction to the Work of Marcel Mauss*, F. Baker (trans.) (London: Routledge, 1987), p.35.
6 Walter Benjamin, 'The task of the translator', *Illuminations*, H. Zohn (trans.) (London: Cape, 1970), p. 75.
7 ibid. For a most useful survey of the issue see Tejaswini Niranjana, *History, Post-Structuralism and the Colonial Context: Siting Translation* (Berkeley, CA: California University Press, 1992).

7

THE 'DIASPORA' DIASPORA

Rogers Brubaker

A radical break?

Having reviewed the changing meanings of 'diaspora', and pointed out differences and tensions in the way core constitutive elements are understood, I want now to raise some more general questions, and to make some analytical suggestions.

What are we to make of the proliferation of diasporas and of diaspora-talk, inside and outside the academy? And how should one interpret it? Are we seeing a proliferation of diasporas in the world, or perhaps even the dawning of an age of diaspora? Or, on the other hand (to put the question in deliberately exaggerated form), are we seeing simply a proliferation of diaspora talk, a change in idiom rather than in the world?

I want to consider two sorts of claims about novelty and discontinuity. One concerns a putatively sharp break in ways of looking at the world, the other a putatively sharp transformation in the world itself. The two claims are, of course, closely related and are usually advanced together: the radical shift in perspective is presented as a way of coming to terms, analytically and politically, with fundamental changes in the world.

On the one hand, the literature on diaspora claims to mark a sharp shift in perspective. The old perspective – it is suggested – was immigrationist, assimilationist, (methodologically) nationalist,[1] and teleological. It took nation-states as units of analysis and assumed that immigrants made a sharp and definitive break with their homelands, that migration trajectories were unidirectional, and that migration inexorably led to assimilation. The new perspective does not make these assumptions. It is said to 'transcend' the old assimilationist, immigrationist paradigm. In one representative statement:

> it is no longer assumed that immigrants make a sharp break from their homelands. Rather, premigration networks, cultures, and capital remain salient. The sojourn itself is neither unidirectional nor final. . . . [M]ovements . . . follow multifarious trajectories and sustain diverse networks. Rather than the singular immigrant, scholars now detail the diversity of immigration circumstances, class backgrounds, gendered transitions, and the sheer multitude of migration experiences.[2]
>
> *(Lie 1995, p. 304)*

This greatly exaggerates the shift in perspective, at least in the American context. Long before 'diaspora' became fashionable, historians and sociologists of immigration had abandoned – if indeed they ever held – simplistic assumptions about unidirectional trajectories, sharp and definitive breaks with home countries, and a singular path of assimilation. If Glazer and Moynihan's (1963, p. v) observation that 'the point about the melting pot . . . is that it did not happen' was iconoclastic when first made, it had become widely accepted by the end of the 1960s. So much emphasis was placed on ethnic persistence in the historical and sociological literature between about 1965 and 1985 – again, before the 'diaspora' explosion – that there has even been, in reaction, a certain 'return of assimilation' (Brubaker 2001) in the last two decades (albeit of a more subtle, multi-dimensional, and normatively ambivalent concept of assimilation).

More important than the alleged novelty and originality of the literature is the alleged novelty and import of the phenomenon itself. Does 'diaspora' – along with kindred terms such as transnationalism, post-nationalism, globalization, deterritorialization, postcolonialism, creolization, transculturalism and postmodernity – name something fundamentally new in the world? Do these terms mark, or at least augur, an epochal shift, as some theorists (Kearney 1991; Appadurai 1996) have suggested? Have we passed from the age of the nation-state to the age of diaspora?

More specifically, does the 'unprecedented porosity' of borders (Sheffer 2003, p. 22) – the unprecedented circulation of people, goods, messages, images, ideas and cultural products – signify a basic realignment of the relationship between politics and culture, territorial state and de-territorialized identities? Does this entail the transcendence of the nation-state, based on territorial closure, exclusive claims on citizens' loyalty, and a homogenizing, nationalizing, assimilationist logic? Does the age of diaspora open up new possibilities for what Clifford has called 'non-exclusive practices of community, politics and difference' (1994, p. 302)? Does it offer 'an alternative to life in territorially and nationally marked groups'?[3]

Obviously, the world has changed, and so have our ways of talking about it. But one should be sceptical of grand claims about radical breaks and epochal shifts (Favell 2001). Can one, in fact, speak of an unprecedented porosity of borders? Not with regard to the movement of people. Over the course of the nineteenth and, especially, the twentieth centuries, states have gained rather than lost the capacity to monitor and control the movement of people by deploying increasingly sophisticated technologies of identification and control including citizenship, passports, visas, surveillance, integrated databases and biometric devices.[4] The shock of 9/11 has only pushed states further and faster along a path on which they were already moving. No liberal state, to be sure, can absolutely seal its borders. On balance, however, the world's poor who seek work or refuge in prosperous and peaceful countries encounter a tighter mesh of state regulation and have fewer opportunities for migration to prosperous and peaceful countries than they had a century ago (Hirst and Thompson 1999, pp. 30–31, 267).

Is migration today unprecedented in volume and velocity? How one answers this question depends, of course, on one's units of analysis. Migrant flows of recent decades to the United States are, in fact, much smaller, in relation both to the population of the United States and to the population of the rest of the world, than those of a century ago. And while contemporary migrations worldwide are 'more geographically extensive than the great global migrations of the modern era', they are 'on balance slightly *less* intensive' (Held *et al.* 1999, p. 326, italics added). Even if there are as many as 120 million international migrants (including refugees and asylum seekers) today, as one expert has suggested, this amounts to less than 2 per cent of the global population (Castles and Miller 1998, pp. 4–5); the mobility of the great majority remains severely limited by the morally arbitrary facts of birthplace and inherited citizenship and by the exclusionary policies of states.

Is migration today neither unidirectional nor permanent? Of course not, in many cases; but it was neither unidirectional nor permanent, in many cases, a century ago. Historians have long highlighted the very high rates of return migration from North America to various European countries of origin in the late nineteenth and early twentieth centuries. Do migrants make a sharp and definitive break with their homelands? Of course not. Nor did they do so a century ago, as an abundant historical literature has made clear. Do migrants sustain ties with their country of origin? They do indeed; but they managed to do so by non-electronic means a century ago (Hollinger 1995, pp. 151 ff; Morawska 2001; Waldinger and Fitzgerald 2004). This is not to say that nothing has changed, or that distance-eclipsing technologies of communication and transportation do not matter; it is, however, to caution against exaggerated claims of an epochal break.

Have the exclusive claims of the nation-state been eroded? They have indeed, but *the* nation-state – as opposed to the multifarious particular nation-states – is a figment of the sociological imagination. 'The' nation-state is the primary conceptual 'other' against which diaspora is defined – and often celebrated (Tölölyan 1991; Clifford 1994, p. 307). But there is a risk of essentializing 'the' nation-state, a risk of attributing to it a timeless, self-actualizing, homogenizing 'logic'. Sophisticated discussions are sensitive to the heterogeneity of diasporas; but they are not always as sensitive to the heterogeneity of nation-states. Discussions of diaspora are often informed by a strikingly idealist, teleological understanding of the nation-state, which is seen as the unfolding of an idea, the idea of nationalizing and homogenizing the population.[5] The conceptual antithesis between nation-state and diaspora obscures more than it reveals, occluding the persisting significance (and great empirical variety) of nation-states (Mann 1997).

Entity or stance?

Like nation, ethnic group or minority – terms with which it shares an overlapping semantic field (Tölölyan 1991, 1996) – diaspora is often characterized in substantialist terms as an 'entity'. As one example among many, consider the beginning of a new book by Gabriel Sheffer:

> The highly motivated Koreans and Vietnamese toiling hard to become prosperous in bustling Los Angeles, the haggard Palestinians living in dreary refugee camps near Beirut and Amman, the beleaguered Turks dwelling in cramped apartments in Berlin, and the frustrated Russians in Estonia, all have much in common. All of them, along with Indians, Chinese, Japanese, Africans, African-Americans. Jews, Palestinians, Greeks, Gypsies, Romanians, Poles, Kurds, Armenians and numerous other groups permanently residing outside of their countries of origin, but maintaining contacts with people back in their old homelands, are members of ethno-national diasporas.
>
> *(2003, p. 1)*

The problem here is with the definite article. Diasporas are treated as 'bona fide actual entities' (ibid, p. 245) and cast as unitary actors. They are seen as possessing countable, quantifiable memberships. And indeed they are counted. We learn from the 'first attempt to estimate the *real numbers* of the main historical, modern and incipient diasporas' that among 'historical diasporas', the Chinese diaspora numbers 35 million, the Indian diaspora 9 million, the Jewish and Gypsy diasporas 8 million each, the Armenian diaspora 5.5 million, the Greek diaspora 4 million, the German diaspora 2.5 million and the Druze 1 million. Among 'modern' diasporas, the African-American diaspora numbers 25 million, the Kurdish diaspora 14 million, the Irish diaspora 10 million, the Italian diaspora 8 million, the Hungarian and Polish diasporas 4.5 million each, the Turkish and Iranian diasporas 3.5 million each, the Japanese diaspora 3 million, the Lebanese (Christian) diaspora 2.5 million and the 'Black Atlantic' diaspora 1.5 million. A similar list with numbers is given for thirty 'incipient diasporas' (Sheffer 2003, pp. 104–6, my italics).

Sheffer, to be sure, distinguishes 'core', 'marginal' and 'dormant' members of diasporas (2003, p. 100), but then goes on to quantify diaspora memberships, without any grounds for indicating that those so counted identify as members of the respective diasporas at all. And the large numbers he provides – 25 million, for example, for the incipient Russian diaspora – suggest that the numbers take no account of these distinctions but are maximally inclusive. The very notion of 'dormant members' of a diaspora is problematic; if they are really dormant – if they have 'assimilated or fully integrated' into a host society (Sheffer 2003, p. 100) and merely 'know or feel that their roots are in the diaspora group' – then why should they count, and be counted, as 'members' of the diaspora at all?

What is it that Sheffer and others are counting when they count 'members' of diasporas? It appears that what is usually counted, or rather estimated, is ancestry. But if one takes seriously boundary maintenance, lateral ties to fellow diaspora members in other states and vertical ties to the homeland, then ancestry is surely a poor proxy for membership in a diaspora. Enumerations such as this suggest that discussions of diaspora opportunistically combine elements of strong and weak definitions.[6] Strong definitions are used to emphasize the distinctiveness of diaspora as a social form; weak definitions, to emphasize numbers (and thereby the import of the phenomenon).

Not all discussions of diaspora, to be sure, emphasize boundary-maintenance. Some discussions, as indicated above, emphasize hybridity, fluidity, creolization and syncretism and offer an alternative to the groupist portrayal of diasporas as tangible, quantifiable and bounded entities (though these discussions, too, tend to speak of diasporas as distinctive communities with distinctive identities, without explaining how such distinctive communities and identities can emerge if all is hybrid, fluid, creolized and syncretic).

Where boundary maintenance and distinctive identity are emphasized, as they are in most discussions, familiar problems of 'groupism' arise (Brubaker 2002). The metaphysics of the nation-state as a bounded territorial community may have been overcome; but the metaphysics of 'community' and 'identity' remain. Diaspora can be seen as an *alternative* to the essentialization of belonging;[7] but it can also represent a non-territorial *form* of essentialized belonging. Talk of the de-territorialization of identity is all well and good; but it still presupposes that there is 'an identity' that is reconfigured, stretched in space to cross state boundaries, but on some level fundamentally the same. Yet if, as Homi Bhaba put it in a discussion of Rushdie's *Satanic Verses,* 'there is no such whole as the nation, the culture, or even the self',[8] then why should there be any such whole as the Indian or Chinese or Jewish or Armenian or Kurdish diaspora?

To overcome these problems of groupism, I want to argue that we should think of diaspora not in substantialist terms as a bounded entity, but rather as an idiom, a stance, a claim. We should think of diaspora in the first instance as a category of practice, and only then ask whether, and how, it can fruitfully be used as a category of analysis.[9] As a category of practice, 'diaspora' is used to make claims, to articulate projects, to formulate expectations, to mobilize energies, to appeal to loyalties.[10] It is often a category with a strong normative change. It does not so much *describe* the world as seek to *remake* it.

As idiom, stance and claim, diaspora is a way of formulating the identities and loyalties of a population. Those who do the formulating may themselves be part of the population in question; or they may be speaking in the name of the putative homeland state.[11] In either case, though, not all those who are claimed as members of putative diasporas themselves adopt a diasporic stance. Indeed, those who consistently adopt a diasporic stance, as Tölölyan (1996, p. 19) has noted, are often only a small minority of the population that political or cultural entrepreneurs formulate as a diaspora. According to one comprehensive sociological analysis (Bakalian 1992, cf Tölölyan 1996, p. 15), for example, what is casually called 'the Armenian diaspora' is, in the US, not very diasporic at all and is becoming less rather than more so over time, as the large majority of those who identify as Armenians distance themselves from diasporic stances, from links to the homeland, and from links to Armenians in other countries. Their 'Armenianness' is closer to what sociologist Herbert Gans (1979) long ago called 'symbolic ethnicity'.

There is, of course, a committed diasporan or diasporic fraction, as Tölölyan (1996, p. 18) calls it, among Armenians and many other dispersed populations. And they have good reason to refer to all dispersed Armenians as a 'diaspora'. For them, diaspora is a category of practice and central to their project. But why should we, as analysts, use diaspora as a category of analysis to refer to all persons of Armenian descent living outside Armenia? The disadvantage of doing so is that it occludes the difference between the actively diasporan fraction and the majority who do not adopt a diasporic stance and are not committed to the diasporic project.

In sum, rather than speak of 'a diaspora' or 'the diaspora' as an entity, a bounded group, an ethnodemographic or ethnocultural fact, it may be more fruitful, and certainly more precise, to speak of diasporic stances, projects, claims, idioms, practices, and so on. We can then study empirically the degree and form of support for a diasporic project among members of its putative constituency, just as we can do when studying a nationalist project. And we can explore to what extent, and in what circumstances, those claimed as members of putative diasporas actively adopt or at least passively sympathize with the diasporic stance,[12] just as we can do with respect to those who are claimed as members of putative nations, or of any other putative collectivity.

Conclusion

One of the virtues of 'diaspora', scholars have suggested, is that it provides an alternative to teleological, nation-statist understandings of immigration and assimilation. But theories of 'diaspora' have their own teleologies. Diaspora is often seen as destiny – a destiny to which previously dormant members (or previously dormant diasporas in their entirety) are now 'awakening' (Sheffer 2003, p. 21). Embedded in the teleological language of 'awakening' – the language, not coincidentally, of many nationalist movements – are essentialist assumptions about 'true' identities. Little is gained if we escape from one teleology only to fall into another.

The point of this analysis has not been to deflate diaspora, but rather to de-substantialize it, by treating it as a category of practice, project, claim and stance, rather than as a bounded group. The 'groupness' of putative diasporas, like that of putative 'nations', is precisely what is at stake in [political, social and cultural] struggles. We should not, as analysts, prejudge the outcome of such struggles by imposing groupness through definitional fiat. We should seek, rather, to bring the struggles themselves into focus, without presupposing that they will eventuate in bounded groups.

Notes

1 On methodological nationalism, see Centre for the Study of Global Governance 2002; Wimmer and Glick Schiller 2003. Although she does not use the term, Soysal (2000) makes a partially similar argument.

2 For related articles about a fundamental shift in perspective, see Glick Schiller *et al.* 1995; Kearney 1995; Beck 2000.

3 Natan Sznaider, opening remarks to the conference on 'Diaspora Today', Schloss Elmau, Germany, 17 July 2003.

4 For a critique of the view that states have lost their ability to control their borders, see Brubaker 1994; Freeman 1994; and, for a more detailed account, Zolberg 1999. On the mid-nineteenth century codification of citizenship as a means of controlling migration, see Brubaker 1992, pp, 64 ff. On the historical development of passports and related techniques of identification, see Torpey 2000 and the studies collected in Caplan and Torpey 2001.

5 For a nuanced argument about 'cosmopolitics' – as a mode of 'thinking and feeling beyond the nation' – that does *not* treat the nation-state and cosmopolitanism as antithetical, see Robbins 1998. David Hollinger has also argued eloquently that the 'nation' need not be antithetical to cosmopolitan or transnational engagements, but can sometimes mediate effectively 'between the ethnos and the species' (1998, p. 87; see also 1995, ch. 6).

6 For an argument that discussions of identity are bedevilled by a mix of strong and weak definitions, see Brubaker and Cooper 2000.

7 The former possibility has been emphasized by Gilroy 1997, p. 328 and by Natan Sznaider, in his opening remarks to the conference on 'Diaspora Today'. Schloss Elmau, Germany. 17 July 2003. The latter possibility has been noted by Anthias 1998, pp. 560, 563, 567.

8 Quoted in Tambiah 2000, p. 178.

9 For a very different argument criticizing the use of diaspora as an analytical category in the study of immigration, see Soysal 2000. For an argument about categories of analysis and categories of practice in the study of ethnicity, race and nation, see Brubaker 2002.

10 Writing on the African diaspora, Patterson and Kelly (2000, p. 19) observe that 'the presumption that black people worldwide share a common culture was not . . . the result of poor scholarship, It responded to a political imperative – one that led to the formation of political and cultural movements premised on international solidarity'. They quote Hall's (1990, p. 224) remark that unitary images of diaspora offered 'a way of imposing an imaginary coherence on the experience of dispersal and fragmentation'.

11 On the changing historical stances of sending states towards emigrant populations and their descendants, see, for example, Smith 2003 (on Mexico, Italy and Poland), Gabaccia 2000 (on Italy), Itzigsohn 2000 (on the Dominican Republic, Haiti and El Salvador), and Wang 1993 (on China).

12 There is no reason to expect that people will be consistent in this respect. They may well adopt a diasporic stance at some moments or in some contexts, and distance themselves from such a stance in other times and contexts.

References

Anthias, Floya 1998 'Evaluating "diaspora": Beyond ethnicity', *Sociology*, vol. 32, no. 3, pp. 557–80.

Appadurai, Arjun 1996 *Modernity at Large: Cultural Dimensions of Globalization*. Minneapolis, MN: University of Minnesota Press.

Bakalian, Anny P. 1992 *Armenian-Americans: From Being to Feeling Armenian*. New Brunswick: Transaction Publishers.

Beck, Ulrich 2000 'The cosmopolitan perspective: Sociology of the second age of modernity', *British Journal of Sociology*, vol. 51, no. 1, pp. 79–105.

Brubaker, Rogers 1992 *Citizenship and Nationhood in France and Germany*. Cambridge, MA: Harvard University Press.

———— 1994 'Are immigration control efforts really failing?', in Wayne A. Cornelius, Philip L. Martin, and James F. Hollifield (eds). *Controlling Immigration: A Global Perspective*. Stanford, CA: Stanford University Press, pp. 227–31.

———— 2001 'The return of assimilation?', *Ethnic and Racial Studies*, vol. 24. no. 4, pp. 531–48.

———— 2002 'Ethnicity without groups', *Archives européenes de sociologie*, vol. XLIII, no. 2, pp. 163–89.

Brubaker, Rogers and Cooper, Frederick 2000 'Beyond "identity"', *Theory and Society*, vol. 29, no. 1, pp. 1–47.

Caplan, Jane and Torpey, John 2001 *Documenting Individual Identity: The Development of State Practices in the Modern World*. Princeton: Princeton University Press.

Castles, Stephen and Miller, Mark J. 1998 *The Age of Migration: International Population Movements in the Modern World*. New York: The Guilford Press.

Centre for the Study of Global Governance 2002 London School of Economics and Political Science. Draft report on 'Workshop on methodological nationalism', 26–27 June 2002.

Clifford, James 1994 'Diasporas', *Cultural Anthropology*, vol. 9, no. 3, pp. 302–38.

Favell, Adrian 2001 'Migration, mobility and globaloney: Metaphors and rhetoric in the sociology of globalization', *Global Networks*, vol. 1. no. 4, pp. 389–98.

Freeman, Gary P. 1994 'Can liberal states control unwanted migration?', *Annals of the American Academy of Political and Social Science*, vol. 534, pp. 17–30.

Gabaccia, Donna R. 2000 *Italy's Many Diasporas*. London: UCL Press.

Gans, Herbert J. 1979 'Symbolic ethnicity: The future of ethnic groups and cultures in America', *Ethnic and Racial Studies*, vol. 2, no. 1, pp. 1–20.

Gilroy, Paul 1997 'Diaspora and the detours of identity', in Kathryn Woodward (ed.), *Identity and Difference*. London and Thousand Oaks. CA: Sage Publications in association with the Open University, pp. 299–343.

Glazer, Nathan and Moynihan, Daniel Patrick 1963 *Beyond the Melting Pot: The Negroes, Puerto Ricans, Jews, Italians, and Irish of New York City*. Cambridge, MA: MIT Press.

Glick Schiller, Nina, Basch, Linda, and Blanc, Christina Szanton 1995 'From immigrant to transmigrant: Theorizing transnational migration', *Anthropological Quarterly*, vol. 68, pp. 48–63.

Hall, Stuart 1990 'Cultural identity and diaspora', in Jonathan Rutherford (ed.), *Identity: Community, Culture, Difference*. London: Lawrence & Wishart, pp. 222–37.

Held, David, Mcgrew, Anthony, Goldblatt, David, and Perraton, Jonathan 1999 *Global Transformations: Politics, Economics, and Culture*. Stanford. CA: Stanford University Press.

Hirst, Paul and Thompson, Grahame 1999 *Globalization in Question*. Cambridge: Polity Press.

Hollinger, David A. 1995 *Postethnic America: Beyond Multiculturalism*. New York: Basic Books.

——— 1998 'Nationalism, cosmopolitanism and the United States', in Noah M. J. Piekus (ed.), *Immigration and Citizenship in the Twenty-First Century*. Lanham: Rowman and Littlcficld, pp. 85–99.

ltzigsohn, José 2000 'Immigration and the boundaries of citizenship: The institutions of immigrants' political transnationalism', *Immigration and the Boundaries of Citizenship*, vol. 34. no. 4, pp. 1126–54.

Kearney, Michael 1991 'Borders and boundaries of state and self at the end of empire', *Journal of Historical Sociology*, vol. 4, no. 1, pp. 52–74.

——— 1995 'The local and the global: The anthropology of globalization and transnationalism', *Annual Review of Anthropology*, vol. 24, pp. 547–65.

Lie, John 1995 'From international migration to transnational diaspora', *Contemporary Sociology*, vol. 24. no. 4, pp. 303–6.

Mann, Michael 1997 'Has globalization ended the rise and rise of the nation-state?', *Review of International Political Economy*, vol. 4. no. 3, pp. 472–96.

Morawska, Ewa 2001 'Immigrants, transnationalism, and ethnicization: A comparison of this great wave and the last', in Gary Gcrstle and John Mollcnkopf (eds), *E Pluribus Unum? Contemporary and Historical Perspectives on Immigrant Political Incorporation*. New York: Russell Sage, pp. l75–212.

Patterson, Tiffany Ruby and Kelley, Robin D. G. 2000 'Unfinished migrations: Reflections on the African diaspora and the making of the modern world', *African Studies Review*, vol. 43, no. 1, pp. 11–45.

Robbins, Bruce 1998 'lntroduction Part 1: Actually existing cosmopolitanism', in Pheng Cheah and Bruce Robbins (eds), *Cosmopolitics: Thinking and Feeling Beyond the Nation*. Minneapolis, MN: University of Minnesota Press, pp. l–19.

Sheffer, Gabriel 2003 *Diaspora Politics: At Home Abroad*. Cambridge: Cambridge University Press.

Smith, Robert C. 2003 'Diasporic membcrships in historical perspective: Comparative insights from the Mexican, ltalian, and Polish cases', *International Migration Review*, vol. 37, no. 3, pp. 724–59.

Soysal, Yasemin 2000 'Citizenship and identity: Living in diasporas in post-war Europe', *Ethnic and Racial Studies,* vol. 23. no. l, pp. 1–15.

Tambiah, Stanley J. 2000 'Transitional movements, diaspora, and multiple modernities', *Daedalus*, vol. 129, no. 1, pp. 163–94.

Tölölyan, Khachig 1991 'The nation-state and its other: In lieu of a preface', *Diaspora*, vol. 1, no. 1, pp. 3–7.

——— 1996 'Rethinking diaspora(s): stateless power in the transnational moment', *Diaspora*, vol. 5, no. 1, pp. 3–36.

Torpey, John 2000 *The Invention of the Passport: Surveillance, Citizenship and the State*. Cambridge: Cambridge University Press.

Waldinger, Roger and Fitzgerald, David 2004 'Transnationalism in question', *American Journal of Sociology*, vol. 109, no. 5, pp. 1177–95.

Wang, Gungwu 1993 'Greater China and the Chinese overseas', *The China Quarterly*, no. 136, pp. 926–48.

Wimmer, Andreas and Glick Schiller, Nina 2003 'Methodological nationalism, the social sciences, and the study of migration: An essay in historical epistemology', *International Migration Review*, vol. 37. no. 3, pp. 576–610.

Zolberg, Aristide 1999 'Matters of state: Theorizing immigration policy', in Charles Hirschman, Philip Kasnitz, and Josh DeWind (eds), *The Handbook of International Migration: The American Experience*. New York: Russell Sage Foundation, pp. 71–93.

8

THE BLACK ATLANTIC AS COUNTERCULTURE OF MODERNITY

Paul Gilroy

Histories of cultural studies seldom acknowledge how the politically radical and openly inter-ventionist aspirations found in the best of its scholarship are already articulated to black cultural history and theory. These links are rarely seen or accorded any significance. In England the work of figures like C. L. R. James and Stuart Hall offers a wealth of both symbols and concrete evidence for the practical links between these critical political projects. In the United States the work of interventionist scholars like bell hooks and Cornel West as well as that of more orthodox academics like Henry Louis Gates, Jr., Houston A. Baker, Jr., Anthony Appiah, and Hazel Carby, points to similar convergences. The position of these thinkers in the contested "contact zones"[1] between cultures and histories is not, however, as exceptional as it might appear at first. We shall see below that successive generations of black intellectuals (especially those whose lives, like James's, crisscrossed the Atlantic Ocean) noted this intercultural positionality and accorded it a special significance before launching their distinct modes of cultural and political critique. They were often urged on in their labor by the brutal absurdity of racial classification that derives from and also celebrates racially exclusive conceptions of national identity from which blacks were excluded as either non-humans or non-citizens. I shall try to show that their marginal endeavors point to some new analytic possibilities with a general significance far beyond the well-policed borders of black particularity. For example, this body of work offers intermediate concepts, lodged between the local and the global, which have a wider applicability in cultural history and politics precisely because they offer an alternative to the nationalist focus which dominates cultural criticism. [. . .]

Getting beyond these national and nationalistic perspectives has become essential for two additional reasons. The first arises from the urgent obligation to re-evaluate the significance of the modern nation-state as a political, economic, and cultural unit. Neither political nor economic structures of domination are still simply coextensive with national borders. This has a special significance in contemporary Europe, where new political and economic relations are being created seemingly day by day, but it is a worldwide phenomenon with significant consequences for the relationship between the politics of information and the practices of capital accumulation. Its effects underpin more recognizably political changes like the growing cent-rality of transnational ecological movements which, through their insistence on the association of sustainability and justice, do so much to shift the moral and scientific precepts on which the modern separation of politics and ethics was built. The second reason relates to the tragic popularity of ideas about the integrity and purity of cultures. In particular, it concerns the relationship between nationality and ethnicity. This too currently has a special force in Europe, but it is also reflected directly in the post-colonial histories and complex, transcultural, political trajectories of Britain's black settlers.

What might be called the peculiarity of the black English requires attention to the inter-mixture of a variety of distinct cultural forms. Previously separated, political and intellectual traditions converged and, in their coming together, overdetermined the process of black Britain's social and historical formation. This blending is misunderstood if it is conceived in simple ethnic terms, but right and left, racist and anti-racist, black and white tacitly share a view of it as little more than a collision between fully formed and mutually exclusive cultural communities. This has become the dominant view where black history and culture are perceived, like black settlers themselves, as an illegitimate intrusion into a vision of authentic British national life that, prior to their arrival, was as stable and as peaceful as it was ethnically undifferentiated. [. . .] However, though it arises from present rather than past conditions, contemporary British racism bears the imprint of the past in many ways. The especially crude and reductive notions of culture that form the substance of racial politics today are clearly associated with an older discourse of racial and ethnic difference which is everywhere entangled in the history of the idea of culture in the modern West. This history has itself become hotly contested since debates about multi-culturalism, cultural pluralism, and the responses to them that are sometimes dismissively called "political correctness" arrived to query the ease and speed with which European particularisms are still being translated into absolute, universal standards for human achievement, norms, and aspirations.

It is significant that prior to the consolidation of scientific racism in the nineteenth century,[2] the term "race" was used very much in the way that the word "culture" is used today. But in the attempts to differentiate the true, the good, and the beautiful which characterize the junction point of capitalism, industrialization, and political democracy and give substance to the discourse of Western modernity, it is important to appreciate that scientists did not monopolize either the image of the black or the emergent concept of biologically based racial difference. As far as the future of cultural studies is concerned, it should be equally important that both were centrally employed in those European attempts to think through beauty, taste, and aesthetic judgment that are the precursors of contemporary cultural criticism.

[. . .]

In opposition to both of these nationalist or ethnically absolute approaches, I want to develop the suggestion that cultural historians could take the Atlantic as one single, complex unit of analysis in their discussions of the modern world and use it to produce an explicitly transnational and intercultural perspective.[3] Apart from the confrontation with English his-toriography and literary history this entails a challenge to the ways in which black American cultural and political histories have so far been conceived. I want to suggest that much of the precious intellectual legacy claimed by African-American intellectuals as the substance of their particularity is in fact only partly their absolute ethnic property. No less than in the case of the English New Left, the idea of the black Atlantic can be used to show that there are other claims to it which can be based on the structure of the African diaspora into the Western hemisphere. A concern with the Atlantic as a cultural and political system has been forced on black his-toriography and intellectual history by the economic and historical matrix in which plantation slavery – "capitalism with its clothes off" – was one special moment. The fractal patterns of cultural and political exchange and transformation that we try and specify through manifestly inadequate theoretical terms like creolization and syncretism indicate how both ethnicities and political cultures have been made anew in ways that are significant not simply for the peoples of the Caribbean but for Europe, for Africa, especially Liberia and Sierra Leone, and of course, for black America.

It bears repetition that Britain's black settler communities have forged a compound culture from disparate sources. Elements of political sensibility and cultural expression transmitted from black America over a long period of time have been reaccentuated in Britain. They are central, though no longer dominant, within the increasingly novel configurations that characterize another newer black vernacular culture. This is not content to be either dependent upon or simply imitative of the African diaspora cultures of America and the Caribbean. The rise and rise of Jazzie B and Soul II Soul at the turn of the last decade constituted one valuable sign of this new assertive mood. North London's Funki Dreds, whose name itself projects a newly hybridized identity, have projected the distinct culture and rhythm of life of black Britain outwards into the world. Their song "Keep On Moving" was notable for having been produced in England by the children of Caribbean settlers and then remixed in a (Jamaican) dub format in the United States by Teddy Riley, an African American. It included segments or samples of music taken from American and Jamaican records by the JBs and Mikey Dread respectively. This formal unity of diverse cultural elements was more than just a powerful symbol. It encapsulated the playful diasporic intimacy that has been a marked feature of transnational black Atlantic creativity. The record and its extra-ordinary popularity enacted the ties of affiliation and affect with articulated the discontinuous histories of black settlers in the new world. The fundamental injunction to "Keep On Moving" also expressed the restlessness of spirit which makes that diaspora culture vital. The contemporary black arts movement in film, visual arts, and theatre as well as music, which provided the background to this musical release, have created a new topography of loyalty and identity in which the structures and presuppositions of the nation-state have been left behind because they are seen to be outmoded. It is important to remember that these recent black Atlantic phenomena may not be as novel as their digital encoding via the transnational force of north London's Soul II Soul suggests. Columbus's pilot, Pedro Nino, was also an African. The history of the black Atlantic since then, continually crisscrossed by the movements of black people – not only as commodities but engaged in various struggles towards emancipation, autonomy, and citizenship – provides a means to re-examine the problems of nationality, location, identity, and historical memory. They all emerge from it with special clarity if we contrast the national, nationalistic, and ethnically absolute paradigms of cultural criticism to be found in England and America with those hidden expressions, both residual and emergent, that attempt to be global or outer-national in nature. These traditions have supported countercultures of modernity that touched the workers' movement but are not reducible to it. They supplied important foundations on which it could build.

Turner's extraordinary painting of the slave ship remains a useful image not only for its self-conscious moral power and the striking way that it aims directly for the sublime in its invocation of racial terror, commerce, and England's ethico-political degeneration. It should be emphasized that ships were the living means by which the points within that Atlantic world were joined. They were mobile elements that stood for the shifting spaces in between the fixed places that they connected.[4] Accordingly they need to be thought of as cultural and political units rather than abstract embodiments of the triangular trade. They were something more – a means to conduct political dissent and possibly a distinct mode of cultural production. The ship provides a chance to explore the articulations between the discontinuous histories of England's ports, its interfaces with the wider world.[5] Ships also refer us back to the Middle Passage, to the half-remembered micropolitics of the slave trade and its relationship to both industrialization and modernization. As it were, getting on board promises a means to reconceptualize the orthodox relationship between modernity and what passes for its prehistory. It provides a different sense of where modernity might itself be thought to begin in the constitutive relationships with outsiders that both found and temper a self-conscious sense of Western civilization.[6] For all these reasons, the ship is the first of the novel chronotopes presupposed by my attempts to rethink modernity via the history of the black Atlantic and the African diaspora into the Western hemisphere.

In the venturesome spirit proposed by James Clifford in his influential work on traveling culture,[7] I want to consider the impact that this outer-national, transcultural reconceptualization might have on the political and cultural history of black Americans and that of blacks in Europe. In recent history this will certainly mean re-evaluating Garvey and Garveyism, pan-Africanism, and Black Power as hemispheric if not global phenomena. In periodizing modern black politics it will require fresh thinking about the importance of Haiti and its revolution for the development of African-American political thought and movements of resistance. From the European side it will no doubt be necessary to reconsider Frederick Douglass's relationship to English and Scottish radicalisms and to meditate on the significance of William Wells Brown's five years in Europe as a fugitive slave, on Alexander Crummell's living and studying in Cambridge, and upon Martin Delany's experiences at the London congress of the International Statistical Congress in 1860.[8] It will require comprehension of such difficult and complex questions as W. E. B. Du Bois's childhood interest in Bismarck, his investment in modeling his dress and moustache on that of Kaiser Wilhelm II, his likely thoughts while sitting in Heinrich Von Treitschke's seminars,[9] and the use his tragic heroes make of European culture.

Notable black American travelers, from the poet Phyllis Wheatley onwards, went to Europe and had their perceptions of America and racial domination shifted as a result of their experiences there. This had important consequences for their understanding of racial identities. The radical journalist and political organizer Ida B. Wells is typical, describing her productive times in England as like "being born again in a new condition."[10] Lucy Parsons is a more problematic figure in the political history of black America,[11] but how might her encounters with William Morris Annie Besant, and Peter Kropotkin impact upon a rewriting of the history of English radicalism? What of Nella Larsen's relationship to Denmark, where George Padmore was held in jail during the early 1930s and which was also the home base of his banned paper the *Negro Worker,* circulated across the world by its supporters in the Colonial Seamen's Association?[12] What of Sarah Parker Remond's work as a medical practitioner in Italy and the life of Edmonia Lewis, the sculptor, who made her home in Rome?[13] What effects did living in Paris have upon Anna Cooper, Jessie Fauset, Gwendolyn Bennett,[14] and Lois Maillou Jones?

It would appear that there are large questions raised about the direction and character of black culture and art if we take the powerful effects of even temporary experiences of exile, relocation, and displacement into account. How for example, was the course of the black vernacular art of jazz changed by what happened to Quincy Jones in Sweden and Donald Byrd in Paris? This is especially interesting because both men played powerful roles in the remaking of jazz as a popular form in the early 1970s. Byrd describes his sense of Europe's appeal as something that grew out of the view of Canada he developed as a young man growing up in Detroit:

> That's why Europe was so important to me. Living across the river from Canada as a kid, I used to go down and sit and look at Windsor, Ontario. Windsor represented Europe to me. That was the rest of the world that was foreign to me. So I always had a feeling for the foreign, the European thing, because Canada was right there. We used to go to Canada. For black people, you see, Canada was a place that treated you better than America, the North. For my father Detroit was better than the South, to me born in the North, Canada was better. At least that was what I thought. Later on I found out otherwise, but anyway, Canada represented for me something foreign, exotic, that was not the United States.[15]

Richard Wright's life in exile . . . has been written off as a betrayal of his authenticity and as a process of seduction by philosophical traditions supposedly outside his narrow ethnic compass,[16] . . . an exemplary instance of how the politics of location and the politics of identity get inscribed in analyses of black culture. [. . .] They are all potential candidates for inclusion in the latest African-American cultural canon, a canon that is conditional on and possibly required by the academic packaging of black cultural studies[17] [. . .]. Du Bois's travel experiences raise in the sharpest possible form a question common to the lives of almost all these figures who begin as African Americans or Caribbean people and are then changed into something else which evades those specific labels and with them all fixed notions of nationality and national identity. Whether their experience of exile is enforced or chosen, temporary or permanent, these intellectuals and activists, writers, speakers, poets, and artists repeatedly articulate a desire to escape the restrictive bonds of ethnicity, national identification, and sometimes even "race" itself. Some speak, like Wells and Wright, in terms of the rebirth that Europe offered them. Whether they dissolved their African-American sensibility into an explicitly pan-Africanist discourse or political commitment, their relationship to the land of their birth and their ethnic political constituency was absolutely transformed. The specificity of the modern political and cultural formation I want to call the black Atlantic can be defined, on one level, through this desire to transcend both the structures of the nation-state and the constraints of ethnicity and national particularity. These desires are relevant to understanding political organizing and cultural criticism. They have always sat uneasily alongside the strategic choices forced on black movements and individuals embedded in national political cultures and nation-states in America, the Caribbean, and Europe.

[. . .]

Black politics and modernity

[. . .] The problem of weighing the claims of national identity against other contrasting varieties of subjectivity and identification has a special place in the intellectual history of blacks in the West. Du Bois's concept of double consciousness [. . .] is only the best-known resolution of a familiar problem which points towards the core dynamic of racial oppression as well as the fundamental antinomy of diaspora blacks. How has this doubleness, what Richard Wright calls the dreadful objectivity[18] which follows from being both inside and outside the West, affected the conduct of political movements against racial oppression and towards black autonomy? Are the inescapable pluralities involved in the movements of black peoples, in Africa and in exile, ever to be synchronized? How would these struggles be periodized in relation to modernity: the fatal intermediation of capitalism, industrialization, and a new conception of political democracy? Does posing these questions in this way signify anything more than the reluctant intellectual affiliation of diaspora blacks to an approach which mistakenly attempts a premature totalization of infinite struggles, an approach which itself has deep and problematic roots within the ambiguous intellectual traditions of the European Enlightenment which have, at different moments, been both a lifeline and a fetter?

[Martin] Delany's work has provided some powerful evidence to show that the intellectual heritage of Euro-American modernity determined and possibly still determines the manner in which nationality is understood within black political discourse. In particular, this legacy conditions the continuing aspiration to acquire a supposedly authentic, natural, and stable "rooted" identity. This invariant identity is in turn the premise of a thinking "racial" self that is both socialized and unified by its connection with other kindred souls encountered usually, though not always, within the fortified frontiers of those discrete ethnic cultures which also happen to coincide with the contours of a sovereign nation-state that guarantees their continuity.

Consider for a moment the looseness with which the term "black nationalism" is used both by its advocates and by skeptics. Why is a more refined political language for dealing with these crucial issues of identity, kinship, generation, affect, and affiliation such a long time coming? A small but telling example can be drawn from the case of Edouard Glissant, who has contributed so much to the emergence of a creole counter-discourse that can answer the alchemy of nationalisms. Discussion of these problems suffers when his translator excises Glissant's references to the work of Deleuze and Guattari from the English edition of his 1981 book *Le Discours antillais,*[19] presumably because to acknowledge this exchange would somehow violate the aura of Caribbean authenticity that is a desirable frame around the work. This typical refusal to accept the complicity and syncretic interdependency of black and white thinkers has recently become associated with a second difficulty: the overintegrated conceptions of pure and homogeneous culture which mean that black political struggles are construed as somehow automatically *expressive* of the national or ethnic differences with which they are associated.

This overintegrated sense of cultural and ethnic particularity is very popular today, and blacks do not monopolize it. It masks the arbitrariness of its own political choices in the morally charged language of ethnic absolutism and this poses additional dangers because it overlooks the development and change of black political ideologies and ignores the restless, recombinant qualities of the black Atlantic's affirmative political cultures. The political project forged by thinkers like Delany in the difficult journey from slave ship to citizenship is in danger of being wrecked by the seemingly insoluble conflict between two distinct but currently symbiotic perspectives. They can be loosely identified as the essentialist and the pluralist standpoints, though they are in fact two different varieties of essentialism: one ontological, the other strategic. The antagonistic relationship between these two outlooks has been especially intense in discussions of black art and cultural criticism. The ontological essentialist view has often been characterized by a brute pan-Africanism. It has proved unable to specify precisely where the highly prized but doggedly evasive essence of black artistic and political sensibility is currently located, but that is no obstacle to its popular circulation. This perspective sees the black intellectual and artist as a leader. Where it pronounces on cultural matters, it is often allied to a realist approach to aesthetic value that minimizes the substantive political and philosophical issues involved in the processes of artistic representation. Its absolutist conception of ethnic cultures can be identified by the way in which it registers uncomprehending disappointment with the actual cultural choices and patterns of the mass of black people. It has little to say about the profane, contaminated world of black popular culture and looks instead for an artistic practice that can disabuse the mass of black people of the illusions into which they have been seduced by their condition of exile and unthinking consumption of inappropriate cultural objects like the wrong hair-care products, pop music, and Western clothing. The community is felt to be on the wrong road, and it is the intellectual's job to give them a new direction, firstly by recovering and then by donating the racial awareness that the masses seem to lack.

This perspective currently confronts a pluralistic position which affirms blackness as an open signifier and seeks to celebrate complex representations of a black particularity that is *internally* divided: by class, sexuality, gender, age, ethnicity, economics, and political consciousness. There is no unitary idea of black community here, and the authoritarian tendencies of those who would police black cultural expression in the name of their own particular history or priorities are rightly repudiated. The ontologically grounded essentialism is replaced by a libertarian, strategic alternative: the cultural saturnalia which attends the end of innocent notions of the essential black subject.[20] Here, the polyphonic qualities of black cultural expression form the main aesthetic consideration and there is often an uneasy but exhilarating fusion of modernist and populist techniques and styles. From this perspective, the achievements of popular black cultural forms like music are a constant source of inspiration. They are prized for their implicit warning against the pitfalls of artistic conceit. The difficulty with this second tendency is that in leaving racial essentialism behind by viewing "race" itself as a social and cultural construction, it has been insufficiently alive to the lingering power of specifically racialized forms of power and subordination.

Each outlook compensates for the obvious weaknesses in the other camp, but so far there has been little open and explicit debate between them. Their conflict, initially formulated in debates over black aesthetics and cultural production,[21] is valuable as a preliminary guide to some of the dilemmas faced by cultural and intellectual *historians* of the modern, Western, African diaspora. The problems it raises become acute, particularly for those who seek to comprehend cultural developments and political resistances which have had scant regard for either modern borders or premodern frontiers. At its worst the lazy, casual invocation of cultural insiderism which frequently characterizes the ontological essentialist view is nothing more than a symptom of the growing cleavages *within* the black communities. There, uneasy spokespeople of the black elite – some of them professional cultural commentators, artists, writers, painters, and filmmakers as well as political leaders – have fabricated a volkish outlook as an expression of their own contradictory position. This neonationalism seems out of tune with the spirit of the novel Africentric garb in which it appears before us today. It incorporates commentary on the special needs and desires of the relatively privileged castes within black communities, but its most consistent trademark is the persistent mystification of that group's increasingly problematic relationships with the black poor, who, after all, supply the elite with a dubious entitlement to speak on behalf of the phantom constituency of black people in general. The idea of blacks as a national or protonational group with its own hermetically enclosed culture plays a key role in this mystification, and, though seldom overtly named, the misplaced idea of a national interest gets invoked as a means to silence dissent and censor political debate when the incoherences and inconsistencies of Africalogical discourse are put on display.

Notes

1 Mary Louise Pratt, *Imperial Eyes* (London and New York: Routledge, 1992).

2 Nancy Stepan, *The Idea of Race in Science: Great Britain, 1800–1960* (Basingstoke: Macmillan, 1982); Michael Banton, *Racial Theories* (Cambridge: Cambridge University Press, 1987).

3 Linebaugh, "Atlantic Mountains." This is also the strategy pursued by Marcus Rediker in his brilliant book *Between the Devil and the Deep Blue Sea* (Cambridge: Cambridge University Press, 1987).

4 "A space exists when one takes into consideration vectors of direction, velocities, and time variables. Thus space is composed of intersections of mobile elements. It is in a sense articulated by the ensemble of movements deployed within it." Michel de Certeau, *The Practice of Everyday Life* (Berkeley and London: University of California Press, 1984), p. 117.

5 See Michael Colin and Michael K. Platzer, *Black Men of the Sea* (New York: Dodd, Mead, 1978). I have been heavily reliant on George Francis Dow's anthology *Slave Ships and Slaving,* publication no. 15 of the Marine Research Society (1927; rpt. Cambridge, MD: Cornell Maritime Press, 1968), which includes extracts from valuable eighteenth and nineteenth-century material. On England, I have found the anonymously published study *Liverpool and Slavery* (Liverpool: A. Bowker and Sons, 1884) to be very valuable. Memoirs produced by black sea captains also point to a number of new intercultural and transcultural research problems. Captain Harry Dean's *The Pedro Gorino: The adventures of a Negro Sea Captain in Africa and on the Seven Seas in His attempts to Found an Ethiopian Empire* (Boston and New York: Houghton Mifflin, 1929) contains interesting material on the practical politics of pan-Africanism that go unrecorded elsewhere. Captain Hugh Mulzac's autobiography, *A Star to Steer By* (New York: International Publishers, 1963), includes valuable observations on the role of ships in the Garvey movement. Some pointers towards what a black Atlantic rereading of the history of Rastafari might involve are to be found in Robert A. Hill's important essay which accentuates complex post-slavery relations between Jamaica and Africa: "Dread History: Leonard P. Howell and Millenarian Visions in Early Rastafari Religions in Jamaica," *Epoché: Journal of the History of Religions at UCLA 9 (1981):* 30–71.

6 Stephen Greenblatt, *Marvellous Possessions* (Oxford: Oxford University Press, 1992). See also Pratt, *Imperial Eyes.*

7 James T. Clifford, "Travelling Cultures," *in Cultural Studies,* ed. Lawrence Grossberg et al. (New York and London: Routledge, 1992), and "Notes on Theory and Travel," *Inscriptions* 5 (1989).

8 *Manchester Weekly Advertiser,* July 21, 1860; *Punch,* July 18, 1860, *Morning Star,* July 18, 1860 and F. A. Rollin, *Life and Public Services of Martin R. Delany* (Boston, MA: Lee and Shepard, 1868), p. 102.

9 Peter Winzen, "Treitschke's Influence on the Rise of Imperialist and Anti-British Nationalism in Germany," in P. Kennedy and A. Nicholls, eds, *Nationalist and Racialist Movements in Britain and Germany before 1914* (Basingstoke: Macmillan, 1981).

10 Ida B. Wells quoted in Vron Ware, *Beyond the Pale: White Women, Racism, and History* (London and New York: Verso, 1992), p. 177.

11 Carolyn Ashbaugh, *Lucy Parsons: American Revolutionary* (Chicago, IL: Charles H. Kerr, 1976). I must thank Tommy Lott for this reference.

12 Frank Hooker, *Black Revolutionary: George Padmore's Path from Communism to Pan-Africanism* (London: Pall Mall Library of African Affairs, 1967).

13 William S. McFeely, *Frederick Douglass* (New York: W. W. Norton, 1991), p. 329.

14 Michel Fabre, *Black American Writers in France, 1840–1980* (Urbana and Chicago: University of Illinois Press, 1991).

15 Ursula Broschke Davis, *Paris without Regret* (Iowa City: University of Iowa Press, 1986), p. 102.

16 I challenge this view in chapter 5. [*Editors' note:* Gilroy refers to chapter 5 of *The Black Atlantic.*]

17 Some of the problems associated with this strategy have been discussed by Cornel West in "Minority Discourse and the Pitfalls of Canon Formation," *Yale Journal of Criticism* 1, no. 1 (fall 1987): 193–201.

18 This phrase is taken from Wright's novel *The Outsider* (New York: Harper and Row, 1953), p. 129. In his book of essays, *White Man Listen!* (Garden City, NY: Anchor Books, 1964), he employs the phrase "dual existence" to map the same terrain. See chapter 5 below. [*Editors' note:* Gilroy refers to chapter 5 of *The Black Atlantic.*]

19 Edouard Glissant, *Le Discours antillais* (Paris: Editions du Seuil, 1981).

20 Stuart Hall, "New Ethnicities," in K. Mercer, ed., *Black Film; British Cinema* (London: ICA Documents 7, 1988), p. 28.

21 See *Ten.8 2,* no. 3 (1992), issue entitled *The Critical Decade.*

CITIZENSHIP AND THE TRANSGLOBAL

Introduction

Like other categories of affiliation, citizenship has responded dynamically to the new forces of globalisation, mass migration and the rise of the new social media. But even a static binary model of diaspora such as William Safran's (see Chapter 1, this volume) had argued that citizenship is a choice as well as a legal status, and not necessarily linked to a single geographical territory or nation. For Michel Laguerre (2009), the dispersed sites outside the homeland (as in trade, labour and imperial diasporas) that retain affiliations with the sovereign territory of the nation-state, argue for the nation/diaspora binary to be reconceived as a 'transglobal network nation' (205). Such a model emphasises multiple, interconnected diasporic locations and borders served by flexible constructions of citizenship and civic belonging, both 'at home' and abroad, such as the category of dual citizenship that allows capital to be returned from the diaspora to the homeland (Quayson and Daswani 2013, 13). These more fluid practices of citizenship are most appropriate for transnational groups who retain traditional strong links to the homeland rather than, for example, the multiply-dispersed groups of the Caribbean diaspora, or those of the Parsi who no longer have a homeland to refer to (Cohen 2008, 124, 135–7). Those who live in transit and in 'a place of transit', as, for example, in present day Haiti, go so far as to subscribe to a notion of citizenship that has been removed from its national foundations and relocated in 'a transnational or global arena' (Laguerre 2009, 205–6).[1]

Global mobility and new types of political participation have exposed the limits and inadequacy of the state-centred distribution paradigm of citizenship that casts citizens as consumers in a territorialised political system. Migratory subjects are shaping new modes of participatory politics at the sub- and supra-national levels, while claiming a place and active role in their social environment and remaining involved in political life via social networks and cyberactivism. One of the major changes in citizenship construction is the abandonment of the focus on national, legal frameworks and the turn to actor-oriented, transnational, transglobal and rights-based approaches and perspectives with a stronger emphasis on norms, practices and identities. Citizenship is recast as 'practiced rather than as given' (Cornwall and Gaventa 2000, 59), and understood as a form of self-agency, for global trends are acknowledged that 'signal a deterritorializing of citizen practices and identities and of discourses about loyalty and allegiance' (Sassen 2003, 42).

As citizenship is increasingly reconceived in terms of global and international human rights that transcend the nation-state, however, its spatial location, postnational identity and relation to diaspora have become topics of debate (Canning and Rose 2002, 2, cited in Fleischmann and Van Styvendale 2011; see Chapter 11 of this volume). For Yasemin Soysal in 'Citizenship and identity' the making and enacting of citizenship in the transglobal sphere does not have to be harnessed to diaspora with its powerful existing links to the nation. Citizenship is more about membership and belonging beyond borders, and about actively performing and enabling, than part of the diaspora community's need to maintain ties with the nation. The rights of citizenship, for example, do not require a national status to enable subjects to practice them, since they were decoupled from nations and their identities after universal statements on human rights such as the United Nations Universal Declaration of Human Rights (December 10, 1948) passed in the post-World War Two era, replacing (national) citizenship rights. Specific rights can now be exercised and legitimated at the local and national levels according to such universal discourses about person-hood. For example, Pakistanis who demand a greater commitment to religious teaching in British state schools mobilise around a Muslim identity but appeal to the universalistic European Court of Human Rights. In Soysal's terms, which are similar to Brubaker's concept of diaspora (see Chapter 7, this volume), citizenship can be identified as a category of practice rather than a category of analysis, one that articulates civic projects, makes claims, engages members, initiates transactions, mobilises identities and appeals to loyalties. Members of migrant communities and organisations are thus able to validate particularistic identities and promote causes by appealing to the universalistic and homogenising discourses of individual rights, equality and emancipation, rather than by participating in the arrangements and transactions of the ethnic diasporas to which they may belong and the nation-states from which they originate.

Soysal identifies a new dynamic in the proliferating sites of making and enacting citizenship, claiming that the public sphere of post-World War Two, rights-based immigration in Europe is broader than the domain of diaspora. Lily Cho, by contrast, in 'Diasporic citizenship', considers that 'the demands of citizenship clash with the desires of diaspora', and she is less convinced that citizenship works effectively for diaspora communities. She attributes the 'unfitness' of the relation between diaspora and citizenship to the lack of a smooth transition into the hostland that would enable citizenship and belonging. Cho develops an analogy between what she perceives as the historical dislocation inherent in Canadian literature (with its division between minority and majority literatures) and the necessary amnesia about past exclusions needed to create the illusion of equality among all citizens. In situating minority literature within the overarching field of Canadian literature, she argues that 'diasporic citizenship' requires recognition of the enabling and disabling features of citizenship; the contingency inherent in making choices for citizenship; and occupation of those 'messy spaces' which evidence the clash between citizenship and diaspora.

With a closer focus on the positive benefits from the practices of citizenship within the nation state, Aloys N.M. Fleischmann and Nancy Van Styvendale in their 'Introduction' to *Narratives of Citizenship* identify an indigenous concept of citizenship that refers to communities that are ex-centric to the normative state of belonging within the nation state. In countries like the USA and Canada where such minority indigenous groups are held on reservations, they can be considered as belonging to an internal diaspora. Often including diaspora groups, these minorities might resist national master narratives that proclaim a monolithic and equal citizenship, displaying an affective register in their struggle to belong. The critical attention to the positioning of indigenous cultures within the nation state and 'loosening the common opposition of "indigenous" and "diasporic" forms of life' (Clifford 2007, 199, cited by Fleischmann and Van Styvendale 2011, xxvi) is a relatively neglected area of diaspora studies (Maracle 2005). The intersection of the field with the work of indigenous studies, as found in Fleischmann and Van Styvendale's collection of essays, helps differentiate diaspora from the transnational by aligning it to diasporas' 'long histories of dislocation' (see Cho, Chapter 9, this volume) of indigenous communities due to colonisation.

Although a modern citizenship implies national belonging, legal equality and a set of rights and duties to be bestowed by the state upon its subjects, the new ideas of civic engagement – ranging from the juridical prescriptions regarding political citizenship, to the cultural performance of citizenship in local and global spheres – testify to the influence of heightened global mobility and transnational political participation. These new forms of civic participation are regulated by various types of (supra)-national legislation, and they include diverse cultural practices, from literary production such as life writing to internet blogging and other forms of cultural expression which raise awareness of citizenship issues. Cumulatively they lay down a challenge to more atavistic, divisive and ethnically conceived constructions of national belonging.

Note

1 On special initiatives that connect the Haitian Government and the Haitian diaspora see 'Introduction' to '(Inter)national Policy and Diaspora', p. 85.

References

Canning, Kathleen, and Sonya O. Rose. 2002. 'Introduction: Gender, Citizenship and Subjectivity: Some Historical and Theoretical Considerations.' In *Gender, Citizenship and Subjectivities*, edited by Kathleen Canning and Sonya O. Rose, 1–17. Oxford: Blackwell.

Clifford, James. 2007. 'Varieties of Indigenous Experience: Diasporas, Homelands, Sovereignties.' In *Indigenous Experience Today*, edited by Marisol de la Cadena and Orin Starn, 197–223. Oxford and New York: Berg.

Cohen, Robin. 2008. *Global Diasporas: An Introduction*, 2nd ed. London and New York: Routledge.

Cornwall, Andrea, and John Gaventa. 2000. 'From Users and Choosers to Makers and Shapers: Repositioning Participation in Social Policy.' *IDS Bulletin* 31 (4): 50–62.

Fleischmann, Aloys N.M., and Nancy Van Styvendale. 2011. 'Introduction.' In *Narratives of Citizenship: Indigenous Diaspora People Unsettle the Nation-State*, edited by Aloys N.M. Fleischmann and Nancy Van Styvendale, xi–xlv. Edmonton, Alberta: University of Alberta Press.

Laguerre, Michel D. 2009. 'The Transglobal Network Nation: Diaspora, Homeland, and Hostland.' In *Transnationalism: Diasporas and the Advent of a New (Dis)Order*, edited by Eliezer Ben-Rafael and Yitzhak Sternberg, 195–210. Leiden and Boston: Brill.

Maracle, Lee. 2005. 'Some Words on Study as a Process of Discovery.' Presentation given at the Trans-Canada: Literature, Institutions conference, held at Simon Fraser University, Vancouver, June 24. Available at: https://web.archive.org/web/20080318161632/http://www.transcanadas.ca/transcanada1/maracle.shtml.

Quayson, Ato, and Girish Daswani. 2013. 'Introduction: Diaspora and Transnationalism: Scapes, Scales, and Scopes.' In *A Companion to Diaspora and Transnationalism*, edited by Ato Quayson and Girish Daswani, 1–26. Oxford: Wiley-Blackwell.

Sassen, Saskia. 2003. 'The Repositioning of Citizenship: Emergent Subjects and Spaces for Politics.' *The New Centennial Review* 3 (2): 41–66.

9

DIASPORIC CITIZENSHIP

Contradictions and possibilities for Canadian literature

Lily Cho

The nation is not necessarily the natural site of citizenship. Recent work on citizenship in fields such as sociology, political theory, and globalization studies unfolds the possibilities for uncoupling the notion of citizenship from the nation. In "The Repositioning of Citizenship," Saskia Sassen questions the collapse of the nation and citizen, and argues for an "unbundling" of this package while still retaining the nation as a reference point for thinking about citizenship (62). Distinguishing between denationalized and postnational citizenship, Sassen proposes a "pluralization" of citizenship that may "explode the boundaries" (2002, 56) of its legal status.[1] Echoing the language of human rights, Keith Faulks argues that the obligations of citizenship demand an understanding of how the concept moves beyond the state. He suggests that "it is becoming clear that the idea of the nation is increasingly a barrier rather than a supporting pillar of citizenship" (2000, 42). Untangling the notion of the citizen from that of the nation reveals the ways in which the nation has bounded citizenship not only geographically but also in terms of understandings of community and identity.

While there may be compelling possibilities to explore in thinking of citizenship either in denationalized or postnational terms, the national literary continues to connect citizenship and literature almost as tightly as the nation has been connected with citizenship. The relationship between citizenship and literature has its clearest articulation most recently in Donna Palmateer Pennee's "Literary Citizenship: Culture (Un)Bounded, Culture (Re)Distributed" where she argues that "national literary studies, understood as a process, provide for a kind of literary citizenship as a form of cultural and civic participation and cultural and civic legitimation in the social imaginary" (2004, 81). Risking both a kind of optimism and a belief in our work as critics, Pennee then suggests that there is a possibility that the "statement—that national literary studies are exclusionary—may be operating at its historical limit" (82). I want to hang on to Pennee's risk even as I am less optimistic about the historical limits of the exclusionary practices of the national literary; but I also want to situate her claims within the context of the untangling of citizenship from the nation. [. . .]

Diasporic citizenship

I want to propose diasporic citizenship as a rubric for thinking through what I understand to be the contradictions and possibilities of Canadian literature. In its most prominent usage to date, Michel Laguerre's notion of diasporic citizenship articulates the ways in which Haitian communities within the US have built a civil society that could not thrive within Haiti itself.

However, I want to use the idea of diasporic citizenship in a slightly different register from that of Laguerre (1998).[2] The current use of diasporic citizenship in the social sciences understands the diasporic as an extension of citizenship practices that tend to be located at the level of the nation-state. While this usage offers a number of possibilities for thinking about transnational forms of identity and belonging, I want to emphasize the inherent dissonance between the terms "diasporic" and "citizenship." I do not see diaspora as a different kind of "container" for citizenship. The idea of diasporic citizenship seems to offer the shimmering possibility of something new, something that might supplant the nation as a site of citizenship and might take into account the underside of transnational mobility, those not accounted for in the idea of Aihwa Ong's (1999) "flexible citizenship."[3] I am deeply unconvinced by this shimmering possibility. A new phrase will not necessarily get us out of old problems. Instead, I want to pursue in my exploration of diasporic citizenship precisely its "unfitness." "Diaspora" and "citizenship" do not fit easily together. The former emerges through collectivities; the latter has been grounded in notions of individual autonomy. The former exists uneasily alongside the nation; the latter emerges within the nation. The subject of diaspora and the subject of citizenship do not map onto one another. This uneasiness and dissonance could be very productive for thinking through the differential histories of dislocation in Canadian literature. I want to explore this dissonance in two ways: first, through the push and pull of history and memory; and second, through the problematic legacy of citizenship itself. [. . .]

I want to examine the conditions of citizenship that we have inherited and the ways in which these conditions signal the inexorability of our choice *for* citizenship. Despite any uneasiness that we might have about the idea of citizenship, despite the ways in which we might point to its legacies of exclusion and even violence, we cannot, given the choice, choose not to be citizens. To do so would be to render ourselves refugees—a state that Agamben identifies as one that illuminates the limit of citizenship. Instead of guaranteeing one's rights, what the 1789 Declaration would term the Rights of Man, the loss of citizenship thus endangers the guarantee of rights. The only claim that can return the refugee to the relative safety and security of a social existence lies in a claim for citizenship. Agamben observes that, "even in the best of cases, the status of refugee has always been considered a temporary condition that ought to lead either to naturalization or repatriation" (2000, 20). Despite the long-term existence of millions of refugees, "illegal" migrants and other stateless persons, statelessness continues to be understood as a form of transience. We must all always either be citizens of somewhere or be on our way to such a condition. Citizenship is indispensable. We can seek to transform the institution of citizenship; indeed, following from the work of Henderson and others, we must continue to struggle for forms of citizenship that might better encompass the vision of a society in which we hope to thrive; but we must still choose to enter into this process of transformation, choosing within the contingencies of a situation, at least in part, not of our own making, of a legacy that is not entirely our own. [. . .]

Diasporas function as a perpetual reminder of the losses that enable citizenship. Diasporic citizenship is then not a new, shiny, improved version of citizenship that might be seen as the underside of cosmopolitan citizenship. Nor can it address the failures of the nation-state to safeguard against the violation of the right to be human. Nor is diasporic citizenship a panacea for the contradiction inherent in the conception of modern citizenship itself. For me, at least in this context, it is something much smaller. As I have been arguing, the profound dissonance between these terms, diaspora and citizenship, enables a dialectical tension between them. The disparity between the subject of diaspora and the subject of citizenship opens up a recognition of the contingencies surrounding our choice for citizenship. Diaspora allows us to be up against citizenship, to embrace it even as we hold it at some distance, to recognize it as both disabling and enabling. To return to where I began, the situating of minority literatures within Canadian literature as a field, it is my hope that diasporic citizenship might allow us to think through the entanglements of a national literary that remains committed to long histories of dislocation even as it exists within the contradictions of citizenship. I understand minority literatures such as Asian Canadian, Black Canadian, and Native literatures as existing in an uneasy lockstep with Canadian literature in much the same way that the subject of diaspora and the subject of citizenship might co-exist in uneasy but nonetheless unavoidable relation. Engaging in what Huhndorf (2001) calls the "rituals of citizenship"[4] reveals an ongoing occupation of diasporic identities as an elaborate act of national forgetting. Being against citizenship, being both intimate and in opposition to it, requires more than a rejection of ritual. It requires an exploration of those messy spaces where the subject of citizenship and the subject of diaspora do not overlap, where they pull and sometimes tear away from each other. The work of diasporic citizenship is thus the work of dwelling in this dissonance between diaspora and citizenship in order to enable memory to tear away at the coherence of national forgettings.

Notes

1 Sassen distinguishes de-nationalized from postnational citizenship and suggests that "The understanding in the scholarship is that postnational citizenship is located partly outside the confines of the national. In considering denationalization, the focus moves on to the transformation of the national, including the national in its condition as foundation for citizenship. Thus it could be argued that postnationalism and denationalization represent two different trajectories. Both are viable, and they do not exclude each other" (2002, 56).

2 See Michel Laguerre, *Diasporic Citizenship: Haitian Americans in Transnational America* (1998).

3 In *Flexible Citizenship,* Ong focusses "on the agency of displaced subjects and attempts by the state to regulate their activities and identities as a way to explore new cultural logics of transnationality" (1999, 23). The subjects of Ong's study are thus mainly multiple-passport-carrying entrepreneurs and other transnational elites.

4 I take the phrase from the title of the final chapter of *Going Native,* "Rituals of Citizenship: Going Native and Contemporary American Identity" (2001, 199–202). Huhndorf argues specifically that the occupation of Native identities by White America is part of a process "of constructing white identities, naturalizing conquest, and inscribing various power relations within American culture" (6). Thus, the rituals of citizenship involve a continual process of "going Native," of taking the place of Native identities in mainstream culture and, in the case of a film such as *Dances with Wolves,* evoking "the conquest of Native America ... only to assuage the guilt stemming from that painful history" (4). As I have argued throughout this paper, Native Canadian identities are not minoritized in the same ways as other racially minoritized identities are, but we can productively think through the relationship of these minority positions within the rubric of diaspora.

References

Agamben, Giorgio. 2000. *Means without End: Notes on Politics.* Trans. Vincenzo Binetti and Cesare Casarino. Minneapolis: U of Minnesota P.

Faulks, Keith. 2000. *Citizenship.* New York: Routledge.

Huhndorf, Shari. 2001. "Rituals of Citizenship: Going Native and Contemporary American Identity." *Going Native: Indians in the American Cultural Imagination.* Ithaca, NY: Cornell UP, 199–202.

Laguerre, Michel. 1998. *Diasporic Citizenship: Haitian Americans in Transnational America.* New York: St. Martin's.

Ong, Aihwa. 1999. *Flexible Citizenship: The Cultural Logics of Transnationality.* Durham, NC: Duke UP.

Pennee, Donna Palmateer. 2004. "Literary Citizenship: Culture (Un)Bounded, Culture (Re)Distributed." *Home-Work: Postcolonialism, Pedagogy, and Canadian Literature.* Ed. Cynthia Sugars. Ottawa: U of Ottawa P, 75–85.

Sassen, Saskia. 2002. "The Repositioning of Citizenship: Emergent Subjects and Spaces for Politics." *Berkeley Journal of Sociology* 46: 41–66.

10

CITIZENSHIP AND IDENTITY

Living in diasporas in post-war Europe?

Yasemin Nuhoglu Soysal

My argument would be that in the post-war era, the boundaries and imperatives within which diasporas are expected to take shape have changed. Particularly in Europe, in response to trans-formations affecting the contemporary politics, economies and institutions of the nation-state system, new forms of citizenship, belonging and claims have emerged. These new forms under-mine the 'national order of things',[1] thus the very premise of diaspora. Diaspora, as an analytical category is too limiting to explicate the contemporary contours of membership and belonging. We have to move beyond the customary and static precepts of diaspora and expand our theoretical and political vocabulary.

A more challenging and productive perspective is achieved by focusing our analytical prov-idence on the proliferating sites of making and enacting citizenship. In a world of incessant migrations, it is in these novel geographies of citizenship that we recognize the dynamics and distribution of rights and identities, and patterns of exclusion and inclusion. My goal is to address the new forms and sites of citizenship and the broader processes that occasion their emergence. I begin by summarizing briefly the developments that contextualize the changes in the institution and practice of citizenship in the post-war Europe. Then, I elaborate the two paradoxes that I see as crucial in understanding the contemporary formations of citizenship, and exclusions and inclusions. The first paradox relates to the rights and identities, the two main components of citizenship, and their increasing decoupling. The second paradox to the ways collective claims are made and mobilized: an increasing tendency towards particularistic and group-based claims and their legitimation through universalistic discourses of personhood and strategies. Finally, I suggest that these two paradoxes warrant a reconsideration of our dominant approaches to immigrants and membership, and categories of exclusion and inclusion.

Post-war changes in the European state system

Contrary to the predominant understandings and conceptualizations in sociology, my work suggests that the limits of citizenship are not singularly located in a nation-state but also encompass the local and the transnational. Contemporary practice of citizenship is increasingly decoupled from belonging in the national collective. Regardless of their historical or cultural ties to the German nation, and even without a formal German nationality, Turkish immigrants in Berlin make claims on Berlin's authority structures and participate in Berlin's public institutions. When they make demands for the teaching of Islam in state schools, the Pakistani immigrants in Britain mobilize around a Muslim identity, but they appeal to a universalistic language of 'human rights' to justify their claims. And, they not only mobilize to affect the local school authorities, but also pressure the national government, and take their case to the European Court of Human Rights. I argue that these examples undermine the predominant models of citizenship, which are normatively predicated upon the integrity of national communities and their boundaries. I suggest that to provide a meaningful understanding of contemporary formations of citizenship, and exclusion and inclusion, we need to incorporate these seeming anomalies into our analytical 'tool-kit'.

The background to the arguments I am now advancing is a series of interlocking legal, institutional, and ideological changes in the European state system in the post-war period. These changes have complicated the national order of citizenship and introduced new dynamics for membership and participation in the public sphere. I elaborated these changes elsewhere (Soysal 1994). Here I briefly cite four developments that have significant implications for the institution of citizenship and the notions of identity and rights:

- First, the transformations in the existing national and ethnic composition of European countries, as a consequence of massive migratory flows not only from the immediate European periphery but also from 'distant lands'.
- Second, the increasing intensification of transnational discourse and legal instruments that codify 'human rights' or personhood as a world-level principle. This elaboration of individual rights, in international agreements and institutions but also in scientific and popular discourses, has laid the ground upon which more expansive claims and rights can be advanced, and led to the introduction of new forms of rights – for women, children, minorities, immigrants, and even for animals and plants (see Turner 1986).
- Third, the increasing legitimacy of the right to 'one's own culture' and identity. This right has been furthered by the massive decolonizations in the post-war period, as well as through the works of international organizations such as the United Nations, UNESCO, and the Council of Europe. Collective identity has been redefined as a category of human rights. Codified as a right, identities have become important organizational and symbolic tools for creating new group solidarities and mobilizing resources (as in the case of women's movements, environmentalists, gays and lesbians, regional identities and interests, indigenous groups and immigrants).
- Lastly, the diffusion of sovereignty and the emergence of multi-level polities, such as we observe with the gradual unfolding of the European Union and the devolution of some European nation-states into culturally and administratively autonomous regions (Schmitter 1992; Marks and McAdam 1996). The diffusion and sharing of sovereignty among local, national and transnational political institutions, enable new actors, open up an array of new organizational strategies, and facilitate competition over resources and definitions.

All these developments, the transformations in the population composition of the European states, the legitimation of rights at the transnational level, the codification of collective identities as rights, and the increasing diffusion of sovereignty, have paradoxical implications for national citizenship. They have paradoxical implications as regards the ways that rights and identities are defined and allocated; and also as regards the ways in which collective claims are made and mobilized. I now turn to the discussion of these paradoxes of citizenship. By doing so, I also aim to clarify my objection to the uncritical reinsertion of the concept of the diaspora into our discussions and analyses.

Paradoxes of citizenship

Decoupling of rights and identity

The first paradox I would like to elaborate is the increasing decoupling of rights and identity. In the nation-state mode of political community, national belonging constitutes the source of rights and duties of individuals; and citizenship is delimited by national collectivity. The post-war era, however, has witnessed an increasing recasting of (national) citizenship rights as human (or personhood) rights (Soysal 1994).[2] Rights that were once associated with belonging in a national community have become increasingly abstract, and legitimated at the transnational level.

The post-war reification of personhood and individual rights expands the boundaries of political community, by legitimating individuals' participation and claims beyond their membership status in a particular nation-state. With the breakdown of the link between the national community and rights, we observe multiple forms of citizenship that are no longer anchored in national collectives, and that expand the sets of right-bearing members within and without the nation-state. These forms are exemplified in the membership of the long-term non-citizen immigrants, who hold various rights and privileges without a formal nationality status; in the increasing instances of dual citizenship, which breaches the traditional notions of political membership and loyalty in a single state; in the European Union citizenship, which represents a multi-tiered form of membership; and in subnational citizenships in culturally or administratively autonomous regions of Europe (for example, Basque country, Catalonia and Scotland).

As the source and legitimacy of rights shift to the transnational level, paradoxically, identities remain particularistic, and locally defined and organized. The same global rules and institutional frameworks which celebrate personhood and human rights, at the same time naturalize collective identities around national and ethno-religious particularisms.

This, as I have already stated, has a lot to do with the works of the international organizations such as the United Nations, UNESCO, the Council of Europe and the like, (as well as the discipline of anthropology), through which the universal right to 'one's own culture' has gained increasing legitimacy, and collective identity has been redefined as a category of human rights. What are considered particularistic characteristics of collectivities – culture, language and standard ethnic traits – have become variants of the universal core of humanness or selfhood. This identity represents the 'unchosen', and is naturalized through the language of kinship, homeland, nation and territory. One cannot help but have identity.[3]

The seeming naturalness and inevitability of diaspora formations (and theorizing immigrant communities as diasporas) are part and parcel of this global and hegemonic discourse of identity. Once institutionalized as natural, the discourse about identities creates ever increasing claims about cultural distinctiveness and group rights. Ethnic/national identities are enacted and improvised for mobilizing and making claims in national and world polities, authenticating diaspora as an idiom for the politics of identity. On the other hand, as exercised in individual and collective actors' narratives and strategies, identity also authorizes ethnic nationalisms and sovereignties. Thus, while rights acquire a more universalistic form and are divorced from national belonging, (thus giving rise to more inclusionary forms of membership), at the same time, identities become intentionally particularistic and exclusionary practices (on the basis of identity) prevail. And this we observe in the increasingly restrictive immigration policies of European countries, the vocalization of ethnic minority and religious groups for cultural closure, and the discriminatory citizenship practices of many of the ex-Soviet republics. So more inclusionary forms of rights clash with more exclusionary practices of identity.

Making particularistic claims through universalistic discourses of personhood and strategies

The second paradox to which I would like to draw attention regards collective claims-making and participation in public spheres; in other words, the practice of citizenship by individuals and groups. With the post-war reconfigurations in citizenship that I described in the previous section, the old categories that attach individuals to nationally defined status positions and distributory mechanisms become blurred. This inevitably changes the nature and locus of struggles for social equality and rights. New forms of mobilizing and advancing claims and participation emerge beyond the frame of national citizenship.

If we recall, our classical notions of citizenship assume the existence of actors whose rights and identities are grounded within the bounds of national collectives. And these collectives constitute the 'authentic' sites for the realization of claims-making and civic participation. My research reveals two trends that diverge from this predominant prescription of citizenship. First, we see an increasing tendency to advance particularistic identities and demands, which, at the same time, are located in and legitimated by the universalistic discourses of human or personhood rights. Second, we see that the mobilization of claims takes place independent of nationally delimited collectives and at different levels (local, national and transnational). In other words, the social and political stages for claims-making proliferate.

I would like to elaborate on these two trends by citing empirical evidence from Muslim immigrant communities and their participation and mobilization in European public spheres. I do not wish to imply that we can observe the emerging forms only in the case of Muslim immigrants. These are broader tendencies, but my focus is on Muslim groups, since these communities are visibly at the centre of contention.

a) The first trend concerns the nature of the claims and discourse. Immigrant groups in Europe mobilize around claims for particularistic provisions and emphasize their group identities. Their claims, however, are not simply grounded in the particularities of religious or ethnic narratives. On the contrary, they appeal to the universalistic principles and dominant discourses of equality, emancipation and individual rights. In other words, the claims that immigrants advance and the identities that they mobilize, though particularistic, derive their legitimacy and authority from universalistic discourses of personhood and human rights. Diaspora theories, with their singular focus on ethnic transactions and community formation, bypass these larger scripts, which activate and energize the very claims and identities. In turn, they misread immigrant mobilization simply as enactments of ethnicity.

Let me expand on this point. When Muslim immigrant associations advocate the rights and needs of immigrant children in school, they employ a discourse that appropriates the rights of the individuals as its central theme. They invoke the international instruments and conventions on human rights to frame their position. They forward demands about mother-tongue instruction, Islamic *foulard,* or *halal* food by asserting the 'natural' right of individuals to their own cultures, rather than drawing upon religious teachings and traditions.

To give an example. In 1989 the issue of Islamic *foulard* erupted into a national crisis and debate in France, when three North African students were expelled from school for insisting on wearing their scarfs in class. In the ensuing debates, the issue became not only a topical contention over immigrant integration and French laicism but entered into the public arena as a matter of rights of individuals. During the debates, the head of the Great Mosque of Paris declared the rules preventing the wearing of scarfs in school to be discriminatory on the ground of individual rights. His emphasis was on personal rights, rather than religious traditions or duties: 'If a girl asks to have her hair covered, I believe it is her most basic right' *(Washington Post,* 23 October 1989). In this case, Muslim identity, while symbolized by the headscarf, was asserted and authenticated by the very categories and language of the host society; that is, through a discourse that accentuates individual rights.

In another episode (in Germany this time), on 12 November 1995, which corresponded to the birthday of Fatima (the daughter of the prophet Muhammad), the Shi'ite *Ehlibeyt* mosque in Berlin invited 'all Muslim women' to a celebration of the World's Women's Day. Speakers to the meeting included not only the (male) clergy of the mosque but 'Muslim' women of different nationalities, Turks, Arabs and Germans. The focal point of the speeches delivered was to highlight women's emancipation, including demands to end discrimination against Muslim women in work places and schools, especially on the basis of their wearing the Islamic headscarf. The issues raised encapsulated the very terms of the contemporary gender discourse. The keynote speaker, a young *imam,* traced the issue of the rights of women to the Qur'an. Making references to the Beijing Conference on Women, he claimed the assertion of 'women's rights are human rights' as an original teaching of Islam and its culture. He declared indignantly: 'In the Beijing conference, when someone said, "women's rights are human rights", thousands of women cheered and clapped. What were they cheering for? We already said that 1400 years ago! That is our word!' The meeting was an instance of linking Islamic moral realm to the contemporary concerns and discourses about women, speaking to and through them.

Let me insert a caveat here: Muslim groups in European countries, obviously, do not speak in a uniform discursive framework. The examples that I have just given by no means exhaust the range of narratives employed by Muslim groups. Again, speaking for the Islamic veil, a Turkish *imam* in Nantua declared the practice as 'God's law' and put pressure on the Turkish families to withdraw their daughters from school. This led to serious divisions among the Turkish immigrant community and to his eventual deportation from France (Kepel 1997, pp. 222–23). It is also possible to find Islamic positions which base their claims on religiously codified family laws that sanction status disparity between genders. These proclamations obviously point to alternative, and often conflicting, claims and leadership among Muslim communities. This is not something I deny. My point here is to delineate the prevalent universalistic forms of making claims by Muslim groups that are commonly overlooked, and to elucidate their implications for our theoretical vistas.

Yet another caveat is warranted here. Granted, there is significant variation in the accommodation of the types of claims advanced. While some claims face organizational resistance, others are more readily accepted and incorporated into formal state structures. The educational authorities in Britain, for example, are more willing to accommodate the claims for Islamic dress codes, or even the teaching of immigrant languages in schools. On the other hand, religiously codified family laws (or polygamy, female circumcision) which create status disparity between genders are not viewed as legitimate demands. Here, the principle of gender equality contests the principle of religious equality, both of which are clearly embedded in European citizenships and transnational frameworks. In Europe, the treatment of women is codified in secular laws and institutions, thus the attempts to subject it to a religious, private domain generates conflict. In my research, I attempt to untangle the contradictory dynamics among different legitimating discourses and principles, and explain how these dynamics lead to conflicting claims and empowerments in the public sphere.[4]

To reiterate my main point, the Muslim organizations that I study do not justify their demands by simply reaching back to religious teachings or traditions but through a language of rights, thus, citizenship. By using the rights language they exercise civic projects and link themselves to the broader public spheres. The projects of citizenship in which they engage, however, are not necessarily nationally bounded. They are both spatially and symbolically multi-referential.

When Muslim associations make demands about veiling in schools, theirs is not a claim for belonging to an existing 'French collectivity', but to the educational system itself, which they see as their most natural right. This, I argue, is not necessarily disengagement from the collective life but the collective is no longer bounded by a preordained national community. Indeed, they try to redefine the very nature of national community.

b) The second trend as regards claims-making is that the organizational strategies employed by immigrant groups increasingly acquire a transnational and subnational character. The terms of their participation extend beyond the limits of the national, span multiple localities, transnationally connect public spheres, thus, diversify the 'spaces for and of politics'.[5] For example, we find political parties, mosque organizations, and community associations which operate at local levels but do not confine their claims only to their localities. During the last elections in Berlin, Turkish immigrant organizations pushed for their local voting rights and demands to vote in European elections, while at the same time, they put pressure on the Turkish government to facilitate their rights to vote in Turkish national elections. As such, they envisage their participation in multiple civic spaces, in Berlin, in Europe and in Turkey. This is increasingly a trend among immigrant populations in other parts of the world. Similar claims are being made by Mexican and Central American immigrant groups in the United States. They demand dual citizenship and dual voting rights in their countries of origin and residence. And, indeed, the governments of Mexico, Columbia and the Dominican Republic recently passed legislation allowing dual nationality.

In pursuing their claims, the mobilization of immigrant groups entails multiple states and political agencies, and they target trans- and sub-national institutions. Again, for example, the Islamic *foulard* issue was not simply a matter confined to the discretion of a local school board, but has traversed the realms of local, national, transnational jurisdictions – from local educational authorities to the European Court of Human Rights. Similarly, in the early 1990s, when the local authorities refused to permit the opening of another Islamic primary school, the Islamic Foundation in London decided to take the issue to the European Court of Human Rights. Indeed, more and more Muslim associations elevate their operations to the European level, establishing umbrella organizations and forums to coordinate their activities and pursue a Europewide agenda (Kastoryano 1996).

So, while the claims and mobilization of Muslim groups aim to further particularistic identities and solidarities, paradoxically, they make appeals to the universalistic principles of human rights and connect themselves to a diverse set of public spheres. As such, their mobilization is not simply a reinvention of ethnic or religious particularisms. Their civic projects and mobilization are not ethnically self-referential but reflect larger scripts of rights and personhood. Drawing upon universalistic repertoires of claims-making, they, at the same time, participate in and contribute to the reification of host-society and global discourses.

All these point to solidarities and participatory forms which cannot be captured by the concept of diaspora. Focusing peculiarly on the ethnic axis of homelands and abroad, the theories of diaspora overlook the transgressions of national boundaries and collectives and forget the new ways by which immigrants experience and enact their membership. In this new topography of membership, what constitutes the grounds for civic projects is no longer the 'horizontal connectedness' among members of an ethnic community (that is, mutual trust and solidarity on the basis of ethnic belonging). Here, the 'ties that bind' manifest themselves through participation in and by 'vertical connection' to common, universalistic discourses that transcend the very ethnic idiom of community.

To complete the picture, let me briefly refer to the second-generation immigrants, who are seen as enigmatic producers of diasporic cultures and identities. Far from being simple extensions of their 'homelands', the second-generation immigrants – Maghrebins, Pakistanis, Turks, Caribbeans, Bengalis living in the immigration capitals of Europe – negotiate and map collective identities which are dissociated from ethno-cultural citizenships (Bauman 1996; Soysal 1999). They appropriate their identity symbols as much from global cultural flows as host or home country cultural practices. As 'youth subcultures', they are increasingly part of the global (Gilroy 1993; Amit-Talai and Wulff 1995; Hannerz 1996), in many ways bypassing the national or traditional. Thus, it should not come as a surprise that Turkish youth in Germany listen to the rap music as much as, if not more than, they listen to Turkish *Sarki* or German *Lied*. Or that the immigrant 'youth gangs' adopt names in English: Two Nation Force, Turkish Power Boys, Cobras and Bulldogs. Or that they form rap groups cleverly called Cartel, Microphone Mafia, and Islamic Force, and that their graffiti on Berlin walls very much replicate the acclaimed styles of New York.

By highlighting this plethora of immigrant experience in a multitude of arenas, I wish to maintain that public spaces within which immigrants act, mobilize, advance claims and produce cultures are broader than the ethnic dominion of diaspora. Their connections to multi-level discourses and their access to diverse citizenship practices are invisible under the *modus operandi* of diasporic theorizing. Nor can the expanse and multi-referentiality of their mobilizing be contained by bi-directional ethnic transactions and arrangements.

Notes

1 The phrase is from Liisa H. Malkki (1995).
2 I use the term 'human rights' in its broad, abstract sense, not necessarily referring to specific international conventions or instruments and their categorical contents.
3 See Anderson (1983), Appadurai (1996), Herzfeld (1992), Malkki (1995), Gupta and Ferguson (1992) and Soysal (1996).
4 By emphasizing the universality of discourses and strategies employed by immigrant groups, I am not taking a naive position and assuming that individuals or groups will bond together and arrive at agreeable positions. Here I diverge from the Habermasian project, according to which the discursive process, when rational, serves to bring reason and will together and create consensus without coercion (Habermas 1962). Public sphere necessarily involves conflict, contestation and incoherent outcomes, however rational. In that sense, the role of the discursive participatory process is to focus on agendas of contestation and provide space for strategic action, rather than consensus building (Eder 1995).
5 I borrow the phrase from Jane Jenson (1993: 138).

References

Amit-Talai, Vered and Wullf, Helena (eds) 1995 *Youth Cultures: A Cross-cultural Perspective*, London: Routledge.

Anderson, Benedict 1983 *Imagined Communities*, London: Verso.

Appadurai, Arjun 1996 *Modernity at Large: Cultural Dimensions of Globalization*, Minneapolis, MN: University of Minnesota Press.

Baumann, Gerd 1996 *Contesting Culture: Discourses of Identity in Multi-Ethnic London*, Cambridge: Cambridge University Press.

Eder, Klaus 1995 'The Institutionalization of Environmentalism: Ecological Discourse and the Second Transformation of the Public Sphere', unpublished manuscript, European University Institute, Florence.

Gilroy, Paul 1993 *The Black Atlantic: Modernity and Double Consciousness*, Cambridge, MA: Harvard University Press.

Gupta, Akil and Ferguson, James 1992 'Beyond "Culture": space, identity, and the politics of difference', *Cultural Anthropology*, vol. 7, pp. 6–23.

Habermas, Jürgen 1962 [1989] *The Structural Transformation of the Public Sphere*, Cambridge, MA: MIT Press.

Hannerz, Ulf 1996 *Transnational Connections: Culture, People, Places*, New York: Routledge.

Herzfeld, Michael 1992 *The Social Production of Indifference: Exploring the Symbolic Roots of Western Bureaucracy*, New York: Berg.

Jenson, Jane 1993 'De-constructing dualities: making rights claims in political institutions', in G. Drover and P. Kerans (eds), *New Approaches to Welfare Theory*, Aldershot: Edward Elgar Publishers.

Kastoryano, Riva 1996 *Négocier l'Identité. La France, l'Allemagne et leurs Immigrés*, Paris: Armand Colin.

Kepel, Gilles 1997 *Allah in the West: Islamic Movements in America and Europe*, Stanford, CA: Stanford University Press.

Malkki, Liisa H. 1995 *Purity and Exile: Violence, Memory, and National Cosmology among Hutu Refugees in Tanzania*, Chicago, IL: University of Chicago Press.

Marks, Gary and McAdam, Doug 1996 'Social movements and the changing structure of political opportunity in the European Union', *West European Politics*, vol. 19, no. 2, pp. 249–87.

Schmitter, Philippe C. 1992 'Interests, powers, and functions: emergent properties and unintended consequences in the European polity', Unpublished manuscript, Department of Political Science, Stanford University.

Soysal, Levent 1999 'Projects of Culture: An Ethnographic Episode in the Life of Migrant Youth in Berlin', PhD thesis, Harvard University.

Soysal, Yasemin Nuhogælu 1994 *Limits of Citizenship: Migrants and Postnational Membership in Europe*, Chicago, IL: University of Chicago Press.

——— 1996 'Boundaries and Identity: Immigrants in Europe', European Forum, Working Paper Series, European University Institute, Florence.

Turner, Bryan S. 1986 'Personhood and Citizenship', *Theory and Society*, vol. 3, pp. 1–16.

11

INTRODUCTION TO *NARRATIVES OF CITIZENSHIP*

Aloys N. M. Fleischmann and Nancy van Styvendale

Delimiting citizenship: Universality and exclusion

Citizenship, scholars agree, is a contested term, "an extremely flexible concept" (Alejandro 1998, 9). "At one level," as Peter Kivisto and Thomas Faist suggest,

> *citizenship can be succinctly defined in terms of two component features. The first is that it constitutes membership in a polity, and as such citizenship inevitably involves a dialectical process between inclusion and exclusion, between those deemed eligible for citizenship and those who are denied the right to become members. In its earliest articulation in ancient Greece, the polity in question was the city-state. In the modern world, it was transformed into the nation-state. Second, membership brings with it a reciprocal set of duties and rights, both of which vary by place and time, though some are universal.*
>
> (2007, 1–2)[1]

In its broadest nationalist sense, citizenship is a term of positive content, a status conferred by the nation-state upon individuals by dint of birth, marriage, or naturalization. It promises affiliation and protection at home and abroad, imposes obligations, and ideally (at least in a democracy) allows the individual to influence government decisions. Beyond its strictly legal sense, citizenship is often understood in terms of loyalty to the nation-state, or may be considered a form of civic responsibility—the "good citizen" works for the collective well-being of any given civil unit, be it the neighbourhood, city, province, etc.[2] For those fortunate enough to be well and truly inside the particular demographics that make citizenship automatic—and they need not necessarily be of a privileged elite, although that certainly helps—citizenship becomes transparent, an invisible narrative that weaves multiple, disparate elements within the nation into a rhetorically coherent whole.

T.H. Marshall famously noted that citizens' rights are not only civic and political, but social as well. He posited an "evolutionary model" in which citizenship is understood to have developed over time to include the previously marginalized and excluded (Yuval-Davis 1997, 12). Feminists have problematized Marshall's definition, pointing out that exclusion is not remedied by citizenship, but is, in fact, fundamental to its constitution. In her discussion of gendered citizenship, for example, Nira Yuval-Davis, drawing on the work of Ursula Vogel, argues that "women were not simply latecomers to citizenship rights. . . . Their exclusion was part and parcel of the construction of the entitlement of men, not only as individuals but also as 'representatives of a family (i.e., a group of non-citizens)'" (12). Iris Marion Young further historicizes the exclusivist foundations of citizenship, noting that before the twentieth century, "the exclusion of groups defined as different was explicitly acknowledged" (1990, 119). European and early American republicans, she details, "found little contradiction in promoting a universality of citizenship that excluded some groups, because the idea that citizenship is the same for all translated in practice to the requirement that all citizens be the same" (121). Accordingly, the "other" of universal citizenship functions as "the referential standpoint we [citizens] check from time to time to make sure we are still *not* them. They serve as a landscape for other people's frustrations and as a permanent scapegoat" (Alejandro 1998, 26). Matteo Gianni, "[u]sing Schmitt's terminology," claims that "citizenship creates its own enemies" (1998, 41).

While, as Bauböck and Rundell stress, contemporary democratic states are based on the assumption that an "integrated citizenry" is "tolerant of its own internal diversity" (1998, 10), a "tolerance" celebrated by the discourse of multiculturalism for example, past and contemporary realities recall the expulsions upon which citizenship is based. Acknowledging this legacy, *Narratives of Citizenship* suggests that national citizenship relies on a liminal zone between the incorporation and disincorporation of the often racialized, internal other. Giorgio Agamben's theory of *homo sacer,* the "sacred man," presents a species of this process of exclusion/inclusion, one taken up in this volume not only as an explanation of how the sovereignty of the nation-state is produced and sustained, but also as a potential site of resistance [. . .]. According to Agamben, *homo sacer* is the person who has been reduced by the juridico-political order to an expression of bare life—a being who is entirely stripped of the protection of citizenship, a body to be regulated as only a biological fact (or resource) with the attendant abuse. Agamben argues that the sovereign claim rests on the incorporation of this entity who is apparently "outside" the law, and insists that there is no externality—no exception—prior to the law. Instead, the law inaugurates its own externality as its founding gesture:

> *Here what is outside is included not simply by means of an interdiction or an internment, but rather by means of the suspension of the juridical order's validity—by letting the juridical order, that is, withdraw from the exception and abandon it. The exception does not subtract itself from the rule; rather, the rule, suspending itself gives rise to the exception and, maintaining itself in relation to the exception, first constitutes itself as a rule.*
>
> (1998, 18)

Citizenship both alienates and assimilates, ostracizes and "equalizes." It rests upon its own categories of exclusion. It is a highly problematic, contested and contestable category, composed as much of negative as positive content, of absence as much as presence, especially for members of the uncountable demographics who find themselves other-than-natural/ized. Persons from diasporic and Indigenous groups are often engaged in protracted struggles to define which of the most basic of human rights should be accorded them by countries that demand their assimilation while insisting upon their separation and, in extreme cases, internment or expulsion. Their narratives of citizenship are atypical and inherently political, challenging many of the discourses of power that serve to entrench vested racial, economic, and juridical interests. [. . .]

The nation-state tends to be the dominant framework through which practices associated with sovereignty and citizenship are articulated. Therefore, a narrative-based critique of the nation-state leads almost inevitably to a critique of the narrative production of citizenship. However, critics who focus on the nation-state alone elide, for instance, the history of the European polis, which preceded the rise of the nation-state; they also risk denying forms of communal identification that carry the same weight as national citizenship for the participants themselves. These forms of identification are often articulated as a qualified form of citizenship for the sake of claiming rights at the national or international level. As Canning and Rose observe, recently "the spatial location of citizenship has been . . . a topic of debate, as citizenship is increasingly conceived in terms of global or international human rights that transcend the nation-state" (2002, 2).[3] In a national context, the flexibility of citizenship can be seen, for example, in the Japanese-Canadian redress movement. As previously mentioned, citizenship-related claims proved a powerful means of uniting the Japanese-Canadian community around the shared experience of internment, even though approximately 25 per cent of those of Japanese ancestry interned were not, in fact, citizens of Canada (Miki 2004, 2).

As Lloyd L. Wong reminds us, "Citizenship is definable in terms of the existence of a political community, civil society, and public sphere. It is not coterminous with a nation-state" (2002, 175). While Wong addresses the "post-national problematic" of an increasingly globalized world, his observations on the limitations of nation-state citizenship are applicable in other contexts. For instance, the terms "sovereignty" and "nation" are contentious ones within North American Indigenous circles, reflecting as they do a Euro-American bias toward hierarchy and centralized power. Yet such terminology can come to embody Indigenous political practice, as Daniel Justice asserts: "Indigenous nationhood is more than simple political independence or the exercise of a distinctive cultural identity; it is also an understanding of a common social interdependence within the community, the tribal web of kinship rights *and* responsibilities that link the people, the land, and the cosmos together in an ongoing and dynamic system of mutually affecting relationships" (qtd. in Weaver 2006, 45–46). Just as globalized citizenship may transcend the nation-state, Indigenous conceptions of the nation exceed comparatively insular European conceptions of nationhood.

While Indigenous peoples retain a distinct legal relationship to their respective settler nations, the call to universal citizenship—in other words, to "inclusion" in the nation-state—often functions to paper over the continuance of Indigenous treaty relations. "First Nations politics," David Chariandy and Sophie McCall state, "often highlight that citizenship can . . . function not only through the violence of exclusion, but by inclusion—by shortchanging previously established provisions through a rhetoric of universal (liberal) rights" (2008, 5). James (Sákéj) Youngblood Henderson argues that "the vague offer of citizenship ignores the fact that the rights of aliens to Canadian citizenship are derived mostly from the Aboriginal sovereign's conditional permission to the British sovereign to provide for settlements, rather than as is frequently argued, from British sovereignty alone and delegated legislative authority" (2002, 419). Crown sovereignty in Canada, regardless of the legislative representatives of that sovereignty, is maintained through treaty with sovereign First Nations. Further, even where treaties were not ratified, as in much of British Columbia, Aboriginal populations maintain a distinct *sui generis* order embedded within the Constitution. To quote Henderson again: "Aboriginal and Treaty rights constitute a jurisprudence of its own, one that is not derived from, but unique and distinct from British, French, or European jurisprudence," a distinct relation that the courts are legally bound to recognize (2007, 7). [. . .]

Other challenges to the state as sole underwriter of citizenship come from the proliferation of non-state actors, as well as the de- and re-territorialization of citizenship—that is, the "delinking of community and identity from place" (Wong 2002, 171) and the re-routing/rooting of citizenship in multiple locales.[4] As Saskia Sassen writes,

> *Insofar as globalization has changed certain features of the territorial and institutional organization of the political power and authority of the state, the institution of citizenship—its formal rights, its practices, its psychological dimension—has also been transformed, even when it remains centered in the national state . . . . [T]his territorial and institutional transformation of state power and*

authority has produced operational, conceptual, and rhetorical openings for nation-based subjects other than the national state to emerge as legitimate actors in international and global arenas that used be exclusive to the state.

(2003, 55)

Global commerce and the politics of transnational migrant labour provide new opportunities to contest for rights and recognition. Just as narrative imagines national community, it can strengthen solidarities and provide "rhetorical openings" for new understandings of both extra-national and practice- rather than legally-based intranational citizenship, unsettling the traditional hegemonic authority of the nation-state. [. . .]

Connecting indigeneity and diaspora

Not all elsewheres are equal, and not all dislocations are the same. It is on the land from which Native communities have been expelled that Chinese labourers have come to work; it is one thing to be displaced from one's homeland by colonialism and another to arrive to work as a coolie. Part of the commitment . . . is to think through the relations between diasporas as well as those between majoritized and minoritized communities.

(Cho 2007, 100) [. . .]

"If there are diasporic aspects of indigenous life," Clifford argues, "the reverse is also true. For something like an indigenous desire animates diasporic consciousness: the search for somewhere to belong that is outside the imagined community of the dominant nation-state. In diaspora," he concludes, "the authentic home is found in another imagined place (simultaneously past and future, lost and desired) as well as in concrete social networks of linked places" (2007, 205).

Reading Indigenous and diasporic perspectives on citizenship together underscores the relevance of borders, boundaries and limits (both geographic and conceptual) to the theorization of citizenship. As Cho's epigraph exhorts, an ethical approach to citizenship studies must think through the similarities between the politics of displacement of what could be termed Indigenous diaspora—meaning the relocation of Indigenous populations within or just ahead of an encroaching settler state—and more commonly recognized extra-national diasporic migrations. This is especially true when considering diasporic subjects not as bilaterally mobile transnationals but as people driven from their countries of origin by economic and/or other social pressures, people "whose agonized relationship to home engenders a perpetual sense of not quite having left and not quite having arrived" (Cho 2007, 99).

While *Narratives of Citizenship* loosens the opposition between Indigenous and diasporic, the articles in this collection also caution against collapsing Indigenous and diasporic concerns, the danger of which is evident in the discourse of multiculturalism. Ann Coleman and Winton Higgins explain:

The notion of contemporary "multiculturalism" plays its own mischievous role in obscuring the contemporary patterns of ethnic conflict. It suggests that all inter-ethnic conflicts spring from the same source (prejudice), admit of the same solutions (acknowledgement and tolerance of cultural difference) and can be treated together. This approach obscures the drastic difference between the moral claims of indigenous peoples on the one hand and those of minority migrant cultures on the other.

(2000, 54)[5]

The "agonized relationship to home" of diasporic subjects is reconfigured in the case of Indigenous populations, especially those who literally have "not left" their ancestral homelands and whose sovereign claim predates the nation-state that has imposed itself around them. Their "elsewhere" may even be "right here," and accepting citizenship in the settler nation amounts to accepting the passport of an occupying power. Marilyn Lake problematizes the inclusiveness of citizenship as a necessary good in an Australian Aboriginal context, reminding us of Chief Don Maracle's comments, in relation to Aboriginal participation in the census, on the irony of "inclusion" in the Canadian context. While the extension of Australian citizenship to the country's Aboriginal people in 1967 can be seen "as the realisation of the modern promise of a non-discriminating citizenship— and thus was important in assuaging the past hurt of exclusion" (2002, 142)—citizenship's inclusiveness, its assimilationist drive, functions to underscore Aboriginal loss. As Lake summarizes, "Aboriginal people had suffered both the hurt of racial discrimination and exclusion *and* the loss of their country and culture"—in other words, the "profound pain" of integration, of being inside as well as outside (142).

Notes

1 See Kaplan (1993) for a brief history of citizenship from ancient Greece, the Roman Empire, and the French and American Revolutions to contemporary times.
2 Referring to Alasdair MacIntyre (MacIntyre 1984), Robert Alejandro (1998, 10) adds to this perspective that citizenship "might refer to a community of friends sharing and pursuing a conception of the human good in opposition to liberal institutions; or to people who see the nation as a project that goes to the past and extends to the future".
3 For more on citizenship in the context of globalization and human rights, see Brysk and Shafir's (2004) *People Out of Place*.
4 Arjun Appadurai uses the term "translocalities" and Avtar Brah "multi-locationality" to "indicate a local embeddedness or 'rootedness' to transnational processes" (Wong 2002, 172).
5 Charles Westin also discusses the tensions and connections between Indigenous and diasporic groups: "Diasporic groups challenge the hegemony of the nation-state, but so do autochthonous or First Nation peoples (Clifford 1994). Autochthonous peoples stress their original attachment to the land, their natural right to the land, and the continuity of their attachment to the territory. Thus tension may arise between conflicting interests of recognition between First Nations and diasporas. Many First Nation peoples have suffered displacement through colonization and land acquisition by powerful settler communities. . . . In a sense, then, First Nation people represent an internal diaspora, and classic diasporas may represent a kind of First Nation people in exile" (77).

References

Agamben, Georgio. 1998. *Homo Sacer: Sovereign Power and Bare Life*. Trans. Daniel Heller-Roazen. Stanford, CA: Stanford University Press. Print.
Alejandro, Roberto. 1998. "Impossible Citizenship." *Citizenship After Liberalism*. Ed. Karen Slawner and Mark E. Denham. New York: Peter Lang. 9–32. Print.
Bauböck, Rainer and John Rundell. 1998. Preface. *Blurred Boundaries: Migration, Ethnicity, Citizenship*. Ed. Rainer Bauböck and John Rundell. Aldershot, Hamps.: Ashgate. 7–13. Print.
Brysk, Alison and Gershon Shafir, eds. 2004. *People Out of Place: Globalization, Human Rights, and the Citizenship Gap*. London and New York: Routledge. Print.
Canning, Kathleen and Sonya O. Rose. 2002. "Introduction: Gender, Citizenship and Subjectivity: Some Historical and Theoretical Considerations." *Gender, Citizenship & Subjectivities*. Ed. Kathleen Canning and Sonya O. Rose. Oxford: Blackwell Publishing. 1–17. Print.
Chariandy, David and Sophie McCall. 2008. "Citizenship and Cultural Belonging." Spec. issue of *West Coast Line* 42.3: 4–14. Print.
Cho, Lily. 2007. "Diasporic Citizenship: Contradictions and Possibilities for Canadian Literature." *Trans. Can.Lit; Resituating the Study of Canadian Literature*. Ed. Smaro Kamboureli and Roy Miki. Waterloo, ON: Wilfrid Laurier University Press, 93–109. Print.

Clifford, James. 1994. "Further Inflections: Toward Ethnographies of the Future." *Cultural Anthropology* 9.3: 302–38. Print.

——— 2007. "Varieties of Indigenous Experience: Diasporas, Homelands, Sovereignties." *Indigenous Experience Today*. Ed. Marisol de la Cadena. Oxford and New York: Berg, 197–223. Print.

Coleman, Ann and Winton Higgins. 2000. "Racial and Cultural Diversity in Contemporary Citizenship." *Citizenship and Democracy in a Global Era*. Ed. Andrew Vandenberg. New York: St. Martin's Press, 51–76. Print.

Gianni, Matteo. 1998. "Taking Multiculturalism Seriously: Political Claims for a Differentiated Citizenship." *Citizenship After Liberalism*. Ed. Karen Slawner and Mark E. Denham. New York: Peter Lang, 33–55. Print.

Henderson, James (Sákéj) Youngblood. 2002. "*Sui Generis* and Treaty Citizenship." *Citizenship Studies* 6.4: 415–40. Print.

——— 2007. *Treaty Rights in the Constitution of Canada*. Toronto: Thomson Carswell. Print.

Kaplan, William. 1993. "Who Belongs? Changing Concepts of Citizenship and Nationality." *Belonging: The Meaning and Future of Canadian Citizenship*. Ed. William Kaplan. Montreal and Kingston: McGill-Queen's University Press, 245–64. Print.

Kivisto, Peter and Thomas Faist. 2007. *Citizenship: Discourse, Theory, and Transnational Prospects*. Malden, MA: Blackwell Publishing. Print.

Lake, Marilyn. 2002. "Citizenship as Non-Discrimination: Acceptance or Assimilationism? Political Logic and Emotional Investment in Campaigns for Aboriginal Rights in Australia, 1940–1970." *Gender, Citizenships & Subjectivities*. Ed. Kathleen Canning and Sonya O. Rose. Oxford: Blackwell Publishing, 140–66. Print.

MacIntyre, Alasdair. 1984. *After Virtue*. 2nd ed. Notre Dame, IN: Notre Dame University Press.

Miki, Roy. 2004. *Redress: Inside the Japanese Canadian Call for Justice*. Vancouver: Raincoast Books. Print.

Sassen, Saskia. 2003. "The Repositioning of Citizenship: Emergent Subjects and Spaces for Politics." *CR: The New Centennial Review* 3.2: 41–66. Print.

Weaver, Jace. 2006. "Splitting the Earth: First Utterances and Pluralist Separatism." *American Indian Literary Nationalism*. Ed. Jace Weaver, Craig S. Womack, and Robert Warrior. Albuquerque: University of New Mexico Press, 1–89. Print.

Wong, Lloyd L. 2002. "Home Away From Home? Transnationalism and the Canadian Citizenship Regime." *Communities Across Borders: New Immigrants and Transnational Cultures*. Ed. Paul Kennedy and Victor Roudometof. London and New York: Routledge, 169–81. Print.

Young, Iris Marion. 1990. "Polity and Group Difference: A Critique of the Ideal of Universal Citizenship." *Feminism and Political Theory*. Ed. Cass R. Sunstein. Chicago: University of Chicago Press, 117–41. Print.

Yuval-Davis, Nira. 1997. "Women, Citizenship and Difference." *Feminist Review* 57: 4–27. Print.

(INTER)NATIONAL POLICY AND DIASPORA

Introduction

The relationship between diasporic communities and their homelands has been a constant feature in all definitions of diaspora. This relationship has consequences in terms of identity and cultural production, but also involves economic and political interventions, seen as 'political transnationalism', that involve at least three stakeholders: the 'country of origin'; the diasporic community itself; and the 'host nation'.

The first point of reference in such discussions of international policy is usually the 'remittances' made to those in the homeland by those in diaspora. It is difficult to assess the value of this flow of capital – just as it is difficult for origin states to control it – but The World Bank (2016) estimated that remittances to low- and middle-income countries were expected to show an annual increase of 0.8% to US$442 billion.

However, all three writers in this section seek to go beyond what Alan Gamlen refers to as the 'blindingly obvious' phenomenon of remittances, towards an assessment of the complex economic and political connections between diasporas and states which, Gamlen argues, 'interact in ways that economic policy makers are only beginning to understand'. Diasporas have been 'leveraged' by the nations to assist in reaching development goals through investment of money and expertise. In the 1990s, links between the Haitian government and the Haitian diaspora were notable for raising much-needed funds through initiatives such as the 'marathon of dignity' *Voye Ayiti Monte* (Send Haiti Upward). Indeed, the Haitian diaspora could be said to have begun to reconceptualize the nation state and its population (Schiller and Fouron 1998, 135–6), and in return for their support President Aristide 'pledged to the diaspora that the Haitian government would be their spokesperson and protector' (Schiller and Fouron 2001, 121).

The three essays collected here explore how nations can maintain positive and productive relations with members of their diasporas through interventions and national policies (such as recognition through awards, efficient and helpful government departments and continued voting rights). Some states solicit the loyalty of their diasporas by extending such rights and trying to 'extract obligations' from them, as Khachig Tölölyan (2010) points out from first-hand experience of Armenia.

Diasporas can be mobilized for politically dubious purposes as well as benign ones, and this tendency is evident with right-wing conservative governments in the 'home' nations. The Hungarian government's very explicit policies of mobilizing its regional diasporas (created as a result of the breakdown of the Austro-Hungarian Empire after 1918, and massive re-drawings of borders in Central Europe) involve offering citizenship rights, but also the stoking up of nationalist and retributive sentiments, which have created regional tensions with Slovakia and Romania, where Hungarian minorities are substantial in number. Eszter Herner-Kovács (2014) has shown how the Hungarian government, through projects launched after 2010, defined as its primary goals: the integration of the 'diaspora individual' into the diaspora community; enhanced connection to Hungary; strengthening the national identity of the diaspora; exploitation of its economic, professional potential as well as its ability to improve the image of Hungary abroad; and reaching the members of the newest diaspora' (67).

Cyberspace, with its ability to facilitate the exchange of ideas, business projects, art and political ideas, and, in the words of Victoria Bernal, to 'elide the global and the local', has had a transformative effect on the notion of participatory democracy as enacted in diaspora. Numerous case studies have been written on this phenomenon, including Anna Everett's (2009) account of 'social relationships across barriers of space and time' in the African diaspora, and Victoria Bernal's (2006) study of 'the Eritrean diaspora online', which suggests how 'through the web the diaspora has mobilized demonstrators, amassed funds for war, debated the formulation of the constitution, and influenced the government of Eritrea' (see also Brinkerhoff 2004).

In 'Why engage diasporas?' Alan Gamlen reviews sending states' engagement strategies, such as bureaucratic reforms, investment policies, political rights, state services abroad and symbolic politics. He notes that such policies are seldom fully thought-out and may result in inefficient and unjust outcomes. It is, nevertheless, in the interest of the sending state to improve diaspora policies, even though attempts to facilitate and capture remittances have been beset with difficulties. Gamlen cites New Zealand and Ireland as examples of states that have successfully enlisted well-connected expatriates in the process of economic and cultural development. He then moves beyond these pragmatic strategies in order to consider the obligations of the sending states towards their diasporas. He argues that claims that this amounts to 'interference' in host states' affairs are not logically justified, and makes the case for mutual cooperation between sender and host states.

Jennifer M. Brinkerhoff addresses the contribution of digital diasporas to homeland socio-economic development, and the way this can be creatively fostered through activities such as diaspora philanthropy, knowledge transfer, diaspora investment, business development and policy influence (although diasporas may also influence regime change and sustain conflict). Similarly, while the internet can help create collective diasporic identity, it can also provide an avenue for 'recruitment into violent activities' (one rationale for the activities of the US Department of Homeland Security). She arrives at policy recommendations 'for homeland governments, adopted country governments, and international development actors', by celebrating optimistically the internet's potential for 'identity negotiation and the representation of liberal values' within diasporic communities. She stresses that internet privacy and access are important in this process – although the article was written three years before Edward Snowden's revelations about the extent of the US Government mass surveillance of its citizens.

Brinkerhoff outlines research that shows the benefits to homelands of 'networking that links the homeland to the diaspora', and the ways in which non-governmental organizations (NGOs) can link into such networks. She makes an important point about agency: that 'diasporas are pioneering their own development models, often coordinated through online communities'. States and agencies need to engage flexibly with these well-informed and astute diasporic communities (although here it might be worth noting, in the wake of Brexit, the more nefarious uses of diasporic communities by the governments of both the home and host nations – as, for instance, the case of the large Polish diaspora in Britain, spoken about as a 'bargaining chip' in future negotiations within the European Union, both by the UK and Poland).

Ronald Skeldon's 'International migration as a tool in development policy: A passing phase?' asks how policies aimed at fostering transnational ties can assist in reaching development goals.

While skilled migration and 'brain drain' might appear to be the other side of the coin from remittances (especially for small countries such as Guyana, Grenada, St. Vincent and the Grenadines), the impact of such migration may have been proportionally less felt in poor rural areas, and attempts to restrict the migration of the highly skilled are unlikely to be effective. Noting that the United Nations tends to prefer the term 'transnational community' to 'diaspora', Skeldon observes that overseas Chinese and expatriate Vietnamese have been important in their countries' development, and that in East Asia generally the number of migrants 'returning home' has been significant since the 1970s. Migration need not necessarily be bad for development, but the heterogeneity of diasporic populations in terms of skills, education and political alignment, as well as the fact that 'those who leave represent a small proportion of the home populations', leads Skeldon to argue that it is possible to place too much emphasis on diasporic interventions, despite the Haitian and Eritrean case studies cited by Schiller and Fouron, and Bernal.

However, Skeldon's argument could be seen as controversial – large numbers of people have left certain countries in East-Central Europe, particularly Poland and Romania, and while some of them will possibly return, most will not, forming rather dense and compact diasporic communities (in the UK and Germany for Poland; in Italy and Spain for Romania). In their home countries, this has led to a much-felt shortage of skills, and a depletion of the able, mobile and flexible working force, with important economic consequences in terms of the ability of home states to extract taxes (a much smaller base of taxation resulting from millions of working-people abroad) and pay for various social amenities. So certain policy interventions might actually be beneficial in incentivizing economic diasporas to return. To cite another example: 22 million Indians live outside India itself, and new categories of citizenship have been introduced to recognize this. Non-Resident Indians (NRIs) are Indian citizens who live in another country. They can get special bank accounts from Indian banks, continue to own land and property in India, with only local earnings in India (interest, rental income) still taxed. A special quota of seats in Indian universities is reserved for NRIs, who can still vote, although they need to be in India to do it. In these and other ways, international policies relating to diaspora continue to be fluid as well as economically and socially significant.

References

Bernal, Victoria. 2006 'Diaspora, Cyberspace and Political Imagination: The Eritrean Diaspora Online.' *Global Networks* 6.2: 161–179.

Brinkerhoff, Jennifer M. 2004. 'Digital Diasporas and International Development: Afghan-Americans and the Reconstruction of Afghanistan.' *Public Administration and Development* 24 (2004): 397–413.

Everett, Anna. 2009. *Digital Diaspora: A Race for Cyberspace.* New York, NY: State University of NY Press.

Herner-Kovács, Eszter. 2014. 'Nation Building Extended: Hungarian Diaspora Politics.' *Minority Studies* 17: 55–67.

Schiller, Nina Glick, and George Fouron. 1998. 'Transnational Lives and National Identities: The Identity Politics of Haitian Immigrants.' In *Transnationalism from Below. Vol. 6, Comparative Urban and Community Research*, edited by Michael Peter Smith and Luis Eduardo Guarnizo, 135–136. Piscataway, NJ: Transaction Publishers.

Schiller, Nina Glick, and George Fouron. 2001. *Georges Woke Up Laughing: Long Distance Nationalism and the Search for Home.* Durham, NC: Duke University Press.

Tölölyan, Khachig. 2010. 'Beyond the Homeland: From Exilic Nationalism to Diasporic Transnationalism.' In *The Call of the Homeland: Diaspora Nationalisms, Past and Present*, edited by Allon Gal, Athena S. Leoussi, and Anthony David Smith, 27–56. Leiden: Brill.

World Bank. 2016. 'Remittances to Developing Countries Expected to Grow at Weak Pace in 2016 and Beyond.' Available at: www.worldbank.org/en/news/press-release/2016/10/06/remittances-to-developing-countries-expected-to-grow-at-weak-pace-in-2016-and-beyond.

12

WHY ENGAGE DIASPORAS?

Alan Gamlen

Why engage diasporas?

One important question is, what kinds of policies 'make' diasporas? Or in other words, what are diaspora policies? In this paper diaspora policies are defined as state institutions and practices that apply to members of that state's society who reside outside its borders. These range from state-sponsored celebrations and awards for expatriates, to bureaucratic units dedicated to the diaspora, to external voting rights and bilateral agreements on social security and pension transferability, right through to the range of mechanisms through which origin states attempt to extract finances, expertise, and influence from their diasporas. In short, they consist of that portion of the state machinery which protrudes beyond territory. Diaspora policies are most often interpreted as facets of 'external' or 'extra-territorial citizenship' (Bauböck 1994; Laguerre 1998; Itzigsohn 2000; Lee 2004; Glick Schiller 2005; Barry 2006): by incorporating the diaspora into the state, these policies redefine or reconfigure what it means to be a member of 'national society'.

There have been a number of different attempts to taxonomize diaspora policies. For example, Østergaard-Nielsen (2003a) and Chander (2006) adopt a straightforward distinction between economic, political and cultural devices of sending states. In the same vein, Barry (2006) identifies legal, economic and political instruments that apply to emigrant citizens. Levitt and De la Dehesa (2003) distinguish between bureaucratic reforms, investment policies, political rights, state services abroad, and symbolic politics. Gamlen (2006) classifies diaspora policies according to how they contribute to expanding citizenship beyond territorial borders, distinguishing two types: 'community building policies' aimed at cultivating or recognizing diaspora communities, and mechanisms aimed at extending membership privileges and obligations to these diaspora communities.

However, it is important to note that there has been an overemphasis on what is novel, transformative or otherwise normal about diaspora policies – and not enough recognition that "all states are to a certain extent deterritorialized" (as Chulwoo Lee has hypothesized[1]). The tools themselves are commonplace; it is the techniques to use them that remain underdeveloped. Relatively few governments see diaspora policy as a distinct issue area, and they do not deliberately pursue coherence between the different state mechanisms through which they impact on diasporas. Most of what goes on is ad hoc and arbitrary, and reflects the different interests and historical trajectories of different institutions. For example, bilateral agreements and consular services reflect foreign policy imperatives despite the fact that emigrant citizens are their end users. Migration policies have domestic scope, despite the fact that every immigrant is also an emigrant. Electoral systems may incorporate diaspora participation, but legislative processes generally do not. The result is that, when it comes to the diaspora dimension of policies and institutions, inefficient and unjust outcomes that would be subject to thought, planning and oversight in a domestic context, are overlooked in diaspora contexts. Thus, improving diaspora policies is in large part a matter of improving the coherence of what is already taking place in the area of state-diaspora relations, rather than doing something entirely new.

I will now highlight three main arguments about why good diaspora policies are important to policy makers at the national and supranational or global level. [. . .]

Interests

There are at least two reasons why it is in the interests of migrant-sending states to form better diaspora policies: firstly because the involvement of diasporas presents sending states with certain policy *imperatives,* and secondly because such policies may offer unique *opportunities.*

Imperatives

As populations become increasing mobile and transnational, political, economic and social dynamics in migrant sending countries undergo profound transformations (see Vertovec, 2004). Institutions that fail to adapt inevitably lose their relevance and legitimacy. For example, the increasing prevalence of extra-territorial political participation influences the composition of legislatures (see Bauböck, 2005; Collyer and Vathi, 2007; Rubio-Marin, 2006; Spiro, 2006). However, because expatriates usually have to vote for a candidate who represents the geo-graphical electorate where they *used to* live, rather than someone who represents their current geographical location, elected representatives face a conflict of interests, and it can be unclear whether they are over- or under-serving extra-territorial voters.

In the realm of economic policy, inward and outward migration patterns interact in complex ways with labour market dynamics and trade and investment patterns – yet economic policy-makers only have decent data on inward migration. They tend not to systematically study the economic impact of their diasporas unless it is a blindingly obvious one (for example, when GDP would be decimated without remittances). Relationships between different types of transnational involvement – such as identification with the homeland or social, economic and political connectedness – interact in ways that economic policy makers are only beginning to understand.

Similarly, social policy has to grapple with the populations that are increasingly mobile and spread their lives across two or more nation-states (and therefore welfare states, tax and fiscal systems) (Lunt, et al. 2006). This raises important questions surrounding the provision of public goods such as education and healthcare. For example, brain drain can be interpreted as a classic free-rider problem: it is individually rational for graduates to emigrate for higher wages, but collectively irrational for states to educate people who spend their working lives in a foreign tax jurisdiction. The absence of parents who retire abroad can increase burdens on young families working and caring for children, with implications for public childcare services. Conversely, outflows of young people who leave permanently increases the number of elderly people with no family support, who then turn to the state for care provision. If not applied coherently and consistently, mechanisms such as bilateral agreements on social security and double taxation can create incentives to free riders and welfare shoppers.

In short, the impact of diasporas on existing public institutions and policies is a complex area, and one that is becoming increasingly important – but it is also one that has traditionally been approached in an arbitrary and ad hoc manner, based on migration data that only shows half the picture. The emigrants are invisible.

Opportunities

The argument that diaspora engagement policies are an opportunity to further national interests can be summarized in one phrase: migration and development. The main thrust of the argument is that specific types of policy intervention can enhance flows of remittances, investments, knowledge transfers and political influence through diaspora groups back into their homelands.

The significance of remittances has become a cornerstone of migration and development literature. To repeat one of the best known development mantras, in 2006 the total value of global remittances flows to developing countries topped US$220 billion (having almost doubled in the previous four years), and only foreign direct investment flows supply poorer countries with more stable currency than remittances. As Ian Goldin and Kenneth Reinert (2006: 176) note, developing-country governments usually welcome remittances as contributions to national development because they reduce poverty and boost living standards among recipients, and can have a stabilizing effect during periods of upheaval.

Many countries have implemented policies to facilitate and capture remittances. These policies range from increasing access to remittance infrastructure and opening up competition in the remittance market (as the World Bank advocated in its 2006 Report; World Bank 2005); to matching each dollar remitted through official channels with state funds (as in Mexico's *tres por uno* scheme); to duty free allowances on goods brought home (along the lines of the Philippines' *balikbayan* boxes); to free passport issuance for remittances over certain amounts (in India and Pakistan).

Enthusiasm for remittances as a development panacea has been tempered by the reminder that they are private, not public, funds. State interference in the form of efforts to 'channel' remittances into national development goals are frowned upon, and it is warned that donor states should not see remittances as a substitute for development aid.

Many countries, whether developing countries like India and China or developed OECD members like Ireland and New Zealand, turn to well-connected expatriates to help attract FDI. For example, the Irish Development Agency pursued an aggressive strategy utilizing Irish-American business connections and arguments about the availability of skilled expatriate labour in order to attract computer-chip giant Intel to Ireland. As an outgrowth of recommendations from Boston Consulting Group surrounding how to increase FDI, New Zealand has set up a 'World Class New Zealander' network of high profile business-people in key markets, hoping to attract wealthy expatriates and 'friends of New Zealand' to invest in the country.

The rise of 'New Growth' economic theories, which conceive of knowledge as the engine of growth, has stimulated interest in promoting transfers of knowledge and technologies from abroad in order to promote economic growth at home. There are two main types of policy. One is based on facilitating returns of a temporary (or sometimes long-term) nature, by providing consultancy or fellowship opportunities for expatriate researchers – the classic example being UNDP's long-standing TOKTEN programme. The other type of knowledge transfer policy is based around cultivating what are sometimes called 'diaspora knowledge networks' – dispersed networks of researchers from the home country who collaborate on scientific projects in the hope of benefiting their home country (Kuznetsov 2006).

In sum, there are imperatives for states to adapt to a transnational world through transnational policy-making, and there may be developmental advantages to doing so. However, these empirical, interest-based arguments are susceptible to at least two rebuttals. Firstly, the empirical link between emigration and development in the sending country is not universally accepted, and it is wise to ask whose interests are really served by asserting such a connection. Is it really a grand bargain among sending states, receiving states and migrants, or are the odds stacked in favour of elites in more powerful receiving countries? Is the 'migration and development' case really *evidence* that national interests can converge over migration, or is it more an *argument* that nation-states should be less self-interested and more open to cooperation for an (imagined?) global collective interest? This leads to the second rebuttal: even if it is empirically true that the interests of states are served by diaspora policies, do these interests trump the territorial norms around which politics is – at least in theory – organized? [. . .]

Obligations

There are three main normative arguments why states should not engage their diasporas; I will call these arguments *external non-interference, internal non-interference* and *non-preference. External non-interference* refers to the international norm that one state should not interfere with a population living within the territory of another state. One could argue that when a migrant-sending state makes policies towards its diaspora, it violates the sovereignty of the receiving state. *Internal non-interference* refers to the liberal norm that someone who does not consent to the authority of the government in one place should be free to leave that place without interference. One could argue that when a migrant-sending state makes diaspora policies, it effectively asserts authority over migrants wherever they are. *Non-preference* refers to the notion that a state should privilege people within its own territory over people who live outside its territory. One could argue that when a state allows diasporas to vote or grants them other social rights in the home country, they are privileging non-resident 'outsiders' at the expense of resident 'insiders'.

There are problems with all three arguments. Firstly, migrant-receiving states do not necessarily feel violated by the diaspora policies of migrant-sending states. Sometimes they welcome these policies because they supplement resources that have been stretched by a large inflow of migrants. For example, local and municipal governments often welcome the efforts of migrant-sending states to provide health and education assistance to immigrants, because this means that they do not have to fight for central state funds to provide those services themselves. Though there are plenty of cases where long-standing ethnic rivalries or territorial disputes engender suspicion of irredentism or fifth columnism (such as the case of Hungary's Status Law), there are also plenty of instances where bilateral relations are warm enough in other areas to prevent diaspora policies from becoming a point of serious bilateral conflict (such as – arguably – Mexico's emigration policies under NAFTA (see Délano, 2006)).

Secondly, diasporas are not always exiles – they have not necessarily rejected the government of their homeland, and even if they have they may not have renounced their role in its politics and institutions. Diaspora groups may be actively involved in politics and seeking incorporation into the state system, and it is therefore problematic to portray them as non-members towards whom the home state must maintain a policy of 'no policy'. On the other hand, if non-residents do wish to escape the reach of the sending state, they have the option of naturalizing in their host country and avoiding any contact with any institutions connected to their homeland. These institutions do not have any coercive power in the host country, so they are relatively easy to escape from.

Thirdly, and for similar reasons, it is not simple to label diasporas as 'outsiders' whose interests should be discounted against those of residents. As increasingly mobile populations move in and out of countries, making contributions in one place and drawing on public resources in other places, it is as much a mistake to differentiate diaspora populations too strictly from domestic ones as to ignore the differences between them. Diasporas often contribute to and draw on the public good in their home country and therefore there are strong arguments that they should be considered part of it. This is a good time to discuss normative arguments *for* diaspora policies.

There are two arguments that states should intervene in diaspora populations in specific ways. Firstly, migrant-sending states should ensure that people who leave still fulfil any outstanding obligations to their sending state. For example, one could argue that people who benefit from publicly subsidised education and healthcare in their dependent youth or old age should be obliged to contribute to the economy during their working lives – even if their career takes them to another country – and that there should be regulatory mechanisms to enforce this reciprocity. As Jagdish Bagwhati – whose proposed expatriate tax has remained a topic of debate since the 1960s – says, rights and obligations must go together (Bhagwati, 2003).

Secondly, the reverse argument for diaspora policies is also valid: migrant-sending states inevitably exert control over diasporas in various ways, and therefore they are obliged to treat diasporas fairly and take their interests into consideration when making decisions. One important example where this argument applies is in the area of pension transferability: many countries have national pension plans that discriminate against people who pay taxes during their working lives but are not eligible for full pensions if they decide to retire in another country (Clark 2002).

In sum, while there are arguments that sending-state policies cannot legitimately apply to extra-territorial populations, it is an empirical fact that such policies do exist, and arguable that policy makers should focus on *how*, rather than *whether*, they should operate.

Co-operation

Arguments about national interests and the norms governing relations between states and their citizens abroad operate within a communitarian normative framework: they assume that moral obligations operate within specific cultural – in this case national – contexts; that members of one's community should occupy a higher moral standing in one's estimation than non-members.

However, there are also cosmopolitan arguments for engaging diasporas. These are based on the view that humans of whatever nationality belong to a common moral community which should organize its affairs in order to promote the good of all, regardless of nationality. One strand of cosmopolitan thinking concerns itself with the desirability of political organization at the world scale – or to use the contemporary parlance, 'global governance' (Rosenau 1999). Recent discussions surrounding globalization have highlighted the absence of a multilateral framework for regulating migration at the global level, and proponents of global governance have argued that such a framework is necessary to ensure states cooperate rather than pursuing their own national interests at the expense of the greater global good (Betts, 2008).

There are at least two cosmopolitan arguments for engaging diasporas; I will refer to them as *global efficiency* and *global multiculturalism*. Global efficiency refers to the argument that cooperation in global migration governance is not possible unless the policies of migrant-sending states are addressed at the same time as those of receiving-states. Both global governance debates and migration studies debates have tended to assume that migration policy is all about regulating inflows of people. This view tends to exclude migrant-sending states from the picture. However, relations between migrant-sending states and diasporas already play a major role in governing international migration: these relations influence how migrants identify and organize themselves, how migrants relate to their sending and receiving states, and how these states interact. To focus on immigration policy is to see half of the picture of global migration governance: every *imm*igrant is also an *em*igrant, with ties to a society and state of origin – ties which should not be overlooked when considering how to increase the efficiency and equity of migration outcomes for the various actors concerned. In short, if global policy makers are serious about improving the way migration is governed at the global level, they must find ways of improving how migrant-sending states relate to their diasporas, and reconciling these relationships with migration policies in receiving states.

Global multiculturalism refers to the argument that national communities should be able to govern their own affairs in ways that are compatible with the global greater good, but not in ways that are contradictory to it. This follows a similar line to Will Kymlicka's argument for liberal multiculturalism at the national level (Kymlicka 1995). Kymlicka distinguishes between types of minority cultural practices that states should protect and types which they should not protect. Under the label "external protection", he argues that states should enforce the liberty of ethnic minorities to pursue their cultural practices without interference from the majority culture. For example, this argument would justify a national law preventing employers from banning turbans in the workplace. On the other hand, under the label of "internal restriction" Kymlicka argues that states should not enforce minority cultural practices that restrict the liberty of their members. For example, this argument would disallow a national law forcing females of a certain cultural background to undergo circumcision. Translating this line of argument to the global context would mean that states – including sending states – should be allowed to protect the rights of 'their' emigrants, but not to restrict their liberty. Such an argument could constitute a normative benchmark for the role of emigration states in the global governance of migration.

Note

1 Personal communication, 2006.

References

Barry, K. 2006. Home and Away: The Construction of Citizenship in an Emigration Context. *New York University Law Review* 81 (1):11–59.

Bauböck, R. 1994. *Transnational Citizenship: Membership and Rights in International Migration.* Cheltenham and Northampton: Edward Elgar.

——— 2005. Expansive Citizenship: Voting Beyond Territory and Membership. *Political Science and Politics*, 38:683–687.

Betts, A. 2008. *Global Migration Governance*, Global Economic Governance WP 2008/43, University of Oxford.

Bhagwati, J. 2003. Borders Beyond Control. *Foreign Affairs* 82, 98.

Chander, A. 2006. Homeward Bound. *New York University Law Review* 81 (1):60–89.

Clark, G. 2002. Country of residence and pension entitlement: the arbitrary geography of UK legal formalism. *Environment and Planning A* 34:2102–06.

Collyer, M. & Z. Vathi. 2007. *Patterns of Extra-territorial Voting*, University of Sussex.

Délano, A. 2006. The politics of the migrant-sending state from an international perspective: A study of the Mexican case, presented at the COMPAS Annual Conference 2006, *International Labour Migration: In Whose Interests?*, Center on Migration Policies and Society, Oxford, July 5-6, 2006.

Gamlen, A. 2006. *What are Diaspora Engagement Policies and what kinds of States Use Them?* Vol. WP0632, *COMPAS Working Papers.* Oxford: Centre on Migration, Policy and Society, University of Oxford.

Glick Schiller, N. 2005. Transborder Citizenship: An Outcome of Legal Pluralism within Transnational Social Fields. In *Mobile People, Mobile Law: Expanding Legal Relations in a Contracting World*, eds. F. Von Benda-Beckmann, K. Von Benda-Beckmann and A. Griffiths, 27–150. London: Ashgate.

Goldin, I., K. A. Reinert, and World Bank. 2006. *Globalization for Development: Trade, Capital, Aid, Migration, and Policy.* Washington, DC and Basingstoke: World Bank and Palgrave MacMillan.

Itzigsohn, J. 2000. Immigration and the Boundaries of Citizenship: The Institutions of Immigrants' Political Transnationalism. *International Migration Review* 43 (4):1126–1154.

Kuznetsov, Y., ed. 2006. *Diaspora Networks and the International Migration of Skills: How Countries Can Draw on Their Talent Abroad, WBI Development Studies.* Washington, D.C.: World Bank.

Kymlicka, W. 1995. *Multicultural Citizenship: A Liberal Theory of Minority Rights.* Oxford: Clarendon Press.

Laguerre, M. S. 1998. *Diasporic Citizenship: Haitian Americans in Transnational America.* Basingstoke: Macmillan.

Lee, C. 2004. The Transnationalization of Citizenship and the Logic of the Nation-State. In *Asian- Pacific Sociological Association 6th Conference on Asia-Pacific Societies in Globalization.* Seoul.

Levitt, P., and R. de la Dehesa. 2003. Transnational Migration and the Redefinition of the State: Variations and Explanations. *Ethnic and Racial Studies* 26 (4):587–611.

Lunt, N., M. McPherson, and J. Browning. 2006. *Les Familles et Whanau sans Frontieres: New Zealand and Transnational Family Obligations.* Wellington: Families Commission.

Østergaard-Nielsen, E. 2003a. International Migration and Sending Countries: Key Issues and Themes. In *International Migration and Sending Countries: Perceptions, Policies and Transnational Relations*, ed. E. Østergaard-Nielsen, 3–32. Basingstoke: Palgrave Macmillan.

Rosenau, J. 1999. Towards an Ontology for Global Governance. In *Approaches to Global Governance Theory*, eds. M. Hewson and T. J. Sinclair, xv, 312. New York: State University of New York.

Rubio-Marin, R. 2006. Transnational Politics and the Democratic Nation-state: Normative Challenges of Expatriate Voting and Nationality Retention of Emigrants. *New York University Law Review*, 81: 117–147.

Spiro, P. J. 2006. Perfecting Political Diaspora. *New York University Law Review*, 81:207–233.

Vertovec, S. 2004. Migrant Transnationalism and Modes of Transformation. *International Migration Review*, 38:971–1001.

World Bank. 2005. Global Economic Prospects 2006: Economic Implications of Remittances and Migration. Washington D.C.: World Bank.

13

MIGRATION, INFORMATION TECHNOLOGY, AND INTERNATIONAL POLICY

Jennifer M. Brinkerhoff

Diaspora identity expression and transnational engagement occur with or without policy inter-ventions, and in those areas where diasporas' economic and political contributions are less noticeable, we are likely to see fewer, if any, government policies and programs. One such area is in the digital arena. The purpose of this chapter is to build upon our cumulative understanding of digital diasporas to generate a series of policy recommendations for homeland governments, adopted-country governments, and international development actors. These recommendations build largely from my own comparative analysis of nine digital diaspora organizations (ibid.).

Adopted-country governments

Migrant integration can be eased when diasporans have opportunities to express their hybrid identities collectively. The Internet provides important opportunities for creating a sense of identity and solidarity around a shared cultural heritage and diaspora experience. The com-munities created serve to combat feelings of marginalization among diasporans, providing them identity and other forms of support as they cope with the diaspora experience. This identity support, in turn, enables diasporans to integrate new ideas, values, and experience into their identity frame of reference, testing the boundaries for what it means to their homeland identity as well as a potentially more modern and individualistic adopted-country identity. At the same time, digital diasporas are important vehicles for disseminating information and advice for accessing public goods and services and easing the transition from newly arrived migrant to productive member of the host society.

The Internet's conducive features for identity negotiation and representation of liberal values (in both form and function) are important contributors that should be sustained and protected. The motivation to express identity is natural and common to all human beings. Whether addressed in cyberspace or in the physical world, diasporans face a psychosocial need to develop and express their hybrid identities and to experiment with the integration of alternative and additional values and conceptions, including those representing liberal values. Given hybridity, affirming the homeland identity and even talk of return do not mean that diasporans do not value or embrace their adopted country and society. An improved public awareness of this complexity could encourage tolerance and, ideally, incentives to seek improved understanding of particular individuals and communities.

Understanding hybridity is crucial in the consideration of social policies. Portes (2006) examines three practical theoretical stances or policy orientation options vis-à-vis migrants in receiving societies. Hard assimilation seeks to completely assimilate migrants to the exclusion of a homeland identity by the second generation. Permanent culturalism emphasizes the homeland identity, sometimes to the exclusion of an adopted country identity. It can lead to ethnic enclaving, which, in turn, can isolate immigrant communities, potentially sending them down a path of downward assimilation, where the second generation and beyond experience a downward spiral of economic and educational opportunities (see Rumbaut and Portes 2001; and Waldinger and Feliciano 2004). Soft assimilation tolerates ethnicity but promotes the ultimate goal of integration. It encourages knowledge and respect of mainstream culture, laws, education, and language. It typically leads to gradual and voluntary integration. Minimal requirements for its success include knowledge of the adoptive country language and observance of its rule of law. It is this model, Portes argues, that leads to the American tolerance and even encouragement of hyphenation. Soft assimilation celebrates hybridity, and digital diasporas are an important vehicle for expressing hybridity. Digital diasporas afford migrants opportunities to embrace their American selves while still maintaining a homeland identity; in other words, digital diasporas contribute to soft assimilation and should thus be allowed to function unencumbered.

Diasporans make implicit cost-benefit analyses with respect to both identity orientation (see, for example, Portes and Zhou 1993; Waters 1999; and Sánchez Gibau 2005) and identity mobilization and its direction (Brinkerhoff 2008). Policy makers can influence the terms of this analysis by attending to the "context of reception." This is typically defined according to three factors: "the state policies directed at a specific migrant group; the reactions to and perceptions of the immigrants by public opinion; and the presence or absence of an established ethnic community to receive the immigrants" (Grosfoguel and Cordero-Guzmán 1998, 357). The importance of a receiving ethnic community confirms the need for solidarity benefits stemming from a shared, collective identity; it further highlights the salience of digital diasporas' contributions.

Policy makers can focus on changing the stakes for identity mobilization, enhancing the possibility of constructive directions by creating an enabling environment for a high quality of life and community for diasporas. Such an enabling environment might include, for example, access to small business and home ownership loans and support for access to vocational training and higher education. For example, Grosfoguel and Cordero-Guzmán's review of the Cuban diaspora experience confirms the importance of both social networks—internal community solidarity—and "broader social structures that constrain or enable access to capital, information, and resources by members of a specific community's micro-networks" for integration and success in the receiving country (1998, 355).

In short, digital diasporas support integration by providing solidarity, combating marginalization, facilitating access to public goods and services, and embracing hybridity and soft assimilation. They are particularly salient to the context of reception, which further supports migrant integration. Two policy recommendations emerge from this discussion. First, information technology (IT) regulation should maintain privacy and access in order not to interfere with opportunities for exploring identity and representing liberal values. Second, and relevant to diasporas beyond cyberspace, policy makers should focus on changing the stakes for identity mobilization by creating an enabling environment for a high quality of life and community for diasporas, thus discouraging ethnic isolation and mobilization for destructive aims.

Host governments are also concerned with the security implications of diasporas. With the recent war on terrorism, migration to industrialized countries has sparked new concerns ranging from the migration of terrorists or the harboring of terrorists by immigrant communities to the

financial support of terrorist activities through charity foundations and the recruitment of terrorists from within seemingly assimilated diaspora communities. These concerns can be partially
addressed through a cooperative strategy with diaspora organizations. Loose partnerships or
cooperative arrangements can create structures for anonymous reporting by concerned diasporans
and associated response procedures by the receiving governing bodies. Not all communities will
equally embrace this idea, and the parameters of what is acceptable will need to be negotiated on a
case-by-case basis. The Internet can be a useful tool in such cooperative reporting.

Homeland governments

This discussion of homeland government policy options focuses on how to interface with established diasporas rather than prevent them in the first place (i.e. through migration management
policies). There is a broad scope for governments to engage with their diasporas to facilitate their
constructive political, social, and economic contributions to the homeland. Proactive efforts and
explicit policies have been slow in coming. Portes, Escobar, and Radford reviewed the experience
and research to date and summarized it as follows: "All empirical evidence indicates that economic,
political, and socio-cultural activities linking expatriate communities with their countries of origin
emerged by initiative of the immigrants themselves, with governments jumping onto the band-
wagon only when their importance and economic potential became evident" (2007, 258; see also
Portes 2003).

Proactive diaspora engagement has been labeled the "diaspora option" and encompasses
several potential approaches. This policy framework conceives the skilled diaspora as an asset to
be captured (Meyer et al. 1997), and encompasses three types of related diaspora engagement
strategies: remittance capture, diaspora networking, and diaspora integration (Gamlen 2005).
Each of these arenas holds policy implications for digital diasporas.

Regarding remittance capture, home governments are increasingly soliciting remittances and
offering policy incentives (e.g. tax-free investment opportunities and matching) and investment
options (e.g. remittance-backed bonds and foreign currency accounts) to encourage diaspora
contributions (see, for example, Orozco with Lapointe 2004; Lowell and De la Garza 2000; and
Pires-Hester 1999). Less attention is given to the importance of an enabling IT infrastructure for
remittance transfer, banking, and other transactions. For example, Thamel.com has evolved a
sophisticated set of remittance services that enable diasporans to make monthly payments directly
to bank accounts with specified purposes, such as making monthly payments to support private
education or home equity loans. Reliable infrastructure and a supportive IT regulatory environment are crucial to the effectiveness of such services.

Diaspora networking refers to networking that links the homeland to the diaspora. This
includes, for example, fulfilling intermediary functions, such as acting as a coordinating body
between the supply and demand of potential contributions (see Meyer and Brown 1999), facilitating the migration process, and ensuring transportability of qualifications (Vertovec 2002).
Diaspora networking can support the capture of diaspora socioeconomic contributions to the
homeland. Outreach and communications, including visiting delegations between home- and
host land, contribute both to networking and to integration strategies. IT is often used to support
these efforts; for example, intermediary organizations (including government agencies) may set up
online databases to fulfill matching functions, governments may set up Web portals specifically to
interface with their diasporas, and e-newsletters may be distributed to diaspora organizations and
individuals abroad.

The diaspora integration strategy recognizes the diaspora as a constituency that is marginalized
from the homeland. Thus, related policies include the extension of citizen rights such as voting

and the organization of diaspora summits and diplomatic visits to diaspora organizations in their host countries. Diaspora integration policies confer social status, political influence, and legitimacy to the diaspora and its potential efforts to contribute to the homeland. Combined with diaspora networking, this strategy may be used to seek endorsement and legitimacy for homeland political agendas.

Digital diasporas are a relatively untapped resource for supporting each of these policy strategies. Beyond databases and their own e-mail Listservs, homeland governments can more systematically use digital diasporas to solicit and possibly influence diaspora contributions, disseminate information about homeland developments, perhaps seeking endorsement (e.g. for postconflict draft constitutions, as in the case of Afghanistan), and stay connected to their diasporas, acknowledging them in ways that may encourage diasporas' further engagement in support of the homeland.

The international development industry

As a practice, international development can be viewed as an industry, driven by international donors, multilateral and bilateral, whose resources are represented by official development assistance (ODA). Universities, private consulting firms, and non-governmental organizations (NGOs) are the major producers of international goods and services, purchased through ODA. Where do diaspora contributions fit in the formal policies and programs of official development assistance?

Globalization has exacerbated many of the challenges to effective development assistance (see Florini 2000), including a declining capacity of national governments, changing private sector and NGO roles, and weak and outmoded global institutions (Brinkerhoff 2004). In response, Lindenberg and Bryant call for a new global NGO architecture, including networks and virtual organizations. However, they conclude, somewhat pessimistically, that "none of the globalizing organizations from any part of the world have a fresh vision of how more genuine, multi-directional global networks for poverty alleviation and conflict reduction might be most realistically developed" (2001, 245). On his part, Dichter (2003) notes some positive advancement outside of the development industry, notably the growing promise of telecommunications and economic remittances from diaspora communities. Digital diasporas hold great potential to meaningfully contribute to the socioeconomic development of their homelands in ways that supplement and may even enhance current industry efforts.

To date, most diaspora-related initiatives originating from the donor community concentrate on research and enhancing the productive benefits of remittances. Isolated experimentation and experiences are accumulating, wherein diaspora organizations are more engaged in the interface with formal development institutions, including providing technical assistance and intermediary services and even as implementing partners (see Brinkerhoff 2004). Diaspora members have individually been engaged in formal development assistance for some time. A more systematic review of options and experience is needed, particularly with the increased role of official development assistance in postconflict reconstruction, where societies have largely lost their human capital to war and forced and elective migration.

Whether through formal partnerships or informally, international development practitioners can tap digital diasporas to solicit information and cultural and technical expertise, disseminate information about their programming for the purpose of constituency building and coordination, and seek intermediary support in order to better reach the diaspora and target communities and those with requisite skills and experience. Independently, diasporas are pioneering their own development models, often coordinated through online communities. The development industry could enhance the effectiveness and impact of these efforts, helping these organizations to scale up these activities, building the organizational capacity of these diaspora organizations, and providing forums for these groups to share experiences and learn from each other, as well as industry development efforts.

References

Brinkerhoff, Jennifer M. 2004. Digital diasporas and international development: Afghan-Americans and the reconstruction of Afghanistan. *Public Administration and Development* 24: 397–413.

————. 2008. Diaspora identity and the potential for violence: Toward an identity-mobilization framework. *Identity: An International Journal of Theory and Research* 8.

Dichter, Thomas W. 2003. *Despite good intentions: Why development assistance to the third world has failed.* Amherst: University of Massachusetts Press.

Florini, Ann, ed. 2000. *The third force: The rise of transnational civil society.* Washington, D.C.: Carnegie Endowment for International Peace.

Gamlen, Alan. 2005. The brain drain is dead, long live the New Zealand diaspora. Working Paper no. 10. Oxford: Oxford University, Centre on Migration, Policy, and Society.

Grosfoguel, Ramón, and Héctor Cordero-Guzmán. 1998. International migration in a global context: Recent approaches to migration theory. *Diaspora* 7: 351–68.

Lindenberg, Marc, and Coralie Bryant. 2001. *Going global: Transforming relief and development NGOs.* Bloomfield: Kumarian Press.

Lowell, B. Lindsay, and Rodolofo O. De la Garza. 2000. *The developmental role of remittances in U.S. Latino communities and in Latin American countries: A final project report.* Washington, D.C.: Inter-American Dialogue and the Tomas Rivera Policy Institute.

Meyer, John-Baptiste, and Mercy Brown. 1999. Scientific diasporas: A new approach to the brain drain. Prepared for the World Conference on Science, unesco-icsu. Budapest, Hungary, June 26–July 1.

Meyer, John-Baptiste, Jorge Charum, Dora Bernal, Jacques Gaillard, José Granés, John Leon, Alvaro Montenegro, Alvaro Morales, Carlos Murcia, Nora Narvaez-Berthelemot, Luz Stella Parrado, and Bernard Schlemmer. 1997. Turning brain drain into brain gain: The Colombian experience of the diaspora option. *Science-Technology and Society* 2. Available at http://sansa.nrf.ac.za/documents/stsjbm.pdf.

Orozco, Manuel, with Michelle Lapointe. 2004. Mexican hometown associations and development opportunities. *Journal of International Affairs* 57: 31–49.

Pires-Hester, Laura. 1999. The emergence of bilateral diaspora ethnicity among Cape Verdean–Americans. In *The African diaspora: African origins and New World identities,* ed. Isidore Okpewho, Carole Boyce Davies, and Ali A. Mazrui. Bloomington: Indiana University Press.

Portes, Alejandro. 2003. Conclusion: Theoretical convergencies and empirical evidence in the study of immigrant transnationalism. *International Migration Review* 37: 874–92.

————. 2006. Remarks at the Bellagio dialogue on migration, closing conference. Bellagio, Italy: German Marshall Fund and the Rockefeller Foundation, July 14–15.

Portes, Alejandro, and Mi Zhou. 1993. The new second generation: Segmented assimilation and its variants (interminority affairs in the U.S.: Pluralism at the crossroads). *Annals of the American Academy of Political and Social Science* 30: 74–97.

Portes, Alejandro, Cristina Escobar, and Alexandria Walton Radford. 2007. Immigrant transnational organizations and development: A comparative study. *Immigration Migration Review* 41: 242–81.

Rumbaut, Rubén, and Alejandro Portes, eds. 2001. *Ethnicities: Children of immigrants in America.* Berkeley and Los Angeles: University of California Press.

Sánchez Gibau, Gina. 2005. Contested identities: Narratives of race and ethnicity in the Cape Verdean diaspora. *Identities: Global Studies in Culture and Power* 12: 405–38.

Vertovec, Steven. 2002. Transnation and skilled labour migration. Presentation at the conference "Ladenburger Diskurs 'Migration' Gottlieb Daimier-und Karl Benz-Stiftung." Ladenburg, February 14–15.

Waldinger, Roger, and Cynthia Feliciano. 2004. Will the new second generation experience "downward assimilation"? Segmented assimilation re-assessed. *Ethnic and Racial Studies* 27: 376–402.

Waters, Mary C. 1999. *Black identities: West Indian immigrant dreams and American realities.* Cambridge: Harvard University Press.

14

INTERNATIONAL MIGRATION AS A TOOL IN DEVELOPMENT POLICY

A passing phase?

Ronald Skeldon

The migrant diaspora

Another major theme in the current migration and development debate is the importance of migrant communities overseas in home-country development. This theme, centred around the concept of "diaspora," essentially brings remittances and the skilled migrants together. The physical and human capital of international migrants can be "leveraged" for the development of the country of origin (Kuznetsov 2006).

The word migration gives the impression of a definitive move: to a destination where the migrant will stay and eventually become a citizen of another country. Diaspora, on the other hand, draws attention to looking back, to the importance of linkages between origins and destinations and to the fact that migrants may return or at least continue their involvement with their countries of origin. Diaspora becomes closely associated with another term that has come to prominence in the migration literature, the "transnational community": migrants maintain close links with their origins and may even operate or live and work in two or more states. In fact, the United Nations uses the term transnational community as a substitute for diaspora. Diaspora also brings together, under a single rubric, migrants and co-ethnics who may have been born in the destination society. It is a small jump from the focus on linkages between origins and destinations to the idea that development can be associated with the diaspora. As seen above, in the migrant diaspora are to be found many of the best and brightest workers that a country of origin has to offer. If a country can take advantage of its population living outside its borders, then these expatriates should be able to contribute to development.

The role of the diaspora has been significant in development in East Asia. The overseas Chinese have for decades supported the construction of infrastructure in southern China; and in Vietnam today, expatriate Vietnamese, the Viet Kieu, are playing a critical role in the country's development. Their investment is much more than remittances, it is foreign direct investment, although, again, a clear distinction between the two is elusive. Moreover, the diaspora plays a much greater role than just financial investment. In the economies of East Asia, many migrants have returned home. As mentioned above, thousands of students from East Asia left in the 1960s, with very few returning initially. The proportion returning has increased markedly from the

1970s on (Tsai 1988). Today in Japan, Taiwan, South Korea, Singapore, and other economies in the region, including China, centers of academic excellence are emerging for the regional and global training of the highly skilled. The role that returned students have played in Asian economies is remarkable. The parliaments of the Asian Tiger economies, and the administrations of those economies, include many senior members who have been trained or have gained experience overseas. For example, of the 45 members of the cabinet of Taiwan in 2006, 25 had completed advanced degrees outside Taiwan, mainly in the United States but also in Japan, France, and the United Kingdom. The father of modern Singapore, Lee Kwan Yew, wrote an article in the late 1940s on the role of the returned student. Return migration and the trend toward a democratization of political systems in East Asia are surely more than coincidental.

Revolutionaries of other persuasions, too, refined their ideologies in Paris in the early 1920s and returned to play key a role in the transformations of China and Vietnam. Ho Chi Minh, Deng Xiaoping, and Zhou Enlai were among the most prominent leaders who returned to their homeland, but more than one thousand young Chinese students traveled to Paris in 1919 and 1920, including some of Mao Zedong's closest associates (Spence 1990: 321). In the words of one Vietnamese revolutionary, "Oppression comes to us from France, but so does the spirit of freedom" (Ta Thu Thau in Van 1995: 123). "Students" who learned their skills in Afghanistan fighting the then Soviet Union moved on to ply their craft in many of today's trouble spots.

Returning to the capitalist development in East Asia, two critical points need to be borne in mind when we assess the role of the diaspora in development. First, there was something for the migrants to return to. It would be simplistic, if not just wrong, to attribute the development of East Asia to the return migration or to the role of the diaspora. Return migrants certainly contributed to that development but they did not cause it. The assumption that the return of some of the highly skilled to Ghana, Chad, or Burkina Faso will automatically bring development is again assigning a primacy to migrant agency that seems totally misplaced. The underlying structures need first to be in place in order for the agency of migrants to function. Where the structures are nonexistent or weakly developed, the return of the highly skilled is likely to be ineffective. Development drives migration, not the other way round, although, clearly, migration can support development.

Second, the diaspora migration back to East Asia was part of a wider migration of the highly skilled from the developed world. The diaspora was not occurring in isolation from other migratory currents. Skilled persons from North America, Australasia, and Europe were also involved. Some of this migration was of nationals from the majority populations of these areas. Another part of this migration was the product of previous moves to these destination societies. Diaspora, as was noted above, deals not just with migrants but with ethnic groups including descendants—first, second, or later generations of children of migrants who may see their migration as a return, short- or long-term, to their ancestral home. Ethnic Koreans are moving from the United States and from China (the *chosungjok*) to Korea; ethnic Japanese (the *nikkeijin*) are moving to Japan from South America. Some may have been born in Korea or Japan but they are the minority, with the vast majority born in the United States, China, Brazil, or Peru, who have returned to the land of their parents or grandparents to participate in the economic dynamism of these economies. In Hong Kong, Singapore, and China we find BBCs (British-born Chinese), ABCs (American-born Chinese), CBCs (Canadian-born Chinese), and, in Vietnam, American-born Vietnamese, who are returning to live and work in their ancestral lands.

Finally, the diaspora is highly heterogeneous in terms of skill and education as well as origins and political persuasion. The diaspora cannot be thought of simply in terms of a resource to be easily mined. Many in the migrant diaspora may not have the interests of current rulers in areas of origin in mind; in fact, they may work to depose them overtly or covertly. Secession movements in the homeland have been supported by diaspora migrants in countries such as India, Ireland, and Sri Lanka. Hence, diaspora becomes associated with security and geopolitical issues, and the concept raises difficult questions of identity and loyalty. Transnationalism is much more than just linkages among co-ethnics or between migrants and communities back home.

Conclusions and a way forward

This essay has examined how current concerns over migration and development have arisen and particularly how a traditional focus in migration studies on causes and consequences of population movement has shifted to a policy focus on types of migration that will promote or inhibit development. Through an examination of the three main areas of current concern—remittances, skilled migration, and diaspora—I have argued that the responsibility for development is being increasingly placed upon the agency of migrants rather than on institutional structures. While it is clear that international migrants can influence institutional structures, they are minorities in any population. Excluding mass forced movements, those who leave represent a small proportion of the home populations, and those who return are minorities of the minority. More fundamentally, there is a danger in reifying migration as something separate from development, specifying that migration itself is a "thing apart" that can be used to promote development. Migration is essentially the responses of thousands of individuals to changing development conditions. That development promotes increased population mobility has been a central theme since the early pioneering works on international migration.

If the results of the voluminous research and the numerous meetings on international migration and development have shown that migration is not generally a negative factor for development, then a major step forward has been achieved. More concretely, if migration becomes accepted as an integral part of development and if it is acknowledged that development itself cannot be used to stop migration, then indeed progress will have been made (de Haas 2006; Skeldon 1997). Giving migration a higher profile has been a positive achievement, but the limitations of this stance also need to be acknowledged. Care has to be taken not to go to the other extreme and promote the idea that facilitating certain types of population mobility will lead to development. The point is not so much that migration can be used to promote development but that governments need to be prepared for the kinds of population migration that development generates. Development will not stop migration, although it can influence the volume and patterns of population movement. Migration has proven singularly intractable to policy intervention. Nevertheless, this fact should not imply that migration policy is irrelevant in an "age of migration" (Castles and Miller 2003).

The discussion in this essay suggests two shifts in thinking about migration and development. First, a shift in thinking is required toward more reactive rather than proactive policies. Accommodationist policies, or those that seek to respond to and plan for the kinds of migration that are likely to occur in any particular development scenario, are likely to be more appropriate than proactive policies that seek to channel migration in a particular direction to promote development. Thus, the migration and development debate needs to shift somewhat back to its intellectual roots. International migration is not a development index in the same way as the millennium development goals, although these goals themselves, like migration, simply reflect broader, deep-rooted elements of economic and social change. It is right to include migration as an integral part of the development process, but it is deceptive to think that it can be manipulated to bring about development itself. Second, a shift in the approaches to migration is required to reincorporate internal migrants into the migration and development debate, thus bringing the majority of migrants into the equation. For an example using data from Asia, see Skeldon (2006).

To consider any linkages between migration and development without taking into consideration the fact that most of those who move do so internally seems misguided.

Hence, research on urbanization, international migration, and development needs to be integrated, and the role of cities and metropolitan governments needs to be given greater prominence in the migration and development debate. Also critical is the creation of new political and economic spaces. The expansion of the European Union eastward incorporated millions of de facto international migrants without their even moving, but they thereby became entitled to move internally within the EU. Some free-trade areas and contiguous states that agree to freedom of movement across their common borders in other parts of the world, too, such as Australia–New Zealand or India–Nepal, achieve similar results. Hence, more important than the relatively small numbers who move internationally are those who are "moved" into new situations because of political and economic agreements. The subject of migration and political development has, perhaps understandably, not been a central part of the recent migration and development debate.

International migration was identified as one of the ten most pressing global challenges facing humankind by an international panel of leading economists (Lomborg 2004), but it was also deemed to be one of the least likely of the ten challenges to respond to cost-effective policy intervention. A sense of skepticism may be setting in about how effective programs of migration management can be in bringing about development. Already a sense exists that the policy debate may be moving on from migration and development to other topics such as migration and climate change. Ultimately, when we are dealing with these global challenges or with the ways in which the millennium development goals are to be achieved, the emphasis must be placed on structures: on establishing the kinds of institutions that will lead to improvements in human well-being. A focus on phenomena that are consequences rather than causes of the process, such as the diaspora, remittances, or skilled migrants, without addressing the causes of a lack of development in the first place, is unlikely to bring success. Migration can be best addressed, paradoxical though this may at first seem, if the current preoccupation with international migration as a tool to promote development becomes a passing phase in the debate on development. Migration should not be eliminated from the equation, but it should be recognized as an integral part of the development process itself and planned for accordingly.

References

Castles, S. and M. J. Miller. 2003. *The Age of Migration*, Third Edition. Basingstoke: Palgrave and Macmillan.
de Haas, H. 2006. "Turning the tide? Why 'development instead of migration' policies are bound to fail," Oxford, International Migration Institute, Working Paper No. 2.
Kuznetsov, Y. (ed.). 2006. *International Migration of Skills and Diaspora Networks: How Countries Can Draw on Their Talent Abroad*. Washington, DC: World Bank.
Lomborg, B. (ed.). 2004. *Global Crises, Global Solutions*. Cambridge: Cambridge University Press.
Skeldon, R. 1997. *Migration and Development: A Global Interpretation*. London: Longman.
Skeldon, R. 2006. "Interlinkages between internal and international migration and development in the Asian region," *Population, Space and Place* 12: 15–30.
Spence, J. D. 1990. *The Search for Modern China*. London: Hutchinson.
Tsai, C. L. 1988. "A study on the migration of students from Taiwan to the United States: A summary report," *Journal of Population Studies* 12: 91–120.
Van, N. 1995. *Revolutionaries They Could Not Break: The Fight for the Fourth International in Indochina 1930–1945*. London: Index Books.

PART III

Identities

SUBJECTIVITY

Introduction

Questions of identity, agency and movement have played a major role in the shift of critical attention away from earlier theories of diaspora linked to geographical models to globalized concepts such as multiply-located and interconnected diaspora sites that require a reconfiguring of citizenship in its relation to the nation-state. These expanded meanings of diaspora include the notion that migrations, whether due to colonialism, imperialism or contemporary forces of globalization, lead to distinctive subjectivities based on the collective experience of displacement. Theories of cultural identity such as Stuart Hall's have stressed how identity is always 'in process', a product that is constantly being made and unmade, experienced as heterogeneous and diverse, fluid and mobile, while also capable of being anchored into fixed moments of being (Hall 1990, 222). This is particularly true of diaspora figures which function 'as mobile social positions, and not fixed identities' (Nail 2015, 3), and are 'creolized, syncretized, hybridized and chronically impure forms' (Gilroy 2000, 129). In considering the construction of the modern subject (Davis 2006, 336) in diaspora, some critics highlight the operation of an 'individual subjective agency' in the reshaping of identity (Ashcroft, Griffiths and Tiffin 2006, 422). Often, as the articles included in this section show, it is external regimes of power that contribute to a traumatic refashioning of subjectivity out of conditions of loss and placelessness, as was the case in the expulsions of the Jewish and Armenian diasporas. These have, in the first instance, weakened the Cartesian assurance of the self, and in the second, caused a play of confusion and bewilderment. Such thinking about subjectivity and agency can be related to the upsurge of research which engages critically with the affective experiences of individuals and collectivities under the pressure of structural forces such as globalization and colonization; notably in trauma theory, memory studies, human rights discourses, psychoanalytic theory focusing on mourning and melancholia (Byrne 2008, 21), and the nostalgia, loss and longing comprising the 'affective economy of diaspora' (Quayson 2013, 147–8).

Lily Cho marks out this new terrain by arguing that diaspora is a condition of subjectivity, so implying that subjectivity and subject formations are constitutive of the meaning of the term diaspora. She sees the Jewish and Armenian diasporas as paradigmatic of the contingencies of diasporic subjectivity because they are marked by the 'histories of displacement and genealogies of dispossession', and embodying the disjunctive condition of being in one place and feeling attached to another. Diaspora, therefore, in Cho's theorization, cannot be defined as a social-historical disciplinary category, because it emerges from the subjective processes of racial memory, the histories and practices of race and racialization that are constitutive of diaspora and part of its emergence. The subjectivity of such collectivities is centrally focused around these buried griefs and unfulfilled longings. Cho draws on Judith Butler's (1997) work to argue that diasporas emerge through power relations which operate externally and internally: the diaspora subject turns away from the basic referents of identity (home, loss, belonging) due to external forces, but also remains subject (playing on the dualism of subjectivity/subjectification) to the internal processes of subject/identity formation through the psychic relations of power. Cho's focus on the subjective experiences associated with the *longue durées* of the paradigmatic victim migrations, postulates that diaspora is closer to the condition of exile – as a forced expulsion with an interdict on a return to the country of origin – than to that of transnational movements with the security of a promised return. The prolonged sense of loss and longing, of difference and disorientation, recalls Raymond Williams's 'structures of feeling', the subjectivities and identities of groups 'on the edge of semantic availability', whose discourse and language do not allow them to fully articulate their experience during the renegotiations of identity with the dominant culture that occur within the new liminal space (Williams 1977).

Although Cho can be criticized for emphasizing the diasporic subject as 'victim' to the exclusion of other subject positions, she nevertheless draws attention to how these structures of feeling help define diaspora, setting it apart from kindred terms like the transnational and transglobal. Her stress on the inheritance of traumatic structures from the earliest diasporas as a condition of subjectivity is a point of departure for understanding the effects of present day movements, as trauma theorists and migration critics have observed: 'We cannot understand new mobilities, without understanding old mobilities' (Cresswell 2010, 28), a comment that can be aligned with Homi Bhabha's view that only in recognizing what is 'old and weary' in those '"long histories" of slavery, colonization, diaspora' (Bhabha 2003, 27, cited by Byrne 2008, 22) can newness enter the world – namely that the past's haunting and shadowing is a necessary condition of the present (see also Craps 2013). Cho's argument that diaspora is deeply rooted in the affective responses of the subject who is caught up in power dynamics has been seminal in recent explorations of this topic.

The other two articles in this section build on and extend Cho's position. Dibyesh Anand suggests a new paradigm for the victim diaspora by arguing that the diasporic subjectivity should be appropriated as an ethical political position; he recommends the formalizing of power relations through analytical frameworks that allow for silenced and marginalized voices within diaspora and culture to be heard. In part this argument is familiar from postcolonial theory, and the assumption that all diaspora communities are necessarily marginal and disadvantaged is a limitation. Nevertheless, Anand draws attention to the fact that the import of an ethical stance is undertheorized and underrepresented in accounts and conceptualizations of diasporas, although they are articulated in relation to the fates of refugees and asylum seekers at the level of international politics.

Colin Davis, like Jane Mummery (Chapter 32, this volume) is one of the first critics to use the lens of European philosophy to examine the concept of a diasporic subjectivity, beginning with the subject's state of innate unbelonging, seen as a failure to keep a proper place. This is understood as crucial to the invention of the modern subject. Recalling Derrida and Sartre, Davis posits the inevitable alienation of the subject in general, who, deprived of home and language, is necessarily diasporic (357, this volume 122), and he demonstrates affinities with Cho's position in alluding to the place of home in the Jewish context as 'the exile of diaspora', and as speaking for all humankind. Davis's concept of the unsettled homeless subject who cannot secure the terms of his existence and, like the biblical Abraham, has no hope of return, creates an alignment between diasporic unbelonging and existentialism (338, this volume 124).

Diasporic subjectivity therefore aligns the affective experience of dislocation due to movement with the *longue durées* of the paradigmatic victim diasporas, and other extreme experiences of trauma; but the critical angles offered by the articles in this section point to its intersection with broader cultural and theoretical formations. It overlaps with philosophical concepts of existential suffering arising out of what is deemed to be the essential human condition of homelessness and unbelonging, while a diaspora subjectivity that is contextualized by the contested and constructed nature of culture in general may include all disempowered marginal social groups, not just those who are materially diasporic on account of their mobility.

References

Ashcroft, Bill, Gareth Griffiths, and Helen Tiffin, eds. 2006. *The Postcolonial Studies Reader*, 2nd ed. London: Routledge.

Bhabha, Homi. 2003. 'Democracy De-Realised.' *Diogenes* 50 (1): 27–35.

Butler, Judith. 1997. *The Psychic Life of Power: Theories in Subjection*. Stanford, CA: Stanford University Press.

Byrne, Eleanor. 2008. 'Diasporic Literature and Theory: Where Now? Passing Through the Impasse.' In *Diasporic Literature and Theory – Where Now?*, edited by Mark Shackleton, 19–34. Newcastle upon Tyne: Cambridge Scholars Publishing.

Craps, Stef. 2013. *Postcolonial Witnessing: Trauma Out of Bounds*. London: Palgrave Macmillan.

Cresswell, Tim. 2010. 'Towards a Politics of Mobility.' *Environment and Planning D: Society & Space* 28 (1): 17–31.

Davis, Colin. 2006. 'Diasporic Subjectivities.' *French Cultural Studies* 17 (3): 335–348.

Gilroy, Paul. 2000. *Between Camps: Nations, Cultures and the Allure of Race*. London: Allen Lane/Penguin.

Hall, Stuart. 1990. 'Cultural Identity and Diaspora.' In *Identity: Community, Culture, Difference*, edited by Jonathan Rutherford, 222–237. London: Lawrence and Wishart.

Nail, Thomas. 2015. *The Figure of the Migrant*. Stanford, CA: Stanford University Press.

Quayson, Ato. 2013. 'Postcolonialism and the Diasporic Imaginary.' In *A Companion to Diaspora and Transnationalism*, edited by Ato Quayson and Girisih Daswani, 139–159. Oxford: Blackwell.

Williams, Raymond. 1977. 'Structures of Feeling.' In *Marxism and Literature* by Raymond Williams, 128–135. Oxford: Oxford University Press.

15

THE TURN TO DIASPORA

Lily Cho

Diaspora must be understood as a *condition of subjectivity* and not as an object of analysis. Thus, my primary aim is not to define diaspora, but to argue strenuously for an understanding of diaspora as first and foremost a subjective condition marked by the contingencies of long histories of displacements and genealogies of dispossession. Diaspora is not divorced from the histories of colonialism and imperialism, nor is it unmarked by race and the processes of racialization. It is not defined by these histories and social practices, but these histories and practices form a crucial part of the condition of diaspora's emergence. Diaspora is related to globalization, transnationalism and postcolonialism, but differentiated from these processes, not by the objective features of demographics and geography, but by the subjective conditions of demography and the longings connected to geographical displacement. Some diasporic subjects do indeed emerge from the processes of globalization, but not all. Some diasporic subjects are indeed transnational, but not all. Diaspora emerges as a subjectivity alive to the effects of globalization and transnational migration, but also attuned to the histories of colonialism and imperialism. Diaspora is not a function of socio-historical and disciplinary phenomena, but emerges from deeply subjective processes of racial memory, of grieving for losses which cannot always be articulated and longings which hang at the edge of possibility. It is constituted in the spectrality of sorrow and the pleasures of "obscure miracles of connection."

In focusing on the problem of subjectivity and subject formation for diaspora, I am suggesting that diasporas are not just there. They are not simply collections of people, communities of scattered individuals bound by some shared history, race or religion, or however we want to break down the definitions and classifications. Rather, they have a relation to power. They emerge in relation to power. This power is both external to the diasporic subject and internally formative. As Judith Butler understands, "power that at first appears as external, pressed upon the subject, pressing the subject into subordination, assumes a psychic form that constitutes the subject's self-identity" (Butler 1997: 3). Crucially, Butler highlights the centrality of *turning* in relation to the power of subjection: "The form this power takes is relentlessly marked by a figure of turning, a turning back upon oneself or even a turn on oneself. . ., the turn appears to function as a tropological inauguration of the subject, a founding moment whose ontological status remains permanently uncertain" (3–4). In exploring what I have noted as the diasporic turn, I am not just talking about the turn to diaspora in academic discussions; I am also proposing that diasporic subjects emerge in turning, turning back upon those markers of the self—homeland, memory, loss—even as they turn on or away from them. In understanding power's relation to diasporic subjectivity as both internal and external, I find Butler's querying of that classic instance of turning in subject formation, Althusser's policeman's hail, to be particularly instructive. "Why," she asks, "does this subject turn towards the voice of the law, and what is the effect of such a turn in inaugurating a social subject?" (5). She goes on to argue that,

> the inaugurative address of state authority presupposes not only that the inculcation of conscience already has taken place, but that conscience, understood as the psychic operation of a regulatory norm, constitutes a specifically psychic and social working of power on which interpellation depends but for which it gives no account.
>
> *(5)*

Thus, it is not just that power presses upon, hails and forms diasporic subjects. It is also the case that diasporic subjects emerge out of psychic relations to power which do not come from without, but are integral to that which is within the processes of subject formation. As Butler understands, "no subject comes into being without power, but that its coming into being involves the dissimulation of power, a metaleptic reversal in which the subject produced by power becomes heralded as the subject who *founds* power" (15–16). This metaleptic reversal functions as a possible answer to the important concerns that Kazanjian and Nichanian raise via Fred Moten when they note that "accounts of subjection risk becoming 'an obsessive recording of mastery' if they do not also attend to the scenes in which subjection is 'cut and augmented'"(Kazanjian and Nichanian 2003: 7). One possibility of cutting and augmenting subjection lies in the ambivalent temporality of subjectivity.

Butler's discussion exposes the ambivalent temporality of subjectivity. It is this temporality which reveals the problematic relationship between diasporas and the conditions of their emergence. Do diasporas exist prior to the experience of scattering? When do people cease to be diasporic? As Butler understands, "The paradox of subjection implies a paradox of referentiality: namely, that we must refer to what does not yet exist" (Butler 1997: 4). This quandary illuminates the strange circularity of the many attempts at defining diaspora. They are at once already there and yet also in the process of becoming and yet again also in the process of dissolving. We cannot presume that a diasporic subject exists prior to the external forces which have produced diasporas. And yet, we cannot also talk about this subject without assuming some kind of prior relation to power. These quandaries signal the necessity of understanding the temporality of diasporic subjectivity as that which is profoundly out of joint, neither before nor after a particular event or experience, haunted by the pastness of the future. [. . .]

I derive my understanding of the conditions of diasporic subjectivity, conditions marked by sorrow and loss as well as by the pleasures of connection, from the specific histories of the classical Jewish and Armenian diasporas. A recognition of the subjective dimensions of diaspora requires a recuperation of the classical principles of diaspora from the histories of Jewish and Armenian communities. While many discussions of diaspora note that Jewish and Armenian diasporas are "ideal" diasporas, this observation suggests that these ideal types of diaspora are outdated and function as little more than an originary point. These gestures toward the origins of diaspora do little to acknowledge the genealogy of the term. Against the language of origins, I follow Jonathan and Daniel Boyarín in understanding diasporic consciousness as something which is marked both by genealogy and contingency (Boyarín and Boyarín 2002: 4). I situate Boyarín and Boyarín's engagement with origins within Walter Benjamin's refining of the term in *The Origins of German Tragic Drama*. Benjamin writes:

> Origin *[Ursprung]*, although an entirely historical category, has, nevertheless, nothing to do with genesis *[Entstehung]*. The term origin is not intended to describe the process by which the existent came into being, but rather to describe that which emerges from the

process of becoming and disappearance. Origin is an eddy in the stream of becoming, and in its current it swallows the material involved in the process of genesis. That which is original is never revealed in the naked and manifest existence of the factual; its rhythm is only apparent to dual insight. On the one hand it needs to be recognized as a process of restoration and re-establishment, but, on the other hand, and precisely because of this, as something imperfect and incomplete.

(Benjamin 2003: 45)

Thus, the question of origins is not one of genesis for an established and fixed past, but of a dialectical emergence from a history that is both restorative and incomplete. Diasporas disappear and reappear through this process of emergence.

Diasporas do not come from nowhere, nor are the conditions of diasporic subjectivity whimsical devices of differentiation. My commitment to locating conditions of diasporic subjectivity within the long histories of Jewish and Armenian diasporic experience emerges from my sense that any theorization of contemporary diaspora must acknowledge and engage with the history of the term and the ways in which this history continues to haunt the construction of contemporary diasporic community. In arguing for an engagement with the classical Jewish and Armenian diasporas, I am not suggesting an unquestioning recuperation of these historical dispersals for the present. Rather, a critical engagement with experiences of Jewish and Armenian diaspora enables an understanding of diaspora as a subjective condition bound by the catastrophic losses inflicted by power and, in the spirit of Butler's metaleptic reversal, productive of power. For example, Jonathan and Daniel Boyarín's reading of diaspora as foundationally queer and feminized in their call to rethink the role of the fable of Masada for Jewish culture illuminates one way in which diasporic subjectivity emerges as a response to power even while it generates the power of diasporic difference. Arguing that the valorization of "the account of the honourable suicide to avoid surrender at Masada was another step in Josephus' self-Romanization" (Boyarín and Boyarín 2002: 49), they contend "that the choice of 'death with (so-called) honour'—as in the Zionist appropriations of the Warsaw Ghetto revolt, harking back to the Masada ideal— represents a cultural capitulation that does not honour Jewish difference, while the choice to live however one can and continue to create as Jews is resistance" (53). Recuperating the queer and the feminine, they further argue:

The notion of dying with a weapon as more beautiful and honourable than dying without one is a surrender of Jewish difference to a "universal," masculinist consensus. Modern Jewish culture (not only Zionist) has assimilated to the macho male ethos of Western civilization.

(53)

Thus, for Boyarín and Boyarín, the power of Jewish diasporic difference lies in understanding "resistance not as the accession to power and dominance, but as resistance *to* the assumption of dominance" (102). This critical engagement with Jewish diasporic difference suggests one way in which the losses inflicted by power, the murders of Jews committed by the Romans at Masada, is a violent instance both of subjection and of the power of diasporic subjectivity generated in this resistance to the "masculinist consensus" of Western civilization. I do not turn to this re-examination of Masada in order to privilege Jewish diasporic experience as exemplary, but rather to engage critically with history and memory in turning to diaspora. As Boyarín and Boyarín propose, "It is important to insist not on the *centrality* of Jewish diaspora nor on its *logical priority* within comparative diaspora studies, but on the need to refer to, and better understand, Jewish diaspora history within the contemporary diaspora rubric" (10). That is, engaging with diaspora's genealogy within Jewish and Armenian experiences is not a process of claiming origins, but one of attending to the ways in which these histories are inextricably bound to contemporary diasporas. I turn to the classical diasporas not because they came first, but because they mark the contingencies of diasporic subjectivity.

Drawing from the models of the Jewish and Armenian diasporas, I propose that there is a vital difference between the transnational and the diasporic. While many discussions of diaspora emphasize the ways in which diasporas challenge national borders and national identities through their crossing of borders, I argue that diasporas are not constituted by transnational movement. Indeed, diasporic subjectivity does not necessarily emerge from the traversing of national boundaries. The subjective experience of what Homi Bhabha calls unhoming, with all the resonances of an uncanny haunting and loss, depends less upon moving from one national space to another than it does the experience and memory of becoming unhomely. In his introduction to *The Location of Culture,* Bhabha explores the "unhomeliness of migrancy" proposing that "[t]o live in the unhomely world, to find its ambivalences and ambiguities enacted in the house of fiction, or its sundering and splitting performed in the work of art, is also to affirm a profound desire for social solidarity" (Bhabha 1994: 18). Bhabha's proposal highlights the psychic dimension of diaspora which is so often overlooked in socio-historical examinations. His mapping of the loss of home to the uncanniness of feeling out [of] place understands dislocation and dispossession as both an affect and an effect. To live in diaspora is to be haunted by histories that sit uncomfortably out of joint, ambivalently ahead of their time and yet behind it too. It is to feel a small tingle on the skin at the back of your neck and know that something is not quite right about where you are now, but to know also that you cannot leave. To be unhomed is a process. To be unhomely is a state of diasporic consciousness.

Diaspora must be differentiated from transnationalism, not only because the crossing of national borders does not necessarily define diasporic subjectivity, but also because to be diasporic is to be marked by loss. In differentiating the diasporic from the transnational, I am thus differentiating between migration and what it means to be marked by the memory of migration. I want to reserve diaspora for the underclass, for those who must move through the world in, or are haunted by, the shadowy uncertainties of dispossession. The difference between the transnational and the diasporic lies in the difference between those whose subjectivities emerge out of the security of moving through the world with the knowledge of a return and those whose subjectivities are conditioned by the knowledge of loss. [. . .]

Another condition marked by "ideal" diasporas lies in the foundational role of traumatic dislocation. In Jewish and Armenian diasporic experience, Jewish and Armenian peoples have been forcibly scattered. While there are numerous accounts of these histories, what matters for my argument is not the specific events of the scattering itself, but its effect as a subjective experience. I recognize the dangers of a perpetual return to a narrative of wounding and victimization. In particular, I recognize the possibility of clinging to these narratives as a mode of retrenchment, as a claim to singularity and as a justification for conservative insularities. But these are the dangers of a fossilized approach to history which does not take into account the ways in which the past lives in the present. An emphasis on subjectivity makes possible a mode of engaging with these histories not as immutable expressions of victimization and wounding, but as crucially productive of subjectivities which straddle the divide between past and present. One of the major challenges to thinking about the formation of diasporic subjectivity lies in understanding the legacies of displacement and dislocation as crucially mutable features of the present. What form does the memory of the Middle Passage take in contemporary diasporic subjectivity? How do we understand the experiences of incarceration in the barracks and the barracoons as part of memory in the present? One of the wagers of this essay, a wager that is shared by many postcolonial and diaspora critics, is that these histories are not merely narratives of a faraway past disconnected from contemporary subjectivities and memories. The question then becomes one of thinking through how it is that these histories are also histories of the present. How do historical experiences of incarceration and bondage in the service of Empire emerge in the formation of contemporary identities? What are the forms of transmission? Who carries these histories into the present? What transformations in these histories occur in the process of transmission and how are these histories transformative?

Those questions can be addressed by thinking through the conditions and formation of diasporic subjectivity. Diasporic subjectivity calls attention to the conditions of its formation. Contrary to studies of diasporas as objects of analysis where race or religion might be considered a defining feature, I have been arguing that no one is born diasporic. Rather, one *becomes* diasporic through a complex process of memory and emergence. Thus, to be black, for example, does not automatically translate into a state of being within the black diaspora. Blackness is not inherently diasporic. Black diaspora subjectivity emerges in what it means to be black and live through the displacements of slavery and to carry into the future the memory of the losses compelled by the legacy of slavery, to be torn by the ambivalences of mourning losses that are both your own and yet not quite your own. Black diasporic subjectivity emerges in relation to other diasporic communities and through the depths of histories that will not rest because they have had no peace. [. . .]

The turn to diaspora illuminates the urgency of and the desire for an engagement with the legacies of colonial displacement which attends to the emergence of subjectivities bound by the disparate geographies of home and away, the past and the present. Diaspora touches upon and is marked by the colonial and the postcolonial, race and redress, culture and history. For if cultural memory in the present is the work of the future in the name of losses not yet redressed and sadnesses not yet recognized, it is also the work of embracing the unrelenting homesickness of the unhomely denizens of diaspora. To turn to diaspora is to turn to the power of relation and the enabling possibilities of difference. To turn to diaspora is to turn away from the seemingly inexorable march of history and towards the secret of memories embedded within the intimacies of the everyday. To turn to diaspora is to turn to restless specters of sorrow bound by that which is lost and to obscure miracles of connection marked by that which is found. Let us turn then to diaspora.

References

Benjamin, Walter. 2003. *The Origin of German Tragic Drama*. London: Verso.
Bhabha, Homi K. 1994. *The Location of Culture*. New York: Routledge.
Boyarín, Jonathan and Danel Boyarín. 2002. *The Powers of Diaspora: Two Essays on the Relevance of Jewish Culture*. Minneapolis: University of Minnesota Press.
Butler, Judith. 1997. *The Psychic Life of Power: Theories in Subjection*. Stanford: Stanford University Press.
Kazanjian, David and Marc Nichanian. 2003. Between Genocide and Catastrophe. In *Loss: the Politics of Mourning*, edited by David Eng and David Kazanjian, 125–47. Berkeley and Los Angeles: University of California Press.

16

DIASPORIC SUBJECTIVITY AS AN ETHICAL POSITION

Dibyesh Anand

Agreeing with works that highlight hybridity and identity politics within diasporas (see Brah 1996; Hall 1990; Radhakrishnan 1996), I argue for conceptualising diasporic subjectivity as an ethical political position that rejects cultural conformity and celebrates culture as a site of contestation.

This position breaks the monopoly of social formation of diasporas over diasporic subjectivity. One need not be socially diasporic to possess diasporic subjectivity. And many members of a diaspora may not possess diasporic subjectivity of the kind I am highlighting here – an approach to culture that refuses to privilege what is shared within a community over erasures and debates that get papered over in dominant narratives. Diasporic ethical subjectivity should serve as a constant reminder to the observers of South Asian diasporas of four things. First, that their investigation is as much about conceptualisation as it is about empirical realities on the ground. Second, an understanding of diaspora entails excavating marginalised, silenced and dissenting voices as well as the dominant ones. Third, what role do the host states and civil societies play in shaping and disciplining the narratives of diaspora? Fourth, belonging and alienation within diaspora is better studied in terms of a mix of politics of identification (that sees identity as always already a political process) and identity politics (that sees identity as a category that can be mobilised for politics; for an extended discussion, see Kaul 2007). To provoke an intellectual debate, I focus on this reimagined diasporic subjectivity as a normative endeavour and make no claim that it is always ethnographically mappable onto actually existing diasporic populations. [. . .]

Diasporas by their very existence problematise the notion of political allegiance because their loyalty can never be unambiguously to one or the other. They are privileged, or condemned, depending on one's point of view, to forever straddle across boundaries. While their existence is tied to one place, their affective connections are with more than one place, including with where they 'come from', their original homeland. This coming from could have taken place a few years, or a few centuries or forever ago. If the people who have moved no longer have emotional connections with their homeland, they are not diasporic. If they live in one place (their hostland) but have complete loyalty to their homeland, they are not diasporic but temporary migrants. Rejecting a comprehensive notion of diaspora that includes all types of migrants, I propose confining the term to those collectivities within which individual subjectivity is marked by an ambiguity, a confusion, a productive anxiety, an affective pull from different directions, all of which creates a hyper-awareness and not a predominant sense of regret. The advantage of this narrow conception of diaspora is that it shifts away the emphasis from ethnicity and identity to a politics of identification and thus foregrounds agency. 'The diaspora experience . . . is defined, not by essence or purity, but by the recognition of a necessary heterogeneity and diversity; by a conception of "identity" which lives with and through, not despite, difference; by hybridity' (Hall 1990, p. 235).

Migrants who have lost all sense of belonging to their homeland and have no connections with it whatsoever except ethnic ties are not diasporic. They might be socially diasporic but their subjectivity is too resolved and settled to be diasporic. For instance, branding all overseas Chinese, including those who have no ties with China at all, as Chinese diaspora privileges an essentialist and primordial conception of ethnicity. In contrast, Chinese diaspora should refer only to those ethnic Chinese people living overseas who retain emotional connections with China and see it as their homeland. Even the most hyper-nationalistic activists within the diaspora who try their level best to ground their identity cannot exorcise the uncertainty that stems from their existence within a different polity. Rather than treating such displacement as only an occasion of loss and regret (for instance, as represented in many Hindi movies and songs), one should accept the diasporic subjectivity as an opportunity. An opportunity to re-read and re-imagine one's own culture is also problematic. This may allow a more nuanced politics of identity and culture that focuses more on routes than roots, for a rooted notion of culture (see Clifford 1997) may foster a sense of irreconcilability with difference. Diasporic condition serves as a reminder to all of 'anxious identities we inhabit' (Kaul 2003). Diaspora thus has a psychogeography of displacement and desire of belonging built into itself. [. . .]

A focus on diasporas as conspicuous phenomena destabilises the familiarity of identity politics underpinning international relations. International relations adopts a jigsaw-puzzle view of the world with discrete and distinct bounded national communities interacting with each other. The ideal subjectivity is that of a nation-state, one where the population = territory = government = sovereignty, but this putative equation is put into question with the presence of diasporas. Diasporas make a neat division of the world into fully formed, clearly demarcated units with a secure sense of national identity impossible. And rightly so. For they could also act as a check against narrow exclusivist notions of national identity. If the state wants stability and security, it cannot afford to be exclusionary. Instead of acting merely as pressure groups working in tandem (as in the case of Jewish diaspora or Indian diaspora in the USA) or in opposition (like the Cuban diaspora in the USA) with their homeland government, diasporas could potentially occupy a role that makes a progressive difference and ensures an inclusionary nationalism within and accommodative foreign relations without. The existence of such diasporas could make the world more peaceful by complicating international relations, by criss-crossing boundaries and making mobilisation of violence around a specific narrow identity difficult. Diasporas, instead of jostling for political power and influence, could transform themselves into interlocutors and negotiators. We recognise that this normative exhortation for diasporas to challenge the key characteristics of international relations – war and peace, statism, national interest, pursuit of power – instead of subscribing to them is far from reality. Diasporas have often acted as extensions of nationalist discourse of the homeland or even encouraged a more exclusionary nationalism than that existing back in the homeland. Diasporas often contribute toward hypernationalism in their homeland. The oft reported financial support by the Hindu Non-Resident Indians to various Hindu nationalist organisations back in India is a case in point (see articles in *Ethnic and Racial Studies* 2000), but this need not be the case as a thought experiment at the very least.

Diasporas have a multifarious relationship with the notion of national identity. The diasporic condition forces one to confront difference. You cannot be comfortable and ignorant about your identity if you are diasporic. Your identity plays an important role in how you negotiate your daily life. You cannot but be aware of how you are similar and different from the majority around you. Some in the diaspora find it hard to reconcile their 'original' beliefs and values in a different context. I put 'original' under scare quotes because what may be perceived as original is often a product of nostalgic imagination and myth-making. Diasporas even when they have striven to be part of the host country's national identity have often found it is easier said than done. Racialised discourses and discomfort with difference often makes diasporic subjects targets of resentment on the part of sections of the 'native' population.

And then there are members of some diasporas who may claim to move beyond national identity to a global one. Rejection of narrow national identity does not automatically indicate a progressive broadening of horizon. The conspicuous examples of some radicalised British Muslims of Asian descent show how loyalty is neither to the host country nor to the original home country, but to the universal *umma*. In practice, their attempt to adopt a universal placeless identity cannot but be mediated through negotiations with concrete places, but these radical Islamists in the West pose an altogether different kind of challenge. Unlike diasporas who negotiate their identity between two particularities (one place *vis-à-vis* another), radical Islamists living outside their place of origin deny the very existence of specificity and locatedness. They fight battles in the name of a place-free notion of Islam and *umma* and are not concerned with homeland–hostland interactions. Even when they wage territorial wars, say in Palestine or Kashmir, they do so in the name of deterritorialised Islam. It is because of this reason, I propose expunging extremism, in the name of globalist ideology, out of the concept of diaspora. Diaspora involves negotiations across boundaries and between particular spatialities (even though imagined) and should not be applicable to universal spatial formations (global jihadi Islamism is one obvious example). Diasporas are always already cultural formations that involve perpetual negotiations between the universal and the particular and not a negation of one or the other. The end of the negotiation is the end of diasporic subjectivity. [. . .]

The dominant understanding of culture is that it is something that a social group shares, that defines the we and us, and allows for recognising the boundaries between us and them, Self and the Other. Culture is not about I but about Us. It is a collective phenomenon. It has various aspects to it but the main one is the common thread (or threads) that bind us together. Culture involves 'objective' commonalities such as language, way of thinking, songs, dances, literature, music, poetry, perceptual lens, morality, ethics, food and dress, sense of history, collective myths and legends, etc. For instance, American culture could be understood in terms of mass consumerism, Coke, KFC, Hollywood, Marilyn Monroe, Andy Warhol, big gas guzzlers, *The Great Gatsby,* Broadway and so on, but culture also involves a *recognition* of commonality, a subjective consciousness of who we are, an awareness of us. Culture cannot just exist, it has to be felt. Without a consciousness of commonality among the collective, culture has little significance. This does not mean that everyone has to be equally conscious for it to exist, but a general consensual consciousness has to be there. [. . .]

Diaspora is an entity whose very existence is a product of interactions across cultures. The presence of diaspora is a constant reminder that there is always more than one culture. At the very least, there are two cultures – one in the host country and another in the home country. For instance, the presence of Iranian diaspora in Canada implies that there is an Iranian culture and there is also a Canadian culture. The Canadians as well as the Iranian diasporic population will be aware of this, but many Iranians when they go back to Iran for a visit are likely to realise that there are at least three cultures – one Canadian, one Iranian and the third that is Canadian–Iranian. Even this ignores wide differences *within* Canadian, Iranian and Canadian–Iranian cultures. Thus, diasporic subjectivity can inculcate an awareness of multiplicity and difference and serve as a caution against narrow self-focused understandings of culture. This is not often the case, for the actually existing diasporic subjects may deny this emancipating diasporic subjectivity promoting humility and go for a different, more commonplace, understanding of culture. How diasporic subjects act toward those not belonging to their culture depends on their notion of culture. [. . .]

Diasporas when they adopt such a notion of culture – as almost a fixed shared sense of belonging – are prone to vacillate between exclusion and inter-cultural dialogue, but they underplay inter-mixing, and any inter-mixing that is inevitable is seen as an impurity and an attack on culture. In contrast, I put forward culture as a site of debate and contestation. Culture is about contestations and conversations within it. The view of an Iranian feminist or a Revolutionary Guard about what is the core of Iranian-Islamic culture would be very different. Some may argue that tea and being reserved is an essential characteristic of British culture, others might argue that it is tolerance and liberty. In this sense, cultures are always in process. They are not the end product which can be easily identified. After all, cultures are about 'circuits of meaning' and different actors always debate these meanings and in the process construct cultures. Such a social constructionist approach studies culture as a constitutive process, as processual (see Hall 1997). It understands identity of culture as well as cultural identity as always in flux and as a product of representations. [. . .]

Reconceptualising diaspora

Thus conceptualising culture as a site of contestation encourages us to read diaspora as a problematic and fragile imagined category and pay more attention to silences, marginalisations and erasures in the dominant narratives coming out of the diaspora. This is ethnographically rigorous as well as ethnically sound. For anything else will make analysts complicit with the dominant narratives in diaspora which often paper over differences within and accentuate differences without. For instance, in the UK context, the dominant narratives are the ones that are often used by the so-called community leaders. These communities – say 'Asian' or 'Black' or 'Bangladeshi' or 'Indian' – are ethnic minorities within Britain while also being diasporic. This is different from the status of minorities in China for instance. Minorities in China are not a product of modern diasporic movements, but because most visible minorities in the West have come to be through recent migrations, they are also diasporic. The interaction between this minority status and diasporic status is pregnant with multiple meanings. We can only point out to some here. The state, the media, the civil society – all use the language of 'community' for ethnic minorities and often talk of 'community elders' and 'community leaders'. This vocabulary needs an unpacking for there are unanswered questions about agency – who defines the community, who selects the community spokesmen (yes, they are almost always men), what are the assumptions behind the institutions and personnels of the host state and host civil society who perceive diasporic-ethnic minorities, how does the language of community reflect and reshape identity politics within the diaspora? How about those members of the diaspora who refuse to conform, who refuse to adhere to the cultural norms, who contest a certain given sense of what it means to belong to their culture? Does the 'community' have a space for them or are they outcasted? We argue for seeing the diaspora, its culture and its identity through the eye of these outsiders. The limits are always fluid and an arena for struggles.

Those who push the boundaries of culture, the limits of diasporic culture, are in a better position to have a critical understanding of 'their culture' (we use this for want of a better phrase) and appreciate commonalities across cultural formations. This does not imply that they are better 'cultural ambassadors' because no one, including they themselves, would see it as such. They are non-ambassadors and dissenters. Note that diplomacy (of which ambassadors are a crucial part) is never questioning of one's own country or identity but always promoting it. An ambassador represents her country, she will only project an uncritical view of her country. A diasporic subject as an ambassador of his native culture or as a representative of her homeland culture – this native culture or homeland could be another country or another sub-national group or even a non-national entity – is similarly involved in shoving under the carpet differences and power relations within his or her own cultural community. In contrast, the figure of the dissenter lends a critical distance. Even if the dissenter is marginalised or outcast, she knows how it feels to bear the burden of culture (non)confirmity, he has felt the culture operate through his body and being in not so pleasant ways. The disciplining, mostly through social and moral sanctions, of dissidents of diaspora reveals the arbitrariness and artificiality of the cultural claims made in the name of diaspora. An understanding of this can also put the other cultures – especially of the hostland – under erasure and questioning. In this, we call for reconceptualising diasporic subjectivity as an ethical political positioning that can be occupied by anyone with a consciousness of the contested and constructed nature of the culture to which they are seen as belonging. This normative take on diaspora allows one to witness and understand the ways in which culture is sought to be manufactured through different voices and silences, through inclusions and exclusion.

References

Brah, A., 1996. *Cartographies of diaspora: contesting identities*. London: Routledge.

Clifford, J., 1997. *Routes: travel and translation in the late twentieth century*. Cambridge, MA: Harvard University Press.

Hall, S., 1990. Cultural identity and diaspora. In: J. Rutherford, ed. *Identity: community, culture, difference*. London: Lawrence & Wishart, 222–237.

Hall, S., 1997. The spectacle of the 'other'. In: S. Hall, ed. *Representation: cultural representations and signifying practices*. London: Sage/Open University, 223–290.

Kaul, N., 2003. The anxious identities we inhabit . . . post'isms and economic understandings. In: D. Barker and E. Kuiper, eds. *Toward a feminist philosophy of economics*. London: Routledge, 194–210.

Kaul, N., 2007. *Imagining economics otherwise: encounters with identity/difference*. London: Routledge.

Radhakrishnan, R., 1996. *Diasporic mediations: between home and location*. Minneapolis, MN: University of Minnesota Press.

17

DIASPORIC SUBJECTIVITIES

Colin Davis

The aim of this article is to analyse some of the conceptual resources of the term diaspora, particularly through its links with subjectivity, language and spectrality. To conclude, the article looks briefly at Camus's short story 'L'Hôte', which explores the deadlock of the diasporic subject unable to belong where it is or to return to a place where it belongs. My starting point here is the observation that the displacement named by diaspora is conceptual as well as geographical; and more specifically it operates within the modern conception of subjectivity originating in Descartes and Kant.[1] Their invention of the modern subject entails a self-conscious failure to locate the subject's proper place. In his Second Meditation Descartes expressed the subject's unshakeable certainty that 'je suis quelque chose', but quite where that 'quelque chose' was to be found is another matter:

> Je ne suis point cet assemblage de membres, que l'on appelle le corps humain; je ne suis
> pas un air délié et pénétrant, répandu dans tous ces membres; je ne suis point un vent,
> un souffle, une vapeur, ni rien de tout ce que je puis feindre et imaginer.
>
> *(Descartes, 1953: 277)*

Descartes expresses, as Christina Howells puts it (Howells, 1992: 322), 'ambivalence with respect to the location of the subject, whether it lies in the "soul" alone or in an intimate union of body and soul'. The subject is both irreducible to and inseparable from physical components; it is not to be found entirely in the body nor anywhere other than in the body. The Cartesian subject of doubt is, as Paul Ricoeur puts it (Ricoeur, 1990: 16), 'désancré' or 'déplacé', succumbing to crisis at the very moment of its constitution. Kant radicalised this impossibility of locating the subject's proper place by revealing a split at its core between its knowable, conditioned, phenomenal dimension and its unknowable, free, noumenal dimension. If Descartes is unsure about the subject's home, Kant more radically describes a subject which cannot be at home because it cannot, and must, simultaneously occupy two incommensurable sites. Ricoeur (Ricoeur, 1990: 27) refers to the *je* of philosophies of the subject as *'atopos, sans place assurée dans le discours'*. It is not merely *decentred,* because this would imply the existence of a centre from which it could be removed (and to which it might conceivably return); rather, it is place-less, deprived of any site that it could occupy as its own. The subject, this article suggests, has something diasporic about it;

and this in turn has ethical and political consequences which bear directly on questions of belonging, nationhood and migration.

The connection between subjectivity and diaspora is made by Sartre in *L'Etre et le néant,* where at one moment he describes what he calls the *pour-soi* as *diasporic.* From the context it is clear that Sartre is thinking specifically of the Jewish Diaspora: 'On désignait dans le monde antique la cohésion profonde et la dispersion du peuple juif du nom de "diaspora". C'est ce mot qui nous servira pour désigner le mode d'être du Pour-soi: il est diasporique' (Sartre, 1943: 176). This observation comes in the course of a discussion of temporality; and as in earlier parts of *L'Etre et le néant* Sartre uses spatial metaphors to suggest the impossibility for the *pour-soi* of achieving self-coincidence in time. The *pour-soi* is 'à distance de soi' (Sartre, 1943: 116), 'un ailleurs par rapport à lui-même' (116–17), or simply 'là-bas' (143). Its proper place cannot be localised. Wherever it is, it is not here; and its lack of rooted self-presence instigates the temporal process by which it launches itself through time. Temporality is the dimension in which the *pour-soi* undertakes the impossible project of attaining itself.

The diasporic *pour-soi* is a kind of ghost within the human machine because it is neither here nor not here, neither present nor absent. Sartre's subject is haunted; and what it is haunted by is itself, and by its knowledge that it can never fully find itself: 'je suis hanté par cet être que je crains de rencontrer un jour au détour d'un chemin, qui m'est si étranger et qui est pourtant *mon être* et dont je sais aussi que, malgré mes efforts, je ne le rencontrerai jamais' (Sartre, 1943: 418). Consciousness is described as *'cet être [qui] implique un être autre que lui'* (Sartre, 1943: 29). Its being consists in its lack of being. The Sartrean *pour-soi* is 'une présence à soi qui manque d'une certaine présence à soi et c'est en tant que manque de cette présence qu'il est présence à soi' (Sartre, 1943: 140); or as Sartre famously puts it (1943: 117), it is a being 'qui n'est pas ce qu'il est et qui est ce qu'il n'est pas'. The *pour-soi* pursues a doomed project of self-coincidence. It desires to be other than it is, but it can never attain what it wants without its desire being instantaneously deflected elsewhere. It strains to be what it can never be, and it can never achieve the impossible status of the *en-soi-pour-soi* in which project and being would be at one.

So the *pour-soi* is haunted and diasporic insofar as it is not at home; it is in exile, expelled from being, unable to return. Sartre's reference to diaspora alludes to the Jewish experience of expulsion at first to Babylon in the sixth century BCE and then from Jerusalem under the Romans in the second century CE. The Jews of the Diaspora are sent away from their home and forced to live elsewhere.[2] On the surface, at least, the notion of diaspora relies on a settled distinction between homeland and exile and a series of related binaries: native/alien, insider/outsider, included/excluded, belonging/intrusion. But this is to simplify both Sartre's use of the term and the experience of the Jewish Diaspora. In the passage which relates the *pour-soi* to diaspora quoted above, Sartre insists that diaspora is 'la cohésion profonde et la dispersion du peuple juif': it is both cohesion and dispersion; it is the manner in which what is dispersed coheres with itself. Nearly 40 years after the publication of *L'Etre et le néant,* in interviews with Benny Lévy recorded shortly before his death, Sartre reiterated this insistence on the link between the Jewish Diaspora and unity: 'Il fallait concevoir l'histoire juive non seulement comme l'histoire d'une dissémination des juifs à travers le monde, mais encore comme l'unité de cette diaspora, l'unité des juifs dispersés' (Sartre and Lévy, 1991: 74). The unity-in-dispersion of the Diaspora has nothing to do with what Sartre calls 'un rassemblement sur une terre historique' (Sartre and Lévy, 1991: 75). Diaspora must be distinguished from exile, if exile is understood as entailing the possibility or the fantasy of return to a lost homeland. The *pour-soi* has nowhere else to be other than not-at-home. When Sartre calls diaspora a 'mode d'être', he is defining it as the mode of being of that which cannot *be,* but which can only *seek to be.* In the Jewish context, the Diaspora is not merely a geographical condition of separation from Israel. The Diaspora and Israel are not just places; they are also communities and spiritual conditions; so Israel is in Diaspora, and Diaspora is the state (if not the State) of Israel. When Sartre says that the *pour-soi* is diasporic, he is also saying that its home, its proper place, is the exile of diaspora; and the Jewish experience of the Diaspora is also the human experience of what it means to be a subject.

The biblical precedent for the term *diaspora* is attributed to Deuteronomy 28:25, translated in the King James Bible as '[thou] shalt be removed into all the kingdoms of the earth'. The Greek translation of the Hebrew Bible known as the Septuagint has, in a literal English version, 'thou shalt be a diaspora in all kingdoms of the earth'. Etymologically *diaspora* refers to the spreading or scattering of seed; it is formed from the Greek verb *diaspeirein,* made up of the prefix *dia-* ('about, across') and *speirein* ('to sow, to scatter'). This etymology prompts two observations. First, already in the etymological sense there is no implication that the place in which the seed originates is the proper place to which it should return; on the contrary, seed fulfils its role by being scattered, by not remaining with its parent stock, and by taking its chances of implanting itself away from its point of departure. Braziel and Mannur underscore the positive connotations of the etymology of *diaspora* when they note (Braziel and Mannur, 2003: 4) that it 'suggests the (more positive) fertility of dispersion, dissemination, and the scattering of seeds'. Second, as is hinted in this quotation (and in Sartre's comment quoted in the previous paragraph), there is an etymological and conceptual link between diaspora and dissemination. The term *dissemination,* which it is now impossible to separate from Derrida's use of it, translates the Greek *diaspora* into a Latinate vocabulary. Dissemination also describes the dispersion of seed or of semen or of sense; so Derrida's reflection on dissemination is also a way of relating to diaspora and to the characteristic tensions of diasporic subjectivity.[3]

In *La Dissémination* Derrida describes dissemination as 'l'impossible retour à l'unité rejointe, réajointée d'un sens, la marche barrée d'une telle *réflexion*' (Derrida, 1972: 299). This impossible return, the impossibility even to think in terms of return, is precisely the diasporic state of the Sartrean *pour-soi,* to which the prospect of self-coincidence is irrevocably blocked. Derrida goes on to insist that dissemination has nothing to do with a *loss* of meaning, which would imply that truth was once available; rather, as he puts it (Derrida, 1972: 300), 'la dissémination *affirme* la génération toujours déjà divisée du sens'. Dissemination, then, is not something that happens to meaning like a hammer blow which shatters a vase; rather it is the inaugural moment, the non-originary origin, out of which meaning is produced. Without the spreading of the seed there is no generation; and there is no opposition here between dissemination and proper meaning, because the notion of proper meaning is precisely what dissemination scatters to the wind. Moreover, this undercuts the temptation of nostalgia; there is no truth, no self, no object of desire, no homeland, which were once possessed and to which we can hope to return. Dissemination is where meaning occurs, albeit in disarray; diaspora is where the subject finds itself, albeit as fractured.

Dissemination and diasporic subjectivity are linked in that both record an originary displacement, so that there is no proper site to which they can long to return. Derrida himself does not make this link between diaspora and dissemination; it is nevertheless implied by his account of his own experience as a Jew of the Diaspora in Algeria. In *Le Monolinguisme de l'autre,* Derrida describes how the Algerian Jews had their French citizenship revoked during the Second World War. They were thereby left literally stateless, isolated both from the indigenous Arab communities and the white French colonials. This sense of not-belonging-here-but-not-belonging-anywhere-else is the state of diaspora when all nostalgia for a lost homeland is abandoned. Language is bound up with the diasporic condition. Derrida was brought up as French-speaking, without a native knowledge either of the Jewish languages of the Diaspora or other languages current in Algeria, notably Arabic or Berber; so French is his only language, but it is also not *his.* It is the language of a colonial power which denied him citizenship, and which therefore excluded him from owning the only language he knew well. This originary loss of French is intensified in the experience of the Algerian Jews, who according to Derrida are subject to a triple loss of language: they were dispossessed of French, which could be a genuine mother tongue; Ladino (Judeo-Spanish, the language of the Jews of Spanish origin) was no longer practised; and Hebrew was not widely taught and understood (Derrida, 1996: 100). Derrida both describes something specific to his own experience and generalises that experience to give it broader validity. As Jane Hiddleston argues (2005: 299–300), for Derrida:

> [a]lienation and lack are not symptoms of a lost wholeness, but are constitutive of all language and culture . . . From this perspective, language is perceived *always* to contain otherness or marginality, and myths of belonging and unmediated identification are revealed as unworkable. The colonised Jews of Algeria were dispossessed of their language in a traumatic and shocking manner, but alienation in language at the same time affects coloniser and colonised alike.

Derrida relates this alienation from his language to a lack, but it is a lack which is not a lack of something that was ever, or could ever, be present. From the specific experience of diaspora emerges a general account of subjectivity which could have come straight out of Sartre's *L'Etre et le néant*:

> Comme le "manque", cette "aliénation" à demeure paraît constitutive. Mais elle n'est ni un manque ni une aliénation, elle ne manque de rien qui la précède ou la suive, elle n'aliène aucune ipséité, aucune propriété, aucun *soi* qui ait jamais pu représenter sa veille.
> *(Derrida, 1996: 47)*

The link here between (the loss of) language and diasporic subjectivity is important. In a key metaphor, Derrida (Derrida, 1996: 91) relates the possession of language to the protection of a *chez-soi*. Having a language is also having a home, but language cannot be possessed. Derrida's triple loss of language makes more acute what he regards as a *constitutive* alienation, shared by both colonisers and colonised (though the former may delude themselves that it is not true). And lacking a *chez-soi* in language is also to be deprived of a *soi,* as Derrida suggests (1996: 108) in a resonant list which links place, home and subjectivity: 'la place, le lieu, le logis du chez-soi, l'*ipse*, l'être chez-soi ou l'être-avec-soi du soi' (Derrida, 1996: 108). To lack language is also to lack a place, a home, a being-at-home and a being.

There are, then, compelling links here between diaspora, the dissemination of meaning, the dispossession of language, the loss of statehood and the lack-which-is-not-a-lack within the subject. The '"aliénation" originaire' (Derrida, 1996: 121) described by Derrida ensures that language always belongs to the other; it can never be the property of any speaking subject. The event of speech, the *phenomenon* by which the subject's intended meaning *(vouloirdire)* is supported by its ability to hear and to understand itself in the intimacy of its subjectivity *(s'entendre-parler),* is instituted and disturbed by this originary alienation. Derrida argues that the *phenomenon* is also a *phantasm,* and, as he goes on to suggest (Derrida, 1996: 48), '*Phantasma,* c'est aussi le fantôme, le double ou le revenant'. The most intimate part of the subject is already haunted by non-present presences which eerily disturb its self-possession. This flourish is evidently linked to Derrida's work on spectrality and in particular to what has proved to be one of the most influential and controversial works of his late period, *Spectres de Marx* (1993). It also looks back to his earlier work on phenomenology, as it disturbs the status of the indispensable building block of phenomenology: the phenomenon itself. The phenomenon, which should be that which is most unquestionably available to experience, is haunted, shadowed, not fully present because it does not coincide with itself any more than we can fully possess it. At this point, despite everything that separates them, Derrida rejoins Sartre. Sartrean phenomenology depicts a world of *apparitions* in which the phenomenon is both nothing other than what it appears to be and never fully present in its appearances; and the Sartrean subject, described as 'hanté par la présence de ce avec quoi il devrait coïncider pour être *soi*' (Sartre, 1943: 140), is also in the thrall of its internalised ghosts.

Diaspora, then, can be taken as a figure for modern, spectral subjectivity, homeless and self-haunted. Derrida is aware that his account of 'alienation without alienation' takes his own exceptional experience as *exemplary;* but as Judith Still has pointed out (2004: 124), in this he is merely replicating the standard move of autobiography: 'Exceptional and everyman – of course the classic autobiographical trope' (Still, 2004: 124). Moreover, Derrida's hesitant embracing of autobiography and his anxious yet frequent use of the first person, his 'lucid self-probing' (Hiddleston, 2005: 303), can be related to the more widespread philosophical return to the subject. This return, though, is a return to something which is now discovered to be displaced. The Cartesian foundation of knowledge on the subject's self-certainty has been eroded, so that subjectivity is now a site where various forms of bewilderment are played out. That this is not just a theoretical issue is indicated by the epistemological anxieties which can be traced in popular culture as much as in Derridean poststructuralism. The *Matrix* trilogy provides a good example of such anxieties in recent film. Neo, the character who may be the One to lead humanity out of computer simulation back into an assured reality, is seen right at the beginning of the first *Matrix* film carrying Baudrillard's *Simulacra and Simulation,* as if the whole series were conceived out of the drive to prove Baudrillard first right (there is only simulation) and then wrong (we can re-conquer the real). The series may point to the possibility of escaping from simulation and returning to the real world in which we belong, but the cost of this may be too heavy to bear. It entails a quasi-religious leap of faith which the films (perhaps inadvertently) make laughably implausible, as if they were themselves willing to embrace belief in a return to the real but in the end find themselves unable to pay the price.

Another sign of such anxieties is the persistence of stories and films of the supernatural. Here, it is as if the haunting of the subject described by Sartre and Derrida were being literalised, again in a double gesture of acknowledgement and repudiation. Such stories give ghosts existence outside the subject, making them more real and in the process re-affirming the distinctions that haunted subjectivity no longer knows for certain: real and imaginary, self and other, subject and object, life and death. Typically, the ghost returns to put things right, to restore an order that had been temporarily disrupted. In this respect, modern stories of the supernatural perform the normative, restorative function described by Keith Thomas in his now-classic *Religion and the Decline of Magic.* Thomas describes (Thomas, 1971: 597) how the ghosts of pre-Reformation Europe returned 'to confess some unrequited offence, to describe the punishment which lay in wait for some heinous sin, or to testify to the rewards in store for virtuous conduct', or 'to denounce an undetected evil-doer'. Even if we no longer have the belief systems which explain such functions, the roles of the ghosts in, for example, *Ghost* or *The Sixth Sense* are not much different, as they return in order to complete unfinished business.

However, if the ghosts return to restore order, the world to which they come back is trans-formed by the very fact of their return, so that the anxieties they were meant to still are also reactivated by their presence. This can be seen graphically in zombie movies. George A. Romero's great zombie series, comprising *Night of the Living Dead, Dawn of the Dead, Day of the Dead* and *Land of the Dead,* illustrates how the repressed returns as both the same and different, repeating the past and in the process showing it for what it was and savagely transforming it. In *The Night of the Living Dead* the zombie attack was an apparently isolated incident, but the subsequent films show these attacks becoming more widespread, as the zombies gradually colonise the land of the living. In *Land of the Dead,* the most recent of the series, the zombies have more or less taken over, with only one walled city remaining as a pocket of human habitation. Here, then, to be alive is to be encircled by the dead, desperately and hopelessly resisting being recruited to their ranks. But to read the film in this way makes firmer oppositions between the living and the dead than it actually supports. The zombies are precisely *not* dead, or not dead enough. Like vampires, they are caught between their first death, which turns them into what they are, and their second death, which will finally destroy them. In the meantime, they are in some sense alive. One sequence from *Dawn of the Dead* shows them wandering around a shopping mall, looking mindlessly in the store windows much as their living counterparts might. And perhaps they are even more alive than the living: they are now pure hunger, pure desire, no longer bound by the paltry courtesies of living social beings. Moreover they are, as Žižek memorably puts it (Žižek, 1992: 22–3),

> not portrayed as embodiments of pure evil, of a simple drive to kill or revenge, but as sufferers, pursuing their victims with an awkward persistence, colored by a kind of infinite sadness (as in Werner Herzog's *Nosferatu,* in which the vampire is not a simple machinery of evil with a cynical smile on his lips, but a melancholic sufferer longing for salvation).

As Žižek says of vampires, 'precisely as "living dead", they *are far more alive* than us'; and, he goes on, 'the real "living dead" are we, common mortals, condemned to vegetate in the symbolic' (Žižek, 1991: 221). The zombie movie disturbs the discrete worlds of the living and the dead. In the process it enacts the constitutive ambiguity of diaspora in that it seems to depend upon a settled opposition (here: between the living and the dead), but it then mercilessly and ruthlessly devours that opposition, just as the zombies devour their prey. And out of the zombie movie emerges, in dramatic form, the question posed, according to Lacan, by the obsessional neurotic: Am I dead or alive?

What is at stake, and what is dispersed, in diasporic subjectivities is, then, the subject's assurance of its place within a settled order which would secure its sense of belonging and even its existence. [. . .]

The displaced subject of Sartre or Derrida, the ghosts and zombies of recent films, and Daru in Camus's story are all in some sense diasporic creatures. As such, the urgency which speaks through them is not to restore or return to a former state, but rather a forwards drive which disturbs, deranges and disseminates the settled knowledge from which they set out. To adapt terms used frequently by Levinas, the diasporic subject is not Odysseus, whose point of departure is also the homeland of Ithaca to which he longs to return; rather, it is Abraham, who obeys a call that comes from nowhere instructing him to set out on a journey into the land of the Other without hope of return. Diaspora names a scattering, an impossible self-coincidence, a dispersion without source, an exile without homeland, and an appalling entanglement of the living and the dead. The subject is diasporic in part because it traverses the anguish of never achieving self-coincidence; but this anguish is also the condition by which it seeks and discovers the new, and in which it comes to know the exquisite pain of encounter, loss and desire.

Notes

1 The following discussion draws substantially on Howells, 'Conclusion: Sartre and the Deconstruction of the Subject' (Howells, 1992).
2 In this paragraph I follow the convention of giving diaspora an initial capital when it refers specifically to the Jewish Diaspora, and using lower case when it refers to the more general sense of the term.

3 For a now classic exploration of dissemination in the context of postcolonial theory, see Bhabha, 'DissemiNation: Time, Narrative and the Margins of the Modern Nation', in *The Location of Culture* (Bhabha, 1994).

References

Bhabha, H. K. (1994) *The Location of Culture*. Routledge: London.

Braziel, J. E. and Mannur, A. (2003) 'Nation, Migration, Globalization: Points of Contention in Diaspora Studies', in J. E. Braziel and A. Mannur (eds), *Theorizing Diaspora: A Reader*, pp. 1–22. Malden, MA: Blackwell.

Derrida, J. (1972) *La Dissémination*. Paris: Seuil.

[Derrida, J. (1993) *Spectres de Marx*. Paris: Galilée.]

Derrida, J. (1996) *Le Monolinguisme de l'autre*. Paris: Galilée.

Descartes, R. (1953) *OEuvres et lettres*. Paris: Gallimard.

Hiddleston, J. (2005) 'Derrida, Autobiography and Postcoloniality', *French Cultural Studies*, 16(3): 291–304.

Howells, C. (1992) 'Conclusion: Sartre and the Deconstruction of the Subject', in C. Howells (ed.), *The Cambridge Companion to Sartre*, pp. 318–52. Cambridge: Cambridge University Press.

Ricoeur, P. (1990) *Soi-même comme un autre*. Paris: Seuil, Points essais edition.

Sartre, J.-P. (1943) *L'Etre et le néant*. Paris: Gallimard, Tel (1980 printing).

Sartre, J.-P. and Lévy, B. (1991) *L'Espoir maintenant: les entretiens de 1980*. Paris: Verdier.

Still, J. (2004) 'Language as Hospitality: Revisiting Intertextuality via Monolingualism of the Other', *Paragraph: A Journal of Modern Critical Theory*, 27(1): 113–27.

Thomas, K. (1971) *Religion and the Decline of Magic: Studies in Popular Beliefs in Sixteenth and Seventeenth-Century England*. London: Weidenfeld and Nicolson.

Žižek, S. (1991) *For They Know Not What They Do: Enjoyment as a Political Factor*. London and New York: Verso.

Žižek, S. (1992) *Looking Awry: An Introduction to Jacques Lacan through Popular Culture*. Cambridge, MA and London: MIT Press.

HYBRIDITY AND CULTURAL IDENTITY

Introduction

Hybridity is one of the most dynamic and productive concepts to have emerged within post-colonial and diaspora studies in recent years, as post-structuralist theory (particularly Jacques Derrida's work on difference) was used to reformulate and reconceptualize the term. In nineteenth-century racialized colonial thinking, hybridity had been associated, as Robert Young (1995) has shown, with miscegenation and cross-racial desire, but more recently it has been used to generate new models of cultural interaction (see Papastergiadis 2000, 3) – so widely that many studies (like Avtar Brah and Annie E. Coombes's *Hybridity and its Discontents* [2000]) open with concerns about the proliferation of meanings it has generated. Paul Gilroy (2000) has also expressed concern that the term 'hybridity' might inevitably imply some earlier 'uncontaminated' purities (250). Thus while hybridity, conceived by Stuart Hall, Homi Bhabha and others as an alternative to essentialism and notions of 'purity', can be seen as a mode of resistance to colonial power and demands for diasporic assimilation, its potency in that respect has been much debated, even contested by diaspora theorists.

Although not included here, Stuart Hall's (1990) essay 'Cultural Identity and Diaspora' is often referred to as an early intervention in the debate about hybridity. Hall talks of cultural identity and representation in terms of the sharing of culture and collectivity. For him, cultural identity, including that experienced in diaspora, is necessarily unstable, fluid and of hybrid formation – certainly when seen in the context of the 'ruptures and discontinuities' (236) of colonization. This 'unsettling' can be a resource of cultural creativity and empowerment; it exists within, not outside, representation, and brings into being a 'diasporic aesthetic', as a structure of postcolonial experience.

Most discussions of hybridity in relation to diaspora reference the work of Homi Bhabha and his view that hybridity 'provide[s] the terrain for elaborating strategies of selfhood [. . .] that initiate new signs of identity, and innovative sites of collaboration and contestation' (1994, 1–2). 'The Third Space', a rare interview conducted with Bhabha in 1990, needs to be seen in terms of his increasingly influential position as an emerging postcolonial thinker. Here he expounds further on his foundational concept of the 'third space' – as drawn from his seminal article 'The Commitment to Theory', first published in 1988 and later reprinted in *The Location of Culture* (Bhabha 1994). Bhabha clarifies the key points: that commitment to 'cultural diversity' is not necessarily positive, since it can be seen as continuing to endorse a 'transparent norm [. . .] given by the host society or dominant culture'; that the alternative notion of 'difference' opens up possibilities for more radical (and in the end more accurate) thinking in this area; that identification is a process of identifying through another object; and that 'all forms of culture are continually in a process of hybridity'. He suggests that hybridity *is* the third space – this is not identity as such, but a continuous and fluid process of identification, and is in general a positive concept. Bhabha's ideas are significant for diaspora studies, since they build on Stuart Hall's advocacy of hybridity as a resource of cultural creativity and empowerment.

Floya Anthias's 'New hybridities, old concepts: The limits of "culture"' argues that Bhabha's notion of hybridity, although it is valuable in challenging 'static and essentialist notions of ethnicity, culture and identity, presents important conceptual and substantive difficulties'. For example, while Bhabha's commitment to post-structuralist thinking leads him to suggest that 'all forms of culture are continually in a process of hybridity', Anthias comments that 'if all cultures are by definition hybrid, the term loses its specific analytic usefulness'. The fact that culture can be celebrated as predominantly hybrid unintentionally ignores the fact that it is still characterized by uneven power structures and hierarchies. Anthias's concept of 'translocational positionality' – whereby we are positioned within the world and all live within social hierarchies – is designed to help us think more critically about the hybrid potential of diaspora. Focusing on cultural production alone or on the positive aspects of the third space subscribes to a view of society that neglects the political and power dimensions of social relations and their inherent inequalities (see also Anthias 2008 and Anthias 2009). Thus analysis of diaspora that focuses on cultural hybridity can lose sight of 'cultural domination; power, as embodied in culture, disappears', and may dwell 'too much on transgressive elements, [underplaying] alienation, exclusion, violence and fundamentalism as part of cultural encounters'. She proposes the notion of 'translocational positionality' as having potential for the exploration of different forms of hybridity.

John Hutnyk's 'Hybridity' criticizes scholars who use 'hybridity talk' to generate a 'jamboree of pluralism and multiplicity'. The problem with this is that differences experienced in diaspora might in fact be flattened out, once they are celebrated, homogenized and globalized. Like Anthias, Hutnyk diagnoses in the enthusiasm for hybridity a tendency to gloss over questions of politics and inequality. He examines the use of the term as a critical tool for the social sciences, and asks sceptically whether these understandings really 'form any sort of basis for political consciousness and a project of emancipation'. Drawing on a number of areas in which hybridity has been deployed in the study of diaspora (such as linguistics, popular culture and politics), he remains unconvinced about its transformative power and notes that dystopic science fiction scenarios, such as Luc Besson's 1997 feature film, *The Fifth Element*, in fact play out a generalized fear of hybridity itself. He concludes that 'a more radical analysis is needed to equip organized groups and achieve [hybridity] in an equitable way'.

Pnina Werbner's essay 'The limits of cultural hybridity: On ritual monsters, poetic licence and contested postcolonial purifications' critiques hybridity in terms similar to those of Anthias and Hutnyk: that cultures cannot be homogenized under an umbrella term of hybridity and that each diasporic culture has its distinctive hybrid forms and modes of transgression. However, Werbner goes on to take a different tack, arguing that transgression of cultural boundaries can become culturally offensive when it is seen as undermining values, decorum and propriety. This can be the case particularly for postcolonial diasporas struggling for recognition in the host nation. Werbner recognizes Bhabha's location of agency in the act of interruptive enunciation as a 'familiar trope' in the discipline of anthropology – and in diasporic poetry. She discusses the celebrated case of the offence given by Salman Rushdie's *The Satanic Verses* to debate 'the creative limits of cultural hybridity' and to give a reminder that even though transgression can be conceived as an attack on cultural essentialism, this can also extend to cultural identity, because cultures themselves are formed of 'ethical values, responsibility and shared sociality'.

It should be noted that the misgivings of Anthias, Hutnyk and Werbner about an undifferentiated or too facile celebration of hybridity in diaspora are shared by a number of postcolonial scholars, particularly those of a more materialist persuasion (for example, Parry 2004; Ahmed 1999; Lazarus 1999). Nevertheless, scholars such as Vanessa Guignery (2011) continue to argue that hybridity 'still matters', since it marks out a ground of 'active, dynamic process of interactions between relational cultures' (6).

References

Ahmed, Sarah. 1999. 'Passing Through Hybridity.' In *Performativity and Belonging*, edited by Vikki Bell, 87–106. London: Sage.

Anthias, Floya. 2008. 'Thinking Through the Lens of Translocational Positionality: An Intersectionality Frame for Understanding Identity and Belonging.' *Translocations, Migration and Change* 4 (1): 5–20.

Anthias, Floya. 2009. 'Translocational Belonging, Identity and Generation: Questions and Problems in Migration and Ethnic Studies.' *Finnish Journal of Ethnicity and Migration* 4 (1): 6–16.

Bhabha, Homi. 1994. *The Location of Culture*. London: Routledge.

Brah, Avtar, and Annie E. Coombes. 2000. *Hybridity and its Discontents: Politics, Science, Culture*. London: Routledge.

Gilroy, Paul. 2000. *Between Camps*. Harmondsworth: Penguin.

Guignery, Vanessa. 2011. 'Introduction: Hybridity, Why It Still Matters.' In *Hybridity: Forms and Figures in Literature and the Visual Arts*, edited by Vanessa Guignery, Catherine Pesso-Miquel and Francois Speck, 1–6. Newcastle upon Tyne: Cambridge Scholars.

Hall, Stuart. 1990. 'Cultural Identity and Diaspora.' In *Identity: Community, Culture, Difference*, edited by Jonathan Rutherford, 222–237. London: Lawrence and Wishart.

Lazarus, Neil. 1999. *Nationalism and Cultural Practice in the Post-colonial World*. Cambridge: Cambridge University Press.

Papastergiadis, Nikos. 2000. *The Turbulence of Migration: Globalization, Deterritorialization and Hybridity*. Cambridge and Malden, MA: Polity Press.

Parry, Benita. 2004. *Postcolonial Studies: A Materialist Critique*. London: Routledge.

Young, Robert. 1995. *Colonial Desire: Hybridity in Theory, Culture and Race*. London: Routledge.

18

THE THIRD SPACE

Interview with Homi Bhabha

Jonathan Rutherford

Homi Bhabha lectures in English and Literary Theory at Sussex University. His writings on colonialism, race, identity and difference have been an important influence on debates in cultural politics. His own essays will be collected into a single volume, *The Location of Culture* and he is editor of another collection of essays, *Nation and Narration* (both published by Routledge).

Homi Bhabha has played a central role in articulating a response from black intellectuals in Britain to the publication of Salman Rushdie's *The Satanic Verses*. His statement, which emerged from the group 'Black Voices', in *New Statesman & Society* (3 March 1989) argues for a position that refutes both fundamentalism and its liberal response. In the statement he poses the question: 'So where do we turn, we who see the limits of liberalism and fear the absolutist demands of fundamentalism?' The following interview attempts to provide some kind of theoretical chart for that journey.

Jonathan: In your essay 'Commitment to Theory'[1] you analyse the processes of cultural change and transformation. Central to this analysis is your distinction between cultural diversity and cultural difference, and alongside your emphasis on difference are the notions of translation and hybridity. Could you say something about these terms you use?

Homi Bhabha: The attempt to conceive of cultural difference as opposed to cultural diversity comes from an awareness that right through the liberal tradition, particularly in philosophical relativism and in forms of anthropology, the idea that cultures are diverse and that in some sense the diversity of cultures is a good and positive thing and ought to be encouraged, has been known for a long time. It is a commonplace of plural, democratic societies to say that they can encourage and accommodate cultural diversity.

In fact the sign of the 'cultured' or the 'civilised' attitude is the ability to appreciate cultures in a kind of a *musée imaginaire;* as though one should be able to collect and appreciate them. Western connoisseurship is the capacity to understand and locate cultures in a universal time-frame that acknowledges their various historical and social contexts only eventually to transcend them and render them transparent.

Following from this, you begin to see the way in which the endorsement of cultural diversity becomes a bedrock of multicultural education policy in this country. There are two problems with it: one is the very obvious one, that although there is always an entertainment and encouragement of cultural diversity, there is always also a corresponding containment of it. A transparent norm constituted, a norm given by the host society or dominant culture, which says that 'these other cultures are fine, but we must be able to locate them within our own grid'. This is what I mean by a *creation* of cultural diversity and a *containment* of cultural difference.

The second problem is, as we know very well, that in societies where multiculturalism is encouraged racism is still rampant in various forms. This is because the universalism that paradoxically permits diversity masks ethnocentric norms, values and interests.

The changing nature of what we understand as the 'national population' is ever more visibly constructed from a range different sorts of interests, different kinds of cultural histories, different post-colonial lineages, different sexual orientations. The whole nature of the public sphere is changing so that we really do need the notion of a politics which is based on unequal, uneven, multiple and *potentially antagonistic,* political identities. This must not be confused with some form of autonomous, individualist pluralism (and the corresponding notion of cultural diversity); what is at issue is a historical moment in which these multiple identities do actually articulate in challenging ways, either positively or negatively, either in progressive or regressive ways, often conflictually, sometimes even *incommensurably* – not some flowering of individual talents and capacities. Multiculturalism represented an attempt both to respond to and to control the dynamic process of the articulation of cultural difference, administering a *consensus* based on a norm that propagates cultural diversity.

My purpose in talking about cultural difference rather than cultural diversity is to acknowledge that this kind of liberal relativist perspective is inadequate in itself and doesn't generally recognise the universalist and normative stance from which it constructs its cultural and political judgements. With the concept of difference, which has its theoretical history in post-structuralist thinking, psychoanalysis (where difference is very resonant), post-Althusserian Marxism, and the exemplary work of Fanon, what I was attempting to do was to begin to see how the notion of the West, itself, or Western culture, its liberalism and relativism – these very potent mythologies of 'progress' – also contain a cutting edge, a limit. With the notion of cultural difference, I try to place myself in that position of liminality, in that productive space of the construction of culture as difference, in the spirit of alterity or otherness.

The difference of cultures cannot be something that can be accommodated within a universalist framework. Different cultures, the difference between cultural practices, the difference in the construction of cultures within different groups, very often set up among and between themselves an *incommensurability.* However rational you are, or 'rationalist' you are (because rationalism is an ideology, not just a way of being sensible), it is actually very difficult, even impossible and counterproductive, to try and fit together different forms of culture and to pretend that they can easily coexist. The assumption that at some level all forms of cultural diversity may be understood on the basis of a particular universal concept, whether it be 'human being', 'class' or 'race', can be both very dangerous and very limiting in trying to understand the ways in which cultural practices construct their own systems of meaning and social organisation.

Relativism and universalism both have their radical forms, which can be more attractive, but even these are basically part of the same process. At this point I'd like to introduce the notion of 'cultural translation' (and my use of the word is informed by the very original observations of Walter Benjamin on the task of translation and on the task of the translator[2]) to suggest that all forms of culture are in some way related to each other, because culture is a signifying or symbolic activity. The articulation of cultures is possible not because of the familiarity or similarity of *contents,* but because all cultures are symbol-forming and subject-constituting, interpellative practices.

We are very resistant to thinking how the act of signification, the act of producing the icons and symbols, the myths and metaphors through which we live culture, must always – by virtue of the fact that they *are* forms of representation – have within them a kind of self-alienating limit.

Meaning is constructed across the bar of difference and separation between the signifier and the signified. So it follows that no culture is full unto itself, no culture is plainly plenitudinous, not only because there are other cultures which contradict its authority, but also because its own symbol-forming activity, its own interpellation in the process of representation, language, signification and meaning-making, always underscores the claim to an originary, holistic, organic identity. By translation I first of all mean a process by which, in order to objectify cultural meaning, there always has to be a process of alienation and of secondariness *in relation to itself*. In that sense there is no 'in itself' and 'for itself' within cultures because they are always subject to intrinsic forms of translation. This theory of culture is close to a theory of language, as part of a process of translations – using that word as before, not in a strict linguistic sense of translation as in a 'book translated from French into English', but as a motif or trope as Benjamin suggests for the activity of displacement within the linguistic sign.

Developing that notion, translation is also a way of imitating, but in a mischievous, displacing sense – imitating an original in such a way that the priority of the original is not reinforced but by the very fact that it *can* be simulated, copied, transferred, transformed, made into a simulacrum and so on: the 'original' is never finished or complete in itself. The 'originary' is always open to translation so that it can never be said to have a totalised prior moment of being or meaning – an essence. What this really means is that cultures are only constituted in relation to that otherness internal to their own symbol-forming activity which makes them decentred structures – through that displacement or liminality opens up the possibility of articulating *different*, even incommensurable cultural practices and priorities.

Now the notion of hybridity comes from the two prior descriptions I've given of the genealogy of difference and the idea of translation, because if, as I was saying, the act of cultural translation (both as representation and as reproduction) denies the essentialism of a prior given original or originary culture, then we see that all forms of culture are continually in a process of hybridity. But for me the importance of hybridity is not to be able to trace two original moments from which the third emerges, rather hybridity to me is the 'third space' which enables other positions to emerge. This third space displaces the histories that constitute it, and sets up new structures of authority, new political initiatives, which are inadequately understood through received wisdom.

Jonathan: I can see how this enables us to elude a politics of polarity and a cultural binarism, but would you call this 'third space' an identity as such?

Homi Bhabha: No, not so much identity as identification (in the psychoanalytic sense). I try to talk about hybridity through a psychoanalytic analogy, so that identification is a process of identifying with and through another object, an object of otherness, at which point the agency of identification – the subject – is itself always ambivalent, because of the intervention of that otherness. But the importance of hybridity is that it bears the traces of those feelings and practices which inform it, just like a translation, so that hybridity puts together the traces of certain other meanings or discourses. It does not give them the authority of being prior in the sense of being original: they are prior only in the sense of being anterior. The process of cultural hybridity gives rise to something different, something new and unrecognisable, a new area of negotiation of meaning and representation. A good example would be the form of hybridity that *The Satanic Verses*[3] represents, where clearly a number of controversies around the origin, the authorship and indeed the authority of the Koran, have been drawn upon in the book.

Within the discourses of theological disputation, what appears in Rushdie's *The Satanic Verses* has all been said and discussed before (about the interpolations in the Koran, the status of those interpolations, the 'Satanic Verses' as illicit intervention and so on). What is interesting is how, using another kind of language of representation – call it the 'migrant metaphor' call it the postmodern novel or what you will – and giving a context of other forms of allegorisation, the metropolitanism of the modern city, contemporary sexuality etc., the knowledges and disputes about the status of the Koran become quite different things in *The Satanic Verses*. Through that transformation, through that form of cultural translation, their values and effects (political, social, cultural) become entirely incommensurable with the traditions of theological or historical interpretation which formed the received culture of Koranic reading and writing.

To think of migration as metaphor suggests that the very language of the novel, its form and rhetoric, must be open to meanings that are ambivalent, doubling and dissembling. Metaphor produces hybrid realities by yoking together unlikely traditions of thought. *The Satanic Verses* is, in this sense, structured around the metaphor of migrancy. The importance of thinking of migration as *literary metaphor* leads us back to the great social offence of the novel (the way it has been read and interpreted, literally, as a Satanic challenge to the authority of Islam), but also permits us to see how it is the *form* of the novel has been profoundly misunderstood and has proved to be politically explosive – precisely because the novel is about metaphor.

Notes

1 In *New Formations*, 'Identities' issue, No.5, Summer 1988, Routledge, London.
2 Walter Benjamin, *Illuminations*, Fontana, London 1982.
3 Salman Rushdie, *The Satanic Verses*, Viking Penguin, London 1988.

19

NEW HYBRIDITIES, OLD CONCEPTS

The limits of 'culture'

Floya Anthias

Approaches that find hybrid social forms to be results of interculturality and diasporic relations, or what Hall (1990) calls cultural diasporization, also claim that these signify new forms of identity. Through a declaration of 'hybridities', they postulate the transcendence of 'old ethnicities' (cf. Hall 1988) and the formation of transgressive cultural formations which *in and of themselves* function to dispel the certainties of fixed location. Contestations over culture are important focuses of struggle as they are part of the exercise of power (Bourdieu 1990). If hybrid social identities are now the characteristic identities of the modern world, then struggles over cultural hegemony and the underlying mechanisms that support it, become increasingly empty signifiers; merely to occupy the space of the 'hybrid' constitutes an emancipatory human condition.[1]

A critical evaluation of hybridity may also be an important frame for evaluating the degree to which change has occurred in the paradigms used to understand forms of migration and settlement in the modern era. The terms hybridity and diaspora open up spaces hitherto foreclosed by traditional approaches to ethnicity and migration, and involve anti-essentialist projects and critiques of static notions of ethnicity and culture. They are terms that seek to overcome the victimology of transnational migrants, empowering them, linking the past and the present. [. . .]

Hybridity is a central term in post-structuralist cultural theory and in some variants of globalization theory. It is, in fact, difficult to understand the importance given to notions of hybridity outside the debate on cultural globalization. Currently debated issues include questions such as: whether it is a new process or an old one, whether it exists or not (Hirst and Thompson 1995), whether its character is imperialistic or democratizing and the extent of hybridization (Pieterse 1995). Hybridity (and diaspora) has been central to the debate about cultural globalization, and has functioned to celebrate it. Such a cultural globalization has been seen as a challenge to ethnic essentialisms and absolutisms. This has occurred at a time when the contradictory nature of globalization vis-à-vis ethnicity, localism, fundamentalism and nationalism has been recognized and explored. Globalization has been seen as a challenge to the nation-state, while concomitantly generating ethnic and cultural parochialisms and localisms, or '*glocalisation*' in Roland Robertson's own 'hybrid' term (Robertson 1995). It has been argued that the boundary of the nation-state is traversed in the multiple ways identified by the movement of capital; the growing penetration over the globe of transnational financial capital; by the growth and penetration of new technologies; by the export and movement of communication modes including media forms and images; by the growth of transnational political and juridical groups (for example, the EU and its potential); by growing international resistance and action groups (for example, the Beijing Conference of Women); by penetration of ideologies producing a 'world system' (Wallerstein 1990) or Global Village (McLuhan 1964). Diasporic and hybridization processes have been related to this.

Hybridity is tied to the idea of cultural syncretism, rather than the cultural difference solidified by multiculturalism, in terms of the inter-penetration of elements. In some versions hybridity is depicted as transgressive, or as enabling a privileged access to knowledge (for example, Bhabha 1990, 1994; Rassool 1997). The argument about multiple belongings in the modern state rests largely on the dismantling of the notion of a unitary identity, partly through a critique of unitary notions of the self and partly through a critique of unitary notions of cultural identity. However, ironically, hybridity arguments need to stress the retention of part of a cultural heritage (that is, the continuities involved), if they are able to identify the cultural identity which is then merged with other aspects to form an organic whole. They thereby share the concern of the old ethnicities with the role of culture in constituting ethnic belonging (for example, Glazer and Moynihan 1963; Shibutani and Khan 1965).

There is a need to desegregate the problematic of culture and that of collective identity and the formation of solidary projects. Identity formation and re-iteration involves the use of narratives of belongingness, but these do not depend solely on cultural practices or beliefs. Hybridization as 'the ways in which forms become separated from existing practices and recombine with new forms of new practices' (Rowe and Schelling 1991, p. 231) may be seen as a depiction of all culture and therefore neither new nor essentially related to diasporic experience or diasporic space (Brah 1996). The forms of 'belonging' hailed by the notion of hybridity therefore require delineating: to what extent does hybridity signal the end of ethnicity, in the sense of struggle and contestation around the ethnic boundary? [. . .]

Modern hybridities: New identities

Hybridity is a key term within mixed-race debates, where it may appear as postulating that the 'races' which become mixed are themselves constituted as essential and non-hybrid. It has been pointed out (Young 1996) that hybridity retains a cultural discourse of racial purity. The new use of the term hybridity implicitly rejects the idea of pre-existing pure categories. Those who object to the use of the term hybrid for making assumptions about the purity of the elements from which it derives are, however, employing semantic rather than substantive objections. On the other hand, if all cultures are by definition hybrid, the term loses its specific analytic usefulness.

It is important to note that 'hybridity' is used in different ways and constitutes for each writer a way of challenging existing paradigms of 'identity'. For Hall, hybridity is particularly linked to the idea of 'new ethnicities' (Hall 1988), which attempts to provide a non-static and non-essentialized approach to ethnic culture. Stuart Hall has been concerned, over the years, to develop an analysis which is non-essentialist, and which validates the search for identity. This is linked to experiences of racialization and posits the importance of narratives of identity for resisting racist exclusions. For Hall (1990), 'histories have their real, material and symbolic effects' (Hall 1990, p. 226). These histories relate to 'the recognition of a necessary heterogeneity and diversity' and 'identity lives with and through, not despite, difference; by hybridity' (Hall 1990, p. 235). In Hall's work, the black subject emerges through history as differently constructed and yet still identifiable on the margins, in the periphery, largely because of racialized experience and subjectivity.

While the 'new ethnicities', it is argued, involve a search for roots and grounding, they are not stymied by a search for identity on the basis of origin. Ethnicity, in this sense, relates both to the homeland, and to the society of settlement and is reconfigured within a diasporic space. It has been argued that this can produce a more effective cultural intervention in racialized discourse (Hall 1990). From this position, it is a small step to argue that such a re-arrangement of identities and cultures opens up a space for interpenetration and translation; this is depicted through the concept of hybridity. Such identities are never complete and are being continuously made and remade. The term hybridity also designates the formation of new identities that may have a more transethnic, and transnational character. For example, new British Muslim identity is not confined to an ethnic group, but is an amalgam, neither purely religious nor specifically ethnic, that may be linked to forging identity as a culture of resistance. Being black, or part of the African diaspora, stresses experience, rather than origins, and constructs a transnational identity (Gilroy 1993). Young white adolescents (Hewitt 1986, Back 1996), have been seen as synthesizing the culture of their white English backgrounds, with the new cultures of the minorities, to forge new cultural forms in music, and inter-racial friendship networks and movements. Young Asians are producing new forms of Anglo-Indian music. Young Greek Cypriots in Britain are keener to abandon the ethnocentricity of their parents, and are forging links with young Turkish Cypriots, and with other marginalized and ethnicized youth (Anthias, forthcoming). [. . .]

I do not have the space to address these problems in detail but I want to summarize two central problems of the debate on cultural hybridity here. Firstly, it privileges the domain of the cultural as opposed to the material or the political (restricting its sense to that of cultural products) and therefore depoliticizes culture. It loses sight of cultural domination; power, as embodied in culture, disappears. Hybridity may not be possible in the colonial encounter (see Spivak 1993). Secondly, it focuses too much on transgressive elements and underplays alienation, exclusion, violence and fundamentalism as part of cultural encounters, particularly where there is social asymmetry as in colonialism.

Given these difficulties, a range of questions needs to be substantively researched: Under what conditions is a synthesis of cultural elements possible? Which elements of culture become destabilized? To what extent do groups assert identity in the face of threat? Which social groups within are most reluctant to negotiate cultural rules and around which aspects of culture? Are some aspects of culture more difficult to mix? How important is the institution of family and kinship, the position of women and religious and moral rules, particularly around sexuality? What are the difficulties of translation? What is implied by the notion of transgressivity? What is the potential for new forms of democracy and citizenship? [. . .]

I argued earlier that hybridity deploys a particular notion of 'culture' (as content or product). Diaspora also deploys a notion of ethnic bonds as primarily revolving around the centrality of 'origin', seeing these being played out in a transnational arena. Therefore, there is a subtext which involves privileging the point of 'origin' in constructing identity and solidarity. If this is the case, then it sits uneasily with the view that diasporas can transcend the orientation to homelands. I have argued elsewhere (Anthias 1998b), that the concept of diaspora fails to pay adequate attention to transethnic, as opposed to transnational, processes. The concept of diaspora also neglects the aspects of ethnicity that are exclusionary, for the commonality constructed by racism is different, and indeed may be transethnic rather than transnational. Transethnic, as opposed to transnational, commonalities and processes are pushed to the background and therefore, in a curious way this sits uneasily with the idea of hybridization as transethnicity. So while hybridity and diaspora are often conjoined within approaches, the connection and tension between them is ignored.

Translocational positionality

While the notion of hybridity focuses on issues of cultural 'cut and mix' and deploys a notion of identity, however multi-layered or fragmented (Anthias 1999), I would like to suggest the continuing importance of the social relations of 'othering' on the one hand, and resource struggles on the other or what I would like to call 'translocational' positionality. These may take particular forms in the period of 'high modernity'. Some of these may yield reflexivity in recognizing multiple selves and others (hybrid/diasporic), but even here there are potentially contradictory processes in terms of struggles around resource allocation; such struggles may take place along the lines of the relations of gender, 'race' and class.

Collective identities involve forms of social organization postulating boundaries with identity markers that denote essential elements of membership (which act to 'code' people), as well as claims that are articulated for specific purposes. The identity markers (culture, origin, language, colour and physiognomy etc.) may themselves function as resources that are deployed contextually and situationally. They function both as sets of self-attributions and attributions by others. By focusing on location/dislocation and on positionality, it is possible to pay attention to spatial and contextual dimensions, treating the issues involved in terms of processes rather than possessive properties of individuals (for example, see Mouffe 1994).

The focus on location and positionality (and translocational positionality) avoids assumptions about subjective processes on the one hand and culturalist forms of determinism on the other. Moreover, it acknowledges that identification is an enactment that does not entail fixity or permanence, as well as the role of the local and the contextual in the processes involved. Narratives of belonging (and its disclaimers) may then be seen as forms of social action, that is, as actively participating in the very construction of subject positionalities. They are also narratives of dislocation, relocation and alterity at multiple levels – structural, cultural and personal. They relate (or more accurately construct) a history and interpellate location and position (social place and hierarchy). Narratives of location/dislocation (and translocation) are produced in interplay with the available narratives that characterize the cultural milieu both in terms of local contexts and the larger epistemological and ontological contexts of a particular Weltanschauung. Such narratives are not given or static, but are emergent, produced interactionally and contain elements of contradiction and struggle that is, they are not unitary (Bakhtin 1986). The construction of difference and identity (as boundaries of difference and sameness), on the one hand, and the construction of hierarchical social positions, on the other, are produced and reproduced in interplay with the narrative structures.

Positionality combines a reference to social position (as a set of effectivities: as outcome) and social positioning (as a set of practices, actions and meanings: as process). The centrality of process involves displacing the binary of agency (thought of as related to human volition) and structure (thought of as a set of determinancies outside individuals), with the specification of sociological relations in terms of practices and outcomes (rather than mechanisms/causes implied by the binary of agency/structure). The focus on location (and translocation), recognizes the importance of context, the situated nature of claims and attributions and their production in complex and shifting locales. It also recognizes variability with some processes leading to more complex, contradictory and, at times, dialogical positionalities than others: this is what is meant by the term 'transnational'. The latter references the complex nature of positionality faced by those who are at the interplay of a range of locations and dislocations in relation to gender, ethnicity, national belonging, class and racialization (see Anthias 1998a). It is therefore able to move more effectively away from the residual elements of essentialization and culturalism retained within the concept of 'hybridities'.

What has usually been thought about as a question of identity (collective identity) can be understood as relating to *boundaries* on the one hand and *hierarchies* on the other. Not only do 'identities' such as ethnicity/'race' (as well as gender and class) entail categories of difference and identity *(boundaries),* they also construct social positions *(hierarchies),* and involve the allocation of power and other resources. What characterizes such categories as boundaries is *relationality, naturalization and collectivization* (for an extended discussion see Anthias 1998a). Relationality involves the construction of categories that involve dichotomy and function as mutually exclusive; to identify is to differentiate from and vice versa. Cultural constructs around these categories tend to use binaries, common in Western thought (self/other, male/female, black/white). Naturalization involves the formation of categories which are taken as indisputable and given. The construction of collective attributions and the production of unitary categories is a particularly salient aspect of ethnic and gender divisions and construct those inside (and often outside) in unitary terms. Constructions of sexual or 'racial' difference in terms of a biological or somatic difference come to signify or postulate necessary social effects, to produce gendered or racialized depictions and dispositions.

What characterizes social identities at the level of positions is *hierarchical difference* (a pecking order of places, symbolically and materially) and *unequal resource allocation* (concrete access to economic, political, symbolic and cultural resources). Hierarchical difference (or hierarchization) relates to the ways in collective identities construct *places* or *positions* in the social order of things. The hierarchization is a complex one because it is not just a matter of a hierarchy of places (and specification of which types of individuals may or may not fill them) within what may be called an ethnic or racialized space. For example, in the category of 'race', there exist class and gender differences that interplay with those of race to produce complex forms of hierarchy. Unequal resource allocation not only references economic resources but also the allocation of power, authority and legitimacy in relation to political, cultural and representational levels, as well as the validation of different kinds of social and symbolic capital (Bourdieu 1990). The boundaries relating to relationality, naturalization and collective attributions are brought into play in a dialogical sense with social position leading to naturalized, collectivized and relational hierarchization and unequal resource allocation.

Positionality relates therefore to the space at the intersection of structure (as social position/social effects) and agency (as social positioning/meaning and practice). The concept involves processes of identification but is not reducible to these, for what is also signalled are the lived practices in which identification is practised/performed as well as the intersubjective, organizational and representational conditions for their existence (Anthias 1998a).

Note

1 The term 'hybridized' as Young points out (1996, p. 25), can be treated in two ways: as a description of a combinatory of elements and as a process whereby (through dialogical means) a permanent space of discontinuities is constructed. It is in the latter sense that the arguments are particularly important. However, such arguments are based on the postulate found in the first definition, that there really is such a mixing and that it is possible to identify its elements.

References

Anthias, Floya 1998a 'Rethinking social divisions: some notes towards a theoretical framework', *Sociological Review*, vol. 46, no. 3, pp. 506–35.
———— 1998b 'Evaluating diaspora: beyond ethnicity?', *Sociology*, vol. 32, no. 3, 557–80.
———— 1999 'Beyond unities of identity in high modernity', *Identities*, vol. 6, no. 1, pp. 121–44.
———— forthcoming 'New British Cypriot identities', unpublished paper.
Back, Les 1996 *New Ethnicities and Urban Culture*, London: UCL Press.
Bakhtin, M.M. 1986 *Speech Genres and Other Late Essays* (edited by M. Holquist), Austin, TX: University of Texas Press.
Bhabha, Homi 1990 *Nation and Narration*, London: Routledge.
———— 1994 *The Location of Culture*, London: Routledge.

Bourdieu, Pierre 1990 *The Logic of Practice*, Oxford: Polity.

Brah, Avtar 1996 *Cartographies of the Diaspora*, London: Routledge.

Gilroy, Paul 1993 *The Black Atlantic*, London: Verso.

Glazer, Nathan and Moynihan, P. Daniel 1963 *Beyond the Melting Pot*, Cambridge, MA: MIT Press.

Hall, Stuart 1988 'New ethnicities', in Kobena Mercer (ed.), *Black film/British cinema*, ICA Document 7, London.

Hall, Stuart 1990 'Cultural identity and diaspora', in James Rutherford (ed.), *Identity: Community, Culture, Difference*, London: Lawrence and Wishart.

Hewitt, Roger 1986 *White Talk, Black Talk: Inter-racial Friendship and Communication amongst Adolescents*, Cambridge: Cambridge University Press.

Hirst, Paul and Thompson, Graham 1995 *Globalisation in Question: The International Economy and the Possibilities of Governance*, Cambridge: Polity.

Mcluhan, Marshall 1964 *Understanding Media*, London: Routledge.

Mouffe, Chantal 1994 'For a politics of nomadic identity', in Roland Robertson et al. (eds), *Travellers' Tales*, London: Routledge.

Pieterse J, Nederveen 1995 'Globalisation as hybridisation' in Mike Featherstone et al. (eds) *Global Modernities*, London: Sage.

Rassool, N 1997 'Fractured or flexible identities? Life histories of "black" diasporic women in Britain', in Heidi Mirza (ed.), *Black British Feminism: A Reader*, London: Routledge.

Robertson, Roland 1995 'Glocalisation: time-space and homogeneity-heterogeneity', in Mike Featherstone et al. (eds), *Global Modernities*, London: Sage.

Rowe, W. and Schelling, V. 1991 *Memory and Modernity: Popular Culture in Latin America*, London: Verso.

Shibutani, T. and Khan, T.M. 1965 *Ethnic Stratification*, New York: Macmillan.

Spivak, Gayatri 1993 'Can the subaltern speak?', in P. Williams and L. Chrisman (eds), *Colonial Discourse and Post-Colonial Theory: A Reader*, Hemel Hempstead: Harvester Wheatsheaf.

Wallerstein, Immanuel 1990 'Culture as the ideological battleground of the modern world-system', in Mike Featherstone (ed.) *Global Culture*, London: Sage.

Young, Robert 1996 *Colonial Desire: Hybridity in Theory, Culture and Race*, London: Routledge.

20

HYBRIDITY

John Hutnyk

Creativity

It is not so strange then that the dynamic of exchange and mixture in the work of contemporary 'hybridity theorists' is intended as a critique of the negative complex of assimilation and integration. Such work insistently affirms the creativity and effervescence of cultural pluralization. This is conceived as a theoretico-political intervention by some major theorists, though it is, of course, never presented uncritically. For example, in Hall's discussion of what he sees as very welcome changes in British cultural life, the term hybridization is used to describe the confluence of black style and the market. With a certain mischievous tone he notes a displacement where 'some sectors of the mobile (and mobile-phoned) black youth' have taken advantage of Thatcherism and the Enterprise Culture of 1990s Britain as part of a general trend towards 'the racial and ethnic pluralisation of British culture and social life'. This process is 'going on, unevenly, everywhere' and through television and other media the 'unwelcome message of cultural hybridization' is being brought into 'the domestic sanctuaries of British living rooms' (Hall 1995, pp. 16–18). While this is good news, it is not unequivocally progressive. The same process can also be seen going on in youth culture where 'black street styles are the cutting edge of the generational style wars' (Hall 1995, p. 22). The question that should be put here has to do not with the evaluation of this diversity, but with the ways its advent leads either to new possibilities in a diasporized polity or, as seems just as likely, to increasing incorporation of the mobile-phoned youth into 'host' society, the culture industry, and more generally into a hybridized mode of capitalism. What is significant here is that the hybrid creativity of black style is affirmed (and it is affirmed also by the market, by the entrepreneurs who want to cash in), and expressions of enthusiasm for this creative change are obvious.

Urbanization-causes-hybridity?

It is my argument, however, that syncretism and hybridity are academic conceptual tools providing an alibi for lack of attention to politics, in a project designed to manage the cultural consequences of colonization and globalization. Where Gilroy calls 'syncretism . . . that dry anthropological word' (Gilroy 1994, p. 54) there might be reason to be suspicious of the ways previous scholarly attention has focused on movements of mixture. The old explanatory routine

of population pressure and subsequent urbanization as the root of all ills for contemporary society
was much discussed in the syncretism literature of anthropology. These themes should feature
prominently in critical discussions of hybridity. Where Papastergiadis writes approvingly of the
'teeming hybridity of the postcolonial city' (Papastergiadis 1998, p. 175), there might be an
opportunity for an incursion that remembers all those excluded from that city and trying to get in.
Garcia Canclini also offers a typical example:

> Undoubtedly urban expansion is one of the causes that intensified cultural hybridiz-
> ation. What does it mean for Latin American cultures that countries that had about
> 10 per cent of their population in cities at the beginning of the century now concentrate
> 60 to 70 per cent in urban agglomerations?
>
> *(Canclini 1995, p. 207)*

Surely, the rural population remains part of any demographic, especially where its movement is
blocked (see the essays on the limits to travel theory in Kaur and Hutnyk 1999), and this in turn
raises questions about who can and who cannot be considered hybrid or open to hybridity. Scare
stories about over-population in the Third World, with subsequent campaigns for fertility
control, and the tightening of immigration restrictions, intractable asylum law, and reduction of
refugee programs, should all be questioned as the nether side of a hierarchical prejudice and
exclusion. Closures abound. In his book *Population and Development,* Frank Furedi offers a cogent
critique of the way population 'paranoia' and 'the goal of population stabilization' and control
'took precedence over that of development' (Furedi 1997, pp. 73, 80–4).

Many of those who had the good sense, relative fortune, or circumstantial luck to escape
agricultural slavery (under feudal lords or under industrialized farming) by means of migration
to the rich metropolis find themselves still to be afflicted by an international division of labour
remapped across multiple zones. In the cities of the rich West as much as in the peripheral
metropoles, the newly industrialized enclaves and the re-pauperised barios, there continues a
comprehensive demarcation. It should be clear that those who escaped the peasant predicament
only to exchange landlords for racists and institutional discrimination are probably marginally
materially better off than their excluded brethren still caught at the sharp end of IMF and World
Bank agricultural policy. Those who remain in the theatre of that peasantry now find the
emigration option replaced by sweatshop micro-production, service subservience or street-
corner begging (perhaps just a few can avail themselves of new romantic tribal ethnicities so as
to attend liberal colloquia on first peoples, but at best it is more likely they will be found
hawking trinkets to backpackers). This does not mean they are the problem; equally, they are
not to be romanticized. We should certainly salute the attempt of those workers who refuse
slavery, and those who struggle under the wire (or risk asphyxiation on a channel tunnel
crossing wedged underneath a lorry, or the danger of drowning on a makeshift raft in the
Florida Keys), but we cannot pretend that running away is the revolution. On the whole,
prospects seem slim for those who want to escape the immiseration of their situations. The issue
is not overpopulation, and to use this as a criterion for limiting redistribution is the ideological
programme excused by the urbanization-causes-hybridity thesis. What must be analysed as
more than a descriptive condition are the turbulent effects of population migration that, glossed
as diaspora and settlement, has rearranged the necessities of struggle and life. Whether it be the
settler colonialists in Australia, Southern Africa or the Americas, the Chinese in Malaysia and
Indonesia, Tamils and Bangladeshis in the Gulf or Punjabis in Britain – and so many more
examples – scholarship has not achieved much in terms of promoting an openness that can
undo exploitation and inequality.

The generalized fear of hybridity is also played out in science fiction urbanization scenarios where the cities of the future are imagined as dystopias of ethnic mixture – urbanization leads to the Asian hybrid future *of Bladerunner* (dir. Ridley Scott, 1982) in Los Angeles 2019 or the Islam-inflected megalopolis of the twenty-fifth century in *The Fifth Element* (dir. Luc Besson 1997). Like sexual mixture, urban crowding is fantasized as a problem to be worked through by agents of law: as with any number of (white, Western) sci-fi heroes, Decker in *Bladerunner,* and Korben Dallas in *The Fifth Element* both fight to preserve the purity of the earth from non-human invasion. The Federation of Star Trek police space with patrols to manage threatening, endlessly multiplying, differences. It was German National Socialism that wanted *Lebensraum,* room to live, and tried to expand the borders of Germany. The Japanese Imperial Government of the 1930s went in for the co-prosperity sphere, which is akin more to economic imperialism than settler colonization. US imperialism today marches to war in the interests of corporate building contracts and resource extraction, yet all these modes of expansion are figured in the off-world adventures of *Bladerunner, The Fifth Element, Star Trek* and many other films where planetary expansion involves 'terra-firming' and conquest or pacification before acclimatization. The task of adapting Mars to human habitation *(Red Planet,* dir. Anthony Hoffman, 2000, *Mission to Mars* dir. Brian de Palma, 2000) is a well-worked variant of the *lebensraum* ambition and is motivated by the same failures to deal justly with the here and now. By displacing thought about life problems 'here' today onto fantasies of the future 'there', what do we avoid?

On this planet it is the local 'aliens' who are a terminological problem for sociological classification as much as for state administration. Talk of urbanization processes reveals the ways descriptions congeal into a conceptual refusal to recognize settlement, opting instead for models of arrivals, second generations, immigrants, hybrids – as if these categories were ever stable and could be applied to really existing groups of people. As always from elsewhere, the lived-in formation of the centre is made subservient to an assumed but unchallenged, original template, as if there were rightful inhabitants. Londoners, in this example, are not those who live in London, but rather the 'residue' of the white 'eastenders' whose brethren mostly decamped to Essex in 'white flight'. The racist cartography of urbanization is clear and can then be mapped on to the class position of advocates of hybridity-talk. Of course then the East end lads' image becomes passé as hybridity is recruited to remake London as the multicultural capital, dining out on its mixed cuisine (expensive venues, underpaid and undocumented service staff) and its multiracial vibe (hints of danger, licentious scenes). It is in the interests of those invested in a certain version of multiculturalism to honour integrated 'ethnic' fractions and well-meaning whites alike in the polite society of the suburban milieu, with excellent services and shopping malls galore – and an indulgent inner urban ghetto-exotica, where fantasy cosmopolitanism can risk a dark inner city evening out. Of course, any political assessment that might carve up the surplus in a more equitable way, locally or globally, is left unconsidered.

Just as we often found anxiety about cross-racial sexuality behind discussions of cultural survival, syncretism, hybridity and mixture, at least historically, in the contemporary period a similar investment provokes concern about diaspora and urbanization. These 'scourges' of cultural homogeneity are seen to operate alongside a hybridity-talk that is unable and unwilling to defend against exclusionary attacks – the theorists of hybridity appear complicit in the middle-class comforts that their own cosmopolitan lives afford, while denying the same to others left to languish in the 'third world' and rural extraction zones. It is an 'unrestful' conclusion that the tranquil discussions of cultural hybridization, diaspora and mixture do little more than confirm middle-class securities and draw others into the hegemony of a fabricated, and commercialized, diversity.

John Hutnyk

Lessons of hybridity?

This might be the place to ask again if the use of a term like hybridity in the social sciences offers understandings hitherto unavailable, and do these understandings then form any sort of basis for political consciousness and a project of emancipation? Or is it merely the case that hybridity offers up no more than festivals of difference in an equalization of cultures that would confirm Adorno's worst fears of a market that sells 'fictitiously individual nuances' (Adorno 1991, p. 35), in a standardized world where each product must claim to be 'irreplaceably unique' (Adorno 1991, p. 68). Canclini is alert to this when he writes:

> When hybridization is the mixing of elements from many diverse societies whose peoples are seen as sets of potential consumers of a global product, the process that in music is called equalization tends to be applied to the differences between cultures.
>
> *(Canclini 2000: p. 47)*

The charge is that a flattening of differences is secured at the very moment that celebrates difference and the creative productivity of new mixings. This flattening has inflected the terms of scholarship to the core. In a provocative volume, *Ethics After Idealism,* Rey Chow suggests that the popularized concepts of hybridity, diversity and pluralism may be grouped with others such as heteroglossia, dialogism, heterogeneity and multiplicity, as well as with notions of the post-colonial and cosmopolitan. Her point is that these concepts all serve to 'obliterate' questions of politics and histories of inequality, thereby occluding 'the legacy of colonialism understood from the viewpoint of the colonized' and so able to 'ignore the experiences of poverty, dependency, subalterneity that persist well beyond the achievement of national independence' (Chow 1998, p. 155). Chow continues in a way that takes to task the metropolitan celebrant of the hybrid:

> The enormous seductiveness of the postmodern hybridite's discourse lies . . . in its invitation to join the power of global capitalism by flattening out past injustices in a way that accepts the extant relations of power and where "the recitation of past injustices seems tedious and unnecessary".
>
> *(Chow 1998, p. 156)*

The same distraction might be discerned in enthusiasm for the figure of the cyborg in Haraway, and science fiction (but be sure to note that this is not to say that this happens in the same way). The consequence, however, is that it becomes possible to forget colonial violence, white supremacy, systematic exploitation and oppression: for those who can join the 'belonging' reserved to the compliant elite fraction of hybridizing capital, hybridity saves. As already noted, it is Spivak who is the most critical thinker here, pointing out that attention to migrancy and hybridity reserves importance to the metropolitan sphere and leaves the zones of exploitation, as arraigned across international divisions of labour, in darkness. In several books, but most explicitly in her *Critique of Postcolonial Reason,* she repeatedly takes to task those hybridized and diasporized members of the cosmopolitan set who market themselves as representatives of the culture they call origin from the luxurious comfort they now call home (Spivak 1999, pp. 191, 361). This is 'going native' in a rather different way: brown employees of the World Bank, IMF and UN conference circuit can only politely be called hybrid. In this conception, hybridity is about the opportunism of diasporic migrants seduced by complicity and advantage. Spivak's critique centres upon the mode of 'post-colonialism' which takes the place of 'the thoroughly stratified larger theatre of the South', by displacing interest and attention to that 'South' by way of a 'migrant hybridism' so that the South 'is once again in shadow, the diasporic stands in for the native informant' (Spivak 1999, pp. 168–9). Subalterneity is occluded or flattened, whatever other problems there might be with subaltern talk, by the celebrated access of hybridity talk. This is achieved with the help of the scholarly enthusiasm for hybridity as discussed above:

> An unexamined cultural studies internationally, joins hands with an unexamined ethnic studies . . . to oil the wheels of what can only be called the ideological state apparatus . . . triumphalist hybridism as well as nostalgic nativism. Business as usual.
>
> *(Spivak 1999, p. 319n)*

The business-as-usual that remains to be studied here is the culture industry co-option of cultural difference. The sophisticated artistic or rustic-ified ethnic performance of culture sits comfortably with an upward mobility of middle-class aspiration in the globalized ecumene. Beneficiaries of surplus while their class underlings succumb, the cultural effervescence of hybridity is indulgent insofar as it no longer contests monoculture but rather facilitates a corporate multiculture.

Surplus

The analytic advances of post-colonial and migration studies, let alone the globalization thematics of an elaborated Cultural Studies, still appear inadequate for thinking strategy and tactics for a political engagement with these issues. This ineffectual discourse of hybridity is here an academic correlate of what Canclini calls a 'tranquillising hybridization' (Canclini 2000, p. 48) that the culture industry develops as panacea for putting up with socio-economic disparities. Hybridity lulls us to sleep.

Thus, the discursive replication of hybridity-talk deserves the critical attention it receives, if only to make explicit what is not being said. Gilroy calls for us to find 'an adequate language for comprehending mixture outside of jeopardy and catastrophe' (Gilroy 2000, p. 217). More than descriptive capacity is needed. Gilroy is correct, but for slightly skewed reasons when he declares his hand:

> We do not have to be content with the halfway house provided by the idea of plural cultures. A theory of relational cultures and of culture as relation represents a more worthwhile resting place. That possibility is currently blocked by banal invocations of hybridity in which everything becomes equally and continuously intermixed.
>
> *(Gilroy 2000, p. 275)*

Let us then not be banal. The problem is that any 'resting place', while the culture industry makes all differences equivalent, is a kind of complicity internal to the problem – capitalist encroachment upon all aspects and varieties of life – mixed or stable, it does not matter which. Resting is not an urgent strategy of a struggle that wants to win. Like descriptive and theoretical competence, this means nothing if unable to examine and work past complicity in its own subsumption and suppression. The plurality of cultures, or the truism that everything is hybrid, surely leads to the torturous reasoning of: 'if so, so what?' Stasis.

Is it true that the synthetic figure of the hybrid is the one who emerges as benefiting from a new cultural surplus?[1] Clearly, the schema of hybridity is one that has often thrived on surplus. The descriptive project of theory-making is itself the conceptual surplus enabling any discussion of hybridity or diaspora in the first place. And though this theory production is most often authorized by the benevolence of the national funding of institutes, universities and national literatures, and so on, it has been important to note that migration and movement also produce much cultural product – writing, film, art. Obviously, it has never been that unusual to accept the nation as the fulcrum of production – it has often been productive in cultural and redistributive terms, however monolithic. But has it not always been the case that travel also generates text? What needs to be examined is how the 'texts' of movement articulate with choices made in the interstices between nations, laws and powers; with actual travels, and blockages to travel; with the day-to-day practicalities of struggle in between secure locations. How do discussions of hybridity co-exist with opinions and policy that impact upon everyday, more or less transient, lives and lifestyles? How do imaginings of hybridity and diaspora constitute or construct communities as dynamic objects in the political, cultural and commercial arena?

Writings of diasporic character, so often marketed under the signature of hybridity, have been among the most often acclaimed, and most debated, items in theorizing the socio-political predicament of our times. High-profile intellectual names on the elite conference circuit testify to this: Bhabha, Hall, Gilroy, Spivak. The impact of this investment in theory is critical. For example, in a post-national register, Hall approves hybridity as forcing an 'unwelcome message' (Hall 1995, p. 18) upon Britain, transforming nationalist complacencies for the better. Bhabha calls this a 'third space'. Gilroy is ambivalent, Spivak scathing. The positions are drawn up and the co-ordinates affirmed – for or against the nation, for or against versions of intellectual and practical politics: the stakes are high. In this context, pluralism is the ideology that conscripts various political movements as mere social interests into an alliance that serves the status quo. Such an alliance assures, through minimal concessions, the success of those already in position to benefit from the cosy comforts of magnanimity. Often intellectuals and similarly culturalist commissars are engaged to carefully efface and subsume, or recruited to bourgeois ends, concepts like difference, hybridity, multiculture. Support by impoverished, undervalued, excluded fractions – what was once called the working class – is engineered by pluralist diversity entrepreneurs from the bourgeoisie without corresponding recognition that they are defending their own established privileges and recruiting others to do the same. Alliances between the well-to-do and those who have nothing seem hard to sustain, yet this is exactly what pluralism and diversity demand if it proceeds from where we are now – an uneven and hierarchical domain. Pluralism on the basis of the current distribution would only be to confirm hierarchy, never its undoing.

Maybe it is the mongrel, interfering, mix that undermines racialist absolutism, and it is the corrosive friction of intercourse and exchange that destabilizes purity and property by right. But is it also perhaps the message of hybridity that reassigns fixed identity into what becomes merely the jamboree of pluralism and multiplicity? These contested themes are often played out in hybridity talk. If some kind of hybridity appears, paradoxically, to be a good thing, a more radical analysis is needed to equip organized groups and achieve it in an equitable way.

Note

1 Perhaps only Gayatri Spivak's work has really taken seriously the privilege of this positioning (Spivak 1999). Her discussion of surplus value is best accessed through the essays 'Scattered Speculations on the Question of Value' (in Spivak 1987) and 'Limits and Openings of Marx in Derrida' (in Spivak 1993).

References

Adorno, Theodor 1991 *The Culture Industry: Selected Essays on Mass Culture*, London: Routledge.
Canclini, Nestor Garcia 1995 *Hybrid Cultures: Strategies for Entering and Leaving Modernity*, Minneapolis: University of Minnesota Press.

———— 2000 'The State of War and the State of Hybridization', in Gilroy, Paul, Grossberg, Lawrence and McRobbie, Angela (eds), *Without Guarantees: In Honour of Stuart Hall*, London: Verso, pp. 38–52.

Chow, Rey 1998 *Ethics After Idealism: Theory-Culture-Ethnicity-Reading*, Bloomington: Indiana University Press.

Furedi, Frank 1997 *Population and Development: A Critical Introduction*, Cambridge: Polity Press.

Gilroy, Paul 1994 'Black Cultural Politics: An Interview with Paul Gilroy by Timmy Lott', *Found Object*, 4: 46–81.

———— 2000 *Between Camps*, London: Penguin.

Hall, Stuart 1995 'Black and White Television', in Givanni, June (ed.) *Remote Control: Dilemmas of Black Intervention in British Film and TV*, British Film Institute, pp. 13–28.

Kaur, Raminder and Hutnyk, John 1999 *Travel Worlds: Journeys in Contemporary Cultural Politics*, London: Zed books.

Papastergiadis, Nikos 1998 *Dialogues in the Diaspora: Essays and Conversations on Cultural Identity*, London: Rivers Oram.

Spivak, Gayatri Chakravorty 1987 *In Other Worlds: Essays in Cultural Politics*, New York: Methuen.

———— 1993 *Outside in the Teaching Machine*, New York, Routledge.

———— 1999 *Critique of Postcolonial Reason: Towards a History of the Vanishing Present*, Cambridge: Harvard University Press.

21

THE LIMITS OF CULTURAL HYBRIDITY

On ritual monsters, poetic licence and contested postcolonial purifications

Pnina Werbner

The limits of cultural hybridity

The objection of Islamists to fun and hybridity is comprehensible in terms of the very narrow yardsticks of religious authenticity that they have set themselves. But what are the limits of cultural hybridity for ordinary people? When do ritual masquerades cease to be revitalizing and enjoyable and become unacceptable? When and why do hybrid postcolonial novels cease to be funny and entertaining and become deeply offensive? After all, poetry, including satirical and agonistic poetry, has long been an integral institution in many Muslim societies.

Writing about Moroccan poetry, Geertz (1983: 117) describes it as 'morally ambiguous because it is not sacred enough to justify the power it actually has and not secular enough for that power to be equated to ordinary eloquence'. The Moroccan oral poet, speaking in Arabic, a sacred language, 'inhabits a region between speech types which is at the same time a region between worlds, between the discourse of God and the wrangle of men'.

In other words, Moroccan oral poetry is a hybrid of social discourses in the Bakhtinian sense, and as such disturbing and interruptive.[1] Hence poets must tread a fine line between delightful transgression and real offence. To judge the response of their audience, they must share a whole number of implicit understandings, experiences, and emotional sensitivities to art, poetry, religion, and life. Geertz (1983: 99 *passim*) calls this aesthetic complex a local 'sensibility'. Extending his insight, we may argue that only someone who fully has such a local sensibility can play upon and transgress a local aesthetic without causing offence. However outrageous the Eid ritual sacrificial goat clowns are, they still observe limits; beyond those limits their actions may arouse hostility or even violence.

But postcolonial societies are no longer intimate societies with 'local' aesthetic sensibilities and, as Gluckman would have it, relatively stable notions of legitimate authority. Aesthetic communities are formed in them through and around mass-produced class and sub-cultural consumer goods and 'neo-tribal' lifestyles (Maffesoli 1995). Moreover, as Bourdieu (1984; especially 1993) in particular has argued, the field of high art has been reconstituted as a discrete field of taste and distinction for a discerning and knowledgeable elite of expert critics. It is a field in which competitive innovation and creativity are accorded high value, and in which novelty and avant-garde transgression are highly rewarded. There is thus, he proposes, a constant attempt to create *disjunctions* between elite tastes and those of the *petit bourgeois* masses. At the same time, even avant-garde novelists would like to reach a mass readership.

Postcolonial diasporic literature in English is produced partly within this rarefied postmodern atmosphere, in which novelists such as Salman Rushdie or Hanif Qureshi are part of a wider cosmopolitan literary cohort of writers, novelists, and poets (see Fowler 2000). Like novelists, postcolonial critics too are included within this enchanted circle of refined tasters. The special contribution that South Asian diasporic writers and critics have made to hybridity theory has been, in their own words, to elaborate the hybrid figure of the postcolonial migrant and, alongside that, to create and invent a hybrid literary style that draws on Indian subcontinental words, images, and tropes and weaves them into the English language in delightfully funny, provocative, or disturbing ways.[2] The originality, in particular, of Rushdie's contribution to the world of English literature, measured by elite canons of high taste, has been breathtaking.

Postcolonial novels, Bhabha has argued, serve to 'interrupt' pure narratives of nation. For Bhabha (1994: 142,158), nationalism is never homogeneous and unitary, it is the liminal space created by the permanent *performative* transgression of national grand narratives, eternal and 'pedagogic', by the 'shreds and patches' of the quotidian 'daily plebiscite' of many national voices, by cultural discourses from the margins. Drawing on Derrida, Bhabha locates agency in the act of interruptive enunciation, as we have seen. As Gilroy (1993: 126, 161–2) also argues, what this does is to create a 'double consciousness', a split subject, a fractured reality – doubly framed (Bhabha 1994: 214). To an anthropologist this echoes familiar tropes. Liminal masks, possessed 'lions' or sacrificial goats, ritual clowns as anomalous creatures from beyond the boundaries, all create such double consciousnesses, except that here the discursive setting is the nation and the marginal, hybrid, anomalous, betwixt-and-between, highly potent creatures are postcolonial migrants; or their creative works of high culture.

One might even suggest that the transgressive and reflexive nature of the modern novel is equivalent to the kinds of 'rituals of rebellion' I have described here, an institutionalized, symbolic form of opposition to the established order. In the case of the novel, this sanctified symbolic interruption is one enshrined by 'enlightened' modern bourgeois society. As such, the novel creates dialogical hybridity and reflexiveness without necessarily being seen to pose a serious threat to a liberal social order. One has only to think of the elaborate ceremonials of publicity accompanying the launch of a new novel, its aesthetic design and set-aside spaces (it must not, of course, either be destroyed or taken too seriously) to unmask its hidden ontology: a ritualized object, hedged with taboos, a modern-day equivalent of liminal sacra, of boundary-crossing pangolins or humanized sacrificial goats.

Artistic creativity is not, however, only the prerogative of cosmopolitan postcolonial elites. In Britain there is also a local diasporic poetry in the vernacular, Urdu. *Mushairas*, poetry readings, are extremely popular among Pakistani settlers. Although not written in Arabic and hence not quite as sanctified linguistically as their Arabic counterparts, Urdu poetry combines high art and satire in an unstable, critical, and potentially transgressive mixture. The bigger *mushairas* include Urdu poets renowned both locally and internationally. Much of the poetry is love poems, *ghazals*, which often deploy stock, formulaic phrases, but now and then poets produce commentaries on the diasporic condition itself. Especially good poems are greeted with loud shouts of appreciation. I use two poems recorded at one such event in Manchester, both by local poets, as an example. The first is clearly written from the perspective of a politically conscious proletarian (words in inverted commas were spoken in English):

Migrant Seasons

Friends, in a 'hotel'[a] I have worked and toiled
For my belly, I carried a bucketful of soil[b]

Consumed by summer heat in the deep cold of winter[c]
I wasted my hard-earned labour on 'pubs', 'clubs', and girls.

[a] restaurant [b] worked extremely hard
[c] suffering the heat of the cooking in cold winters

A second poem reveals the sense of loss and nostalgia which first generation Pakistani migrant settlers experience:

'Why is it that only I cannot sleep?'

The bed is warm and the room is cosy
No fear of tomorrow, no work worry
'Ruby' is sleeping, so is 'Rosy'
'Cheeky' is asleep, so is 'Nosy'[a]
It is only I who cannot sleep
Why is it that only I cannot sleep?

[a] nicknames of his children, born and brought up in Britain

The fifth and sixth lines are famous, written by the poet Mirza Ghalib, the nineteenth-century Urdu poet who witnessed the decline of Muslim power and the rise of British colonialism. In the original version the previous line was 'I know death will come one day'. Stunned by the scale of the loss, Ahmed (1997: 45) tells us, 'in an often quoted verse, perhaps one of the first political poems in Urdu, Ghalib vividly reveals the darkness of the Muslim mind confronting the disintegration: "There is no hope in the future / Once I could laugh at the human condition / Now there is no laughter"', and elsewhere (1997: 172), '"There is no solution in sight / Once there was mirth in the heart / Now nothing makes me smile"'.

The poet implicitly evokes the despair of the colonial experience in lamenting his exile:

They all are happy, speaking English
With sweet 'Lancashire' 'accents'.
They do not understand us, nor we them
Even 'communication' is broken
'Ti, tu, ta, tatar'[b] – I do not understand
Why is it that only I cannot sleep?

We cry not just about speaking –
Eating, drinking, washing, sleeping,[c]
How easy to be without God,
How can one be *with* God?[d]
We cannot see our way through this
Why is it that only I cannot sleep?

I went to the 'GP' to tell my woes
They all sleep, but I cannot
So what have you been thinking of?
Only of what has been gained and lost[e]
But even thinking helps me not
Why is it, Oh healer, that only I cannot sleep?

I took a 'valium' last night
I even put 'baan'[f] on my eyes
I've done all I can to find a remedy
Talking about Rumi, Sanai, and Razi[g]
Now no talk helps
Why is it that only I cannot sleep?

I even watched 'television'
And all the 'season' 'Christmas' 'films'
What is the cause of my dead heart?
Having performed the 'recitation'
Still, the heart's voice fails
Why is it that only I cannot sleep?

We like to display our piety
While doing deeds that should not be done
Having done them, we repent
And we repent our repentances
Nor do we feel ashamed
Why is it that only I cannot sleep?

[b] terms of address in Urdu
[c] All these are different in England.
[d] The poet implies that his children have lost their
     faith, and living with them he himself has difficulty
     retaining his Islamic faith in Britain.
[e] by coming to England [f] an ointment
[g] names of famous Muslim poets

Both of these hybrid poems mix English and Urdu words and phrases satirically, while commenting ironically on the predicaments of a poet's exile, in which dreams of success have been displaced by a reality of sweating in restaurant kitchens or failing to communicate with one's children. At the same time, the second poem also expresses a sense of pain and nostalgic yearning for a less hybrid culture and faith. The question is: is this yearning in some sense wrong? Theories that celebrate hybridity as an attack on cultural essentialism and criminalize culture as a source of evil fail to recognize that the matrices of culture are also, for subjects themselves, the matrices of ethical value, responsibility, and shared sociality (see also Lévi-Strauss 1994: 422–3).[3] In the present deconstructive moment, any unitary conception of a bounded culture is pejoratively labelled naturalistic and essentialist. But the alternatives seem equally unconvincing: if 'culture' is merely a false intellectual construction, an inauthentic nostalgic imaginary, or a bricolage of artificially designed capitalist consumer objects, this leaves most postmodern subjects stripped of an ethical life world. One might even argue that cultural hybridity is powerful *because* it originates from that life world and the orders and separations it prescribes. Moreover, ethnic and religious minorities use culture strategically as a rallying banner to demand equal rights and symbolic citizenship in the public domain. Culture thus becomes a tool in an emancipatory battle.

The Satanic Verses

The question of culture versus hybridity came to the fore in debates about the Muslim response to the publication of *The Satanic Verses* and the offence it evidently caused Muslim feelings.

The Satanic Verses was a book about hybridity written in a hybrid mode that challenged both pure theories of religion (Islamic fundamentalism) and pure theories of the nation (racism or cultural racism). But it seemed to spill over beyond the ritualized, sacred domain of high art and to become a political intervention which generated intolerance rather than tolerance. Partly as a result, a critical anthropological literature has evolved that reflects on the limitations of the postcolonial celebration of cultural hybridity and religious syncretism, as though these were panaceas for religious communalism, ethnic racism, and cultural intolerance.

Criticizing a tendency of elite Indian intellectuals such as Nandy (1983; 1990) to see a prior religious syncretism (Hindu, Muslim, or Buddhist) as more tolerant than current fundamentalist Hindu religious revivalist movements, van der Veer (1994) has argued that syncretism disguises inequalities under a veneer of openness and universal eclecticism. There is always, he maintains, a dominant or hegemonic element in syncretic cults, for example, Sufi saints' cults in South Asia or Gandhian universalism, and in practice also unequal participation and inclusion of different groups in such discourses. In relation to *The Satanic Verses,* van der Veer (1997: 102) criticizes Bhabha's (1994: chap. 11) celebration of the book as a great text of migration and self-renewal, and argues that its provocative insulting of the Prophet and the Qur'an simply intensified the marginalization of a Muslim underclass in Britain and Europe, already suffering racism and economic subordination. The image of fanatical Muslims, which their collective response to the novel provoked, set back the course of race relations in Britain and Europe, he says, by many years.

Echoes of van der Veer's position are found in other work by anthropologists, all of whom stress the vulnerability, backwardness, and deprivation of a Muslim diasporic underclass in Britain. It was the sense of alienation and marginalization of this underclass, the argument goes, that pushed them to defend their culture and sacred icons against what was perceived to be a deliberate insult (Asad 1993; Fischer & Abedi 1990; Friedman 1997). Fischer and Abedi (1990) see this response as part of an ongoing class war in Muslim society itself, in which satirical poetry has always been used as a dissenting tool by intellectual elites, while being rejected by *petit bourgeois* conservatives. Friedman (1997) focuses on postcolonial intellectuals in the West whom, he argues, are a small, self-congratulatory elite having little notion of the problems faced by proletarian migrants living in urban poverty. The same point is echoed by Ahmed (1992: 164–6) in his critique of the snobbery and cronyism of this relatively secularized, South Asian Muslim elite. The disjunction and lack of communication between elites and masses is also one stressed by Fowler (2000), who suggests that Rushdie as a novelist was primarily responsive to the demands of the art field for avant-garde innovation. In his ivory tower, he failed entirely to anticipate the wholly negative response to the novel by fellow Pakistanis in Britain, even though the novel was supposedly about them and even though it narrates almost prophetically the reaction to it.

My own response to the book has been somewhat different. First, I have seen no grounds for describing local Pakistanis as merely an underprivileged, deeply religious underclass. In my observation, Pakistanis in the diaspora form an aesthetic community which celebrates 'fun' in the forms of music, dance, satire, and masquerade, much to the disapproval of a relatively small group of religious reformists. Pre-wedding *mehndi* (henna) celebrations by women include ritual masquerading and clowning, in which the women often dress up as disgusting old men and in which arranged marriage, sexuality, and men in general are spoofed and satirized, while romantic love is celebrated in singing and sensual dancing (P. Werbner 1986; 1990: chap. 9; see also Raheja & Gold 1994). The satirical spoofing of Pakistani inter-generational relations in British Pakistani movies such as 'East is East' exemplifies Asian celebration of self-critical, transgressive laughter. Cricket and, as we have seen, poetry readings, are extremely popular pursuits (on cricket and hybridity, see P. Werbner 1996b; 1997b). In addition, Pakistanis in the diaspora consume an unadulterated diet of Bombay films and of audio-cassettes of film music, *bhangra,* or jazzed-up *qawwali* Sufi devotional singing, which are all extremely popular.

My reading of *The Satanic Verses* also differs from the usual run of interpretations. I have argued (P. Werbner 1996a) that the figure of the Prophet depicted in the novel is one of tolerance and almost-perfection, set against a host of counter-selves who are all deeply flawed. The confrontation with, and ultimate execution of, the poet Baal, a figure who is, for most of the novel, entirely devoid of moral fibre despite his artistic talents, highlights the ambiguous authority of amoral poetry *vis-à-vis* religious morality, without resolving this dilemma fully. It also raises the question of the limits of tolerance.

The Satanic Verses is not, then, simply a novel that celebrates hybridity, epitomized by that familiar trope of diasporic writing, the figure of the postcolonial migrant. If this were all the novel was, it would not be worth defending. For Rushdie, migration, *hijra,* is a more profound experience of conversion and ethical search for a new reality. But even if we take the novel as a serious critique of religious intolerance and not just a postmodern spoof, this does not do away with the question of whether it should have been written, and written in such an obscure way that its serious meanings are completely lost to all but a tiny minority of readers. The fact that it appears to be a sacrilegious attack on Islam and the Prophet makes this the truth of the novel for the majority. Given the clash of emotional aesthetics that the novel has created, and the deep offence it generated even among elite and relatively liberal, fun-loving Muslims (at least in Britain), the question that needs to be asked is not whether it challenges a puritanical religious fundamentalism. The real question is this: in a global context, when does transgressive hybridity facilitate, and when does it destroy, communication across cultures for the sake of social renewal?

Conclusion

How does one tread the line of acceptable interruptive hybridity in the postcolonial world? This is a world in which all identities are 'palimpsest', overlaid and reinscribed (Bauman 1997). Given these historical inscriptions and reinscriptions of different subjective identities, differentially positioned, the analysis of postcolonial struggles for authority in public life presents a daunting challenge (see R. Werbner 1996: 4). Debates about cultural hybridity necessarily rest on notions of right and wrong. But in reality, hybridity is not essentially good, just as cultural essentialism is not intrinsically evil. When women or minorities struggle to gain recognition for 'their' culture in the public domain, they are making legitimate claims to symbolic citizenship in the nation-state.

More than just celebrating hybridity, we need to ask whether cultural movements are critical and emancipatory or conservative and exclusive, whether they recognize difference and allow cultural creativity, or deny the right to be different. But poetic licence is not unlimited; to be effective, it must walk the fine line between social languages so that humour is not read as painful mockery. It must retain a local sensibility in a globalizing world. Otherwise, rather than leading to a double consciousness, a global cultural ecumene (Hannerz 1996) which some scholars optimistically evoke, such hybrid transgressions can lead only to a polarization of discourses.

One of the important points arising from the anthropological study of ritual hybrids is that critical consciousness does not necessarily emerge solely from the encounter between discrete cultures or from a position of strangerhood on the margins of the nation. A key issue is that of reflexivity within, as well as in the encounter between, cultures. Ewing (1997: 20) has argued against the assumption by some anthropologists and sociologists of 'a prior [pre-colonial] existence of an unreflective plenitude in which tradition is hegemonic and simply reproduced'. So, too, there have been many instances in the history of the English novel, for example, in which transgressive critiques of the social order have come from within, from English novelists, just as indigenous Moroccan poetry and ritual serve to heighten consciousness of a local moral order beyond the West.

This is where an anthropological theory of hybridity is crucial. It makes clear that the encounter of order with disorder, however culturally constructed, is always contextual and sited, no matter if this be in the micro-political gendered and generational divisions of village life or in the meeting of a local culture and Western colonialism, as in the ceremony by the bridge in modern Zululand. Whether cultural hybridity is generative and fertilizing depends on how its varied audiences interpret it. For some, multiculturalism, cultural borrowings and mixings, constitute an attack on their felt subjectivity. In a world in which local people feel their culture to be under threat from globalizing Western cultural forces or from incoming stranger migrants, interruptive hybridity may be experienced not as revitalizing and fun, but as threatening a prior social order and morality. The line between respect and transgression, as anthropologists studying joking relations have long recognized, is an easy one to cross. This is ever more so in postcolonial nations and the ambivalent encounters they generate.

Notes

1 Interestingly, Bakhtin (1981) denies that poetry can be hybrid, a characteristic he attributes to the novel.
2 Ironically, it was Rudyard Kipling, an English colonial writer, who initiated this exuberant linguistic hybridization, for instance in *Kim*.
3 Thus Lévi-Strauss (1994: 422) says: 'one has to agree to pay the price: to know that cultures, each of which is attached to a lifestyle and value system of its own, foster their own peculiarities, and that this tendency is healthy and not – as people would like to have us think – pathological'.

References

Ahmed, A.S. 1992. *Postmodernism and Islam: predicament and promise*. London: Routledge.
———— 1997. *Jinnah, Pakistan and Islamic identity: the search for Saladin*. London: Routledge.
Asad, T. 1993. *Genealogies of religion*. Baltimore: Johns Hopkins University Press.
Bakhtin, M. 1981. *The dialogic imagination* (trans. C. Emerson & M. Holquist). Austin: University of Texas Press.
Bauman, Z. 1997. The making and unmaking of strangers. In *Debating cultural hybridity: multi-cultural identities and the politics of anti-racism* (eds) P. Werbner & T. Modood, 46–57. London: Zed Books.
Bhabha, H.K. 1994. *The location of culture*. London: Routledge.
Bourdieu, P. 1984. *Distinction*. London: Routledge & Kegan Paul.
———— 1993. *The field of art production*. Cambridge: Polity Press.
Ewing, K. 1997. *Arguing sainthood: modernity, psychoanalysis and Islam*. Durham, N.C.: Duke University Press.
Fischer, M. & M. Abedi 1990. *Debating Muslims*. Madison: University of Wisconsin Press.
Fowler, B. 2000. A sociological analysis of *The Satanic Verses* affair. *Theory, Culture and Society* 17: 1, 39–62.
Friedman, J. 1997. Global crises, the struggle for cultural identity and intellectual porkbarrelling: cosmopolitans versus locals, ethnics and nationals in an era of de-hegemonisation. In *Debating cultural hybridity: multi-cultural identities and the politics of anti-racism* (eds) P. Werbner & T. Modood, 70–89. London: Zed Books.
Geertz, C. 1983. *Local knowledge*. London: Fontana.
Gilroy, P. 1993. *The Black Atlantic: modernity and double consciousness*. London: Verso.
Hannerz, U. 1996. *Transnational connections*. London: Routledge.
Lévi-Strauss, C. 1994. Anthropology, race and politics: a conversation with Didier Eribon. In *Assessing cultural anthropology* (ed.) R. Borowski, 420–9. New York: McGraw-Hill Inc.
Maffesoli, M. 1995. *The time of the tribes*. London: Sage.
Nandy, A. 1983. *The intimate enemy: loss and recovery of self under colonialism*. Delhi: Oxford University Press.
———— 1990. The politics of secularism and the recovery of religious tolerance. In *Communities, riots and survivors in South Asia* (ed.) V. Das, 69–93. New Delhi: Oxford University Press.

Raheja, G.G. & A.G. Gold 1994. *Listen to the heron's words: reimagining gender and kinship in North India.* Berkeley: University of California Press.

Van der Veer, P. 1994. Syncretism, multiculturalism and the discourse of tolerance. In *Syncretism/ anti-syncretism: the politics of religious synthesis* (eds) C. Stewart & R. Shaw, 196–211. London: Routledge.

——— 1997. 'The enigma of arrival': hybridity and authenticity in the global space. In *Debating cultural hybridity: multi-cultural identities and the politics of anti-racism* (eds) P. Werbner & T. Modood, 90–105. London: Zed Books.

Werbner, P. 1986. The virgin and the clown: ritual elaboration in Pakistani weddings. *Man* (N.S.) 21, 227–50.

——— 1990. *The migration process: capital, gifts and offerings among British Pakistanis.* Oxford: Berg.

——— 1996a. Allegories of sacred imperfection: passion, hermeneutics and magic in *The Satanic Verses. Current Anthropology* 37 (Anthropology in Public, supplement), 55–86.

——— 1996b. Fun spaces: on identity and social empowerment among British Pakistanis. *Theory, Culture and Society* 13: 4, 53–80.

——— 1997b. 'The Lion of Lahore': anthropology, cultural performance and Imran Khan. In *Anthropology and cultural studies* (eds) S. Nugent & C. Shore, 34–67. London: Pluto Press.

Werbner, R. 1996. Introduction: multiple identities, plural arenas. In *Postcolonial identities in Africa* (eds) R. Werbner & T. Ranger, 1–26. London: Zed Books.

INTERSECTIONALITY

Introduction

Intersectionality as a concept had its beginnings in feminist theory, and is often traced back, as Avtar Brah says in an essay specially written for this section of the *Reader*, to the work of Kimberlé Williams Crenshaw (1989). However, the concern it reflects – that focusing on conceptual frames such as feminism or diaspora can obscure distinctions *within* those categories – is present in the background of earlier thinking (Brah uses the example of Sojourner Truth's challenge to nineteenth-century American feminism). Ange-Marie Hancock's (2016) study of the intellectual history of inter-sectionality brings an admirable detail and clarity to the topic, and highlights the number of non-governmental organizations (NGOs), social movements and non-profit organizations around the world that have explicitly used intersectional strategies in their activism (37–71).

Within diaspora studies, as is seen in the first section in Part I of this *Reader*, James Clifford's critique of William Safran raised the question of the gendered nature of diasporic experience, and Robin Cohen refers in his taxonomy to what he calls 'a multi-nodal collective identity': aspects of identity-formation, social experience and oppression that constitute the diasporic experience. In other words, diaspora is experienced differentially according to class, gender, race, sexual orientation, caste, age and a number of other determining factors. The use of the verb 'to intersect' is intended to draw attention to the way these factors cut across and influence each other. They form a number of 'axes', to use Avtar Brah's term, and while paying attention to these axes may involve mapping intersecting forms of discrimination, and raise awareness of resistance and resourcefulness in diasporic communities. Intersectionality suggests that the ways in which such communities are conceived need to be more dynamic. Floya Anthias's (1998) essay 'Evaluating "diaspora"' observed that earlier sociological studies of diaspora had not allowed much space for issues of class, gender, age and trans-ethnic alliances, favouring instead some sort of veiled ethnic belonging over any other kind of belonging to transnational categories, such as gender and class; the idea of intersectionality has promoted systematic discussion of how those categories interact.

Since Anthias wrote her essay, intersectionality has informed many studies of diaspora. David L. Eng (2003), for example, assesses American Korean Deann Borshay Liem's 2000 autobio-graphical documentary, *First Person Plural*. Eng explores the way that the issue of transnational adoption confronts us with:

an interlocking set of gender, racial, national, political, economic, and cultural questions. Is the transnational adoptee an immigrant? Is she, as in those cases such as Borshay Liem's, an Asian American? Even more, is her adoptive family Asian American? How is the "otherness" of the transnational adoptee absorbed into the intimate space of the familial? And how are international and group histories of gender, race, poverty, and nation managed or erased within the "privatized" sphere of the domestic?

(1–2)

Like a number of other writers on intersectionality, Eng reflects on the different power relations that are set into play in a given context. In a related manner, two of the essays chosen for this section discuss how far 'queer', as a way of addressing the restrictiveness of categories such as lesbian, gay, bisexual, etc., is related to the contesting, *dis*organizing and rupturing of categories that characterizes intersectionality (see Sullivan 2003; Jagose 1997; and Hall, Jagose, Bebell and Potter 2013). Eve Kosofsky Sedgwick's (1993) widely-cited definition of 'queer', from her 1993 book *Tendencies*, makes clear why the concept can be brought together fruitfully with intersectionality and diaspora. For Sedgwick, queer can signify 'the open mesh of possibilities, gaps and overlaps, dissonances and resonances, lapses and excesses of meaning when the constituent elements of anyone's sexuality aren't made (or can't be made) to signify monolithically' (8). Like sexuality, diaspora cannot be made to signify 'monolithically', and in fact Sedgwick goes on to suggest how 'queerness' can be related to ethnicity, race and postcolonial nationalism.

Avtar Brah's essay, 'Multiple axes of power: Articulations of diaspora and intersectionality', seeks to clarify the notion of intersectionality, outline its usefulness and assess the objections which have been levelled against it. For her, diasporas are necessarily intersectional in nature, since they are cut by gender, race, class, caste, ethnicity and sexuality. She invokes Donna Haraway's (1988) term 'situated knowledge' as a way of seeing diaspora as an articulation of diverse narratives enunciated from various 'situated' positions, and stresses that it is always bound up in 'historically specific modalities of power'. Brah defines four 'axes' through which intersectionality is marked, constructed and maintained in a diasporic context: social relations, identity, subjectivity and experience. While acknowledging that the concept has its critics, some of whom see it as potentially 'exclusionary', she closes by noting that scholarly explorations of intersections can reveal creative processes as well as repressive ones – a point that is also taken up by Gayatri Gopinath and Meg Wesling in their respective essays.

Gayatri Gopinath uses an intimate scene from the film *My Beautiful Laundrette* to examine queer subjects in diaspora, seeing how the 'queer racialized body becomes a historical archive for both individuals and communities'. The controversy surrounding that film's release in 1985 is emblematic of the debates around queer sexuality and dominant notions of communal identity (Gopinath also cites the South Asian Lesbian and Gay Association's battle throughout the 1990s over the right to march in the annual India Day parade in New York City). Queer bodies must be understood in terms of the production and reproduction of notions of 'culture', 'tradition' and communal belonging. Discourses of sexuality, Gopinath argues, are always deeply linked to colonialism, nationalism, racism and migration. Queer diasporic cultural forms and practices seldom indulge in nostalgia for 'home'; rather, they provide a platform for 'clandestine countermemories' which contest the 'fictions of purity' that inhabit nationalistic and diasporic discourses. Furthermore, the oedipal and male underpinnings of diasporic identity (implied even in the diasporic etymology of 'scattered seeds') which elide female diasporic subjects can be disrupted by queer diasporic texts. Gopinath's project is to attend to 'queer female subjectivity in diaspora', rather than privileging the perception of structures of kinship and community as heteronormative and patriarchal. In her book as a whole, which goes on to analyse queer South Asian and South Asian diasporic texts, Gopinath is concerned to reveal how dominant nationalist and diasporic identities are invested in rendering queer female desire and subjectivity 'impossible'.

155

Instead, she shows how queer pleasure and desire emerge precisely from the 'friction between [. . .] various competing discourses'.

Meg Wesling explicitly addresses the relationship between queer theory and diaspora studies, asking what it might mean to 'queer' diaspora studies. She argues for the importance of global mobility and the mobile subject to the understanding of sexuality and gender identity. Wesling points to an increasing number of studies that in the late 1990s and early twenty-first century saw the 'sexile', or gay cosmopolitan subject, as 'exiled from national space'. Both diasporic and queer subjects were seen as challenging and resisting boundaries, and disrupting stable identity categories. In her view, such an identification risks mystifying the material and psychic relations between queerness and diaspora, and overlooking the experience of labour. The diasporic queer subject may appear paradigmatic of globalization in being doubly mobile and transgressive, but the linking of queer and diasporic tends to downplay other intersecting axes such as gender and labour, by treating migration as necessarily transgressive and disruptive of nation, home and family. To this end, Wesling analyses how two visual texts, *Butterflies on the Scaffold* and *Remote Sensing*, imply the unevenness of the way in which locales can be perceived as 'global', and critique 'the political and material conditions of mobility that become the conditions of possibility for sexuality'. One text deals with the sexual trafficking of women across the globe (*Remote Sensing*); the other depicts Cuban drag in a settlement outside of Havana, and locates it within the global economy (*Butterflies on the Scaffold*). Wesling, like some of the critics of hybridity, seeks to test concepts (here those of globalization, diaspora, intersectionality and queerness) against the shifting material, national and global contexts in which they are configured, asking 'how forms of desire and sexual identity that are transgressive in certain contexts can function [. . .] coercively in others'.

References

Anthias, Floya. 1998. 'Evaluating "Disapora": Beyond Ethnicity?' *Sociology* 32 (3): 557–580.

Crenshaw, Kimberlé Williams. 1989. 'Demarginalising the Intersections of Race and Sex: A Black Feminist Critique of Antidiscrimination Doctrine, Feminist Theory, and Antiracist Politics.' *University of Chicago Legal Forum* 1989 (1): 139–167.

Eng, David L. 2003. 'Transnational Adoption and Queer Diasporas.' *Social Text* 21 (3): 1–37.

Hall, Donald. E., Annamarie Jagose, Andrea Bebell, and eds. 2013. *The Routledge Queer Studies Reader*. Abingdon: Routledge.

Hancock, Ange-Marie. 2016. *Intersectionality: An Intellectual History*. Oxford: Oxford University Press.

Haraway, Donna. 1988. 'Situated Knowledges: The Science Question in Feminism and the Privilege of Partial Perspective.' *Feminist Studies* 14 (3): 575–599.

Jagose, Annamarie. 1997. *Queer Theory: An Introduction*. New York, NY: New York University Press.

Sedgwick, Eve Kosofsky. 1993. *Tendencies*. Durham, NC: Duke University Press.

Sullivan, Nikki. 2003. *A Critical Introduction to Queer Theory*. New York, NY: New York University Press.

22

EVALUATING 'DIASPORA'

Beyond ethnicity?

Floya Anthias

The problem of intersectionality: Class, gender, trans-ethnic alliances and power relations

I argued earlier that unless attention is paid to *difference* and then material is presented to show that these differences are transcended by commonalities of one sort or another and in certain contexts, the idea of a community of Jews, Greeks or others even as 'imagined community' cannot be sustained. I have indicated in my discussions of Cohen and Clifford, that there appears to be a general failure to address class and gendered facets within the diaspora problematic. The image of the diasporic individual in Bhabha (1990) is of the cosmopolitan rootless but routed intellectual. This raises the question of class differences: what are the commonalities between a North Indian upper-class Oxbridge-educated university teacher and a Pakistani waiter or grocer? How meaningful is it to refer to them as part of the Asian diaspora in Britain let alone the Asian diaspora more globally?

For Cohen diasporas are particularly adaptive forms of social organisation and they are at a distinctive advantage in the global era: 'Compared with the members of the host society, those who belong to a diaspora characteristically have an advantageous occupational profile . . . they are less vulnerable to adverse shifts in the labour market' (1997:172). This may be true, though Cohen has not provided adequate evidence for it, but it cannot be true of all diasporas and of all the members of particular diasporas. In addition, even if this were true at the substantive level, it does not of itself say anything about the advantages of being a *diaspora,* though it may reflect the economic and cultural capital that members of particular territorial origins may bring with them, the opportunities or exclusions of location and the success of the strategies they have employed to counter disadvantage, such as ethnic communality and gender strategies (Anthias 1992a). The commonality constructed by racism or other factors that determine social positioning is different to that constructed by notions of the shedding of seeds. The *differentiated* ethnicity and cultural syncretism and the different uses to which it is put by different class categories of transnational migrants needs investigating.

Gendering the diaspora

With regard to gender, the role of men and women in the process of accommodation and syncretism may be different. Women are the transmitters and reproducers of ethnic and national ideologies and

157

central in the transmission of cultural rules (Anthias and Yuval Davis 1989). At the same time they may have a different relation to the nation or ethnic group since they are not represented by it and are generally in a subordinate relation to hegemonic men who are also classed (Kandiyoti 1991, Walby 1994, Anthias 1992a). Women may be empowered by retaining home traditions but they may also be quick to abandon them when they are no longer strategies of survival (Anthias 1992a, Bhachu 1988). What is clear is that they experience two sets of gender relations or patriarchal relations, those of their own classed and gendered group and those of the main ethnic group represented in the state.

To what extent do women of all social classes and groupings have access to 'global' thinking, on the one hand, and to what extent do specific gendered social relations lead to a greater incentive for grasping the global mettle, on the other? How central are women to the ethnic projects of diaspora groups? There is a great deal of evidence (Anthias and Yuval Davis 1989, Anthias 1992a, Brah 1996) that the cultural elements around gender, particularly relating to women's roles and sexuality are central concerns of ethnic projects, both inside and outside diasporas. Transnational and trans-ethnic communities of women are key areas of exploration here that have yet to be fully undertaken. However, again, central in any such exercise is the development of the understanding of the relations between gender, ethnicity and nation in order to investigate the gendered nature of diaspora groups: my argument here is that a diaspora is a particular type of ethnic category, one that exists across the boundaries of nation states rather than within them. If the 'diaspora' notion is to claim the capacity to be gendered, it must do this by clarifying the 'ethnic' dimension that lies at its heart.

The issue of gendering the diaspora can be understood at two different levels. At the first level of analysis, it requires a consideration of the ways in which men and women of the diaspora are inserted into the social relations of the country of settlement, within their own self-defined 'diaspora communities' and within the transnational networks of the diaspora across national borders. For example, some of the work done on women migrants and their descendants in employment (Phizacklea 1983, Anthias 1992a, Westwood and Bhachu 1988) within national labour markets is one facet of such a concern. Such work indicates the distinctiveness of the labour market experiences of 'diasporic' women in relation to that of men and is able to investigate the interactions of gender, ethnicity and racialisation in the labour market, for example. It may also be able to address the extent to which the cultural and structural shifts involved for such women produce more emancipatory and liberating experiences, and it may help to fight entrenched systems of gender subordination (or not). However, this focus on the distinctive experiences of diasporic women is only one level of analysis.

The other level of analysis, regarding gendering the diaspora notion, relates to an exploration of how gendered relations are constitutive of the positionalities of the groups themselves, paying attention to class and other differences within the group, and to different locations and trajectories. Such an analysis will consider the ways in which gender relations will enable a group to occupy certain economic niches, for example, or to reproduce dynamically, in a selective way (in terms of the selective accommodation that Clifford refers to) the cultural, symbolic and material relations it lives within. Here gender lies at the very heart of the social order.

I want to summarise an agenda for gendering the diaspora here:

> Firstly, one set of foci could explore the extent to which ethnic cultures are constituted as travelling and syncretic cultures through rules about sex difference, gender roles, sexuality and sexism. This includes the role of the family and other institutions and discursive formations in the reproduction and dynamic transformation of central facets of culture. This also includes specific analyses of the ways in which gender relations mark the boundaries between one group and another and the extent to which

determinants of 'authenticity', of being regarded as a 'true' member of the group, within transnational movements, may be defined through conformity to gender stereotypes. For example a 'true' Cypriot man is one who conforms to gender specific rules concerning sexually appropriate behaviour (Anthias 1989).

Secondly, more substantive work is needed to research the extent to which diasporic or racialised groups (like all subordinated social groups including those of class), may be subjected to two sets of gender relations: those of the dominant society and those internal to the group. For example, gender rules may construct women as mainly responsible for the domestic domain, and endow them with a particular burden of 'femininity' within dominant discourses and practices in the receiving countries, and within the diaspora. However, they may be gendered in different ways within their own ethnic groups, or countries of origin. This suggests that both the gender relations, and the ethnic cultural processes of the group, will be affected by mainstream rules about gender relations. This also entails exploring how the social and economic position of men and women, within the 'diaspora', is partially determined by the ways in which gender relations, both within the ethnically specific cultures of different groups, and within the wider society, interact with one another. This interaction has implications for both the positioning of men and women from these groups, for the whole of the group, and for social relations more generally. These gender relations may produce a particular class structuration for different migrant and ethnic minority groups, in conjunction with labour-market processes and racialisation.

Thirdly, in the case of diasporic groups, women's labour-market participation and their use as cheap or family labour within their own ethnic group may act to counter some of the exclusionary effects of racialised labour markets (Anthias 1983, 1992b). This use of women, which is dependent on strong familial networks, may give rise to particular forms of economic activity and adaptation (such as self-employment, small-scale family enterprises and so on). This is manifested in the development of ethnic economies, small-scale entrepreneurship, and *petit bourgeois* class formation. The forms of the appropriation are culturally specific, however, and work in interplay with local markets (Anthias 1983). They may lead to particular forms of class structuration within the migrant group itself. Researching such issues more extensively may develop understanding of the different incorporation of men and women within the diaspora and the differences between minority ethnic groups.

Fourthly, a further set of foci, relates to issues of state and nation. Some analyses have suggested that women may have a different relation to the nation, and the nationalist project, as well as to globalisation processes. For example, in my own work, I have argued that women may be related to the project of the nation in diverse ways: as mothers of patriots, as symbolic of boundaries and as carrier of culture (for an analysis see Anthias and Yuval Davis 1989). Women are often used to symbolise the nation, depicting it as a woman mourning her loss. One example is found in the case of Cyprus (Anthias 1989). After the 1974 coup and Turkish invasion of the island, posters appeared everywhere of a black clothed woman weeping, but bravely with fist held high, and the caption underneath read 'Cyprus, our martyred motherland'. How does diasporic positionality relate to these processes?

A further dimension of such a set of foci would explore the multi-faceted relations of gender and the state. On the one hand, women may be constructed by the state as members of collectivities, institutions or classes. They may be seen, alongside men, as participants in the social forces that set the state its given political projects in any specific historical context (Anthias and Yuval Davis 1989), and as an integral category within wider social forces. On the other hand, they may be relegated to the private sphere and be a special focus of state concerns. This may be exemplified by special rules denoting their role in human reproduction, by particular kinds of ideological and discursive positioning, and by particular forms of economic incorporation. Furthermore, diasporic women may be constructed as outside the proper boundaries of the nation and, through racialisation, may be positioned in a particularly disadvantageous position in social relations, having limited rights to citizenship (Anthias and Yuval Davis 1989).

The kinds of foci for gendering the diaspora, suggested above, pinpoint the need, in substantive research, for a framework that pays full attention to the centrality of gender on the one hand, and to intersectionality, on the other. Firstly it may be possible to see ethnicity, gender and class as crosscutting and mutually *reinforcing* systems of domination and subordination, particularly in terms of processes and relations of hierarchisation, unequal resource allocation and inferiorisation (Anthias 1996, 1998). Racialised or diasporic working-class women may be particularly subordinated, through an articulation of social divisions, which produces a coherent set of practices of sub-ordination within a range of social, economic and political contexts. Secondly, the intersections of ethnicity, gender and class may construct multiple, uneven and *contradictory* social patterns of domination and subordination; human subjects may be positioned differentially within these social divisions. For example, white working-class men may be seen to be in a relation of dominance over racialised groups, and over women, but may themselves be in a relation of subordination in class terms. This leads to highly contradictory processes in terms of positionality and identity. The exploration of *reinforcing aspects of the divisions, and their contradictory articulations,* opens up fundamental political questions also. In other words the discussion of connecting social divisions is not purely theoretical. It has a direct relevance in terms of how inequalities, identities and political strategies are conceptualised and assessed.

Trans-ethnicity

Diaspora has a transnational referent: that is certain. But its capacity to be trans-ethnic in terms of forging solidary bonds with crosscutting groups, both from within the dominant category or with other groups also on the margins, is more difficult to sustain. A truly trans-ethnic solidarity must reject all forms of ethnic fundamentalism, for it requires dialogue. If for Cohen, diasporic groups are old forms of social organisation that precede and will outlive the nation state and particularly 'fit' with the new global era, then it is the old solidaristic bonds of a deterritorialised ethnicity that are central: trans-ethnicity is not on the agenda. If for Clifford and others from within the postmodern frame, to borrow Ali Rattansi's words (Rattansi 1994), the diasporic condition leads to breaking the essentialised mould of the nation and the indigene, then why is the theme of home and homing such a powerful metaphor in this approach?

To what extent is the hailing of the commonality of black diaspora across space (found in the work of Gilroy 1993), conducive to forging inter-ethnic bonds between Caribbeans and other groups who share a social and economic position within a particular nation state and across the boundaries of nation states? Asians and Afro Caribbeans are both racialised albeit in different ways. To claim *transnational* bonds for the African diaspora may function to politically weaken *trans-ethnic* bonds with other groups sharing a more local or national context of contestation and struggle. The question is then raised about the capacity of the diaspora claim for entailing the political mobilisation of racialised, subordinated or oppressed groups within nation states. It also raises the question of the forms of political mobilisation, in an international context, if they are to be mediated by claims to ethnic commonality which may have precedence over struggles around economic and other material resources.

Regarding trans-ethnicity as hybridity there are a number of difficulties that I have explored elsewhere (Anthias 1997), particularly with regard to the conception of 'culture' that is involved. The main problems relate to the assumption that non-diasporic ethnic culture is itself non-hybrid, and constituted as an essence; that cultural elements can all freely mix through the voluntaristic agency of individuals; that all cultural components are compatible and therefore a pick-and-mix of elements is possible; that all components of the cultural *melange* are equal in terms of power and that all subjects have equal access to the totality of cultural components. A range of questions are then raised:

1   Under what conditions is a synthesis of cultural elements possible?
2   Which elements of culture become destabilised?
3   To what extent do groups seek to affirm their existing identity in the face of threat by the receiving culture?
4   Which social groups are most reluctant to negotiate their cultural rules and which aspects of culture do they wish to protect?
5   Are some aspects of culture more difficult to 'mix'?
6   How important are the institution of the family and kinship, the position of women and religious and moral rules, particularly around sexuality, for this?
7   What are the difficulties encountered in terms of 'translation'?
8   To what extent is there a truly politically radicalising potential in this 'condition' and what are the different forms that the condition takes?

Conclusion

Through an examination of some of the terms that are prominent in research on issues of transnational migration and settlement, it is evident that the categories we use have implications for defining the bounds of the object and the social relations around it.

The resurrection of the old term 'diaspora' has been partially prompted by the impasse that the notions of 'racial and ethnic minorities' created with their emphasis on inter-group processes and their static notions of culture and difference. Diaspora draws part of its impetus from the difficulties identified with existent ethnic and 'race' paradigms, particularly with regard to recognising highly differentiated transnational population movements and synthetic or 'hybrid' forms of identity. [. . .]

The concept of 'diaspora', however, cannot replace a concern with racialised social relations. I have argued in fact that 'diaspora' turns the analytical gaze away from the dimensions of trans-ethnic relations informed by power hierarchies and by the cross-cutting relations of gender and class. The relationship between forms of exclusion, and indeed differentiated inclusion, and the emergence of diasporic solidarity and political projects of identity, on the one hand, and dialogue (as in hybridisation), on the other, are important foci for research. Such hybridisations may be uncomfortable as well as empowering, alienating as well as emancipatory. The contours of these need much more research. The research needs to be undertaken not only in terms of 'cultural syncretism' but also in terms of the relations of subordination and exclusion embodied in 'ethnic', 'race', class and gender processes.

'Diaspora' has turned the gaze to broader social relations that can encompass politics, economy and culture at the global, rather than national level. It pays attention to the dynamic nature of ethnic bonds, and to the possibilities of selective and contextual cultural translation and negotiation. However, the lack of attention to issues of gender, class and generation, and to other inter-group and intra-group divisions, is one important shortcoming. Secondly, a critique of ethnic bonds is absent within diaspora discourse, and there does not exist any account of the ways in which diaspora may indeed have a tendency to reinforce absolutist notions of 'origin' and 'true belonging'. Finally, the lack of attention given to trans-ethnic solidarities, such as those against racism, of class, of gender, of social movements, is deeply worrying from the perspective of the development of multiculturality, and more inclusive notions of belonging. For a discourse of anti-racism and social mobilisation of a trans-ethnic (as opposed to transnational) character, cannot be easily accommodated, within the discourse of the diaspora, where it retains its dependence on 'homeland' and 'origin', however reconfigured. Unless used with caution, it may close the space of interrogating inter-ethnic allegiances within the nation state, the systematic appraisal of forms of racism, and the problems of anti-racist strategy, both within, and outside, national borders. It fails to provide a radical critique of ethnic rootedness and belonging, as exclusionary mechanisms, in social relations. It also fails to provide a systematic theorisation of the intersections between ethnicity, gender and class.

The critical eye I have cast on the notion of diaspora indicates that the concept of 'diaspora' can only act as a heuristic advance if it is able to overcome the very problems found in earlier notions of ethnicity. It therefore needs to be formulated within a paradigm of 'social divisions and identities' (Anthias 1996, 1998) that is able to treat collective solidaristic bonds as emergent and multiple, and to acknowledge the political dynamics of these processes. Such an approach requires looking at the location of 'ethnic' solidary bonds within other ontological spaces, such as those of gender and class, and must pay full attention to issues of power. A refining and reworking of the terms we use is urgent, but, as we have seen, given the complexity of the phenomena, it is not an easy task. Clearing the space for such an enterprise is but a beginning.

References

Anthias, F. 1983. 'Sexual Divisions and Ethnic Adaptation: Greek Cypriot Women in Britain', in A. Phizacklea (ed.), *One Way Ticket*. London: Routledge & Kegan Paul.

Anthias, F. 1989. 'Women and Nationalism in Cyprus', in N. Yuwal-Davis and F. Anthias (eds), *Women, Nation, State*. Basingstoke: Routledge.

Anthias, F. 1992a. *Ethnicity, Class, Gender and Migration*. Aldershot: Avebury.

Anthias, F. 1992b. 'Connecting "Race" and Ethnic Phenomena', *Sociology* 26: 421–38.

Anthias, F. 1996. *Rethinking Social Divisions*. Inaugural lecture series, Greenwich University Press.

Anthias F. 1997. 'Globalisation, Hybridity and Diaspora: Debates on Culture'. Paper given to Conference on 'Globalisation and Ethnicity: Challenges to the Nation State?' ASEN, LSE.

Anthias, F. 1998. 'Rethinking Social Divisions: Some Notes Towards a Theoretical Framework', *Sociological Review* 46(2): August.

Anthias, F. and Yuval Davis, N. 1989. 'Introduction', in N. Yuval Davis and F. Anthias (eds), *Woman, Nation State*. Basingstoke: Macmillan.

Bhabha, H. 1990. *Nation and Narration*. London: Routledge.

Bhachu, P. 1988. 'Apni Marzi Kardhi: Horne and Work: Sikh Women in Britain', in S. Westwood and P. Bhachu (eds) *Enterprising Women*. London: Routledge.

Brah, A. 1996. *Cartographies of the Diaspora*. London: Routledge.

Cohen, R. 1997. *Global Diasporas: An Introduction*. London: UCL Press.

Gilroy, P. 1993. *The Black Atlantic*. London: Verso.

Kandiyoti, D. (ed.) 1991. *Women, Islam and the State*. Basingstoke: Macmillan.

Phizacklea, A. 1983. *One Way Ticket*. London: Routledge & Kegan Paul.

Rattansi, A. 1994. 'Modern Racisms, Racialised Identities', in A. Rattansi and S. Westwood (eds), *Racism, Modernity and Identity*. Cambridge: Polity.

Walby, S. 1994. 'Is Citizenship Gendered?', *Sociology* 28: 379–95.

Westwood, S. and Bhachu, P. (eds) 1988. *Enterprising Women*. London: Routledge.

23

MULTIPLE AXES OF POWER

Articulations of diaspora and intersectionality

Avtar Brah

It is evident that migrations form a key phenomenon in the contemporary globalised world. According to figures from the Organisation for Economic Co-operation and Development-United Nations Department of Economic and Social Affairs (OECD-UNDESA) there were 232 million international migrants living in the world in 2013. The proportion of female migrants ranged from 52% in the global north to 43% in the global south. The UN Sustainable Development web site (United Nations 2016) notes that the number of migrants living abroad worldwide reached 244 million in 2015. This figure includes 20 million refugees. These global migrants range from economic migrants, through trafficked persons to refugees and asylum seekers (Braziel and Mannur 2003; Braziel 2008; Knott and McLoughlin 2010). These migrations create a plethora of diasporas. Of course, not all migrations comprise diasporas. There has been considerable debate surrounding the criteria that may be used to define a particular migration as a diaspora. Scholars such as William Safran (1991), James Clifford (1994) and Robin Cohen ([1997] 2008) have been centrally involved in these discussions. At minimum, diasporas are not temporary sojourns; rather they are about settling down elsewhere, putting roots and creating a 'home' away from the place of origin. Over the last two decades, considerable effort has gone into theorising and analysing different formations of diaspora. There have been major shifts in conceptualising diaspora with dynamic conceptions acquiring greater salience (Hall 1990; Bhabha 1994; Brah 1996; Cohen [1997] 2008; Gilroy 1993). The study of diasporas is largely a transdisciplinary endeavour. I have sought to describe transdisciplinarity as 'creolised theory'. That is to say that, analysis of diasporic projects calls for the use of conceptual tools and analytical insights from different subject disciplines, theoretical paradigms and political movements.

Diaspora/Intersectionality articulations

It is my claim in this article that diasporas are inherently intersectional, and that the study of diaspora and intersectionality is intrinsically connected. For instance, as an empirical trajectory diaspora cannot be understood as a homogeneous category. A specific diaspora is differentiated according to factors such as gender, race, class, caste, ethnicity and sexuality. As a concept too, diaspora is an articulation of diverse narratives enunciated from various 'situated' positions, or from a 'situated and embodied knowledge' to use the formulation posed by Donna Haraway (1988). This 'positionality of location' is one of dispersal along multiple axes of differentiation.

And the situated positions and knowledges are the terrains upon which the embodiment of our specificity is constructed. We become a 'woman', a 'classed individual' or a 'gay person' in and through the interplay of intersecting axes of differentiation. I have argued elsewhere that the concept of diaspora centres on the configurations of historically specific modalities of power which undergird, mark and differentiate diasporas internally as well as situate them in relation to one another (Brah 1996). The concept of diaspora is a genealogical one, and it signals the historically variable analysis of economic, political and cultural forms in their inter- and intra-relationality. That is to say, this genealogical analysis is intersectional. There is some concern in the field of diaspora studies that the concept of diaspora overemphasises mobilities, and that routes are foregrounded at the expense of roots. In my view the two aspects are not mutually exclusive: diasporas are simultaneously about 'space' and 'place', about movement as well as settling down and 'living side by side' as Bhabha (2013) puts it. It is important to pay attention to both features of diaspora. I have described articulation of the 'genealogies of dispersal' with those of 'staying put' as 'diaspora space'. Within this conception of 'diaspora space' multi-locationality, home, homing desire and belonging are juxtaposed with historical temporalities and diasporic spatialities. How does a site of migration become home? How do we come to 'feel at home'? This is a complex question, one which brings the social and the psychic simultaneously into play. A home, whether in the sense of a dwelling in which we reside or a country or region in which we live, is often *assumed* to be a 'safe' place, but this is not always the case, something which physically and psychologically abused persons know all too well. In terms of a nation-state, a region or locality immigrants may reside in a given place but they may often be constructed and represented as the 'Other'. They may experience all manner of discrimination. They could be denied citizenship rights. Or, they may have legal rights but may not be seen to belong to the larger community or the nation. There could well be terror on the streets directed against racialised, ethnicised people who may or may not be immigrants. All this mitigates against 'feeling at home' on the part of diasporic groups. Yet there are also the intimacies of everyday life – kinship bonds, friendships, relations of conviviality, neighbourliness, collegiality, inter-connections of love – which make a place a home. Feeling at home is essentially about feeling secure and having a sense of belonging – but this cannot be taken for granted, may have to be struggled over, and it is an on-going project rather than a once-and-for-all established fact. The concept of diaspora space addresses the complexity of encounters between those who have migrated and those others who might regard themselves as indigenous. Diaspora space emphasises the interactions between the psychic and the social, between subjectivity and identity, and between the material, the imaginary and the imaginative. As Kim Knott (2010) notes:

> It is necessary, then, for scholars of diaspora to adopt and work with a multidimensional understanding of space and movement that does not restrict to actual physical migration but makes room also for imagined, discursive, material, cultural, virtual, and socially net-worked places and travels [. . .]. A key challenge for diaspora studies is to engage with the realities of settlement, the political contingencies and relationships of diaspora space, as well as the narratives of travel and circulation, and the location of diasporic subjectivity.
>
> *(79–83)*

So far, I have been concerned with issues to do with diaspora. But what do we mean when we invoke the term intersectionality? Where does this idea and concept emerge from? The concept of intersectionality has been mobilised primarily within feminist discourse and practice. It grew out of feminist critiques of those discourses which failed to address the fact that 'woman' is a heterogeneous category. There were class differences amongst women. Different groups of women were differently racialised. Women comprised different ethnicities. They were hetero-sexual, queer or trans. They were rich or poor, and so on. These have been longstanding debates which remain relevant today not only because they highlight and signal diversity, important though that fact is, but because they raise the somewhat contentious issue as how best to theorise and understand such differences. That challenge is equally pertinent today, every time we embark on a new study. In what ways do we tackle the concept of 'difference' and how is it best to analyse clusters of differences across various and variable but intersecting dimensions? I shall return to this point.

In 2004, Ann Phoenix and I wrote about the discourses on intersectionality, and we started with nineteenth-century debates which pre-empt what today goes by the name of intersectionality. We started the article with the well-known nineteenth-century locution in the USA, 'Ain't I a woman?', and I wish to start with it again for it places questions of intersectionality into stark relief. Nineteenth-century contestations among feminists involved anti-slavery struggles and campaigns for women's suffrage, and they showed how untenable essentialist notions of the category 'woman' / 'man'/ 'trans'/ 'intersex' are. These categories and positionalities are inscribed within and across social divisions such as racism, gender, ethnicity, sexuality and disability. Ann Phoenix and I described the concept of 'intersectionality' as 'signifying the complex, irreducible, varied and variable effects which ensue when multiple axes of differentiation – economic, political, cultural, psychic, subjective and experiential – intersect in historically specific contexts' (Brah and Phoenix 2004). I still hold to this way of looking at intersectionality. It challenges the additive models of discussions on the subject. There are those who argue that debates on intersectionality fail to take on board issues of colonialism, imperialism and postcolonialism. But this patently would not be the case in the above definition. Historically specific relations categorically address questions of colo-niality, postcoloniality and imperialisms in their various varieties. There is also academic criticism that intersectional studies may not always attend to transnational and global concerns (Purkayastha 2010; Anthias 2012). This is an important point, yet when *diasporic* intersectional analysis is con-ducted questions of transnationalism become central. Scholars such as Jasbir K. Puar have drawn attention to the importance of the postrepresentional, posthuman or postsubject conceptualisations of the body which interrogate the emphasis on the 'subject' in much intersectional theorisation, including my own (Puar 2012). I am sympathetic to several aspects of her critique but would suggest that such alternatives as the postsubject perhaps decentre but do not replace the 'subject'.

A recent helpful definition of 'intersectionality' has been provided by Patricia Hill Collins and Sirma Bilge (2016). They note:

> Intersectionality is a way of understanding and analyzing the complexity in the world, in people and, in human experiences. The events and conditions of social and political life and the self can seldom be understood as shaped by one factor. They are generally shaped by many factors in diverse and mutually influencing ways. When it comes to social inequality, people's lives and the organization of power in a given society are better understood as being shaped not by a single axis of social division, be it race, or gender or class, but by many axes that work together and influence each other. Intersectionality as an analytic tool gives people better access to the complexity of the world and of themselves.
>
> *(2)*

It is worth pointing out that the question 'Ain't I a woman?' was first articulated by Sojourner Truth, a woman freed from slavery. She took this name, instead of her original name Isabella, when she became a travelling preacher. It is also important to bear in mind that the first anti-slavery society was formed in 1832 by Black women in Salem, Ohio in the USA. Yet a decade later, Black women were absent from the Seneca Falls Anti-Slavery convention of 1848 where White middle-class women debated the motion for women's suffrage. Sojourner Truth campaigned for both the abolition of slavery and women's rights, and her speech at the 1851 Women's Rights convention in Akron, Ohio addressed these two forms of oppression as her primary target. Referring to the prevailing codes of sexualised chivalry amongst white communities, this ex-slave said:

> That man over there says that women need to be helped into carriages, and lifted over ditches, and to have the best place everywhere. Nobody helps me into carriages, or over mud-puddles, or gives me any best place! And ain't I a woman? Look at me! Look at my arm! I have ploughed and planted, and gathered into barns, and no man could head me! And ain't I a woman? I could work as much and eat as much as a man – when I could get it – and bear the lash as well! And ain't I a woman? I have borne thirteen children, and seen most all sold off to slavery, and when I cried out with my mother's grief, none but Jesus heard me! And ain't I a woman?
>
> *(https://sourcebooks.fordham.edu/mod/sojtruth-woman.asp)*

This speech had a resounding impact at the conference and it circulated widely amongst political activists and other opinion makers. What is particularly significant is that it embodies a powerful critique of pre-capitalist economic, political and cultural relations. It castigates dehumanising effects of patriarchal gender relations and racism in slave societies. Its powerful diasporic imagination poses a challenge to hegemonic moves of all kinds, and it remains pertinent today. It pre-figures contemporary debates on the interlinks between racism, gender, pre-capitalist social relations, sexuality, questions of embodiment and so on.

The second half of the twentieth century witnessed a variety of social movements – anti-colonial struggles for independence, Civil Rights and Black Power movements, Peace movements, Student protests, the Workers' Movements. Together, they expressed a serious disaffection with the vision of a centred universal subject of humanism. Within the academy, critiques of the self-referencing, unified subject of modernity flourished across academic disciplines. Within feminism, there was a systematic decentring of the 'normative subject' of other earlier phases of feminism. One of the first of such critiques was that mounted in 1977 by the Combahee River Collective, the Black lesbian feminist organisations from Boston, USA. They spoke against the many ways in which the experience of women who were not white, middle class or heterosexual was marginalised. Importantly for subsequent discussions of inter-sectionality, they argued against privileging a single dimension of experience as if it were the whole of life. Instead they spoke of being 'actively committed to struggling against racial, sexual, heterosexual and class oppression' and advocated 'the development of integrated analyses and practice based upon the fact that the major systems of oppression are interlocking' (Combahee River Collective 1977). This conceptualisation of 'interlocking oppressions' was one of the most productive insights of post-World War Two feminism. At the same time, while lesbian feminist activists were challenging the heteronormative focus of much feminist writing and politics, they were themselves being taken to task for treating some women's experiences as if they were marginal. In the anthology, *This Bridge Called My Back: Writings by Radical Women of Colour,* Cherríe Moraga and Gloria Anzaldúa (1981) argued that lesbian feminism itself was enacting exclusions and overlooking the experience of lesbians of colour by not fully taking on board issues of racism. According to Kira Kosnic, there would seem to be similar reservations about and within queer studies today (Kosnick in Lutz *et al.* 2011), although increasingly queer studies is using intersectional analyses of heteronormativity (Braziel 2008). Queer intersectional studies, Kosnick argues, bring a deconstructive/post-structuralist perspective to bear upon intersectional modalities of subordination and privilege.

In Britain during the 1970s similar issues were raised by women who formed a coalition of Women of African, Caribbean and Asian heritage under the common emblem of the 'Black'. They formed an organisation called OWAAD – Organisation of Women of Asian and African Descent. Its member organisations worked around a wide variety of issues such as wages and conditions of paid work, immigration law, fascist violence, reproductive rights, domestic violence and many manifestations of racism and class inequality. It foregrounded unequal global relations between North and South in its postcolonial formations. It undertook 'integrated analysis' of racism, gender and class whilst remaining sensitive to questions of cultural specificities. Yet it took very little notice of lesbian and gay concerns. And when these concerns were raised at a conference, it created a huge controversy. During the 1970s and 1980s the major contestation between what was then known as 'black' and 'white' feminisms prefigured later theories of 'difference' and those of intersectionality.

Thinking through difference

There have been many debates about questions of difference. Apart from the commonsense binary of difference/commonalities there are other meanings associated with different discourses of difference. Who has the power to define difference? What is the nature of the normativities to which difference is ascribed? By what processes is difference marked, constructed, maintained or eroded? How are social groups represented in varying discourses? How are hierarchies of difference powered? What are the effects of social difference on the constitution of psychic modalities? Such questions have produced the terrain where new ways of thinking about difference can be considered.

Diaspora studies and intersectionality share a common focus on difference. It is within the crucible of difference that the two categories converge. Much has been written on the subject of difference across different disciplines. In my own case, I have tried to work through this concept by suggesting that difference may be theorised along four axes: difference construed in terms of a social relation; difference understood as subjectivity; difference theorised as identity; and difference conceptualised as experience (Brah 1996). Importantly, each of these axes is in turn marked by intersectionality. Although for analytic purposes these axes are presented as separate, they cross-cut and enmesh in practice. Experience, for instance, cannot be understood independently of social relations, nor do social relations exist without bearing on identity and subjectivity. Indeed, the four axes are centrally implicated in the constitution of each other.

As a social relation, difference is to be understood in structural terms along economic, political and cultural discourses and institutional practices. Here it references the macro and micro regimes of power within and across which forms of differentiation such as class, racism and gender, for instance, are produced as structured formations. Social relations foreground systemic and systematic dimensions of social hierarchies and regimes of power. Structural features undergird our social positions and mark the many and variable ways that historical genealogies impact on everyday experiences. Social relations such as difference underscore the structured materiality of social life.

In terms of the second axis of difference, namely subjectivity, we need to explore the means by which the subject is produced. Here, the linguistic approach has been especially influential, analysing 'difference' (as in relation to Derrida's *différance*) which is at the very heart of language itself, at the centre of meaning production. Though of course the question of affect and emotion and preverbal experiences remains critical even as language remains important in making verbal sense of these experiences. Within Saussurian and post-Saussurian linguistics, language represents a way of differentiating between things and relating them to one another. It is argued that meaning is neither intrinsic nor referential; rather it is relational and differential. That is to say, each sign derives its meaning from its difference from all other signs in the chain. As we develop our sense of ourselves in and through language, language is the site of the formation of sub-jectivity. Issues of 'difference' have therefore figured prominently in debates about subjectivity. These debates have been accompanied by various critiques of humanist conceptions of the subject as a unified, unitary, rational and rationalist 'point of origin', as centred in consciousness, and in terms of the Universal Man as the embodiment of an ahistorical essence. Post-structural approaches question the view that consciousness is an origin, treating it instead as an effect of signification (Belsey 2002; Weedon 1987). Overall, in relation to subjectivity, there has been considerable contestation about the relative merits of critical discourse analysis as compared with psychoanalytic approaches to the constitution of subjects and subjectivity. I believe that both approaches are relevant. Psychoanalysis too disrupts a notion of a centred, unitary rational self by foregrounding an inner world permeated by fantasy, conflict, non-rational and unruly responses, and desire. Difference as subjectivity, then, is neither unified nor fixed but fragmented, and continuously in process.

In relation to the third axis of difference, namely difference understood as experience, this is yet another arena of debate, as the concept of experience has been highly contested. It is now generally agreed that experience is not transparent. In other words it does not transparently reflect a pre-given reality, it is not an unmediated guide to some pre-given transparent truth. Rather, experience is a cultural construction and it is the site of subject formation. Indeed experience is a process of signification which is the very condition for the constitution of that which we call 'reality'. Experience, as a signifying or meaning-making practice, is embedded within symbolic and narrative means of making sense. This links with the idea of diaspora as a confluence of diverse and different narratives, both complimentary and contradictory. As I have argued before, experiences do not happen to a fully constituted subject, rather experience is the site of subject formation. Experience is mediated through intersectional formations such as our positionality in terms of gender, class, generation, sexuality and so on. As Joan W. Scott (1992) argues, conceptualising experience 'entails processes of identity formation, insisting on the discursive nature of experience, and on the politics of construction. Experience is at once always already an interpretation and in need of interpretation' (37).

Finally we may consider 'difference' understood as identity. Indeed struggles over identities are in part contestations over meaning. The problematic of 'difference' is also the problematic of identity. As Stuart Hall (1996), drawing on Derrida's concept of *différance*, suggests, identity is always in process and not an established fact. He raises the question:

> If 'identities' can only be read against the grain – that is to say, specifically *not* as that which fixes the play of difference in a point of origin and stability, but as that which is constructed in or through *différance* and is constantly destabilised by what it leaves out, then how can we understand its meaning and how can we theorize its emergence?
>
> *(5)*

Although he is persuaded by the Foucauldian notion that the subject is constructed in discourse, Hall remains cautious in so far as this perspective fails to fully address how and why the subject identifies with some subject positions and not others. His answer, like that of Judith Butler, is to advocate the use of psychoanalysis alongside the discursive approach for the task of thinking through the problematic of identity.

As I noted earlier, the four axes of difference just described always articulate. For example, identities are inscribed through experiences which are culturally constructed within social relations. Subjectivity – our sense of ourselves and of our relation to the world – is the modality in which the precarious or contradictory nature of the subject in process is experienced as identity. Hence, identity is neither fixed nor singular; rather it is a changing relational multiplicity that assumes a specific pattern, as in a kaleidoscope, against particular sets of personal and socio-historical circumstances. But, I think that it is important to differentiate between identity as it pans out in its intimate relationship with unconscious processes of subjectivity, and the highly conscious and reflexive acts of political identity. Political identity is a conscious avowal of specific positions.

Diasporic contestations

So far I have argued that questions of intersectionality have been directly or indirectly tied up with theorisation of the concept of difference that intersectionality shares with the concept of diaspora. Having explored issues associated with 'difference', I now turn attention to some key debates surrounding the notion of intersectionality. Although, as we saw earlier, the concept of social divisions and that of the articulation of different axes of power have been around for a long time, the term 'intersectionality', as we know it today within feminism, was coined by Kimberlé Williams Crenshaw in 1989. Her primary focus was on legal studies, but since then the term has gained currency across a number of disciplines across the humanities and social sciences, although primarily through the lens of feminist studies. It is now widely accepted that intersectional analysis explores how different axes of differentiation articulate at multiple and, crucially, on simultaneous levels in the emergence of context-specific modalities of exclusions, inequality and subject formation. The term has been valorised not only within the academy, but has also made a significant impact in policy circles during the last decades. For example, during 2001, Kimberlé Crenshaw was invited to the World Conference Against Racism in Durban in South Africa to discuss her ideas. Nira Yuval-Davis (2006) notes that during the non-governmental organisation (NGO) session of the conference, Radhika Coomarswamy, the special rapporteur of the UN secretariat on violence against women, stated how the term 'intersectionality' had become extremely popular and used in various UN and NGO forums. Indeed, at the 58th session of the UN Commission of Human Rights on 23 April 2002, the resolution on the human rights of women in its first paragraph stated that it: 'recognised the importance of examining the intersection of multiple forms of discrimination, including their root causes from a gender perspective' (Resolution E/CN.4/2002/l.59).

Within the European Union, anti-discrimination policy was embedded in the legislation of those countries that had not as yet incorporated it. The process of the adaptation of the European Non-Discriminatory Directives into the national law of member states allowed for a discussion of multiple forms of discrimination and the intersectionality approach was debated for the first time. Hence, according to the European Commission Report of 2007, a certain notion of multiple discrimination is characterised as 'intersectional discrimination' (European Commission 2007).

Overall, as Collins and Bilge (2016) note, intersectionality frameworks are utilised not only within diverse academic disciplines, but also by human rights activists, government officials, grassroots organisations, bloggers on digital and social media, and practitioners in education and welfare. They discuss its global dispersion across these fields.

Within the academy, there has been a proliferation of discourses of intersectionality, especially, within feminism. In recent years, an increasing number of special issues of journals, books, conferences, PhD courses and programmes have been devoted to the study of the topic.

Despite its popularity in certain circles, intersectionality has not, as we noted earlier, been without its critics. I have already mentioned that at a debate held at a conference at Goldsmiths ('Feminist Genealogies' conference held on 11 May 2012) some scholars such as Beverly Skeggs considered that the preoccupation with intersectionality draws attention away from the relevance of colonialism and imperialism, but my position is that this is far from the case. Skeggs also suggests that it deflects attention from work on social class. I am not clear how this criticism can be sustained given that social class is considered a crucially important feature of intersectionality. In line with this, it is also alleged that intersectionality emphasises categories of identity at the expense of structures of inequality. But, axes of differentiation may not be understood as identity categories but rather as modalities of asymmetrical power. Another criticism, which has some validity, has been whether the metaphor of 'intersection' – with its image of roads crossing – is adequate for the critical task of analysing power differentials, normativities and identity formation across multiple fields of gender, racism, class, sexuality and so on. Scholars such as Kum Kum Bhavnani prefer the term 'configuration' rather than 'intersection'. But if intersection is seen as an *articulation*, the term may remain productive. There has also been some reservation as to whether or not there is a need for a specific theory and methodology of 'intersectionality' (Nash 2008). Leslie McCall (2005) has developed a threefold clustering of approaches to the study of inter-sectionality: the intercategorical complexity, intracategorical complexity and anticategorical complexity. Intercategorical approach presumes the existence of intersections, and then attempts to map the relationship between different social groups and how these are changing. The intracategorical approach is alive to the shortcomings of existing categorisations and interrogates the way in which they mark boundaries of distinction. The anticategorical approach is concerned with a critique of the presumption that categories are a pre-given. Rather it deconstructs the categories, paying attention to the regimes of power in and through which the categories are constituted in the first place. Here social categories are seen as historically, culturally and lin-guistically produced. I am sympathetic to the anticategorical approach. This is not to suggest, however, that categories themselves are meaningless. Far from it. Rather, they are not already existing formations but take form through socio-cultural, economic and psychic processes. 'Woman' is not a pre-constituted category but one which takes meaning in varying and variable form within discourse. Non-additive models of intersectionality foreground these varying and variable formations of meaning. This broad categorisation by McCall is helpful, but does not provide a specific methodology. In my view, there cannot be a single methodology which all intersectional analysis may follow. Intersectional analysis is first and foremost an interdisciplinary endeavour. Different disciplines have varying methodologies. That which one chooses is dependent upon the problematic that one is addressing and the subject discipline(s) within which one is operating. It cannot by definition have a single, overarching set of methods as tools of analysis. My position gains support from the introduction to a special issue of the journal *Signs*, where Lily Cho, Kimberlé Williams Crenshaw and Leslie McCall (2013) state that 'inter-sectionality is best framed as an analytic sensibility' (795).

Some analysts working with this concept locate their work within feminist standpoint theory. Standpoint feminism argues that feminist social science foregrounds the standpoint of women, that they are better able to understand certain features of the world. Because of their location as a subordinate group, it is argued, they hold a different type of knowledge from men, one which challenges male-biased conventional wisdom. This perspective has been characterised by some as being essentialist, and, in some measure, contrary to the demands of intersectionality in so far as women are not simply equivalent to their gender. In a much more nuanced perspective which does not fix knowledge construction along a single axis, Donna Haraway, as we noted earlier, has used the notion of 'situated knowledge' which is produced, circulated and challenged via intersectional articulations. This concept is akin to what Chandra Talpade Mohanty (1992) calls the 'politics of location' understood as 'historical, geographical, cultural, psychic and imaginative boundaries which provide the ground for political definition' (74). This debate also has a bearing on the processes of embodiment, in which I include the workings of the psyche. People are much more than an amalgam of subject positions – there are emotions, yearnings, unruly and precarious workings of the psyche, and the intersectional excess of 'experience'.

Another question which scholars of intersectionality have raised is whether perspectives informed by standpoint theory and others which take inspiration from post-structuralist theoretical formulations are mutually exclusive?

Despite their major differences, I would argue that there is some overlap and that intersectionality offers the opportunity to reconcile these two perspectives with each other in so far as both decentre the collective subject 'woman'. Both require us to integrate marginalised life-experiences as well as highlight the importance of understanding power and privilege in its manifold manifestations. Through the lens of intersectionality, both perspectives caution against reciting the race, class, gender and sexuality mantra without due attention to the complexity entailed when processes of social division, inequality and subjection formation intersect and articulate.

What are the prospects for the future of intersectionality? Nira Yuval-Davis (2011), for instance, sees the concept of intersectionality as having a great deal of potential. According to her, intersectionality is far better equipped to do justice to the analysis of complex relations of inequality than stratification theory in sociology. Floya Anthias (2012) argues along similar lines, and offers a critique of traditional stratification theories with an emphasis on translocational lens. Kathy Davis (in Lutz *et al.* 2011) finds that, paradoxically, the very vagueness and open-endedness of the framework of intersectionality is the secret of its success and this portends well for its future. One of its strengths lies in the way in which it demands that those engaged in theoretical work embed their meta-narratives in the concrete social and political contexts whilst simultaneously asking generalist researchers to appreciate the importance of theory in feminist inquiry. Nina Lykke (in Lutz *et al.* 2011) provides a qualified assessment of intersectionality. She conceptualises intersectionality as a 'nodal point', and favours it only so long as it remains an 'open ended framework for comparing different feminist conceptualisations of intersecting power differentials, normativities and identity formations – a discursive site where different feminist positions are in critical dialogue or productive conflict with one another' (208).

It is important to bear in mind that from its inception, intersectionality has been an antiracist framework. But a travelling theory or practice may change during the course of its translocation to a different context. Gail Lewis (2013) addresses this question through an analysis of a conference held in Frankfurt in Germany for the purpose of assessing the achievements of intersectionality. She analyses how such situations marked by travelling concepts and methods of intersectionality create deep anxiety and emotionality which are underpinned by fears and anxieties about multiculturalism. She points to the ways in which the 'terminological category of race is disavowed as unspeakable in parts of Europe' (874), and feminists of colour become Othered and positioned outside Europe. These outcomes are likely to be unintended but their effects are palpable. So even a highly inclusive project such as that of intersectionality could have exclusionary effects and this possibility calls for much vigilance.

Diaspora and intersectionality then are mutually articulating. Diaspora – a dispersal of bodies, cultures, imaginaries – is inscribed by the multiple modalities of power constituted in the play of different markers of differentiation. All relations, Foucault has argued, are relations of power. So, diaspora must be understood in terms of the power dynamics which undergird it. A starting point for our analysis is the identification of the different power relations that are set into play in a given context. How are class, racialisations or gender, for example, figured in the lives of diasporic individuals or groups? Power, Foucault tells us, is both coercive and productive. So we analyse, on the one hand, the nature of discrimination or exploitation experienced in given circumstances, and, on the other hand, the nature of the subjects produced – resistant to oppression or complicit with it. Hence we are able to address both the creative dimensions of power as well as its negative features. These various power dynamics raise questions such as: What are the pains and pleasures of a specific cluster of diasporicity? What type of social and cultural life does a diasporic group create within the historical circumstances it faces? What kind of diasporic spaces are mobilised in these circumstances? In my theorisation of diaspora space I have argued that it is the site where the concepts of diaspora, border and multi-axial locationality articulate as a point of confluence of the economic, cultural, political and the psychic processes. Here multiple modalities of power interweave, and questions of belonging and un-belonging are interrogated in and through the inscription of many subject positions, subjectivities and identities. And this diasporicity, I have argued, is always permeated by intersectionality. Taking the two together, I believe, marks new directions in research.

Bibliography

Anthias, Floya. 2012. 'Hierarchies of Social Location, Class and Intersectionality: Towards a Translocational Frame.' *International Sociology* 28 (1): 121–38.

Belsey, Catherine. 2002. *Poststructuralism: A Very Short Introduction.* Oxford: Oxford University Press.

Bhabha, Homi K. 1994. *The Location of Culture.* London: Routledge.

Bhabha, Homi K. 2013. 'Living Side by Side: On Culture and Security.' Keynote Presentation at CoHaB International Conference on Diasporic Constructions of Home and Belonging, Munster University, Germany, September 23.

Brah, Avtar. 1996. *Cartographies of Diaspora: Contesting Identities.* London and New York: Routledge.

Brah, Avtar, and Anne Phoenix. 2004. '"Ain't I A Woman"? Revisiting Intersectionality.' *Journal of International Women's Studies* 5 (3): 75–86.

Braziel Evans, Jana. 2008. *Diaspora: An Introduction.* Oxford: Blackwell.

Braziel Evans, Jana, and Anita Mannur, A., eds. 2003. *Theorizing Diaspora.* Oxford: Blackwell.

Cho, Sumi, Kimberlé Williams Crenshaw, and Leslie McCall. 2013. 'Toward a Field of Intersectional Studies: Theory, Applications, Praxis.' *Signs* 38 (4): 785–810.

Clifford, James. 1994. 'Diasporas.' *Cultural Anthropology* 9 (3): 302–38.

Cohen, Robin. [1997] 2008. *Global Diasporas: An Introduction.* London: Routledge.

Collins, Patricia Hill, and Sirma Bilge. 2016. *Intersectionality.* Cambridge and Malden, MA: Polity Press.

Combahee River Collective, The. 'Combahee River Collective Statement.' 1977. Available at: http://circuitous.org/scraps/combahee.html (accessed 13 November 2016).

Crenshaw, Kimberlé Williams. 1989. 'Demarginalising the Intersections of Race and Sex: A Black Feminist Critique of Antidiscrimination Doctrine, Feminist Theory, and Antiracist Politics.' *University of Chicago Legal Forum* 1989 (1): 139–67.

Davis, Kathy. 2011. 'Intersectionality as Buzzword: A Sociology of Science Perspective on What Makes a Theory Successful.' In *Framing Intersectionality: Debates on a Multi-faceted Concept in Gender Studies*, edited by Helma Lutz, Maria Teresa Herrera Vivar, and Linda Supik, 43–55. London: Ashgate.

European Commission. 2007. *Tackling Multiple Discrimination: Practices, Policies and Laws.* Luxembourg: Office for Official Publications of the European Communities. Available at: http://ec.europa.eu/social/main.jsp?catId=738&pubId=51.

Gilroy, Paul. 1993. *The Black Atlantic: Modernity and Double Consciousness.* London: Verso.

Hall, Stuart. 1990. 'Cultural Identity and Diaspora.' In *Identity, Community, Culture*, edited by Jonathan Rutherford, 222–37. London: Lawrence and Wishart.

Hall, Stuart. 1996. 'Who Needs Identity?' In *Questions of Cultural Identity*, edited by Stuart Hall and Paul du Gay, 1–17. London, Thousand Oaks, CA and New Delhi: Sage.

Haraway, Donna. 1988. 'Situated Knowledges: The Science Question in Feminism and the Privilege of Partial Perspective.' *Feminist Studies* 14 (3): 575–99.

Knott, Kim. 2010. 'Space and Movement.' In *Diasporas: Concepts, Intersections, Identities*, edited by Kim Knott and Sean McLoughlin, 79–83. London: Zed Press.

Knott, Kim, and Sean McLoughlin. 2010. *Diasporas: Concepts, Intersections, Identities.* London: Zed Press.

Lewis, G. 2013. 'Unsafe Travel: Experiencing Intersectionality and Feminist Displacements.' *Signs* 38 (4): 869–92.

Lutz, Helma, Maria Teresa Herrera Vivar, and Linda Supik, eds. 2011. *Framing Intersectionality: Debates on a Multi-faceted Concept in Gender Studies.* London: Ashgate.

Lykke, Nina. 2011. 'Intersectional Analysis: Black Box or Useful Critical Feminist Thinking Technology?' In *Framing Intersectionality: Debates on a Multi-faceted Concept in Gender Studies*, edited by Helma Lutz, Maria Teresa Herrera Vivar, and Linda Supik, 207–20. London: Ashgate.

McCall, Leslie. 2005. 'The Complexity of Intersectionality.' *Signs* 30 (3): 1771–800.

Mohanty, Chandra Talape. 1992. 'Feminist Encounters: Locating the Politics of Experience.' In *Destabilizing Theory: Contemporary Feminist Debates*, edited by Michèle Barrett and Anne Phillips, 74–92. Stanford, CA: Stanford University Press.

Moraga, Cherríe, and Gloria Anzaldúa, eds. 1981. *This Bridge Called My Back: Writings by Radical Women of Colour.* London: Persephone Press.

Nash, Jennifer. 2008. 'Re-thinking Intersectionality.' *Feminist Review* 89 (1): 1–15.

Puar, Jasbir K. 2012. 'I Would Rather Be a Cyborg than a Goddess: Becoming Intersectional in Assemblage Theory.' *Philosphia: A Journal of Feminist Philosphy* 2 (1): 49–66.

Purkayastha, Bandana. 2010. 'Interrogating Intersectionality: Contemporary Globalisation and Racialised Gendering in the Lives of Highly Educated South Asian Americans and their Children.' *Journal of Intercultural Studies* 31 (1): 29–47.

Safran, William. 1991. 'Diasporas in Modern Societies: Myths of Homeland and Return.' *Diaspora: A Journal of Transnational Studies* 1 (1): 83–99.

Scott, Joan W. 1992. 'Experience.' In *Feminists Theorize the Political*, edited by Judith Butler and Joan W. Scott, 22–40. New York: Routledge.

United Nations. 2016. Sustainable Development Blog. '244 million international migrants living abroad worldwide, new UN statistics reveal.' January 12. Available at: www.un.org/sustainabledevelopment/blog/2016/01/244-million-international-migrants-living-abroad-worldwide-new-un-statistics-reveal/.

Weedon, Chris. 1987. *Feminist Practice and Poststructuralist Theory.* Oxford, UK: Blackwell.

Yuval-Davis, Nira. 2006. 'Intersectionality and Feminist Politics.' *European Journal of Women's Studies* 13 (3): 193–209.

Yuval-Davis, Nira. 2011. *Politics of Belonging: Intersectional Contestations.* London: Sage.

24

IMPOSSIBLE DESIRES

Queer diasporas and South Asian public cultures

Gayatri Gopinath

Impossible desires

In a particularly memorable scene in *My Beautiful Laundrette* (dir. Stephen Frears, 1985), British Pakistani screenwriter Hanif Kureishi's groundbreaking film about queer interracial desire in Thatcherite Britain, the white, working-class gay boy Johnny moves to unbutton the shirt of his lover, the upwardly mobile, Pakistan-born Omar. Omar initially acquiesces to Johnny's caresses, but then abruptly puts a halt to the seduction. He turns his back to his lover and recalls a boyhood scene of standing with his immigrant father and seeing Johnny march in a fascist parade through their South London neighborhood: "It was bricks and bottles, immigrants out, kill us. People we knew . . . And it was you. We *saw* you," Omar says bitterly. Johnny initially recoils in shame as Omar brings into the present this damning image from the past of his younger self as a hate-filled skinhead. But then, as Omar continues speaking, he slowly reaches out to draw Omar to him and embraces Omar from behind. The final shot frames Omar's face as he lets his head fall back onto Johnny's chest and he closes his eyes.

The scene eloquently speaks to how the queer racialized body becomes a historical archive for both individuals and communities, one that is excavated through the very act of desiring the racial Other. For Omar, desiring Johnny is irrevocably intertwined with the legacies of British colonialism in South Asia and the more immediate history of Powellian racism in 1960s Britain.[1] In his memory of having seen Johnny march ("we *saw* you"), Omar in a sense reverses the historical availability of brown bodies to a white imperial gaze by turning the gaze back onto Johnny's own racist past. The scene's ambiguous ending—where Omar closes his eyes and succumbs to Johnny's caresses—may suggest that Omar gives in to the historical amnesia that wipes out the legacies of Britain's racist past. Yet the meaning and function of queer desire in the scene are far more complicated than such a reading would allow. If for Johnny sex with Omar is a way of both tacitly acknowledging and erasing that racist past, for Omar, queer desire is precisely what allows him to remember. Indeed, the barely submerged histories of colonialism and racism erupt into the present at the very moment when queer sexuality is being articulated. Queer desire does not transcend or remain peripheral to these histories but instead it becomes central to their telling and remembering: there is no queer desire without these histories, nor can these histories be told or remembered without simultaneously revealing an erotics of power.

Upon its release in 1985, *My Beautiful Laundrette* engendered heated controversy within South Asian communities in the UK, some of whose members took exception to Kureishi's matter-of-fact depiction of queer interracial desire between white and brown men, and more generally to his refusal to produce "positive images" of British Asian lives.[2] The controversy surrounding its release prefigured the at times violent debates around queer sexuality and dominant notions of communal identity that took place both in South Asia and in the diaspora over the following decade.[3] In New York City for instance, the South Asian Lesbian and Gay Association waged an ongoing battle throughout the 1990s over the right to march in the annual India Day Parade, a controversy I will return to later in this chapter. And in several Indian cities in December 1998, as I discuss in detail in chapter 5, Indian-Canadian director Deepa Mehta's film *Fire* was vociferously attacked by right-wing Hindu nationalists outraged by its depiction of "lesbian" sexuality. These various battles in disparate national locations speak to the ways in which queer desires, bodies, and subjectivities become dense sites of meaning in the production and reproduction of notions of "culture," "tradition," and communal belonging both in South Asia and in the diaspora. They also signal the conflation of "perverse" sexualities and diasporic affiliations within a nationalist imaginary, and it is this mapping of queerness onto diaspora that is the subject of this book. [. . .]

My Beautiful Laundrette presents a useful point of departure in addressing many of the questions that concern me throughout this book. As the film makes apparent, all too often diasporas are narrativized through the bonds of relationality between men. Indeed, the oedipal relation between fathers and sons serves as a central and recurring feature within diasporic narratives and becomes a metaphor for the contradictions of sameness and difference that, as Stuart Hall has shown, characterize competing definitions of diasporic subjectivity.[4] For Freud, the oedipal drama explains the consolidation of proper gender identification and heterosexual object choice in little boys, as masculine identification with the father is made while feminine identification with the mother is refused. In his 1952 work *Black Skin, White Masks,* Frantz Fanon resituates the oedipal scenario in the colonial context and shows how, for racialized male subjects, the process whereby the little boy learns to identify with the father and desire the mother is disrupted and disturbed by the (black) father's lack of access to social power.[5] Fanon's analysis, which I engage with more fully in chapter 3, makes evident the inadequacy of the Oedipus complex in explaining the construction of gendered subjectivity within colonial and postcolonial regimes of power. While I am interested in identifying how queer diasporic texts follow Fanon in reworking the notion of oedipality in relation to racialized masculinities, I also ask what alternative narratives emerge when this story of oedipality is jettisoned altogether. For even when the male–male or father–son narrative is mined for its queer valences (as in *Laundrette* or in other gay male diasporic texts I consider here), the centrality of this narrative as the primary trope in imagining diaspora invariably displaces and elides female diasporic subjects. [. . .]

This book, then, begins where Kureishi's text leaves off. *Impossible Desires* examines a range of South Asian diasporic literature, film, and music in order to ask if we can imagine diaspora differently, apart from the biological, reproductive, oedipal logic that invariably forms the core of conventional formulations of diaspora. It does so by paying special attention to *queer female subjectivity in the diaspora,* as it is this particular positionality that forms a constitutive absence in both dominant nationalist and diasporic discourses. More surprisingly perhaps, and therefore worth interrogating closely, is the elision of queer female subjectivity within seemingly radical cultural and political diasporic projects that center a gay male or heterosexual feminist diasporic subject. *Impossible Desires* refuses to accede to the splitting of queerness from feminism that marks such projects. By making female subjectivity central to a queer diasporic project, it begins instead to conceptualize diaspora in ways that do not invariably replicate heteronormative and patriarchal structures of kinship and community. [. . .]

The imbrication of diaspora and diasporic cultural forms with dominant nationalism, on the one hand, and corporate globalization on the other, takes place through discourses that are simultaneously gendered and sexualized. Feminist scholars of nationalism in South Asia have long pointed to the particular rendering of "woman" within nationalist discourse as the grounds upon which male nationalist ideologies take shape.[6] Such scholarship has been instructive in demonstrating how female sexuality under nationalism is a crucial site of surveillance, as it is through women's bodies that the borders and boundaries of communal identities are formed. But as I argue in chapter 5, this body of work has been less successful in fully addressing the ways in which dominant nationalism institutes heterosexuality as a key disciplinary regime. Feminist scholarship on South Asia has also, for the most part, remained curiously silent about how alternative sexualities may constitute a powerful challenge to patriarchal nationalism.[7] Nor has there been much sustained attention paid to the ways in which nationalist framings of women's sexuality are translated into the diaspora, and how these renderings of diasporic women's sexuality are in turn central to the production of nationalism in the home nation.[8] In an article on Indian indentured migration to Trinidad, Tejaswini Niranjana begins this necessary work by observing that anticolonial nationalists in India in the early twentieth century used the figure of the amoral, sexually impure Indian woman abroad as a way of producing the chaste, virtuous Indian woman at "home" as emblematic of a new "nationalist morality."[9] The consolidation of a gendered bourgeois nationalist subject in India through a configuration of its disavowed Other in the diaspora underscores the necessity of conceptualizing the diaspora and the nation as mutually constituted formations. However, as I elaborate in chapter 6, Niranjana's article still presumes the heterosexuality of the female diasporic and female nationalist subject rather than recognizing institutionalized heterosexuality as a primary structure of both British colonialism and incipient Indian nationalism. The failure of feminist scholars of South Asia and the South Asian diaspora to fully interrogate heterosexuality as a structuring mechanism of both state and diasporic nationalisms makes clear the indispensability of a queer critique. A queer diasporic framework insists on the imbrication of nation and diaspora through the production of hetero- and homosexuality, particularly as they are mapped onto the bodies of women.

Just as discourses of female sexuality are central to the mutual constitution of diaspora and nation, so too is the relation between diasporic culture and globalization one that is mediated through dominant gender and sexual ideologies. Feminist theorists have astutely observed that globalization profoundly shapes, transforms, and exploits the gendered arrangements of seemingly "private" zones in the diaspora such as the "immigrant home."[10] But while much scholarship focuses on how global processes function through the differentiation of the labor market along gendered, racial, and national lines, how discourses of sexuality in the diaspora intersect with, and are in turn shaped by, globalization is only beginning to be explored.[11] Furthermore, the impact of globalization on particular diasporic locations produces various forms of oppositional diasporic cultural practices that may both reinscribe and disrupt the gender and sexual ideologies on which globalization depends.

The critical framework of a specifically *queer* diaspora, then, may begin to unsettle the ways in which the diaspora shores up the gender and sexual ideologies of dominant nationalism on the one hand, and processes of globalization on the other. Such a framework enables the concept of diaspora to fulfill the double-pronged critique of the nation and of globalization that Braziel and Mannur suggest is its most useful intervention. This framework "queers" the concept of diaspora by unmasking and undercutting its dependence on a genealogical, implicitly heteronormative reproductive logic. Indeed, while the Bharatiya Janata Party-led Hindu nationalist government in India acknowledged the diaspora solely in the form of the prosperous, Hindu, heterosexual NRI businessman, there exists a different embodiment of diaspora that remains unthinkable within this Hindu nationalist imaginary. The category of "queer" in my project works to name this alternative rendering of diaspora and to dislodge diaspora from its adherence and loyalty to nationalist ideologies that are fully aligned with the interests of transnational capitalism. Suturing "queer" to "diaspora" thus recuperates those desires, practices, and subjectivities that are rendered impossible and unimaginable within conventional diasporic and nationalist imaginaries. A consideration of queerness, in other words, becomes a way to challenge nationalist ideologies by restoring the impure, inauthentic, nonreproductive potential of the notion of diaspora. Indeed, the urgent need to trouble and denaturalize the close relationship between nationalism and heterosexuality is precisely what makes the notion of a queer diaspora so compelling.[12] A queer diasporic framework productively exploits the analogous relation between nation and diaspora on the one hand, and between heterosexuality and queerness on the other: in other words, queerness is to heterosexuality as the diaspora is to the nation. If within heteronormative logic the queer is seen as the debased and inadequate copy of the heterosexual, so too is diaspora within nationalist logic positioned as the queer Other of the nation, its inauthentic imitation. The concept of a queer diaspora enables a simultaneous critique of heterosexuality and the nation form, while exploding the binary oppositions between nation and diaspora, heterosexuality and homo-sexuality, original and copy.

If "diaspora" needs "queerness" in order to rescue it from its genealogical implications, "queerness" also needs "diaspora" in order to make it more supple in relation to questions of race, colonialism, migration, and globalization. An emerging body of queer-of-color scholarship has taken to task the "homonormativity" of certain strands of Euro-American queer studies that center white gay male subjectivity, while simultaneously fixing the queer, nonwhite racialized, and/or immigrant subject as insufficiently politicized and "modern."[13] My articulation of a queer diasporic framework is part of this collective project of decentering whiteness and dominant Euro-American paradigms in theorizing sexuality both locally and transnationally. On the most simple level, I use "queer" to refer to a range of dissident and non-heteronormative practices and desires that may very well be incommensurate with the identity categories of "gay" and "lesbian." A queer diasporic formation works in contradistinction to the globalization of "gay" identity that replicates a colonial narrative of development and progress that judges all "other" sexual cultures, communities, and practices against a model of Euro-American sexual identity.[14] Many of the diasporic cultural forms I discuss in this book do indeed map a "cartography of globalization," in Sharpe's terms, in that they emerge out of queer communities in First World global cities such as London, New York, and Toronto. Yet we must also remember, as Lisa Lowe and David Lloyd point out, that "transnational or *neo-colonial* capitalism, like colonialist capitalism before it, continues to produce sites of contradiction that are effects of its always uneven expansion but that cannot be subsumed by the logic of commodification itself."[15] In other words, while queer diasporic cultural forms are produced in and through the workings of transnational capitalism, they also provide the means by which to critique the logic of global capital itself. The cartography of a queer diaspora tells a different story of how global capitalism impacts local sites by articulating other forms of subjectivity, culture, affect, kinship, and community that may not be visible or audible within standard mappings of nation, diaspora, or globalization. What emerges within this alternative cartography are subjects, communities, and practices that bear little resemblance to the universalized "gay" identity imagined within a Eurocentric gay imaginary.

Reading various cultural forms and practices as both constituting and constituted by a queer South Asian diaspora resituates the conventions by which homosexuality has traditionally been encoded in a Euro-American context. Queer sexualities as articulated by the texts I consider here reference familiar tropes and signifiers of Euro-American homosexuality—such as the coming-out narrative and its attendant markers of secrecy and disclosure, as well as gender inversion and cross-dressing—while investing them with radically different and distinct significations. It is through a particular engagement with South Asian public culture, and popular culture in particular, that this de-familiarization of conventional markers of homosexuality takes place, and that alternative strategies through which to signify non-heteronormative desire are subsequently produced. These alternative strategies suggest a mode of reading and "seeing" same-sex eroticism that challenges modern epistemologies of visibility, revelation, and sexual subjectivity. As such, the notion of a queer South Asian diaspora can be understood as a conceptual apparatus that poses a critique of modernity and its various narratives of progress and development.[16] A queer South Asian diasporic geography of desire and pleasure stages this critique by rewriting colonial constructions of "Third World" sexualities as anterior, premodern, and in need of Western political development—constructions that are recirculated by contemporary gay and lesbian transnational politics. It simultaneously interrogates different South Asian nationalist narratives that imagine and consolidate the nation in terms of organic heterosexuality.

The concept of a queer South Asian diaspora, then, functions on multiple levels throughout this book. First, it situates the formation of sexual subjectivity within transnational flows of culture, capital, bodies, desire, and labor. Second, queer diaspora contests the logic that situates the terms "queer" and "diaspora" as dependent on the originality of "heterosexuality" and "nation." Finally, it disorganizes the dominant categories within the United States for sexual variance, namely "gay and lesbian," and it marks a different economy of desire that escapes legibility within both normative South Asian contexts and homonormative Euro-American contexts. [. . .]

Impossibility

Because the figure of "woman" as a pure and unsullied sexual being is so central to dominant articulations of nation and diaspora, the radical disruption of "home" that queer diasporic texts enact is particularly apparent in their representation of queer female subjectivity. I use the notion of "impossibility" as a way of signaling the unthinkability of a queer female subject position within various mappings of nation and diaspora. My foregrounding of queer female diasporic subjectivity throughout the book is not simply an attempt to merely bring into visibility or recognition a heretofore invisible subject. Indeed, as I have suggested, many of the texts I consider run counter to standard "lesbian" and "gay" narratives of the closet and coming out that are organized exclusively around a logic of recognition and visibility. Instead, I scrutinize the deep investment of dominant diasporic and nationalist ideologies in producing this particular subject position as impossible and unimaginable. Given the illegibility and unrepresentability of a non-heteronormative female subject within patriarchal and heterosexual configurations of both nation and diaspora, the project of locating a "queer South Asian diasporic subject"—and a queer female subject in particular—may begin to challenge the dominance of such configurations. Revealing the mechanisms by which a queer female diasporic positionality is rendered impossible strikes at the very foundation of these ideological structures. Thus, while this project is very much situated within the emergent body of queer-of-color work that I referenced earlier, it also parts ways with much of this scholarship by making a queer female subject the crucial point of departure in theorizing a queer diaspora. In so doing, *Impossible Desires* is located squarely at the intersection of queer and feminist scholarship and therefore challenges the notion that these fields of inquiry are necessarily distinct, separate, and incommensurate.[17] Instead, the book brings together the insights of postcolonial feminist scholarship on the gendering of colonialism, nationalism, and globalization, with a queer critique of the heteronormativity of cultural and state nationalist formations.[18]

Notes

1 For an analysis of the racist ideology espoused by the British politician Enoch Powell in the 1960s, see Anna Marie Smith, *New Right Discourse on Race and Sexuality*.

2 See Ian Iqbal Rashid, "Passage to England," for a discussion of *My Beautiful Laundrette's* reception by the "cultural left" in the UK in the 1980s.

3 In its most general sense, the term "communal" is used here and throughout the book to reference notions of community and collectivity; more specifically, my use of "communal" is meant to evoke the term "communalism," which in the South Asian context names a politics of religious nationalism and the persecution of religious minorities, particularly on the part of the Hindu right.

4 Hall, "Cultural Identity and Diaspora," 245.

5 Frantz Fanon, *Black Skin, White Masks*, 151–3.

6 Some of the most influential works in the broad field of gender and nationalism in South Asia include the following: Kumkum Sangari and Sudesh Vaid, eds., *Recasting Women*; Zoya Hassan, ed., *Forging Identities*; Lata Mani, *Contentious Traditions*; Ritu Menon and Kamala Bhasin, eds., *Borders and Boundaries*.

7 Key exceptions include Ruth Vanita, ed. *Queering India*; Giti Thadani, *Sakhiyani*; Shohini Ghosh, "*Hum Aapke Hain Koun . . . !*"; Paola Bacchetta, "When the (Hindu) Nation Exiles its Queers."

8 See Purnima Mankekar, "Brides Who Travel," for an examination of representations of diasporic women's sexuality in Hindi cinema.

9 Tejaswini Niranjana, "Left to the Imagination." See also Madhavi Kale, *Fragments of Empire*, for a discussion of Indian women's sexuality in the British Caribbean and discourses of both Indian and British nationalism.

10 See, for instance, Lisa Lowe's analysis of Asian immigrant women's labor in "Work, Immigration, Gender."

11 For collections that begin to map out this terrain, see Arnaldo Cruz Malavé and Martin Manalansan, eds, *Queer Globalizations*; Elizabeth Povinelli and George Chauncey, eds, *Thinking Sexuality Transnationally*.

12 Following from George Mosse's groundbreaking analysis of sexuality in Nazi Germany in *Nationalism and Sexuality*, an important body of work has emerged over the past decade that has unraveled the complex interrelation between discourses of sexuality and those of the nation. For a few key examples of this increasingly large and complex field, see Andrew Parker, ed., *Nationalisms and Sexualities*; M. Jacqui Alexander, "Erotic Autonomy as a Politics of Decolonization"; Anne McClintock, *Imperial Leather*; and more recently Licia Fiol Matta, *A Queer Mother for the Nation*.

13 Some exemplary instances of this growing body of literature in US ethnic studies include the following: Martin Manalansan, *Global Divas*; José Muñoz, *Disidentifications*; Juana María Rodríguez, *Queer Latinidad*; Robert Reid Pharr, *Black Gay Man*; Philip Brian Harper, *Are We Not Men?*; David L. Eng, *Racial Castration*; Roderick Ferguson, *Aberrations in Black*; Nayan Shah, *Contagious Divides*.

14 See Martin Manalansan, "In the Shadow of Stonewall," for an important interrogation of contemporary gay transnational politics.

15 Lowe and Lloyd, *The Politics of Culture in the Shadow of Capital*, 1.

16 The imbrication of narratives of "progress," "modernity," and "visibility" is made obvious in what Alexander terms "prevalent metropolitan impulses that explain the absence of visible lesbian and gay movements [in non-Western locations] as a defect in political consciousness and maturity, using evidence of publicly organized lesbian and gay movements in the U.S. . . . as evidence of their originary status (in the West) and superior political maturity." Alexander, "Erotic Autonomy as a Politics of Decolonization," 69.

17 As such, I trace the genealogy of this project back to the rich body of radical women of color scholarship of the late 1970s and 1980s that insistently situated lesbian sexuality within a feminist, antiracist, and anticolonial framework. Such work includes Audre Lorde's *Zami*; Cherríe Moraga, *Loving in the War Years*; Cherríe Moraga and Gloria Anzaldúa, eds, *This Bridge Called My Back*; Gloria Anzaldúa, *Borderlands/La Frontera*; Barbara Smith, ed., *Home Girls*.

18 Queer Euro-American scholarship has done the crucial work of revealing the heteronormativity of dominant US nationalism. Such work includes Gayle Rubin's groundbreaking essay "Thinking Sex"; Michael Warner, *The Trouble with Normal*; Lisa Duggan, *Sapphic Slashers* and *The Twilight of Equality?*

References

Alexander, M. Jacqui. "Erotic Autonomy as a Politics of Decolonization: An Anatomy of Feminist and State Practice in the Bahamas Tourist Economy." In *Feminist Genealogies, Colonial Legacies, Democratic Futures*, edited by M. Jacqui Alexander and Chandra T. Mohanty. New York: Routledge, 1997.

Anzaldúa, Gloria. *Borderlands/La Frontera*. San Francisco: Spinsters/Aum Lute, 1987.

Baccheta, Paola. "When the (Hindu) Nation Exiles its Queers." *Social Text* 61 (Winter 1999): 141–61.

Duggan, Lisa. *Sapphic Slashers: Sex, Violence and American Modernity*. Durham: Duke University Press, 2000.

———. *The Twilight of Equality? Neoliberalism, Cultural Politics and the Attack on Democracy*. Boston: Beacon, 2003.

Eng, David. L. *Racial Castration: Managing Masculinity in Asian America*. Durham: Duke University Press, 2001.

Fanon, Frantz. *Black Skin, White Masks*. New York: Grove Press, 1967.

Ferguson, Roderick. *Aberrations in Black: Toward a Queer of Color Critique*. Minneapolis: University of Minnesota Press, 2003.

Fiol Matta, Licia. *A Queer Mother for the Nation: The State and Gabriela Mistral*. Minneapolis: University of Minnesota Press, 2002.

Ghosh, Shohini. "*Hum Aapke Hain Koun . . . !*: Pluralizing Pleasures of Viewership." *Social Scientist* 28: 2–3 (March–April 2000): 83–90.

Hall, Stuart. "Cultural Identity and Diaspora." In *Theorizing Diaspora*, edited by Jana Evans Braziel and Anita Mannur. Malden, Mass.: Blackwell, 2003.

Harper, Philip Brian. *Are We Not Men? Masculine Anxiety and the Problem of African American Identity*. London: Oxford University Press, 1998.

Hassan, Zoya, ed. *Forging Identities: Gender, Communities and the State*. New Delhi: Kali for Women, 1994.

Kale, Madhavi. *Fragments of Empire: Capital, Slavery and Indian Indentured Labor Migration in the British Caribbean*. Philadelphia: University of Pennsylvania Press, 1998.

Lorde, Audre. *Zami: A New Spelling of My Name*. Freedom, CA: Crossing Press, 1982.

Lowe, Lisa. "Work, Immigration, Gender: Asian 'American' Women." In *Immigrant Acts: On Asian American Cultural Politics*. Durham: Duke University Press, 1996.

Lowe, Lisa, and David Lloyd. "Introduction." In *The Politics of Culture in the Shadow of Capital*, edited by Lisa Lowe and David Lloyd. Durham: Duke University Press, 1997.

Malave, Arnaldo Cruz, and Martin Manalansan, eds. *Queer Globalizations*. New York: New York University Press, 1999.

Manalansan, Martin. "In the Shadows of Stonewall: Examining Gay Transnational Politics and the Diasporic Dilemma." In *The Politics of Culture in the Shadow of Capital*, edited by Lisa Lowe and David Lloyd. Durham: Duke University Press, 1997.

———. *Global Divas: Filipino Gay Men in New York City*. Durham: Duke University Press, 2003.

Mani, Lata. *Contentious Traditions: The Debate on Sati in Colonial India*. Berkeley: University of California Press, 1998.

Mankekar, Purnima. "Brides Who Travel: Gender, Transnationalism, and Nationalism in Hindi Film." *positions* 7, no. 3 (1999): 731–61.

McClintock, Anne. *Imperial Leather: Race, Gender and Sexuality in the Colonial Contest*. New York: Routledge, 1995.

Menon, Ritu, and Kamala Bhasin, eds. *Borders and Boundaries: Women and India's Partition*. New Delhi: Kali for Women, 1998

Moraga, Cherríe. *Loving in the War Years: Lo que nunca paso por sus labios*. Boston: South End Press, 1983.

Moraga, Cherríe, and Gloria Anzaldúa, eds. *This Bridge Called My Back: Writings by Radical Women of Color*. New York: Kitchen Table, 1983.

Mosse, George. *Nationalism and Sexuality: Middle-Class Morality and Sexual Norms in Modern Europe*. Madison: University of Wisconsin Press, 1985.

Muñoz, Jose. *Disidentifications: Queers of Color and the Performance of Politics*. Minneapolis: University of Minnesota Press, 1999.

Niranjana, Tejaswini. "Left to the Imagination: Indian Nationalisms and Female Sexuality in Trinidad." In *A Question of Silence? The Sexual Economies of Modern India*, edited by Mary John and Janaki Nair. New Delhi: Kali for Women, 1998.

Parker, Andrew, ed. *Nationalisms and Sexualities*. New York: Routledge, 1992.

Povinelli, Elizabeth, and George Chauncey, eds. "Thinking Sexuality Transnationally." Special issue, *GLQ* 5, no. 4 (1999).

Rashid, Ian Iqbal. "Passage to England." *Trikone Magazine* 16, no. 3 (July 2001): 10–12.

Reid-Pharr, Robert. *Black Gay Man: Essays*. New York: New York University Press, 2001.

Rodriguez, Juana María. *Queer Latinidad: Identity Practices, Discursive Spaces*. New York: New York University Press, 2003.

Rubin, Gayle. "Thinking Sex: Notes for a Radical Theory of the Politics of Sexuality." In *Pleasure and Danger: Exploring Female Sexuality*, edited by Carole Vance. New York: Routledge, 1984.

Sangari, Kumkum, and Sudesh Vaid, eds. *Recasting Women: Essays in Colonial History*. New Delhi: Kali for Women, 1989.

Shah, Nayan. *Contagious Divides: Epidemics and Race in San Francisco's Chinatown*. Berkeley: University of California Press, 2001.

Smith, Anna Marie. *New Right Discourse on Race and Sexuality: Britain 1968–1990*. Cambridge: Cambridge University Press, 1994.

Smith, Barbara, ed. *Home Girls: A Black Feminist Anthology*. New York: Kitchen Table, 1983.

Thadani, Giri. *Sakhiyani: Lesbian Desire in Ancient and Modern India*. London: Cassell, 1996.

Vanita, Ruth, ed. *Queering India: Same-Sex Love and Eroticism in Indian Culture and Society*. New York: Routledge, 2002.

Warner, Michael. *The Trouble with Normal: Sex, Politics and the Ethics of Queer Life*. New York: Free Press, 1999.

25

WHY QUEER DIASPORA?

Meg Wesling

Each of these frameworks unites the queer with the diasporic in a privileged relation of transgressivity, begging the question about the critical function of such an analogy. Both, it would seem, are fundamentally disruptive of static categories of being, of the hegemonic categories through which proper, normative subjects are produced. Taking this analogy a step further, the queer subject, as a fundamentally diasporic figure, becomes synonymous with globalization itself. Within this analogy, the queer diasporic body is doubly disarticulated from the stasis of sexual and national normativity; likewise, he (gendered male) is doubly privileged as the site for interrogating the assimilative function of heteronormativity and national identity.

To be sure, inasmuch as the work of queer globalization scholars looks to foreground sexuality as a necessary category for thinking the material, psychic, and social effects of globalization, these interventions are both necessary and significant. At the same time, the emphasis on the queer diasporic subject as the central figure of that analysis produces a critical discourse that reinvests in the very categories it would seem to want to challenge. First, the structure of analogy between the queer and the diasporic establishes a tenuous partnership; here the work of Black feminist critics usefully reminds us that such critical analogies fail to attend to the complexities of differentially lived experiences (Crenshaw, 1991; Collins, 2000; Zack, 2005). Moreover, in focusing on mobility over stasis, these interventions have less to say about the conditions that enable or disable the body's mobility. In this way, such theories replicate what other feminist critics have isolated as a gendered dynamic in which women occupy, implicitly, the static role of the local, as well as a critical trend in which queer theory more generally has looked to disarticulate itself from feminism by positing 'queer' as mobile, in relation to feminism's presumed fixity (Martin, 1997). They replicate, as well, the critical paradigm evidenced in macroanalyses of globalization, which have had little to say about gender as an organizing category (Harvey, 1989; Waters, 1995; Appadurai, 1996). The result is 'the implicit, but powerful, dichotomous model in which the gender of globalization is mapped in such a way that the global: masculine as local: feminine' (Freeman, 2001: 1,008).

Such work would thus do well to attend to the critical history of mobility as a liberatory paradigm. This is the challenge offered by Sara Ahmed (2000), who warns against the reification of 'migrant ontologies' in which migration is understood as a necessarily transgressive mode of existence. Likewise, while recognizing the new patterns of movement that are characteristic of post-Fordist regimes of production and consumption, several feminist critics insist upon the importance of groundedness as well, questioning 'the presumption that rootless mobility is the defining feature of contemporary experience' (Ahmed *et al.,* 2003: 2).

As I have argued, this collapsing of the queer and the diasporic prevents us from forging a politics that could recognize the patterns of contradiction and complicity between the psychic and the social, the cultural and the economic, that converge to produce the formations of queerness we recognize today. The claim for the mobile transgressivity of queerness as its own diasporic category – the idea that it is necessarily disruptive of categories of nation, home, and family – misses the ways in which queer desire is necessarily constituted in relation to such categories and can offer us no assurance of their disruption. The point is not to deny the power of mobility as a condition of modern existence, but to resist its epistemological centrality in contemporary scholarship and, in so doing, mark the specificity of forms of rootedness and movement as coincidental, not oppositional categories (Brah, 1996; Fortier, 2003; Gopinath, 2005). As Roger Rouse has observed, 'the cultural politics of domination always concerns the regulation of desire' (1995: 376); as such, queer desire, no less than other forms, must be understood to be fundamentally implicated in the social reproduction of globalization. To take the regulation of desire and domination seriously, then, I suggest we start by abandoning our sense of the forms that such regulation might take. Our starting point would thus take seriously Amy Villarejo's warning that 'there is no confident way of predicting *how* gender will be consolidated in the service of regulatory mechanisms in any given place or moment' (2003: 16). It is precisely in the spirit of such unpredictability that the critical insights of queer theory might be brought to bear upon the political, social, and economic transformations of globalization, not only to push the boundaries of what we might understand as queer, but also to offer new insight into the regulatory mechanisms and the forms of desire such global transformations produce.

[. . .]

Butterflies on the Scaffold thus joins *Remote Sensing* in offering inventive readings of the relations between gender, sexuality, and globalization, readings in which, importantly, labour figures centrally. While *Remote Sensing* offers a suggestive look at sex work as a mobile, gendered form of labour, *Butterflies* asks that we consider how gender itself is a kind of labour – one that drag makes explicit but that is nevertheless part of the production of all gendered bodies. As such, it insists that gender is a part of a material process, linked to the reproduction of nations, the formation of the 'new man', and to the broader patterns of global production and exchange. What these films share is a compelling sense of the material, psychic, and physical costs that comprise the everyday productions of gender, of sexuality, and of desire. Such productions might at first seem out of context in a critical evaluation of queer diaspora, for neither film takes as its focus the queer diasporic subject. However, in each film's careful interrogation of the production of the sexual subject within the particular geographical locations and dislocations of globalization, they offer the opportunity to reconsider this alignment between queerness and mobility, pushing us to consider how each of our contemporary articulations of sexual and gender identity are produced within, and in relation to, globalization. That is to say, the work of queer globalization studies is not simply to seek out liberatory positions for queer subjects in the shifting material, national, and geographical configurations of globalization, though some such liberatory spaces may indeed be found there. It is, as well, and perhaps more pressingly, to understand whether or not the material changes that attend the conditions of globalization, mobility, and diaspora engender new notions of the normative and the queer, new forms of discipline and liberation, and new articulations of desire, identity and sexuality. To 'queer' diaspora is thus to reopen the question of the relation between the sexual and the global, without knowing in advance whether or not the forms that sexual identity might take will even be fully recognizable to us as queer or straight, normative or not. Such possibilities, I would say, are the most critically viable ones available.

References

Ahmed, S. (2000) *Strange Encounters: Embodied Others in Post-Coloniality*, London and New York: Routledge.

Ahmed, S., Casañeda, C., Fortier, A. and Sheller, M. (2003) 'Introduction' in Ahmed, S., Castañeda, C., Fortier, A. and Sheller, M. (2003) editors, *Uprootings/Regroundings: Questions of Home and Migration*, New York: Berg.

Appadurai, A. (1996) *Modernity at Large: Cultural Dimensions of Globalization*, Minneapolis: University of Minnesota.

Brah, A. (1996) *Cartographies of Diaspora: Contesting Identities*, New York: Routledge.

Collins, P.H. (2000) 'Gender, black feminism, and black political economy' *Annals of the American Academy of Political and Social Science*, No. 568: 41–53.

Crenshaw, K. (1991) 'Mapping the margins: Intersectionality, identity politics, and violence against women of color' *Stanford Law Review*, Vol. 43: 1241–1299.

Fortier, A. (2003) 'Queer migrations and motions of attachment' in Ahmed, S., Castañeda, C., Fortier, A. and Sheller, M. (2003) editors, *Uprootings/Regroundings: Questions of Home and Migration*, New York: Berg.

Freeman C. (2001) 'Is local: global as feminine: masculine? Rethinking the gender of globalization' *Signs: Journal of Women in Culture and Society*, Vol. 26, No. 4: 1007–1037.

Gopinath, G. (2005) *Impossible Desires: Queer Diasporas and South Asian Popular Cultures*, Durham, NC: Duke University Press.

Harvey, D. (1989) *The Conditions of Postmodernity: An Enquiry into the Origins of Cultural Change*, Cambridge, MA: Blackwell.

Martin, B. (1997) *Femininity Played Straight: The Significance of Being Lesbian*, New York: Routledge.

Roger Rouse, R. (1995) 'Thinking through transnationalism: notes on the cultural politics of class relations in the contemporary United States' *Public Culture*, Vol. 7: 353–402.

Villarejo, A. (2003) *Lesbian Rule: Cultural Criticism and the Value of Desire*, Durham, NC: Duke University Press.

Waters, M. (1995) *Globalization*, New York: Routledge.

Zack, N. (2005) *Inclusive Feminism: A Third Wave Theory of Women's Commonality*, Lanham, MD: Rowman & Littlefield.

PART IV

Cultural production

DIASPORA LITERATURE

Introduction

Literature, when it is not used in its broad definition of 'printed matter of any kind' (*OED*), but of a specifically defined kind of text as an art form and hence usually spelt with a capital 'L', is conceptually very much a product of the nineteenth century. When Thomas Warton set out to write his comprehensive literary history (never completed), he still entitled it *History of English Poetry* (4 vols, 1774–81), and university professors of English still typically held chairs in 'Poetry' (Thomas Warton in Oxford, for instance) or in 'Rhetoric and Belles Lettres' (Hugh Blair's regius chair in Edinburgh, for example). When Robert Chambers published the first complete history of British literature in 1836, he chose *History of English Language and Literature* as its title and clearly set out to project English Literature as a historical development and an ongoing endeavour to unite and educate the British (Stierstorfer 2005), a project which the then evolving discipline of 'Eng. Lit.' was to follow up throughout the rest of the nineteenth century. The modern concept of 'Literature' must thus be seen as firmly set in the context of a national agenda from which it cannot easily be extracted.

Since the appearance of a diaspora within a national framework based on the idea of a homogenous national culture is widely recognized as an irritation and a challenge, questioning the basic tenets of nationhood and citizenship, the emergence of diasporic literature must also be expected to challenge and irritate the very basis of how we understand 'Literature' today: its functions and cultural significance, its forms and genres, its production and marketing and its reception. Such foundational research into the impact of a now burgeoning diaspora literature – literature written by diasporic writers or about diasporic themes, and sometimes specifically targeting a diasporic market – and on the very of concept of 'literature', i.e. in a wider theory or philosophy of literature, is still missing. The texts by Yogita Goyal and Yoon Sun Lee reprinted here are, however, good indicators of the new direction and orientation that such research might take.

A distinct set of issues gravitates around the question of the uses and functions which can be ascribed to literature in a diasporic context. Here, Theodor W. Adorno's claim that literature is home comes to mind as one with particular relevance to diasporic writers. Adorno ([1951] 2005) states in *Minima Moralia*:

> In the text, the writer sets up house. Just as he trundles papers, books, pencils, documents
> untidily from room to room, he creates the same disorder in his thoughts. They become

pieces of furniture that he sinks into, content or irritable. He strokes them affectionately, wears them out, mixes them up, re-arranges, ruins them. For a man who no longer has a homeland, writing becomes a place to live.

(87)

The uses of literature as home-making which Adorno describes for the individual writer on the production side can also be credited as functions of literature in diasporic contexts on the reception side. If, following Benedict Anderson (1983), nations are to be understood as 'imagined communities', and if literature plays a major role in the processes of such 'imagining', then the same must hold true for diasporic communities, with the further twist that such processes of the transnational literary imagination will pose an irritation and complication for the analogous processes occurring in the host country as well as in the country of origin. And it is arguably these irritations and complications that make diaspora literature so productive and interesting today.

Generally, literature can provide a powerful forum for investigating and presenting the diasporic experience from various angles and for raising and negotiating important issues affecting life in diaspora and life of diasporic groups within a host country. Thus, religion and culture of the Muslim diaspora in Britain can receive such different and highly sophisticated literary attention as offered by Hanif Kureishi's *My Son the Fanatic* (1997; first published in 1994) on the one hand and by Leila Aboulela's novel *Minaret* (2005) on the other. Where Kureishi almost prophetically describes the dangers of fundamentalism in second-generation Muslim immigrants as a reaction to the lack of acceptance of their parents and integration into British society, Aboulela projects her female protagonist's orthodox Muslim belief as a mainstay of her identity, enabling her to navigate her way as a diasporic person in Britain. Such literary interventions in negotiating diasporic existence at large, but also in very specific, national or local contexts, can influence and guide the understanding of diasporas in their political, social and cultural importance. They can also help to re-evaluate what literature is for our time and culture and what it can achieve in such present-day contexts.

In her monograph *Romance, Diaspora and Black Atlantic Literature*, the introduction of which is partly reprinted in the following, Yogita Goyal (2010) exemplifies the 'traffic' of ideas between black diasporic intellectuals throughout the twentieth century as it crystallizes around the contrastive figures of Franz Fanon and Marcus Garvey as the main theorists of black Atlantic exchange. She points out that 'Garvey's race-based nationalism and Fanon's non-racial, non-ethnic anti-colonial revolution simply cannot be understood through received understandings of either nation or diaspora' (7). She therefore perceives the need 'to excavate a larger tradition of diasporic debate over Africa' which has the three hallmarks of 'the synthesis of national and transnational concerns, the centrality of Africa, and the significance of romance and realism' (7). Goyal's subsequent argument then becomes a good instance of diaspora and literature, as she identifies and illustrates the contrastive approaches epitomized by Garvey and Fanon by an analysis of the literary form where they are, as Goyal finds, 'sedimented'. Using the insight to be gained from the premises of Fredric Jameson's genre theory, she is able to cast the 'two competing modes' of 'nationalist realism and diasporic romance' as the source from which 'black Atlantic fiction gains its energy' (8). Goyal provides insight into how 'genre analysis can help call attention to both politics and aesthetics at once' (12, this volume 191).

Yoon Sun Lee's (2016) contribution on 'The postcolonial novel and diaspora' is another of the generally rare instances where diaspora is productively researched using instruments and concepts specific to literature and literary scholarship. Rather than merely exploring the particular subject in individual diasporic novels or even in the diasporic novel as a kind of subgenre in the field, Lee looks at the characteristics of the novel as a literary form. Identifying 'dispersal, disintegration and the "affirmation of a distance"' (133) as central features of the genre, she then goes on to show how the diasporic novel takes up literary heritage and creatively transforms it, constituting 'a mature dialectical engagement with the formal horizons of the novel as a genre'. This results in interesting observations that, 'rather than revealing how a whole emerges out of multiple parts, then, diasporic novels seem to focus more on the performativity of social dimensions of identity' (145, this volume 198). An overdue generic profiling of the diasporic novel is started here with a wider field of further research in diasporic literature clearly apparent on the horizon.

References

Aboulela, Leila. 2005. *Minaret*. London: Bloomsbury.

Adorno, Theodor W. [1951] 2005. *Minima Moralia: Reflections on a Damaged Life*. Trans. by E.F.M. Jephcott. London and New York: Verso.

Anderson, Benedict. 1983. *Imagined Communities: Reflections on the Origin and Spread of Nationalism*. London: Verso.

Goyal, Yogita. 2010. *Romance, Diaspora and Black Atlantic Literature*. Cambridge: Cambridge University Press.

Kureishi, Hanif. [1994] 1997. 'My Son the Fanatic.' In *Love in a Blue Time*, edited by Hanif Kureishi, 119–131. London: Faber.

Lee, Yoon Sun. 2016. 'The Postcolonial Novel and Diaspora.' In *The Cambridge Companion to the Post-colonial Novel*, edited by Ato Quayson, 133–151. Cambridge: Cambridge University Press.

Stierstorfer, Klaus. 2005. 'Vestiges of Nineteenth-Century Biology and Literature: Robert Chambers.' In *Evolving Networks: Biology, Literature and Culture in the Nineteenth Century*, edited by Christa Jansohn and Anne Zwierlein, 27–39. London: Anthem Press.

26

ROMANCE, DIASPORA AND BLACK ATLANTIC LITERATURE

Yogita Goyal

The connection between the novel and the nation is well documented in cultural studies. Drawing from the work of Benedict Anderson in *Imagined Communities*, we are accustomed to thinking about the inextricable relation between the modern nation and the realist novel.[1] Realism has been thought of as the perfect analogue for the project of producing a modern nation, along calendrical, clock time and faith in ideas of progress. On the other hand, the question of the literary form of diaspora narratives is more open-ended. (As Gilroy suggests, in black Atlantic narratives time stops and starts: there is no clear faith in progress, rather the coordinates are the void of the Middle Passage and the horizon of the Jubilee.) In this study, I suggest that diaspora is commonly tied to a break in the form of the realist novel and may be linked to the genre of the romance, implying a non-linear, messianic temporality. Black Atlantic literature expresses both the teleological, modernizing impulse of nationalist realism and the recursive logic of diasporic romance. To imagine a community that is characterized by both national and transnational concerns, black Atlantic texts constitute an eclectic genre, where the realist narrative of the nation is interrupted by the romance of the diaspora. The peculiar nature of black nationalism – its necessary constitution in diaspora – entails such complexity of form.

Reading romance as a mode of representation across twentieth-century black Atlantic novels, my study argues that romance provides two potentially contradictory understandings of diaspora. On the one hand, romance allows black Atlantic writers to imagine diaspora as a utopian horizon, one that breaks away from existing forms of social organization such as nation or ethnic group. On the other hand, romance – as a form that can harmonize seemingly irreconcilable opposites – helps black Atlantic writers collapse distances of time and space to imagine a simultaneity of experience. While the first mode theorizes diaspora as difference, the second mode implies a certain wholeness of vision that refuses to accommodate any sense of difference at all (spatial, temporal, historical, or geographical). Instead of identifying texts as belonging to either one approach, I suggest that they inhabit the two modes in constant tension, offering varying fictional or (what Jameson would call) magical resolutions. My point is not to argue for the essentially escapist or subversive quality of the romance form, but to excavate its precise contribution to the construction of a global black imagined community. Thus, I suggest that romance enables black Atlantic writers to create certain partitions of space between the domestic and the foreign, and partitions of time between the modern and the primeval. Instead of accepting the binary opposition of romance and realism, and coming down on one side as for or against romance, I wish to inhabit and stretch to the breaking point the oppositions romance helps these writers to con-struct, dismantle, or otherwise perform. To render what such writers see as real, magical, or mythic, or to try to change reality by using romance to posit alternatives, or to disturb the boundaries between the real and the fictional, romance becomes an infinitely malleable form. Thinking of genre as the presence of the past in the present, my study highlights constant transformation, as earlier forms are constantly returning, being displaced, inverted, or reproduced. Impure at its very origin, romance inevitably implies a repatterning and rebeginning, rather than the birth of something wholly original, as the writers of diasporic romance compose narratives that function both as a recovery and as an imaginative projection. In this respect, romance allows these writers to collapse time and space to give us a whole, or to shine a beam of light onto one moment, or even to give us a progressive history read backwards from a future point of redemption.

In *Playing in the Dark*, Toni Morrison has written eloquently of the centrality of romance to American literature, urging scholars to decipher its racial coding and the significant work romance is called upon to perform in imaginings of the national community. Morrison insists that an "American Africanism" haunts American literature, figuring blackness as a blank empty space, always available for carrying out the duties of exorcism, reification, and mirroring. "Through the simple expedient of demonizing and reifying the range of color on a palette," Morrison argues, "American Africanism makes it possible to say and not say, to inscribe and erase, to escape and engage, to act out and act on, to historicize and render timeless."[2] Extending her insights in a global frame, this study investigates the ways in which romance produces Africa in the diasporic imagination. Certainly, for African-Americans and others in the diaspora, Africa occurs not just as a dark mirror but as a more complicated sign, which has the power to give or withhold meaning – to return value to the past and to give shape to the future.[3] In excess of common colonial and imperial constructions of Africa as well as of American ones of blackness in general, black diasporic writers turn to Africa to garner cultural solace, to construct a usable past, or to search for the means to create a political future through the sense of a shared destiny. Veering between and across racial nationalism and universalism, they neither simply invert nor adopt existing notions of either formation, but attempt to transform their meaning to suit specific goals.

It is worth noting as well that romance has long held a privileged place in studies of American literature as an analytic tool for gauging the national character as expressed in literature. The romance theory of American fiction forwarded by Richard Chase and other mid-century thinkers has become discredited in the revisionist critique of the New Americanists who point out Chase's interest in creating an exclusionary canon.[4] More broadly, genre criticism is seen as an outmoded or apolitical way of reading material that is better served by historicist and inter-dis-ciplinary approaches, inflected by an awareness of race, class, gender, and sexuality. But romance, as Morrison points out, is deeply implicated in and produced by heavily racialized tropes, and to limn the nature of the tropological work of race in US literature, it is necessary to turn again to the forms that literature takes. Discussions of genre often turn on the issue of aesthetic pleasure. It is not that I am unconcerned with the imaginative force of literature, but my focus lies elsewhere; I am interested in questions of aesthetic style as epistemology, as grounds for knowledge pro-duction, as the site on which questions of power play out. We need only recall the tussle between Booker T. Washington and Du Bois at the beginning of the twentieth century to note that questions of culture were at the heart of African-American struggles for equal rights. We may bear in mind as well Fanon's lengthy discussions of national literature and an appropriate aesthetic form for the nationalist revolution in his manifesto, *The Wretched of the Earth*, or Richard Wright's insistence on avoiding sentimentalism in the portrayal of race relations. Writers as varied as Chinua Achebe, Pauline Hopkins, and Ama Ata Aidoo invariably entangle their aesthetic choices with weighty political and historical questions. It is my belief that by exploring the deep investment of black Atlantic writers in such literary and aesthetic strategies, we can add to the exciting array of possibilities opened up by transnational studies. To assume that genre is not pertinent to the study of race is to suppose that the minority text exists as itself, without institutional identity or pressures. Genre categories frame the expectations both readers and writers bring to a literary text, embedding within themselves a veritable social history of narrative conventions, patterns, and modes of representation. Excavating the cultural work of genre, then, helps highlight aesthetic form as well as epistemological possibility. No genre is inherently conservative or radical, but insofar as genres and their circulation across various national and transnational literatures can be understood through historicist methods of analyzing form, genre analysis can help call attention to both politics and aesthetics at once. To truly globalize American studies, a catalog of what might constitute a black Atlantic canon can help revitalize the sometimes flat oppositions that characterize the field, as attention to the aesthetic may return us more fully and with greater subtlety and texture to the politics and ideologies at the heart of conceptions of the African diaspora.

Diaspora is a term notorious for its semantic expandability, often coming in to stand in for a host of related terms, including transnationality, cosmopolitanism, transatlanticism, exile, expatriation, postcoloniality, migrancy, and globality. Clearly, the term is now a keyword in the manner defined by Raymond Williams. In black studies, the term "diaspora," as Brent Edwards points out, emerges out of the pan-African movement of the mid-twentieth century, though of course, one could easily point to earlier forms of black transnational activity that would also be encompassed by the term, such as the Ethiopianist, Emigrationist, and African Colonization movements of the nineteenth century.[5] The range of ideas and movements the rubric calls into play could vary from the sociological and historical work of Du Bois, St. Clair Drake, George Shepperson, and Arturo Schomburg to the anthropological inquiries into African survivals conducted by Melville Herskovits and Jean-Price Mars. One could also turn to any number of historical moments to track a genealogy of the term, its relation to Jewish concepts of diaspora, or to socialist or communist forms of internationalism. In terms of naming diaspora, then, one could summon an infinitely large body of intellectual work dedicated to thinking through the connections between African-descended peoples. Such a process of nominalization is not my concern here. Rather, precisely because the term can as easily allude to a historical experience of displacement as to a figure for hybridity in cultural studies, I wish to insist on a rigorous and careful stratification.[6] Historicizing the term involves realizing that diaspora is not simply a sign of hybridity, postmodern plasticity, or a logical result of the increasing mobility of ideas, people, and objects in a late capitalist world. In sharp contrast to those who would empty the term of its long and muddled history in discourses of racial essentialism, nationalism, or black Zionism and point solely to its emancipatory qualities, I would like to keep alive the political indeterminacy and richness of that very history.

Romance is another particularly nebulous and historically capacious term, variously interpreted as a genre, a mode, a set of representational strategies, a host of narrative conventions, or even a kind of literary shorthand. As a recent attempt to define romance puts it, it is perhaps easiest to say of romance that we know it when we see it, even as defining it precisely is a much more difficult, even impossible endeavor.[7]

In broad terms, romance refers to a shift outside of realism into the sphere of the marvelous rather than the mundane, often organized around the motif of a quest into unknown territories (both physical and the uncanny zone of the self). Often seen as dealing with the eternal rather than the historical, the ontological rather than the political, romance suggests a movement outside of the linearity of time and history into the cyclic nature of myth and prophecy. Romance encompasses multiple resonances, from the medieval quest-romance, to the sentimental or domestic allegory of love and marriage, to the heroic narrative of struggle and redemption. As Northrop Frye has suggested, it often involves nostalgia for an idealized past, in part to search for alternatives to the social ideals of the here and now.[8] In the words of Jameson, romance offers "the possibility of sensing other historical rhythms" free "from that reality principle to which a now oppressive realistic representation is the hostage."[9] But rather than accepting romance's self-presentation as timeless, unearthing the ideological contexts that govern its premises can help successfully assess its representational work across various times and places. To do so is not to curtail its meaning, but to note how it tries to manage the proliferation of such meanings in order to produce a set of desired cultural and political configurations.

In thinking of the changing uses and functions of romance, it is worth recalling that the role of literature in black Atlantic societies has long exceeded the aesthetic alone, as literature is expected to carry out the work of both history and prophecy. Romance fits the elasticity and semantic openness required for such activities of cultural reconstruction and remembrance, but also for its ability to signal the freedom of possibilities beyond the degraded reality of the present. Once mimetic fidelity, consistency of plot or characterization, and plausibility can be jettisoned as the only criteria through which to judge a text, representations of excess in both form and content may be seen as offering greater possibilities for the political visions that prompt the questions: what is real, what is possible?

My goal, then, in assessing the work of romance in this study is to open up rather than to foreclose interpretive possibilities by attending to the array of meanings encapsulated in the term itself. It is an expansive term, fit for the reach of diasporic visions, which themselves accept no limit or boundary of time or space. In suggesting that romance is the paradigmatic genre of diaspora, my point is not to be prescriptive or to invoke some notion of purity of genre. Categorizing modern prose into the genres of realism and romance is, of course, a messy process.[10] And after all, not all diaspora fictions are romances, and there is no reason at all why there could not be realist representations of diaspora. But most often over the twentieth century, the genre that writers have turned to over and again to represent the black diaspora is that of romance. Even writers like Du Bois, to take just one example, whose concerns are largely sociological, philosophical, and historiographic, have sought the genre of romance for their representations of diaspora. My point is also neither empirical nor taxonomic: to note the proliferation of non-realist strategies of representation in diaspora literature is not to say very much. Rather, by elaborating the varied and surprising work black Atlantic writers put romance to, I want to track these strategies to show how they construct a particular relation of diaspora to modernity by creating partitions of time and space, and by suggesting especially that traversing space can equal movement in time. The study thus offers not a comprehensive study of these explorations but a carefully selected and precise genealogy across various historical conjunctures of a group of writers who produce a distinct historical logic and make visible a particular theoretical and conceptual purchase of diaspora. As specific kinds of representational acts, and also as ways of conceptualizing the world, black Atlantic literature's shifts between the genres of realism and romance call for a nuanced analysis of the cultural contradictions being mapped and managed therein. In this way, the book attempts to treat literary style politically, as a supple and disputed concept within twentieth-century black culture, by replacing static models of racial identity formation and national formation with more flexible, more dynamic ones of migration, circulation, and entanglement. In tracking the history of a genre, I call attention to the way in which genres exist in time, and so provide a means of reviving a kind of historical thinking, in order to stress the relationship between cultural texts located in different times and places. Each writer I look at remakes the form so that it will be adequate to a changing experience of modernity. In addition to offering new ways to read the place of Africa, then, my study of black Atlantic literature also aims

to alter our understanding of how these writers use diverse narrative forms to make sense of –
indeed, to make – our world.

Framed as it is by a discussion of black modernity and counter-modernity, this study is also an
exploration of the politics of time and space. If nation time is linear and developmental (albeit
interrupted by what Arjun Appadurai calls disjunctive and difference), how may we theorize the
time of diaspora?[11] Similarly if nationalist investments are invariably territorial, can the fluid
spatiality of diaspora constitute a viable alternative? While for Gilroy, a black Atlantic space
emerges as an unstable web of identifications that are marked neither territorially nor temporally,
in my analysis, temporality and territoriality both remain central to discussions of diaspora.
I suggest that shifts in genre index specific temporalities – linear and developmental in the case of
nationalist realism, and recursive and messianic in the case of diasporic romance. While nation
time links past, present, and future in a march towards progress, diaspora time emphasizes the
breaks and discontinuities in such a movement, recalling the trauma of the Middle Passage and
looking forward to the Jubilee. In Walter Benjamin's terms, we may say that diaspora time works
differently from nation time as "the time of the now" is shot through with the memory of the
Middle Passage. Instead of defining diaspora time as the "homogenous, empty time" of progress,
it is more appropriate to see it as a time that is characterized by rupture, but also by various kinds of
imagined or projected simultaneities.[12]

That nationalism paradoxically presents itself both as new and old has been pointed out by
several scholars. If, as Tom Nairn suggests, nationalism can be thought of as a modern Janus,
facing back into history in order to move into the modern, every nationalist project must invent
and codify a tradition.[13] In black nationalist discourse, this doubleness is further complicated
by the break of the Middle Passage which ensures that the immemorial past being hailed is
geographically located in Africa, while the future being willed into existence is securely in the
New World. Here it is helpful to recall Benjamin's theory of history as a catastrophe, a notion that
permeates black Atlantic literature, countering the Enlightenment notion of history as progress.
Instead of an understanding of the past as a "chain of events" in the fashion of a positivist historian,
Benjamin offers "one single catastrophe which keeps piling wreckage upon wreckage." Benjamin
asks for the historical materialist to break the myth of continuity in history, and to "brush history
against the grain."[14] To accomplish this redemptive task, the storyteller creates images that fuse
past and present, images that make visible that which has been left out and must now be
reclaimed. These dialectical images confront the experience of the past with the reality of the
now, and momentarily achieve a halt in the progress of history. Accordingly, rather than simply
dismissing diasporic accounts that view Africa as the source of redemption, I draw on Benjamin to
excavate the political potential, if any, of such redemptive fantasies. How might we read diasporic
romances against their grain to find the alternate future that we desire? Instead of viewing these
dreams through the positivist lens of their eventual failure, we need to revisit them and find their
potential, in order to redeem what Benjamin calls our "*weak* messianic power"[15] We can then
understand our present not only in the terms of the hegemonic past but also in light of the
counter-discourses that have been suppressed in the histories of the past. A Benjamin-influenced
reading would release the alternatives that a single line of narrative has to suppress in order to
constitute itself as dominant.

Notes

1 Benedict Anderson, *Imagined Communities: Reflections on the Origin and Spread of Nationalism* (London and
  New York: Verso, 1991).
2 Toni Morrison, *Playing in the Dark: Whiteness and the Literary Imagination* (New York: Vintage, 1992), 7.

3 See Edward Said, *Orientalism* (New York: Pantheon, 1978) and Christopher Miller, *Blank Darkness: Africanist Discourse in French* (Chicago: University of Chicago Press, 1985).

4 Richard Chase defines romance as "an assumed freedom from the ordinary novelistic requirements of verisimilitude, development, and continuity; a tendency towards melodrama and idyll; a more or less formal abstractness and, on the other hand, a tendency to plunge into the underside of consciousness; a willingness to abandon moral questions or to ignore the spectacle of man in society, or to consider these things only indirectly or abstractly" (*The American Novel and Its Tradition* [New York: Anchor-Doubleday, 1957], ix). Chase's argument relies on tropes common in transnational studies, as he draws a distinction between imperial English fiction, concerned with bringing order to disorder, and American fiction, interested in exploration, discovery, and escape, and so more fittingly called "border fiction" (19). For a trenchant critique of the romance thesis, see Nina Baym, "Concepts of Romance in Hawthorne's America," *Nineteenth-Century Fiction* 38 (1984), 426–443. See also Frederick Crews, "Whose American Romance?" *New York Review of Books* 35 (1988), 16 and Michael Davitt Bell, *The Development of American Romance: The Sacrifice of Relation* (Chicago: University of Chicago Press, 1980).

5 For a thorough map of the genealogy of the term "diaspora," see Brent Edwards, "The Uses of Diaspora," *Social Text* 66 (Spring 2001), 45–73. For definitions of black diaspora, see Stuart Hall, "Cultural Identity and Diaspora" in Patrick Williams and Laura Chrisman (eds), *Colonial Discourse and Postcolonial Theory: A Reader* (New York: Columbia University Press, 1994); "New Ethnicities" in David Morley and Kuan-Hsing Ching (eds), *Stuart Hall: Critical Dialogues in Cultural Studies* (London: Routledge, 1996); "Thinking the Diaspora: Home-Thoughts from Abroad," *Small Axe* 6 (1999), 1–18; David Scott, "'An Obscure Miracle of Connection': Discursive Tradition and Black Diaspora Criticism," *Small Axe* 1 (1997), 19–38; Jonathan Elmer, "The Black Atlantic Archive," *American Literary History* 17.1 (2005), 160–170; and Xiomara Santamarina, "'Are We There Yet?': Archives, History, and Specificity in African-American Literary Studies," *American Literary History* 20.1–2 (2008), 304–316. For discussions of diaspora in cultural studies, see Khachig Tololyan, "Rethinking Diaspora(s): Stateless Power in the Transnational Moment," *Diaspora* 5.1 (1996), 3–36, who argues that "cultural studies discourse has found in the diasporic subject a figure for double and multiple consciousness, for a split, even dispersed subject-in-process that crisscrosses boundaries and resists totalization." In this way, diaspora becomes a trope for the hybridity of the postcolonial or postmodern condition, a move that disregards a longer history where the term has a different resonance (such as the nineteenth-century writings of Blyden, Crummell, Delany, and Turner, and the twentieth-century activity of Garvey, Chief Sam, George Padmore, and the poets and thinkers of *négritude*). See also James Clifford, "Diasporas" in *Routes: Travel and Translation in the Late Twentieth Century* (Cambridge, MA: Harvard University Press, 1997), 244–278; Arjun Appadurai, *Modernity at Large: Cultural Dimensions of Globalization* (Delhi: Oxford University Press, 1997); and Homi Bhabha, *The Location of Culture* (London: Routledge, 1994).

6 It is important to note that "black Atlantic" and "diaspora" are not interchangeable terms, as Colin Palmer has argued ("Defining and Studying the Modern African Diaspora," *Perspectives* 36.6 [1998], 24–25). But the two terms – though different in their historical and geographical moorings – often end up doing a similar kind of conceptual work in literary and cultural studies. For Gilroy, using the frame of the Atlantic rather than that of diaspora was an attempt to escape the suggestion of return that older conceptions of diaspora may carry. And yet, the Atlantic cannot preclude the difficult question of origins or of myths of return. See Alasdair Pettinger, "Enduring Fortresses: A Review of *The Black Atlantic*" *Research in African Literatures* 29.4 (1998), 142–147; Charles Piot, "Atlantic Aporias: Africa and Gilroy's Black Atlantic," *The South Atlantic Quarterly* 100.1 (2001), 155–170; and Elliott Skinner, "Dialectic between Diasporas and Homelands" in Joseph E. Harris (ed.), *Global Dimensions of the African Diaspora* (Washington, DC: Howard University Press, 1993).

7 Barbara Fuchs writes, "Romance is a notoriously slippery category. Critics disagree about whether it is a genre or a mode, about its origins and history, even about what it encompasses. Yet, paradoxically, readers are often able to identify romance almost tacitly: they know it when they see it" (*Romance* [New York and London: Routledge, 2004], 1–2). Also see Bell, *Development of American Romance;* Winfried Fluck, "The American Romance and the Changing Functions of the Imaginary," *New Literary History* 27.3 (1996), 415–457; Northrop Frye, *Anatomy of Criticism* (Princeton: Princeton University Press, 1957) and *The Secular Scripture: A Study of the Structure of Romance* (Cambridge, MA: Harvard University Press, 1976); Geraldine Heng, *Empire of Magic: Medieval Romance and the Politics of Cultural Fantasy* (New York: Columbia University Press, 2003); and Amy Kaplan, *The Anarchy of Empire in the Making of US Culture* (Cambridge, MA: Harvard University Press, 2002).

8 See Frye, *Secular Scripture*.

9 [Fredric] Jameson, *The Political Unconscious: Narrative as a Socially Symbolic Act)*, (Ithaca: Cornell University Press, 1981) 104.

10 See Ian Duncan, *Modern Romance and Transformations of the Novel: The Gothic, Scott, Dickens* (Cambridge: Cambridge University Press, 1992).

11 Appadurai, *Modernity at Large*, 27–47.

12 Walter Benjamin, *Illuminations*, ed. Hannah Arendt, trans. Harry Zohn (London: Fontana, HarperCollins, 1992), 255.

13 Tom Nairn, *The Break-up of Britain: Crisis and Neo-Nationalism* (London: Verso, 1981). On time and nation, see Anderson's *Imagined Communities*; Bhabha's *Location of Culture*; Partha Chatterjee's *The Nation and Its Fragments: Colonial and Postcolonial Histories* (Delhi: Oxford University Press, 1995); and Eddie Glaude, Jr. (ed.), *Is it Nation Time? Contemporary Essays on Black Power and Black Nationalism* (Chicago: University of Chicago Press, 2002).

14 Benjamin, *Illuminations*, 248, 249.

15 *Ibid.*, 246.

27

THE POSTCOLONIAL NOVEL AND DIASPORA

Yoon Sun Lee

Theorists have extensively examined the relation of diasporic social formations to hegemonic ideologies, including those of nation-state and empire. My concern here is not to discover a political orientation inherent in diasporic identity; rather, I will examine the structures of feeling and imagination found in novels written by and about populations characterized by a conscious, persistent sense of displacement. The key aspects of the diasporic imaginary highlighted in sociological and theoretical accounts can also be found in the novels of diaspora. Most important is the dialectic of host nation and homeland, the recursive mutual structuring of memory and discovery, the myth of the homeland and the experience of the host nation. This dialectic structures space, identity, and attitudes toward the material world, including the body.[1] These dimensions, which this essay will examine, can be aligned with traditional aspects of the realist novel: its setting or what Fredric Jameson has called its floor plan, the models of subjectivity and sociality that underlie its character system, and its overall plot trajectory. But the diasporic novel is more deeply marked by the recursive shaping of here and there, former selves and future selves. These features allow us to see in it the heir to the cultural revolution that Jameson identifies with the nineteenth-century realist novel. If the prose of Balzac and Flaubert helped to bring about the disenchantment or "desacralization of the older precapitalist life world," undoing hierarchies and erasing pluralities of qualitative experience, the diasporic novel carries on that work.[2] This is not to say that the diasporic novel portrays the world as uniform. In fact, it is driven by the discovery in the host nation of deeply embedded, highly consequential forms of difference, whether racial, gendered, or socioeconomic. But what results from this discovery is far from the reassertion of fixed relations, identities, or locations. Instead, the diasporic novel questions the hierarchy of center and periphery, uncouples movement from space in an era of accelerating travel, and articulates a striking ambivalence toward identity, property, and even material embodiment. In its more radical moments, its aim even appears to be dissolution: a dissolving of the bonds that hold bodies together.

The diasporic imaginary rests on space: space traversed, experienced, and registered as distance. As such, it constitutes a particularly rich and complex dimension of this genre: space is rarely if ever a simple backdrop, setting, or container. Uncoupled from actual place, space is often oddly impervious to experience or knowledge. It is marked by internal divisions, invisible barriers as well as impossible contiguities. Labyrinths, a frequent figure in these novels, are as intensive as they are extensive, a matter of a private inability either to escape or to enter a place. To begin to illuminate this dimension of the diasporic novel, we can turn to the idea of the nonplace described by the anthropologist Marc Augé. Anthropological place, Augé argues, provides a stable principle of meaning: associated with origin and identity, it encodes social relations both internal and external to a group, and constitutes a link with the past.[3] Nonplaces, by contrast, result from the hypermobility, eventfulness, and individualism of what Augé calls "supermodernity." Empirical nonplaces, which include "air, rail, and motorway routes, the mobile cabins called 'means of transport' . . . airports and railway stations, hotel chains, leisure parks, large retail outlets," create a "solitary contractuality," in which the individual enjoys a temporary anonymity in her role as simply customer, user, or passenger. As Augé argues, the nonplace "creates neither singular identity nor relations; only solitude and similitude."[4] Nonplaces, in other words, belong to the realm of seriality and superficial resemblance, while anthropological places reinforce singular identities.

If anthropological places as well as theoretical world systems are internally ordered around central nodes, diasporic novels reflect serial displacement, entrapment, and dissolution. The diasporic imaginary often lacks the sense of a center through which peripheralized locations or persons can mediate their identity. By way of contrast, the centrality of the metropolis can be clearly felt in Samuel Selvon's *The Lonely Londoners*, for example: "just to say 'Charing Cross' have a lot of romance in it . . . that place that everybody in the world know about." The clock in Piccadilly Circus, likewise, "what does tell the time of places all over the world," is "a place that everybody know . . . a meeting place," where "the big life" can be experienced.[5] In Naipaul's *A Bend in the River*, likewise, the "colonial rage" that fills a character as he enters India House in Trafalgar Square reflects a similar sense of a place that defines his own identity as a postcolonial subject: "in that building . . . I had been granted the most cruel knowledge of where I stood in the world."[6] Many diasporic novels of more recent decades, however, find in the host nation a series of nonplaces, as defined by Augé. Train and subway station platforms, subway cars, supermarkets, strip malls, and other serialized places define the landscape. Airports and fast-food franchises offer little sense of where one stands in the world. Dinaw Mengestu's Ethiopian immigrants inhabit "twenty-story slabs of gray concrete apartment buildings [that] line an overly congested road developed to the point of breaking with a dozen strip malls" in a suburb of Washington, D.C.[7] Ha Jin's *A Free Life* carefully locates its immigrant protagonist's Chinese restaurant in "a half-deserted shopping center" in a suburb of Georgia containing "a fabric store, a Laundromat, a photo studio, a pawnshop, and a fitness center" together with a supermarket that comes to be replaced by a Goodwill store – a small inventory of nonplaces in which aspiration and failure, the unmade and the discarded blur together."[8] Le Thi Diem Thuy's *The Gangster We Are All Looking For* jumps from one non-place to another, from a refugee camp in Singapore to the deserted midnight aisles of a Safeway supermarket in San Diego. The "fluorescent-lit city bus," and the series of apartments that the novel's Vietnamese family occupies in southern California are equally devoid of the characteristics of anthropological place. [. . .]

In many diasporic novels, movement figures a permanent state or relation rather than an event. Rather than simply going from one point to another expressing intention or desire, bringing about change, or mapping out the lineaments of a world, such movements simply prolong a condition of dislocation and can even collapse a Cartesian sense of space. Choi's two primary characters find themselves most at home only in Katherine's car while driving, often aimlessly. Cole's narrator, in his ceaseless walks, experiences motion through space as an illusion.[9] Le's characters in *The Gangster We Are All Looking For* note "how sky and sea follow you from place to place as if they too were traveling."[10] At times the persistence of homeland spaces results through the actions of the diasporic coethnic community, the "villagers" as Maxine Hong Kingston calls them. In this uncanny condition of permanent dislocation, ideas of homeland become at best "mythologies of home."[11] The transformation of movement into stasis appears to be a product of history itself. Mengestu's narrator sees his Congolese friend Joseph at his job as a waiter inside a restaurant named "the Colonial Grill," "He stands there frozen in the middle of a busy restaurant designed to look like a nineteenth-century English dining room."[12] Acts of accounting, of remembering particular temporal or spatial locations, feel outdated. Maps and globes feel obsolete in a condition of permanent movement. The spaces that are most strikingly rendered cannot be given coordinates – as in the extraordinary internal and external placelessness experienced by the protagonist of John Okada's *No-No Boy* (1956), banished both from the imaginary homeland of his Japanese parents and from the American nation that has rejected him for his refusal to participate in its war. In the diasporic imaginary, space has less to do with external coordinates than with the intensive experience of movement, relocation, recollection.

As Ato Quayson has pointed out, "the question of identity – who am I? – is necessarily entangled with that of place" in the diasporic novel.[13] But identity is not determined by spatial location in any simple manner. Space and place are themselves extraordinarily complex, as we have seen: divided, layered, unmappable. Through the pressures of diaspora, other social wholes undergo a similar stretching and distortion. As nations and families are spread apart, the question of belonging becomes both urgent and difficult to ascertain. In the host nation, class undergoes a reshuffling, and unfamiliar categories of racial difference make themselves impossible to ignore. Identities are sometimes assigned to you, and just as often denied. Belonging to a larger whole cannot be taken for granted. In these novels, identity emerges as something radically contingent on performance, on performing certain types of acts, gestures, or styles. Yet to do so is not to earn admission to some predefined collective entity. What is striking is the absence of a part–whole dialectic, as will be argued in the following. Rather than thinking of themselves as a part of something complete or absolute, characters find themselves more often than not confronting a possible double, a mirror figure whose performance seems to hold a clue to selfhood or belonging. Diasporic identity seems to comprise ceaseless performances by means of which selves with gender, class, and even racial characteristics emerge temporarily.

The idea that seems to be notably missing in diasporic novels is the notion that everything belongs necessarily to a larger whole. The latter idea is brilliantly embodied in Rushdie's consideration of postcolonial identity in *Midnight's Children*. That novel's treatment of identity rests on the part–whole dialectic. By anchoring itself to the trope of birth, the novel offers the ideal of a whole body that is simultaneously that of the individual, the family, the nation, and the narrative itself. That wholeness is, of course, both playfully withheld and more seriously denied; the recurring image of the perforated sheet does the former work, while the frame of narratorial disintegration performs the latter. Nevertheless, the novel rests on the question of what it means to be a part: whether a body part, a part of a family or tribe, or a part of a nation. The dialectic is inescapable: to reject the whole is still to belong to it conceptually. To lose a part is still to assert the whole. For instance, nothing bespeaks the body's essential wholeness more than to lose a part – something that happens multiple times to the narrator. The novel's reenactments of scenes of birth draw attention to the illusory nature of natality. Birth and the emergence of a body only appear to present something new; larger, older, and more entangled wholes have already ruled out complete independence. At the same time, the wholeness of the body, family, or nation is constantly challenged by the unruliness and entropy of its parts. In the end, only obsessive repeating, reminding, and anticipation create wholeness at the narrative level, there to remain as a formal ideal. [. . .]

Rather than revealing how a whole emerges out of multiple parts, then, diasporic novels seem to focus more on the performativity of social dimensions of identity. Jessica Hagedorn's *Gangster of Love* rests on a notion of identity as a series of performances, some of which are stylized versions of former selves, while others are clearly attempts to rebel against lingering homeland ideologies. The narrator, Rocky, pursues a "stylish and dangerous" life in a rock band, while her Filipina mother "reigns from her rundown San Francisco apartment as if she were still the privileged wife." The unnamed elderly Filipino immigrants on Kearny Street follow the unwritten diasporic rule of theatricalizing identity: "they exude gangster flash and style, chewing on fat cigars . . . acting like millionaires and preening like peacocks. . . . Fiercely determined to keep up appearances at any cost, strutting proudly to their graves. . . . All that bragging and pretending, all that posturing and face-saving."[14] Whether identity at its deepest level can be considered performance, however, remains a question, as the trope of nostos suggests. The desire to return to the homeland, as well as the struggle to negate that desire, suggest a self that may reside at a deeper level. Changrae Lee's novel *A Gesture Life* explores this question of performative identity from a different angle. Its narrator, an ethnic Korean Japanese who had been a medic in the Japanese Imperial Army and has long been settled in a quiet suburban American existence, comes to realize that the notion of merely performing his duty, on which he had relied in complex and contradictory ways during the war, has left him without a sense of self: "I sometimes forget who I really am. . . . I forget what it is I do, the regular activity of my walk and my swim and my taking of tea, the minor trappings and doings of my days, what I've made up to be the token flags of my life. I forget why it is I do such things, why they give me interest or solace or pleasure."[15] Performance can be a temporary escape from questions of identity as well as an answer to those questions. It can take the place of essence in more permanent ways. [. . .]

The rejection of materiality is an enduring theme in diasporic novels. In Ha Jin's *A Free Life,* the protagonist achieves material success in America and then radically disavows it in favor of pursuing his dream of writing poetry; poetry is valued for its immateriality, its weightless transparency, and most of all, it seems, for its unprofitability: "What was the meaning of an existence that was altogether bodily?"[16] In the final scene, he gives away all his money to a homeless man. Chang-rae Lee's *Aloft* expresses a similar uneasiness about the ties of both flesh and property, and an ethical preference for the barest or merest forms of life as it emerges at the very beginning or the end of life. Asceticism is acknowledged as an ideology, a salutary way of life, albeit an unfamiliar one to American families, in Gish Jen's *Love Wife.* Its newly arrived Chinese nanny states, "Better to want nothing. . . . Then nothing means nothing," and the novel ulti-mately affirms this "wanting to want nothing."[17]

Plots of divestiture are frequent in diasporic novels. In Jhumpa Lahiri's *The Namesake,* for example, "diasporic life" is constituted by a permanent suspension. The novel is punctuated by scenes in which apartments and houses are emptied of their belongings. The many scenes of methodical preparation, often preparation for social events, seem in the end merely to rehearse the novel's final leave-taking, in which the woman who had arrived as a young bride in 1968 prepares, thirty-two years later, to return to India. She methodically sorts through her possessions, discarding and donating all of them, erasing the traces of her family's life. Through this austere sentimental inventory, the occasional scrap of connection to past identities is "salvaged . . . by chance."[18]

Yet the deaccessioning of both materiality and meaning is rarely complete. In a familiar paradox, distance and emptiness reveal themselves to be full. Anzia Yezierska's *Bread Givers* begins in an apartment "packed with furniture . . . packed with Father's books," with "junk."[19] Leaving behind the crowded, over-stuffed environment and bulging bodies of these immigrant tene-ments, the protagonist finally acquires her own space, which she leaves conspicuously empty: "No carpet. . . . No pictures on the wall. Nothing but a clean, airy emptiness."[20] But she realizes that "this beautiful, clear emptiness I had created for myself" is still full of "the crowded dirt from where I came." Returning to see her family at the end, she still feels "the generations who made my father whose weight was still upon me."[21] Jamaica Kincaid's *Lucy* likewise traces a girl's deliberate attempt to leave behind her homeland. Her solitude at the end of the novel is described as an achievement: "I was alone in the world. It was not a small accomplishment." Desire has apparently been replaced with freedom; she tells her former employer, "I wanted nothing . . . everything she had reminded me . . . of the weight of the world."[22] Yet such announcements are performative failures. "The object of my life now was to put as much distance between myself and [my mother] as I could manage. For I felt that if I could put enough miles between me and the place from which that letter came . . . would I not be free to take everything just as it came and not see hundreds of years in every gesture, every word spoken, every face?"[23] The question is never answered.

The diasporic novel is capacious in its imagination and equally generous in its disavowals. The ideal of place, narratives of accomplished movement, collective forms of shared essence, and the material burdens and gains of history are disavowed but never completely denied or forgotten. Diasporic novels seem to represent a mature dialectical engagement with the formal horizons of the novel as a genre. They remind us of a longer history of novel writing about coerced and willful travel of subjects to all corners of the globe.

Notes

1 See Ato Quayson and Girish Daswani, "Introduction," in *A Companion to Diaspora and Transnationalism*, ed. Ato Quayson and Girish Daswani (New York: Blackwell, 2013), p. 3, as well as *The Cambridge Companion to Postcolonial Literary Studies*, ed. Neil Lazarus (Cambridge: Cambridge University Press, 2004).
2 Fredric Jameson, "The Realist Floor-Plan," in *On Signs*, ed. Marshall Blonsky (Baltimore, MD: Johns Hopkins University Press, 1985), pp. 373–83, 379.
3 Marc Augé, *Non-Places: An Introduction to Supermodernity* (London:. Verso, 1995), p. 44.
4 Augé, *Non-Places*, pp. 64, 76, 83. Despite his references to refugee camps as well as luxury hotels, Augé's paradigm is clearly that of the privileged traveler in possession of passport and credit card, rather than the undocumented migrant. Augé's insistence that nonplaces are defined by economic rather than political function is usefully criticized by R. Davidson.
5 Samuel Selvon, *The Lonely Londoners* (New York: Longman, 1956), pp. 84–5.
6 V.S. Naipaul, *A Bend in the River* (New York: Random House, 1989, c. 1979), p. 146.
7 Dinaw Mengestu, *The Beautiful Things That Heaven Bears* (New York: Penguin, 2007), p. 96.
8 Ha Jin, *A Free Life* (New York: Random House, 2007), p. 169.
9 Teju Cole, *Open City* (New York: Random House, 2011), p. 52.
10 Le Thi Diem Thuy, *The Gangster We Are All Looking for* (New York: Alfred A. Knopf, 2003), p. 89.
11 Chimamanda Adichie, *Americanah* (New York: Alfred A. Knopf, 2013), p. 118.
12 Mengestu, *Beautiful Things*, p. 172.
13 Ato Quayson, "Postcolonialism and the Diasporic Imaginary," in Quayson and Daswani, *A Companion*, pp. 140–59, 148.
14 Jessica Hagedorn, *The Gangster of Love* (New York: Penguin, 1997), pp. 67, 210, 200, 211.
15 Chang-rae Lee, *A Gesture Life* (New York: Riverhead, 1999), p. 285.
16 Ha Jin, *Waiting* (New York: Pantheon Books, 1999), p. 520.
17 Gish Jen, *The Love Wife* (New York: Knopf), pp. 86–7.
18 Jhumpa Lahiri, *The Namesake* (Boston: Houghton Mifflin, 2003), p. 291.
19 Anzia Yezierska, *Bread Givers* (New York: Persea Books, 2003), p. 8.
20 Ibid., p. 240.
21 Ibid., 297.
22 Jamaica Kincaid, *Lucy* (New York: Penguin, 1990), pp. 161–2.
23 Ibid., 31.

DIASPORA AND VISUAL CULTURE
Introduction

Studies of diaspora and visual culture show a conceptual and semantic overlap with those of diaspora literature in their reference to theories of nation and society that advocate replacing 'static models of racial identity formation and national formation with more flexible, dynamic ones of migration, circulation and entanglement' (see Goyal, Chapter 26, this volume). The privileging of diaspora as an unruly and interventionist force in the life of the nation state in the cultural theories of the 1990s offered new frames for interpreting the diverse ethnic cultures of diaspora collectivities. They point to the historical experience of displacement, often extending to the third generation, and the complex multi-axial, cross-cultural positioning of such groups both within and beyond national borders. In Great Britain, black culture began to challenge the equation of whiteness with Englishness (see Goyal, Chapter 26, this volume) by representing identity as multiple, contradictory and hybrid. Aiming to expose racial ideologies, heterogeneous marginal voices began to unify in developing a contestatory politics of representation. Often aesthetically experimental, such black cultures of the diaspora can be seen as promoting cross-cultural fertilisation by appropriating and creolising the dominant referential codes of the master culture.

The three articles in this section situate their arguments with reference to these revised concepts of cultural hybridity, and the global netscapes of the new media and communication technologies. They focus on the cross-border activities of film-making that exists at a tangent to or outside the paradigms of national cinema, and which thereby promotes ideas and representations of ethnic difference. Among the conceptual categories used to describe such films the most common are transnational cinema, world cinema and accented or diasporic/exilic cinema. All the alternative film-making practices draw on 'a dual inheritance from both Third World and First World film cultures' (Mercer 2003, 249), and are implicitly or explicitly engaged in a 'dialogue' with Hollywood cinema (Cooke 2007), the dominant type commercially, stylistically and ideologically.

Like Yogita Goyal (Chapter 26, this volume), who finds that in the postcolonial/diaspora novel features of the romance genre deliberately interrupt the realist forms associated with existing structures of nation or the ethnic group, and who argues that such contestation helps to construct a global black community, Kobena Mercer (1988), in his contribution, identifies a new antirealist aesthetic in the avant garde black independent cinema in Britain of the 1980s. This was a time of the emergence of black politics, and 'Black' as a political rather than an ethnic term came to signify the symbolic unity of Asian Caribbean and African peoples who had shared forms of racism (Mercer 1990, 55). Comparable to the explosion of Black Power in the USA in the 1960s, new forms of collective subjectivity and imagined community were being mobilised, and, like African-American art of the 1960s, experimentation went beyond the usual categories of the mainstream (Zabunyan 2005, 121). Mercer points out that, in questioning the limits of referential codes of documentary realism and in favouring a more expressive aesthetic that 'interrupts' the naturalistic illusion of the mimetic, black independent films such as *Handsworth Songs* (1986), *Passion of Remembrance* (1986) and *Territories* (1984) articulate a counter discourse and acknowledge the filmic signifier as a reality in its own right. They thus open an affective cognitive space for critical reflection and dialogism. Mercer draws on the historic frames of diaspora culture, contemporary black practices and Bakhtin's notions of carnival and dialogism to advocate artistic modes that encourage recognition of pluralism and contradiction, rather than monologic models that might thematise blackness, or essentialise the black experience. Despite the alternative aesthetics of stylistic polyvalency, and multiplicity in repertoires of cinema-making that is based on a double identity consciousness (Zabunyan 2005, 245), however, Mercer's model still situates identity and 'difference' within the binary of mainstream and margins (Zabunyan 2005, 220).

Hamid Naficy (2001) in his celebrated study of diasporic film-making introduces this type as 'Accented Cinema', a term also used by Stuart Hall to refer to the different 'accent' of the same word used in the class and race struggle (e.g. how the derogatory overtones of the word 'black' became the enhanced value 'black', as in the catch-phrase 'Black is beautiful' [Mercer 1990, 56]). To Naficy such cinema is accented because it aims to reproduce the sounds and voices of its authentic culture prior to displacement, and so oppose mainstream and national cinematic models like Hollywood with their apparently 'neutral' style. Naficy privileges the trajectory of art and culture that encompasses the migratory route from the Third World to the dominant metropolitan centres of the First World where greater opportunities for film production, distribution and dissemination are possible, and where economic, financial and ideological forces create a degree of assimilation. Accented cinema, like independent black British cinema, embodies structures of hybridity, multiplicity and plurality. As a cinema of displacement it engages with the experience of deterritorialisation; its film-makers may be liminal and interstitial as well as exilic or diasporic, but their political aims to oppose entrenched social and cultural structures, as well as their generic hybridisation and the low budget cost of artisanal film-making, align these endeavours with the aesthetics of Third Cinema.

Both Mercer and Naficy focus on artistic practices and aesthetic forms of alternative diaspora cinema that stress the cultural, racial and linguistic differences of minority migrant groups, and which undertake negotiation with the dominant national culture, whether as explicit contestation or as covert resistance, through appropriation of the dominant signifying codes. In writing about Taiwanese-born, but Hollywood-located, film director Ang Lee, Song Hwee Lim challenges Naficy's model, exposing the limits of its underpinning First World/Third World hierarchy with reference to modern Chinese and Taiwanese history. He refers to Ang Lee's early trilogy of displacement, 'Father knows best', about the Chinese and Taiwanese diasporas in the US and the Chinese diaspora in Taiwan, to introduce alternative migratory routes to those privileged by Naficy and Mercer, based on different configurations of the homeland–host relationship: for example, when a migrant community seeks to return to the homeland, or an intra-national path creates a new nation-state at a distance from the original, one that claims hegemonic power and produces an exilic cinema in nationalist form (as the Nationalist or Kuomintang regime [KMT] did by locating a new nation state across the Taiwan Strait), or cinema that travels within the Third World, or directors at home who use themes of exile or displacement.[1] This argument that diaspora cinema is multiply located in alternative sites to those of dispersion, and to cultures that are hybridised and deterritorialised, and that it blends plural vernacular traditions with imported ones, complicates received notions of nation and diaspora, elite and popular, high and low culture (Boehmer and Chaudhuri 2011, 15–18). Lim draws attention to the way Lee reterritorialises the dominant cinematic culture of Bollywood through speaking in the multiple accents, tropes and voices of his Taiwanese language and assimilating to the 'other'.

Note

1 Lim (2012) points out that Ang Lee descends from the *waishengren*, the populations from the outer provinces of China who were settled in Taiwan under the regime of the Republic of China from 1949, and his early trilogy shows the structures of diminishing hope of return of these groups, as well as the accents of voices from Chinese provinces outside Taiwan (132–3).

References

Boehmer, Elleke and Rosinka Chaudhuri, eds. 2011. *The Indian Postcolonial: A Critical Reader*. London: Routledge.

Cooke, Paul, ed. 2007. *World Cinema's "Dialogues" with Hollywood*. Basingstoke: Palgrave MacMillan.

Lim, Song Hwee. 2012. 'Speaking in Tongues: Ang Lee, Accented Cinema, Hollywood.' In *Theorizing World Cinema*, edited by Lucia Nagib, Chris Perriam and Rajinder Dudrah, 129–142. London: I.B. Tauris & Co.

Mercer, Kobena. 1990. 'Welcome to the Jungle: Identity and Diversity in Postmodern Politics.' In *Identity: Community, Culture and Difference*, edited by Jonathan Rutherford, 43–72. London: Lawrence and Wishart.

Mercer, Kobena. 2003. 'Diaspora Culture and the Dialogic Imagination: The Aesthetics of Black Independent Film in Britain.' In *Theorizing Diaspora*, edited by Jana Evans Braziel and Anita Mannur, 247–260. Malden MA: Blackwell. Reprinted from *Blackframes: Critical Perspectives on Independent Black Cinema*, edited by Mbye Cham and Claire Andrade-Watkins, 50–61. Massachusetts Institute of Technology. 1988.

Naficy, Hamid. 2001. *An Accented Cinema: Exilic and Diasporic Filmmaking*. Princeton: Princeton University Press.

Zabunyan, Elvan. 2005. *Black is a Color (A History of African American Art)*. Trans. by Paul Black and Catherine Petit. Paris: Editions Dis Voir.

28

DIASPORA CULTURE AND THE DIALOGIC IMAGINATION

The aesthetics of black independent film in Britain

Kobena Mercer

The question of aesthetics arises today as a crucial issue for black filmmaking practices in Britain for two important reasons. First, significant changes in the material conditions of black politics since the early 1980s have enabled a prolific upsurge in black filmmaking activity in recent years. The emergence of a new generation of cinematic activists – Ceddo, Sankofa, Retake, Black Audio Film Collective – symbolizes a new threshold of cultural struggle in the domain of image-making. Their work deepens and extends the narrative and documentary frameworks established by Horace Ove, Lionel Ngakane, and Menelik Shabazz in the 1960s and 1970s. The emergence of a new experimental approach has also widened the parameters of black independent film practice, bringing a new quality of diversity to black cinema.

Until now, black film in Britain has emphasized the radical content of its political message over the politics of representation inherent in the medium. Certain aesthetic qualities generated by self-consciously cinematic strategies at work in new forms of black filmmaking today, however, indicate significant shifts and critical differences in attitudes to the means of representation. In this context it becomes necessary to think through the political implications of choices and decisions made at the level of film form. If such shifts and changes may be momentarily grasped as an accentuation of the expressive over the referential, or as an emphasis on the complexity rather than homogeneity of black experiences in Britain, then what is at stake is not a categorical break with the past but the embryonic articulation of something new which does not fit a pregiven category.

Second, insofar as aesthetics concerns conceptual criteria for evaluating artistic and cultural practices, it now becomes necessary to reflect more rigorously on the role of critics and criticism. This need arises with urgency not simply because the increase in quantity at the point of production necessitates clarification of qualitative distinctions at the point of reception, but more importantly because of the bewildering range of conflicting responses provoked by new work such as *Handsworth Songs* (Black Audio Film Collective, 1986) and *Passion of Remembrance* (Sankofa, 1986).

[. . .]

"In dreams begin responsibilities," wrote Delmore Schwartz. It seems to me to be crucially important to recognize the multi-accentuated character of the voices that speak in these new modes of black filmmaking because as Volosinov/Bakhtin pointed out,

> The social *multi-accentuality* of the ideological sign is a very crucial aspect [of class struggle in language] . . . Each living ideological sign has two faces, like Janus . . .

This *inner dialectical quality* of the sign comes out fully into the open only in times of social crisis or revolutionary changes.[1]

To the extent that this view echoes Frantz Fanon's insight that the ideological fixity of the signs of colonial authority become increasingly unstable, uncertain, and ambivalent at the point where struggles for national liberation reach a new threshold of intensity,[2] the emergence of this quality in black film discourse today implies a qualitative intensification of the cultural struggle to decolonize and deterritorialize cinema as a site of political intervention. The liberation of the imagination is a precondition of revolution, or so the Surrealists used to say. Carnival is *not* "the revolution," but in the carnavalesque aesthetic emerging here we may discern the mobility of what Bakhtin called "the dialogic principle in which the possibility of social change is pre-figured in collective consciousness by the multiplication of critical dialogues".[3] What is at issue can be characterized as the critical difference between a *monologic* tendency in black film which tends to homogenize and totalize the black experience in Britain, and a *dialogic* tendency which is responsive to the diverse and complex qualities of our black Britishness and British blackness – our differentiated specificity as a diaspora people.

[. . .]

We return therefore to confront the paradox, which is that the mimetic mode as of cinematic expression can be seen as a form of cultural mimicry which demonstrates a neocolonized dependency on the codes, which valorize film as a commodity of cultural imperialism.[4] The problem of imitation and domination was confronted in literary debates around aesthetics and politics in the African, Caribbean, and Afro-American novel in the 1940s and 1950s, which highlighted the existential dilemma of dependent expressivity: how can the "colonized" express an authentic self in an alien language imposed by the imperial power of the "colonizer"?[5]

There is, however, another response to this problematic, inscribed in aesthetic practices of everyday life among black peoples of the African diaspora located in the new world of the capitalist West, which explores and exploits the creative contradictions of the clash of cultures. Across a whole range of cultural forms there is a powerfully *syncretic* dynamic which critically appropriates elements from the master-codes of the dominant culture and *creolizes* them, dis-articulating the given signs and rearticulating their symbolic meaning otherwise. The subversive force of this hybridizing tendency is most apparent at the level of language itself where creoles, patois, and Black English decenter, destabilize, and carnivalize the linguistic domination of "English" – the nation-language of master discourse – through strategic inflections, reaccen-tuations, and other performative moves in semantic and lexical codes. Such patterns of linguistic subversion in Caribbean practices of interculturation have been rigorously examined by Edward Brathwaite.[6] Creolizing practices of counter-appropriation exemplify the critical process of *dialogism* as such practices are self-consciously aware that, in Bakhtin's terms,

> The word in language is half someone else's. It becomes "one's own" only when . . . the speaker appropriates the word, adapting it to his own semantic and expressive intention. Prior to this moment of appropriation the word does not exist in a neutral or impersonal language . . . but rather it exists in other people's mouths, serving other people's intentions: it is from there that one must take the word and make it one's own.[7]

Today, the emergence of this dialogic tendency in black film practice is important as it has the potential to renew the critical function of "independent" cinema. Since former generations of black intelligentsia have now entered the media marketplace and broadcasting institutions, and some appear to have happily embraced commonsense notions of "artistic excellence,"[8]

I would argue that the creole versioning and critical dialogue with selective elements from Euro-American modernism is infinitely preferable to the collusion with the cultural conservatism inherent in such conformist positions (which continue the great British tradition of anti-intellectualism).

There is, on the other hand, a powerful resonance between the aspirations of the new work, which seeks to find a film language adequate to the articulation of our realities as third-generation black people in Britain and the critical goals advocated by the concept of Third Cinema, which seeks to combat the values of both commercialism and auteurism.[9] Aware of the pernicious ethnologocentric force which Clyde Taylor has shown to be inherent in the very concept of "aesthetics" within the dominant European philosophical tradition,[10] my aim has been precisely to avoid setting up a monolithic system of evaluative criteria (itself neither useful nor desirable). Rather, by appropriating elements of Bakhtin's theory of discursive struggle I have tried to differentiate *relational* tendencies in the way black films perform their critical function. Evaluating this function is always context-dependent. The lucid immediacy of *We Are the Elephant* (Ceddo, 1987), for example, not only articulates an incisive account of South African realities of repression and resistance, but in doing so it strikes a dialogic blow against the censorship and control of image and information flows imposed by apartheid and by the alienating spectacle of epics like *Cry Freedom* (director Richard Attenborough, 1986). Which is to say that if there are dialogic moments within films conceived in a conventional documentary realist mode, there are also a few profoundly monologic moments in some of the new work, such as the "speaker's drama" in Sankofa's *Passion of Remembrance* and the remorseless repetition of Black Audio's earlier tape-slide *Signs of Empire* (1984). We are dealing, then, not with categorical absolutes but the relative efficacy of strategic choices made in specific conjunctures and contexts of production and reception.

I would argue that new modes of black British filmmaking are instances of "imperfect cinema," in Julio Garcia Espinosa's phrase:[11] conducting research and experiments, adopting an improvisational approach, and hopefully learning from active mistakes through trial and error. In this sense, Stuart Hall's comment that the originality of the new work is "precisely that it retells the black experience as an *English* experience" must be amplified. In place of reductionist tendencies in the monologic single-issue approach – which often creates a binary "frontier effect" in its political analysis of reality, as if black subjects confront white society as our monolithic Other – critical dialogism gestures towards a counter-hegemonic perspective which assumes that questions of race cannot be isolated from wider social politics. In Hall's terms,

> The fact of the matter is that it is no longer possible to fight racism as if it had its own, autonomous dynamic, located between white people or the police on the one hand and blacks on the other. The problem of racism arises from *every single political development* which has taken place since the New Right emerged.[12]

Critical dialogism has the potential to overturn the binaristic relations of hegemonic boundary maintenance by multiplying critical dialogues *within* particular communities and *between* the various constituencies that make up the "imagined community" of the nation. At once articulating the personal and the political, such dialogism shows that our "other" is already inside each of us, that black identities are plural and heterogeneous, and that political divisions of gender and sexual identity are to be transformed as much as those of race and class. Moreover, critical dialogism questions the monologic exclusivity on which the dominant version of national identity and collective belonging are based. Paul Gilroy has shown how the sense of mutual exclusivity or logical incompatibility between the two terms *black* and *British* is one essential condition for the hegemony of racism over the English collective consciousness.[13] New ways of interrupting this hegemonic logic are suggested by the dialogic movement of creolizing appropriation.

Fully aware of the creative contradictions, and the cost, of our outside-in relation to England, cultural work based on this strategy gives rise to the thought that it is possible to turn dominant versions of Englishness inside out. Gramsci argued that a political struggle enters its hegemonic phase when it goes beyond particular economic interests to forge alliances among different classes of the people so as to redirect the collective will of the nation ("state + civil society"). On this view, counter-hegemonic strategy depends on the struggle to appropriate given elements of the common sense of the people and to rearticulate these elements out of the discourse of the dominant bloc and into a radical democratic direction, which used to be called "equality." At a microlevel, the textual work of creolizing appropriation activated in new forms of black cultural practice awakens the thought that such strategies of disarticulation and rearticulation may be capable of transforming the democratic imaginary at a macrolevel by "othering" inherited discourses of British identity.

Aware that "there is a Third World in every First World and vice versa" (Trinh T. Minh-ha), the diaspora perspective has the potential to expose and illuminate the sheer heterogeneity of the diverse social forces always repressed into the margin by the monologism of dominant discourses – discourses of domination. In a situation where neo-conservative forces have deepened their hold on our ability to apprehend reality, and would have us believe that "It's great to be Great again" (1987 Tory election slogan), we must encourage and develop this critical potential. It might enable us to overcome reality.

Notes

1 V. N. Volosinov, *Marxism and the Philosophy of Language* (New York: Seminar Press, 1973), p. 19.

2 See Frantz Fanon, "On National Liberation," in *The Wretched of the Earth* (Harmondsworth: Penguin Books, 1967), and see also Homi Bhabha's introduction, "Remembering Fanon," in the reprint of *Black Skin/White Masks* (London: Pluto Press, 1986).

3 See M. Bakhtin, "Discourse in the Novel," *The Dialogic Imagination* (Austin: University of Texas Press, 1981, trans. C. Emerson and M. Holquist), and see also Tvetzan Todorov, *Mikhail Bakhtin: The Dialogical Principle* (Manchester: Manchester University Press, 1984).

4 The imitation of Hollywood form in initial developmental phases of various "national" cinemas is discussed in Roy Armes, *Third World Film-making and the West* (Berkeley: University of California Press, 1987). The transfer of professional ideology is discussed in Peter Golding, "Media Professionalism in the Third World" in James Curran and others (eds), *Mass Communication and Society* (London: Edward Arnold, 1977).

5 See Homi K Bhabha, "Representation and the Colonial Text" in Frank Gloversmith, *The Theory of Reading* (Brighton: Harvester Press, 1984). These debates have been recently revived in Ngugi wa Thiong'o, *Decolonising the Mind: The Politics of Language in African Literature* (London: John Currey/ Heinemann, 1986).

6 On creolization and interculturation, see Edward K. Brathwaite, *The Development of Creole Society in Jamaica* (Oxford: Oxford University Press, 1971), *Contradictory Omens* (Mona, Jamaica: Savacou Publications, 1974), and on linguistic subversion in the formation of "nation-language," *The Story of the Voice* (London: New Beacon Publications, 1983).

7 Bakhtin, *The Dialogic Imagination*, pp. 293–4.

8 Farrukh Dondy (Commissioning Editor for Multicultural Programming, Channel Four Television) on UBC "ethnic minority" magazine *Ebony*, transmitted November 1986. Darcus Howe and Tariq Ali edit *The Bandung File*, a black/Third World current affairs programme, Channel Four.

9 The concept of Third Cinema proposed by Latin American independent film practice in the 1960s – see F. Solanas and O. Getino, "Towards a Third Cinema," in Bill Nichols (ed.) *Movies and Methods* (Berkeley: University of California Press, 1976) – and subsequently developed with reference to African cinema by Teshome Gabriel, *Third Cinema in the Third World: The Aesthetics of Liberation* (Ann Arbor: University of

Michigan Research Press, 1982), was the focus of the conference held at the 40th Edinburgh International Film Festival (EIFF), 1986. For two versions of this real event see my reflections on "Third Cinema at Edinburgh," *Screen*, vol. 27, no. 6, 1986, and David Will's account in *Framework*, no. 32/33, 1986.

10 Clyde Taylor's paper "Black Cinema/White Aesthetics" was presented at the EIFF conference "Third Cinema. Theories and Practices" (organized by Jim Pines, Paul Willemen, and June Givanni). Dialogic elucidation of Taylor's argument is provided in his counter-reply to Will in "Eurocentrics VS, New Thought at Edinburgh," *Framework*, no. 34, 1987.

11 See Julio Garcia Espinosa, "Meditations on Imperfect Cinema . . . Fifteen Years Later," *Screen*, vol. 26, no. 3–4, May–August 1985.

12 Stuart Hall, "Cold Comfort Farm" (on Tottenham and Handsworth "riots") *New Socialist*, no. 32, November 1985.

13 See Paul Gilroy, *There Ain't No Black in the Union Jack* (London: Hutchinson 1987), especially ch 2. Ch. 5, "Diaspora, utopia and the critique of capitalism," provides further clarification of Bakhtin's relevance for thinking a diasporan aesthetic.

29

SITUATING ACCENTED CINEMA

Hamid Naficy

Diasporic filmmakers

Originally, "diaspora" referred to the dispersion of the Greeks after the destruction of the city of Aegina, to the Jews after their Babylonian exile, and to the Armenians after Persian and Turkish invasions and expulsion in the mid-sixteenth century. The classic paradigm of diaspora has involved the Jews, but as Peters (1999), Cohen (1997), Tölölyan (1996), Clifford (1997, 244–77), Naficy (1993), and Safran (1991) have argued, the definition should no longer be limited to the dispersion of the Jews, for myriad peoples have historically undergone sustained dispersions—a process that continues on a massive scale today. The term has been taken up by other displaced peoples, among them African-Americans in the United States and Afro-Caribbeans in England, to describe their abduction from their African homes and their forced dispersion to the new world (Gilroy 1993, 1991, 1988; Mercer 1994a, 1994b, 1988; Hall 1988). In these and other recodings, the concept of diaspora has become much closer to exile. Consequently, as Khachig Tölölyan notes, "diaspora" has lost some of its former specificity and precision to become a "promiscuously capacious category that is taken to include all the adjacent phenomena to which it is linked but from which it actually differs in ways that are constitutive" (1996, 8).

Here I will briefly point out the similarities and differences between exile and diaspora that inform this work. Diaspora, like exile, often begins with trauma, rupture, and coercion, and it involves the scattering of populations to places outside their homeland. Sometimes, however, the scattering is caused by a desire for increased trade, for work, or for colonial and imperial pursuits. Consequently, diasporic movements can be classified according to their motivating factors. Robin Cohen (1997) suggested the following classifications and examples: victim/refugee diasporas (exemplified by the Jews, Africans, and Armenians); labor/service diasporas (Indians); trade/business diasporas (Chinese and Lebanese); imperial/colonial diasporas (British, Russian); and cultural/hybrid diasporas (Caribbeans). Like the exiles, people in diaspora have an identity in their homeland *before* their departure, and their diasporic identity is constructed in resonance with this prior identity. However, unlike exile, which may be individualistic or collective, diaspora is necessarily collective, in both its origination and its destination. As a result, the nurturing of a collective memory, often of an idealized homeland, is constitutive of the diasporic identity. This idealization may be state-based, involving love for an existing homeland, or it may be stateless, based on a desire for a homeland yet to come. The Armenian diaspora before and after the Soviet era has been state-based, whereas the Palestinian diaspora since the 1948 creation of Israel has been stateless, driven by the Palestinians' desire to create a sovereign state.

People in diaspora, moreover, maintain a long-term sense of ethnic consciousness and distinctiveness, which is consolidated by the periodic hostility of either the original home or the host societies toward them. However, unlike the exiles whose identity entails a vertical and primary relationship with their homeland, diasporic consciousness is horizontal and multisited, involving not only the homeland but also the compatriot communities elsewhere. As a result, plurality, multiplicity, and hybridity are structured in dominance among the diasporans, while among the political exiles, binarism and duality rule.

These differences tend to shape exilic and diasporic films differently. Diasporized filmmakers tend to be centered less than the exiled filmmakers on a cathected relationship with a single homeland and on a claim that they represent it and its people. As a result, their works are expressed less in the narratives of retrospection, loss, and absence or in strictly partisanal political terms. Their films are accented more fully than those of the exiles by the plurality and performativity of identity. In short, while binarism and subtraction in particular accent exilic films, diasporic films are accented more by multiplicity and addition. Many diasporic filmmakers are discussed here individually, among them Armenians. Black and Asian British filmmakers are discussed collectively.

Postcolonial ethnic and identity filmmakers

Although exilic, diasporic, and ethnic communities all patrol their real and symbolic boundaries to maintain a measure of collective identity that distinguishes them from the ruling strata and ideologies, they differ from one another principally by the relative strength of their attachment to compatriot communities. The postcolonial ethnic and identity filmmakers are both ethnic and diasporic; but they differ from the poststudio American ethnics, such as Woody Allen, Francis Ford Coppola, and Martin Scorsese, in that many of them are either immigrants themselves or have been born in the West since the 1960s to nonwhite, non-Western, postcolonial émigrés. They also differ from the diasporic filmmakers in their emphasis on their ethnic and racial identity within the host country.

The different emphasis on the relationship to place creates differently accented films. Thus, exilic cinema is dominated by its focus on there and then in the homeland, diasporic cinema by its vertical relationship to the homeland and by its lateral relationship to the diaspora communities and experiences, and postcolonial ethnic and identity cinema by the exigencies of life here and now in the country in which the filmmakers reside. As a result of their focus on the here and now, ethnic identity films tend to deal with what Werner Sollors has characterized as "the central drama in American culture," which emerges from the conflict between descent relations, emphasizing bloodline and ethnicity, and consent relations, stressing self-made, contractual affiliations (1986, 6). In other words, while the former is concerned with being, the latter is concerned with becoming; while the former is conciliatory, the latter is contestatory. Although such a drama is also present to some extent in exilic and diasporic films, the hostland location of the drama makes the ethnic and identity films different from the other two categories, whose narratives are often centered elsewhere.

Some of the key problematics of the postcolonial ethnic and identity cinema are encoded in the "politics of the hyphen." Recognized as a crucial marker of ethnicity and authenticity in a multicultural America, group terms such as black, Chicano/a, Oriental, and people of color have gradually been replaced by hyphenated terms such as African-American, Latino-American, and Asian-American. Identity cinema's adoption of the hyphen is seen as a marker of resistance to the homogenizing and hegemonizing power of the American melting pot ideology. However, retaining the hyphen has a number of negative connotations, too. The hyphen may imply a lack, or the idea that hyphenated people are somehow subordinate to unhyphenated people, or that they are "equal but not quite," or that they will never be totally accepted or trusted as full citizens. In addition, it may suggest a divided allegiance, which is a painful reminder to certain groups of American citizens.[1] The hyphen may also suggest a divided mind, an irrevocably split identity, or a type of paralysis between two cultures or nations. Finally, the hyphen can feed into nativist discourses that assume authentic essences that lie outside ideology and predate, or stand apart from, the nation.

In its nativist adoption, the hyphen provides vertical links that emphasize descent relations, roots, depth, inheritance, continuity, homogeneity, and stability. These are allegorized in family sagas and mother–daughter and generational conflict narratives of Chinese-American films such as Wayne Wang's *Eat a Bowl of Tea* (1989) and *The Joy Luck Club* (1993). The filmmakers' task in this modality, in Stuart Hall's words, is "to discover, excavate, bring to light and express through cinematic representation" that inherited collective cultural identity, that "one true self (1994, 393). In its contestatory adoption, the hyphen can operate horizontally, highlighting consent relations, disruption, heterogeneity, slippage, and mediation, as in Trinh T. Minh-ha's *Surname Viet Given Name Nam* (1985) and Srinivas Krishna's *Masala* (1990). In this modality, filmmakers do not recover an existing past or impose an imaginary and often fetishized coherence on their fragmented experiences and histories. Rather, by emphasizing discontinuity and specificity, they demonstrate that they are in the process of becoming, that they are "subject to the continuous 'play' of history, culture and power" (Hall 1994, 394). Christine Choy and Rene Tajima's award-winning film *Who Killed Vincent Chin?* (1988) is really a treatise on the problematic of the hyphen in the Asian-American context, as it centers on the murder of a Chinese-American by out-of-work white Detroit autoworkers who, resentful of Japanese car imports, mistook him for being Japanese.

Read as a sign of hybridized, multiple, or constructed identity, the hyphen can become liberating because it can be performed and signified upon. Each hyphen is in reality a nested hyphen, consisting of a number of other intersecting and overlapping hyphens that provide inter- and intraethnic and national links. This fragmentation and multiplication can work against essentialism, nationalism, and dyadism. Faced with too many options and meanings, however, some have suggested removing the hyphen, while others have proposed replacing it with a plus sign.[2] Martin Scorsese's *ITALIANAMERICAN* (1974) cleverly removes the hyphen and the space and instead joins the "Italian" with the "American" to suggest a fused third term. The film title by this most ethnic of New Hollywood cinema directors posits that there is no Italianness that precedes or stands apart from Americanness. In this book, I have retained the hyphen, since this is the most popular form of writing these compound ethnic designations.

The compound terms that bracket the hyphen also present problems, for at the same time that each term produces symbolic alliance among disparate members of a group, it tends to elide their diversity and specificity. "Asian-American," for example, encompasses people from such culturally and nationally diverse roots as the Philippines, Vietnam, Cambodia, Korea, Japan, Thailand, China, Laos, Taiwan, Indonesia, Malaysia, India, Bangladesh, and Pakistan. To calibrate the term, such unwieldy terms as "Southeast Asian diasporas" have also been created. Similar processes and politics of naming have been tried for the "black" British filmmakers.

Independent film distributors, such as Third World Newsreel, Icarus-First Run Films, and Women Make Movies, exploit the hyphen and the politics of the identity cinema by classifying these films thematically or by their hyphenated designation. Such classifications create targets of opportunity for those interested in such films, but they also narrow the marketing and critical discourses about these films by encouraging audiences to read them in terms of their ethnic content and identity politics more than their authorial vision and stylistic innovations. Several postcolonial ethnic and identity filmmakers are discussed individually and collectively.

Diaspora, exile, and ethnicity are not steady states; rather, they are fluid processes that under certain circumstances may transform into one another and beyond. There is also no direct and predetermined progression from exile to ethnicity, although dominant ideological and economic apparatuses tend to favor an assimilationist trajectory—from exile to diaspora to ethnic to citizen to consumer. [. . .]

Accented style

If the classical cinema has generally required that components of style, such as mise-en-scène, filming, and editing, produce a realistic rendition of the world, the exilic accent must be sought in the manner in which realism is, if not subverted, at least inflected differently. Henry Louis Gates Jr. has characterized black texts as "mulatto" or "mulatta," containing a double voice and a two-toned heritage: "These texts speak in standard Romance and Germanic languages and literary structures, but almost always speak with a distinct and resonant accent, an accent that Signifies (upon) the various black vernacular literary traditions, which are still being written down" (1988, xxiii). Accented films are also mulatta texts. They are created with awareness of the vast histories of the prevailing cinematic modes. They are also created in a new mode that is constituted both by the structures of feeling of the filmmakers themselves as displaced subjects and by the traditions of exilic and diasporic cultural productions that preceded them. From the cinematic traditions they acquire one set of voices, and from the exilic and diasporic traditions they acquire a second. This double consciousness constitutes the accented style that not only signifies upon exile and other cinemas but also signifies the condition of exile itself. It signifies upon cinematic traditions by its artisanal and collective modes of production, which undermine the dominant production mode, and by narrative strategies, which subvert that mode's realistic treatment of time, space, and causality. It also signifies and signifies upon exile by expressing, allegorizing, commenting upon, and critiquing the conditions of its own production, and deterritorialization. Both of these acts of signifying and signification are constitutive of the accented style, whose key characteristics are elaborated upon in the following. What turns these into attributes of style is their repeated inscription in a single film, in the entire oeuvre of individual filmmakers, or in the works of various displaced filmmakers regardless of their place of origin or residence. Ultimately, the style demonstrates their dislocation at the same time that it serves to locate them as authors. [. . .]

Accented structures of feeling

Since the accented style is not a programmatic, already formed style, one may speak of it as an emergent "structure of feeling," which, according to Raymond Williams, is not a fixed institution, formation, position, or even a formal concept such as worldview or ideology. Rather, it is a set of undeniable personal and social experiences—with internal relations and tensions—that is

> still in process, often indeed not yet recognized as social but taken to be private, idiosyncratic, and even isolating, but which in analysis (though rarely otherwise) has its emergent, connecting, and dominant characteristics, indeed its specific hierarchies. These are often more recognizable at a later stage, when they have been (as often happens) formalized, classified, and in many cases built into institutions and formations.
> *(1977, 132)*

The accented style is one such emergent category—not yet fully recognized or formalized. Its structure of feeling is rooted in the filmmakers' profound experiences of deterritorialization, which oscillate between dysphoria and euphoria, celibacy and celebration. These dislocatory feeling structures are powerfully expressed in the accented films' chronotopical configurations of the homeland as utopian and open and of exile as dystopian and claustrophobic (to which I devote two chapters of this book).

In some measure, what is being described here is similar to the feeling structures of postmodernism. In speaking about the formation of a new mass audience for postmodernist art, Fred Pfeil notes that experiencing such art is characterized by

> a very unstable play between a primal delight and primal fear, between two simultaneous versions of the primary aggressive impulse, that which seeks to incorporate the world into itself and that which struggles to prevent its own engulfment. This dialectic is the postmodern 'structure of feeling'.
>
> *(1988, 386)*

To the extent that the accented and postmodernist cinemas both immerse us in these dystopic and euphoric moments of unresolved polarity, they are similar. However, not all postmodernist films are diasporically or exilically accented, while all accented films are to some extent postmodernist. Accented films differ from other postmodernist films because they usually posit the homeland as a grand and deeply rooted referent, which stops the postmodernist play of signification. Since exile (more than diaspora) is driven by the modernist concerns and tropes of nationalism and state formation, which posits the existence and realness of the earth, mountains, monuments, and seas as well as of the peoples, histories, politics, and cultures of the homeland, many exilically accented films are intensely place-bound, and their narratives are driven by a desire either to recapture the homeland or to return to it. As a result, during the liminal period of displacement, the postmodernist playfulness, indeterminacy, and intertextuality have little place in exilic politics and cinema. The referent homeland is too powerfully real, even sacred, to be played with and signified upon. It is this powerful hold of the homeland that imbues the accented structures of feeling with such sadness and sense of terminal loss as described by Edward Said:

> Exile is strangely compelling to think about but terrible to experience. It is the unhealable rift forced between a human being and a native place, between the self and its true home: its essential sadness can never be surmounted. And while it is true that literature and history contain heroic, romantic, glorious, even triumphant episodes in an exile's life, these are no more than efforts meant to overcome the crippling sorrow of estrangement. The achievements of exile are permanently undermined by the loss of something left behind for ever.
>
> *(1990, 357)*

Sadness, loneliness, and alienation are frequent themes, and sad, lonely, and alienated people are favorite characters in the accented films.

Only when the grand return to the homeland is found to be impossible, illusory, or undesirable does the postmodernist semiosis set in. Then the nostalgia for the referent and the pain of separation from it may be transformed into a nostalgia for its synecdoches, fetishes, and signifieds—the frozen sounds and images of the homeland—which are then circulated in exilic media and pop culture (including wall calendars, as in Egoyan's *Calendar*).[3]

Multiple sites, cultures, and time zones inform the feeling structures of exile and diaspora, and they pose the representation of simultaneity and multisitedness as challenges for the accented films. Citing Sergei Eisenstein, George Marcus offered montage as a methodology that not only encodes multiple times and sites but also self-consciously problematizes the realist representation of the world. In the accented cinema, as in the multisited ethnography that Marcus describes, this is achieved by critical juxtapositions of multiple spaces, times, voices, narratives, and foci (1994). [. . .]

Third cinema aesthetics

The genealogy of the accented style may be traced not only to the epochal shifts of post-colonialism and postmodernism but also to the transformation of cinematic structures, theories, and practices since the 1960s. Specifically, it begins with the emergence and theorization of a Latin-American cinema of liberation, dubbed "Third Cinema," and its later elaboration by Teshome H. Gabriel and others. Drawing upon the Cuban revolution of 1959, Italian neorealist film aesthetics, Griersonian social documentary style, and Marxist analysis, Brazilian filmmaker Glauber Rocha issued his passionate polemic, "The Aesthetics of Hunger," and Argentinean cinéastes Fernando Solanas and Spanish-born Octavio Getino, makers of the massive film *The Hour of the Furnaces (La Hora de los Hornos,* 1968), published their famous manifesto, "Towards a Third Cinema." These were followed by an avant-gardist manifesto, "For an Imperfect Cinema," written by the Cuban filmmaker Julio Garcia Espinosa.[4] Other "revolutionary" cinematic manifestos were issued in North Africa and the Middle East.[5] In France, the SLON (later ISKRA) and Dziga Vertov groups, among others, and in the United States, Newsreel and other groups picked up the clarion call of these manifestos and issued their own summons for new radical cinematic practices. The Latin-American polemics and manifestos in particular, including *The Hour of the Furnaces,* critiqued the mainstream, capitalist, "first cinema" and the petit bourgeois, authorial "second cinema"; in their place they proposed a new research category of "Third Cinema"—a cinema that is not perfect, polished, or professional.[6] Indeed, in its formal practices, *The Hour of the Furnaces* is a clear progenitor of the accented style.

The accented cinema is one of the offshoots of the Third Cinema, with which it shares certain attributes and from which it is differentiated by certain sensibilities. As Gabriel elaborated, although Third Cinema films are made chiefly in the Third World, they may be made anywhere, by anyone, about any subject, and in a variety of styles and forms, as long as they are oppositional and liberationist (1982, 2–3). As a cinema of displacement, however, the accented cinema is much more situated than the Third Cinema, for it is necessarily made by (and often for) specific displaced subjects and diasporized communities. Less polemical than the Third Cinema, it is nonetheless a political cinema that stands opposed to authoritarianism and oppression. If Third Cinema films generally advocated class struggle and armed struggle, accented films favor discursive and semiotic struggles. Although not necessarily Marxist or even socialist like the Third Cinema, the accented cinema is an engagé cinema. However, its engagement is less with "the people" and "the masses," as was the case with the Third Cinema, than with specific individuals, ethnicities, nationalities, and identities, and with the experience of deterritorialization itself. In accented cinema, therefore, every story is both a private story of an individual and a social and public story of exile and diaspora. These engagements with collectivities and with deterritorialization turn accented films into allegories of exile and diaspora—not the totalizing "national allegories" that Jameson once characterized Third World literature and cinema to be (1986).

Third Cinema and accented cinema are alike in their attempts to define and create a nostalgic, even fetishized, authentic prior culture—before contamination by the West in the case of the Third Cinema, and before displacement and emigration in the case of the accented cinema.

Like *The Hour of the Furnaces*, accented films are hybridized in their use of forms that cut across the national, typological, generic, and stylistic boundaries. Similarly, many of them are driven by the aesthetics of provisionality, experimentation, and imperfection—even amateurness—and they are made in the artisanal, low-cost mode of "cinema of hunger." In sum, despite some marked differences, both accented films and Third Cinema films are historically conscious, politically engaged, critically aware, generically hybridized, and artisanally produced. The affinity of the two cinemas and the impact of the one on the other are paralleled in the lives of some of the film-makers, such as Fernando Solanas from Argentina and Miguel Littin from Chile, who moved from the Third Cinema in the 1960s to the accented cinema of the 1980s and beyond. [. . .]

Like all approaches to cinema, the accented style attempts to reduce and to channel the free play of meanings. But this approach is driven by its sensitivity to the production and consumption of films and videos in conditions of exilic liminality and diasporic transnationality. The style designation also allows us to reclassify films or to classify certain hitherto unclassifiable films. Thus, Mekas's *Lost. Lost, Lost*, which has been variously regarded as documentary, avant-garde, or diary film, will yield new insights if reread as an accented film. If one thinks of Buñuel as an exilic filmmaker, as does Marsha Kinder (1993), further understanding about his films, hitherto unavailable, will be produced. Likewise, a rereading of Miguel Littin's docudrama *The Jackal of Nahueltoro* (*El Chacal de Nahueltoro*, 1969), turns it into a protoexilic film containing many components of the accented style in emergent form, even though at first blush the story does not warrant such an interpretation.

The accented style helps us to discover commonalities among exilic filmmakers that cut across gender, race, nationality, and ethnicity, as well as across boundaries of national cinemas, genres, and authorship. References to filmmakers in this book range far and wide, from Godard to Mekas, from Akerman to Med Hondo, and from Solanas to Trinh. Approached stylistically, films can be read, reread, and back-read not only as individual texts but also as sites of struggle over meanings and identities. By problematizing the traditional schemas and representational practices, this approach blurs the distinction, often artificially maintained, among various film types such as documentary, fictional, and avant-garde. All of these types are considered here.

The accented style is not a fully recognized and sanctioned film genre, and the exilic and diasporic filmmakers do not always make accented films. In fact, most of them would wish to be in Egoyan's place, to move out of marginal cinema niches into the world of art cinema or even popular cinema. Style permits the critics to track the evolution of the work of not only a single filmmaker but also a group of filmmakers. As I discuss in the chapters on mode of production, Asian Pacific American filmmaking has gradually evolved away from an ethnic focus toward diasporic and exilic concerns, while Iranian exilic filmmakers have evolved toward a diasporic sensibility. These evolutions signal the transformation of both filmmakers and their audiences. They also signal the appropriation of the filmmakers, their audiences, and certain features of the accented style by the mainstream cinema and by its independent offspring. Because it goes beyond connoisseurship to situate the cinéastes within their changing social formations, cultural locations, and cinematic practices, the accented style is not hermetic, homogeneous, or autonomous. It meanders and evolves. It is an inalienable element of the social material process of exile and diaspora and of the exilic and diasporic mode of production.

Notes

1 This is particularly true for the Japanese-Americans whose loyalty to the United States was questioned during World War II and to the Muslim Americans whose loyalty is often questioned in contemporary times.

2 Peter Feng suggests removing the hyphen from "Asian-American," while Gustavo P. Firmat recommends replacing it with a plus sign for "Cuban + American" (1994, 16). Some insert a forward slash between the two terms. On the politics of the hyphen, especially for Asian-Americans, see Feng 1995, 1996; Lowe 1991.

3 For more on the phenomenon of exilic nostalgia and fetishization, see Naficy 1993, chap. 4.

4 These Latin-American and Third Cinema polemics and manifestos are collected in Martin 1997.

5 For some of these, see Willemen 1989, 5–6; for others, see Martin 1995.

6 There is disagreement over what constituted the first and second cinemas. Gabriel, for example, assigned First Cinema to the products of the mainstream film industry in capitalist market economies, while consigning Second Cinema to the products of the communist/socialist command economies (1982, chap. 1).

References

Clifford, James. 1997. *Routes: Travel and Translation in the Late Twentieth Century*. Cambridge, MA: Harvard University Press.

Cohen, Robin. 1997. *Global Diasporas: An Introduction*. London: UCL Press.

Feng, Peter. 1995. "In Search of Asian American Cinema." *Cinéaste* 21 (1–2): 32–36.

Feng, Peter. 1996. "Becoming Asian American: Chinese American Identity, Asian American Subjectivity, and Chan is Missing." *Cinema Journal* 35 (4): 88–118.

Firmat, Gustavo Pérez. 1994. *Life on the Hyphen: The Cuban-American Way*. Austin, TX: University of Texas Press.

Gabriel, Teshome. 1982. *Third Cinema in the Third World: The Aesthetics of Liberation*. Ann Arbor, MI: UMI Research Press.

Gates, Henry Louis, Jr. 1988. *The Signifying Monkey: A Theory of African-American Literary Criticism*. New York: Oxford University Press.

Gilroy, Paul. 1988. "Nothing But Sweat Inside My Head: Aesthetics and Black Arts in Britain." *ICA Documents*, no. 7: 44–46. (Special issue on black film, British cinema.)

Gilroy, Paul. 1991. *"There Ain't no Black in the Union Jack": The Cultural Politics of Race and Nation*. Chicago: Chicago University Press.

Gilroy, Paul. 1993. *The Black Atlantic: Modernity and Double Consciousness*. Cambridge, MA: Harvard University Press.

Hall, Stuart. 1988. "New Ethnicities." *ICA Documents*, no.7: 27–31. (Special issue on black film, British cinema.)

Hall, Stuart. 1994. "Cultural Identity and Diaspora." In *Colonial Discourse and Post-colonial Theory: A Reader*, edited by Patrick Williams and Laura Chrisman, 392–403. New York: Columbia University Press.

Jameson, Fredric. 1986. "Third-World Literature in the Era of Multinational Capitalism." *Social Text* 15 (Fall): 65–88.

Kinder, Marsha. 1993. "Exile and Ideological Reinscription: The Unique Case of Luis Buñuel." In *Blood Cinema: The Reconstruction of National Identity in Spain*. Berkeley, CA: University of California Press.

Lowe, Lisa. 1991. "Heterogeneity, Hybridity, Multiplicity: Making Asian American Difference." *Diaspora* 1 (1): 24–44.

Marcus, George E. 1994. "The Modernist Sensibility in Recent Ethnographic Writing and the Cinematic Metaphor of Montage." In *Visualizing Theory: Selected Essays from V.A.R.*, edited by Lucien Castaing-Taylor, 37–53. London: Routledge.

Martin, Michael T., ed. 1995. *Cinema of the Black Diaspora: Diversity, Dependence and Opposition*. Detroit, MI: Wayne State University Press.

Martin, Michael T., ed. 1997. *New Latin American Cinema*. 2 vols. Detroit, MI: Wayne State University Press.

Mercer, Kobena. 1988. "Recording Narratives of Race and Nation." *ICA Documents*, no.7: 4–14. (Special issue on black film, British cinema.)

Mercer, Kobena. 1994a. "Diaspora Culture and the Dialogic Imagination: The Aesthetics of Black Independent Film in Britain." In *Welcome to the Jungle: New Positions in Black Cultural Studies*, 53–68. London: Routledge.

Mercer, Kobena. 1994b. *Welcome to the Jungle: New Positions in Black Cultural Studies*. London: Routledge.

Naficy, Hamid. 1993. *The Making of Exile Cultures: Iranian Television in Los Angeles*. Minneapolis, MN: University of Minnesota Press.

Peters, John. 1999. "Exile, Nomadism, and Diaspora: The Stakes of Mobility in the Western Canon." In *Home, Exile, Homeland: Film, Media and the Politics of Place*, edited by Hamid Naficy, 17–41. New York: Routledge.

Pfeil, Fred. 1988. "Postmodernism as a 'Structure of Feeling'." In *Marxism and the Interpretation of Culture*, edited by Cary Nelson and Lawrence Grossberg, 381–403. Irbana, IL: University of Illinois Press.

Safran, William. 1991. "Diasporas in Modern Societies: Myths of Homeland and Return." *Diaspora* 1 (1): 83–99.

Said, Edward. 1990. "Reflections on Exile." In *Out There: Marginalization and Contemporary Cultures*, edited by Russell Ferguson, Martha Gever, Trin T. Mih-ha, and Cornel West, 357–66. Cambridge, MA: MIT Press.

Sollors, Werner. 1986. *Beyond Ethnicity: Consent and Descent in American Culture*. New York: Oxford University Press.

Tölölyan, Khachig. 1996. "Rethinking Diaspora(s): Stateless Power in the Transnational Moment." *Diaspora* 5 (1): 3–36.

Willemen, Paul. 1989. "The Third Cinema Question: Notes and Reflections." In *Questions of Third Cinema*, edited by Jim Pines and Paul Willemen, 1–29. London: British Film Institute.

Williams, Raymond. 1977. "Structure of Feeling." In *Marxism and Literature*, 128–35. London: Oxford University Press.

30

SPEAKING IN TONGUES

Ang Lee, accented cinema, Hollywood[1]

Song Hwee Lim

Recent scholarship in film studies has increasingly acknowledged the limitations of the 'national cinema' paradigm to the extent that, if it is not entirely jettisoned, it must at least be problematized, rather than taken as a self-evidential category of analysis (Higson 2000). Several other conceptual categories have been mooted in its place, including transnational cinema, world cinema and accented cinema (encompassing exilic and diasporic cinemas), all of which highlight the various forms of filmmaking practice that cross national borders, and unsettle the notion of the national from both within and without. In an age of globalization that has witnessed massive migration of peoples, capital, cultures and ideologies, the national (and national cinema) can no longer sustain its myth of unity, coherence and purity. Rather, the disjunctive order of the global cultural economy (Appadurai 1990) must be brought to bear on the specificities of each case study of national and cross-border filmmaking activity.

All the above categories, implicitly or explicitly, are engaged in a 'dialogue' with Hollywood (Cooke 2007), a cinema which remains a dominant force in the production, distribution and exhibition of mainstream, commercial films in many parts of the world. Whether we like it or not, Hollywood, as a 'shorthand for a massively industrial, ideologically reactionary, and stylistically conservative form of "dominant" cinema' (Shohat and Stam 1994: 7), is often embedded in the discursive construction of these new categories of analysis, at times as the undesired Other to be distinguished against, or otherwise as an unmentionable shadow lurking in the dark. My intention to bring Hollywood into play in this chapter is borne out of both theoretical and conceptual imperatives. While Lee can variously be claimed as a national (Taiwanese) director, a transnational Chinese director, a world cinema director and an accented (diasporic) director, I believe all these categories cannot be fully accounted for 'unless we also consider his career in the United States, where he has directed films (including a blockbuster) in a globally dominant mode of production. Speaking in multiple tongues, Ang Lee epitomizes a director who can not only move between different cinemas, but is also simultaneously located in all of them, thus exposing these categories of analysis as neither mutually exclusive nor all-encompassing.

More importantly, via the example of Ang Lee's career, I want to rethink the notion of accented cinema which, in Hamid Naficy's construction at least (2001), only concerns itself with filmmaking activities situated in an exilic or diasporic condition emerging from migratory routes from Third World and postcolonial societies to Western cosmopolitan centres. I propose to reconfigure Naficy's restrictive definition and narrow specificity, which 'preclude full realization of its critical potential' (Suner 2006: 377), in three ways. First, that the route of migration for accented directors should not be limited to a hierarchical one from the Third World to the First World, and this will be illustrated through the specificity of modern Chinese and Taiwanese history; second, what happens to the notion of accented cinema when a filmmaker from the Third World begins making films in the mode of 'dominant cinema . . . without accent' (Naficy 2001: 4) such as Hollywood? Finally, instead of being assumed as having no accent, Hollywood must be reconceptualized as bearing an accent that has been, for historical reasons, dominant to an extent that it passes as universal (read unaccented) in many parts of the world, including Taiwan where Lee grew up, when it is just as culturally specific and accented as any other cinema. As a result of this interrogation, the very notion of 'accent', and the discourses and mechanisms that sustain the distinction between accented and non-accented cinemas, will also be challenged.

[. . .]

Speaking in tongues: Ang Lee as Hollywood director

Ang Lee made his firat foray into English-language filmmaking with *Sense and Sensibility* in 1995. Indeed, Lee's career post-'father knows best' trilogy has been mainly in a different tongue, as he followed *Sense and Sensibility* with five more English-language films (*The Ice Storm*, 1997; *Ride with the Devil*, 1999; *Hulk*, 2003; *Brokeback Mountain*, 2005; *Taking Woodstock*, 2009), and he has made only two more Chinese-language films since (*Crouching Tiger, Hidden Dragon* (*Wohu canglong*, 2000); *Lust, Caution* (*Se, jie*, 2007)). In this sense, Lee's filmmaking trajectory is not that dissimilar from those of émigré directors past and present, who have forged a new career in Hollywood making films in a language different from their mother tongue. While Naficy notes the careers of those he calls 'great transplanted directors', such as Alfred Hitchcock, Douglas Sirk and F.W. Murnau (2001: 19), his exclusive focus on filmmaking practices that are marked by displacement, decentredness and deterritorialization fails to illuminate the trajectories of transplanted film-makers whose careers in Hollywood negotiated a different set of dynamics, that of acculturation, integration and reterritorialization. In other words, Naficy is more concerned with filmmakers who bring their accents to, and who preserve their displaced selfhoods in, their host countries. This theoretical model, however, does not adequately address filmmakers such as Ang Lee, who have spoken in different tongues and accents in the process of being assimilated and becoming the other.

Given that Taiwan was shielded by the United States during the Cold War era, the process of acculturation may have begun even before one has travelled to the other shore. In the case of Ang Lee, Shu-mei Shih proposes that knowledge of American culture has become a given for educated Taiwanese, 'to the extent-that a national subject from Taiwan can be readily trans-formed into a minority subject in the US' (Shih 2000: 91). Doubly displaced, Lee has emphasized in an interview his identity as a second-generation mainlander, and the alienation that this group feels in Taiwan and in the United States (Berry 2005: 331–2). Multiple displacements, however, can be both a consequence of and a condition for what Aihwa Ong terms 'flexible citizenship' (1999), and it is precisely this flexibility that has made possible Lee's versatile career.

What does it entail to be flexible, especially in relation to speaking in a different language and working in a different film industry? Lee has spoken candidly about how he struggled to com-mand respect while directing *Sense and Sensibility*, this being his first English-language film and set in a time and place that were unfamiliar to him, and how Emma Thompson and the production designer gave him tutelage in the art and history of the Regency period (Berry 2005: 338). Lee's first attempt to speak in a different tongue reveals an unequal power relation, for to acquire a new language or to put on a different accent is to place oneself constantly in the inferior position of being judged, scrutinized, examined. Like passing a test, one has to also pass as native/authentic, in much the same way that actors and actresses have to sound convincing when playing roles set in a different context, or transgendered people trying to pass as the other gender in appearance and mannerism. This position, however, is a double-edged one, as one's acquisition of the accent/language could be judged to have passed (in both senses) and thus welcomed into the host family, or the remnants of one's original accent/language could be celebrated under the logic of multi-culturalism so that one's cultural difference is not perceived as a hindrance to integration, but, paradoxically, as hybridizing and rejuvenating the host culture.

[. . .]

Unaccented cinema? Provincializing Hollywood

Ang Lee's career clearly demonstrates the limitations of Naficy's model of accented cinema, whose remit is confined not just to films made in exile and diaspora, but also to filmmakers whose location remains liminal and interstitial (Naficy 2001: 20). As I have argued from the outset, this model fails to take into consideration filmmakers like Ang Lee whose careers begin as diasporic and liminal, but have, via strategies of flexibility, gained full citizenship in mainstream film-making. Moreover, by privileging only one route of migration, that from the Third World to the First World, Naficy's model neglects the other myriad forms of migration deserving equal attention, and risks valorizing the First World as the only desired destination. As Suner rightly points out in her critique of Naficy's model: 'As long as it takes emigration to the West as a prerequisite for the entitlement to speak universally, however, this approach would leave the hierarchical division between the West and the rest intact' (2006: 378).

More problematic, for me, is Naficy's distinction between accented and unaccented cinema that leaves the latter category completely unquestioned. On current theoretical paradigms for discussing films, Naficy argues, via Rick Altman, that classificatory approaches are not neutral structures, but 'ideological constructs' masquerading as neutral categories (2001: 19). However, his only mention of unaccented cinema in his book is one line in the introduction, in which he states: 'If the dominant cinema is considered universal and without accent, the films that diasporic and exilic subjects make are accented' (4), without qualifying what is dominant cinema, who considers it as without accent and why, or critiquing this distinction. Naficy, therefore, does not question the masquerading neutrality of what he calls a dominant cinema without accent. As a result, his theoretical model contributes to a widespread but erroneous distinction between Hollywood and the rest, which continues to plague discussions of national cinemas in general and of world cinema in particular. It also allows the dominant (Hollywood) cinema to pass as the norm against which all other cinemas must be measured, without questioning its unqualified hegemonic position, its discursive legitimacy and the violence it inflicts on other cinemas by the sheer force of its capitalist power, which is essentially a form of cultural imperialism.[2]

In this regard, the false dichotomy between accented and unaccented cinema is analogous to the linguistic one from which it draws its metaphor, that of received pronunciation (RP) as standard/unaccented, and regional pronunciation as bearing an accent, even though the idea that a standard English accent had some special claim to be a model has long been questioned (Honey 1989: 11). More disturbingly, given its reinforcement of the distinction between the West and the rest, with its privileging of the one route of migration that begins in the Third World and ends in the First World, the false dichotomy is also analogous to the construction of the white race as universal, neutral, unraced, and the other races as particular, different, 'coloured'. In his seminal book on whiteness, Richard Dyer notes the paradoxical situation in which there is an 'absence of reference to whiteness in the habitual speech and writing of white people in the West', despite the fact that whites, in Western representation, 'are overwhelmingly and disproportionately pre-dominant, have the central and elaborated roles, and above all are placed as the norm, the ordinary, the standard' (1997: 2–3). He goes on to argue that 'there is something especially white in this non-located and disembodied position of knowledge, and thus it seems especially important to try to break the hold of whiteness by locating and embodying it in a particular experience of being white' (1997: 4). Following Dyer, I would propose that Hollywood, rather than being considered as dominant and unaccented, must be recast in film studies in light of its particularities, its cultural specificities, its situatedness, its difference. Similar to the historian Dipesh Chakrabarty's effort to provincialize Europe (2000), a dislodging of Hollywood from its presumed centrality and universality will illuminate the discourses, processes and mechanisms through which it has come to occupy this dominant position. In other words, we need to provincialize Hollywood.

Ang Lee's journey from Taiwan to the United States is not simply the process of losing one accent and acquiring a different, more exalted one, even though those in East Asia have been accustomed, after more than a century of experience of different forms of colonialism and cultural imperialism, to regard Lee's success in Hollywood as 'the pride of all Chinese people'. As the level of migration continues to intensify in the age of globalization, as more and more people – and cinemas – are able to speak in multiple tongues, we also need to dismantle the self/other distinction that continues to perpetuate the myth of the West versus the rest, Hollywood versus world cinema. While Lee's career could be split along linguistic lines, it is worth recalling that film was celebrated as a utopian universal language in its early years, albeit before the introduction of sound brought to it a Babelistic turn. As Miriam Hansen points out, the celebration of film as a universal language was accompanied by, on the one hand, the American film industry's efforts to ensure US films' dominance on both domestic and world markets, and, on the other hand, the emerging codes of classical narrative cinema (1991: 78–9). By projecting the career of Ang Lee through the lens of Naficy's notion of accented cinema, I hope to have demonstrated that the phenomenon of speaking in multiple tongues in cinema must challenge us not only to break down those aforementioned binaries, but ultimately to also rethink the very language of film itself, to question its presumed universality, and to treat all cinemas as particular, peculiar and provincial, while not discounting their abilities to communicate and connect beyond their cultural, linguistic and formal specificities.

Notes

1 I would like to thank Kien Ket Lim for inviting me to a conference on Ang Lee in Taiwan in December 2006, where this chapter took its embryonic form, and Lúcia Nagib for inviting me to the Theorising World Cinema Workshop II in Leeds in November 2007, where the chapter then took a different incarnation. Thanks also to Chris Perriam for his insightful suggestions as discussant at Leeds and to participants at both workshops for their useful comments.
2 As Judith Mayne also argues: 'The classical Hollywood cinema has become the norm against which all other alternative practices are measured. Films which do not engage with the classical Hollywood cinema are by and large relegated to irrelevance. Frequently, the very notion of an "alternative" is posed in the narrow terms of an either-or: either one is within classical discourse and therefore complicit, or one is critical of and/or resistant to it and therefore outside of it' (in Yoshimoto 2006: 36).

References

Appadurai, Arjun (1990) 'Disjuncture and difference in the global cultural economy', *Theory, Culture & Society* 7: 2–3, pp. 295–310.
Berry, Michael (2005) *Speaking in Images: Interviews with Contemporary Chinese Filmmakers* (New York, Columbia University Press).

Chakrabarty, Dipesh (2000) *Provincializing Europe: Postcolonial Thought and Historical Difference* (Princeton, Princeton University Press).

Cooke, Paul (ed.) (2007) *World Cinema's 'Dialogues' with Hollywood* (Basingstoke, Palgrave Macmillan).

Dyer, Richard (1997) *White* (London and New York, Routledge).

Hansen, Miriam (1991) *Babel and Babylon: Spectatorship in American Silent Film* (Cambridge and London, Harvard University Press).

Higson, Andrew (2000) 'The limiting imagination of national cinema', in Mette Hjort and Scott MacKenzie (eds) *Cinema and Nation* (London, Routledge), pp. 63–74.

Honey, John (1989) *Does Accent Matter? The Pygmalion Factor* (London and Boston, Faber & Faber).

Naficy, Hamid. (2001) *An Accented Cinema: Exilic and Diasporic Filmmaking* (Princeton and Oxford, Princeton University Press).

Ong, Aihwa (1999) *Flexible Citizenship: The Cultural Logics of Transnationality* (Durham and London, Duke University Press).

Shih, Shu-mei (2000) 'Globalisation and minoritisation: Ang Lee and the politics of flexibility', *New Formations* 40, pp. 86–101.

Shohat, Ella and Stam, Robert (1994) *Unthinking Eurocentrism: Multiculturalism and the Media* (London and New York, Routledge).

Suner, Asuman (2006) 'Outside in: "accented cinema" at large', *Cultural Studies* 7:3, pp. 363–82.

Yoshimoto, Mitsuhiro (2006) 'National/international/transnational: the concept of trans-Asian cinema and the cultural politics of film criticism', in Valentina Vitali and Paul Willemen (eds) *Theorising National Cinema* (London, BFI Publishing), pp. 254–61.

PART V

Community

HOME AND BELONGING
Introduction

In the English-speaking world, the saying that 'an Englishman's home is his castle' is, perhaps, the most common summary of what 'home' epitomizes or, colloquially, what home means 'when it's at home'. Dating back in its proverbial form to time out of mind, it can be documented as far back as the sixteenth century.[1] It was famously inscribed in law in Chapter 3 of Sir Edward Coke's *Institutes of the Laws of England* (published in 1628): 'For a man's house is his castle, et domus sua cuique est tutissimum refugium [and each man's home is his safest refuge]'. In her study of the Victorian home, Judith Flanders (2006) points out how this legal and political concept had transformed into a 'social description' (22) in that period, quoting its famous literary illustration in Charles Dickens' *Great Expectations*:

> Wemmick's house was a little wooden cottage in the midst of plots of garden, and the top of it was cut out and painted like a battery mounted with guns. [. . .] I think it was the smallest house I ever saw: with the queerest gothic windows (by far the greater part of them sham), and a gothic door, almost too small to get in at.
>
> "That's a real flagstaff, you see," said Wemmick, "and on Sundays I run up a real flag. Then look here. After I have crossed this bridge, I hoist it up – so – and cut off the communication."
>
> The bridge was a plank, and it crossed a chasm about four feet wide and two deep. But it was very pleasant to see the pride with which he hoisted it up, and made it fast; smiling as he did so, with a relish, and not merely mechanically.
>
> At nine o'clock every night, Greenwich time," said Wemmick, "the gun fires. There he is, you see! And when you hear him go, I think you'll say he's a Stinger."
>
> The piece of ordnance referred to was mounted in a separate fortress, constructed of lattice-work. It was protected from the weather by an ingenious little tarpaulin contrivance in the nature of an umbrella.
>
> *(Dickens [1860–1] 1989, 195)*

The quotation is relevant in the context of diaspora, as it shows how concepts of home not only serve to provide safety and comfort for those falling within the 'home' perimeter, but also how functions of exclusion and 'othering' are massively inscribed in them. Again, neither of the two contrastive perspectives on 'home' can be seen as monolithic, but each has its own implications, as for instance Michael McKeon's (2005) magisterial study of domesticity as the 'interior' aspect of home documents. The negative, exclusionary side of 'home' has been pointed out by Edward Said (2000a), with a specific edge given to the position of the exile or the diasporic: 'I suppose part of my critique of Zionism is that it attaches too much importance to home. Saying, we need a home. And we'll do anything to get a home, even if it means making others homeless'.

As Said goes on to show, the diasporic situation is further complicated:

> Most people are principally aware of one culture, one setting, one home; exiles are aware
> of at least two, and this plurality of vision gives rise to an awareness of simultaneous
> dimensions, an awareness that – to borrow a phrase from music – is *contrapuntal.*
>
> *(2000b, 186)*

For diasporic subjects, home has this double dimension: of referring to their current place of diasporic residence where they try to make themselves at home as best they can, and to their place of origin, which is often referred to in a gesture of diasporic nostalgia. Again, these dimensions are complicated and intricately interwoven. The diasporics' attempts at establishing home in the 'host' country not only changes the society and culture of that country, but also the conceptualization of home as such, pointing towards the emergence of what Alison Blunt and Robyn Dowling (2006) describe as 'transnational homes' (196–252). Such reverberations are also felt in the society and culture of the diasporic subjects' country of origin, as diasporics relate to it and change, not only their own concept of home, but also that of those in their host country who might still feel securely settled in that country's society and culture.

Such transformations of home are succinctly summarized by Avtar Brah in the text included in this section as 'the homing of diaspora, the diasporising of home'. Continuing in this line of argument, Brah opens up the full dialectic of diaspora and home as she shows that, on the one hand, 'home' is a 'mythic place of desire in the diasporic imagination' (this volume 236), but on the other hand appears also as 'the lived experience of a locality' (this volume 236); it is based on 'processes of inclusion or exclusion' and it is about 'roots and routes', as she quotes Paul Gilroy (this volume 236), with the concept of diaspora gesturing towards '*processes of multi-locationality across geographical, cultural and psychic boundaries*' (this volume 237; italics in the original). Brah again follows up these observations to their influence on concepts of identity and concludes that 'identity is always plural and in process, even when it might be construed or represented as fixed' (this volume 238), an insight much supported from the experience of diasporics and diaspora studies.

Brah's critical deconstruction of diasporic home and identity is taken up by Robin Cohen, whose article casts Brah in a line of scholars questioning the solidity of home as an indispensable component of a diaspora. He describes how, after a foundational phase epitomized by the pioneering figure of William Safran, when the Jewish experience was the diasporic prototype and the idea of homeland hence central, a phase of constructivist approaches to home followed in the 1990s. This he sees represented in Avtar Brah's positioning but also in Floya Anthias's and Yasemin Nuhoğlu Soysal's, as they all look at diasporic configurations of home in more metaphoric and less material or solid ways. Surveying these various standpoints, Cohen categorizes them in conceptualizations of a 'solid homeland', which is concrete and material, such as the biblical promised land; of 'ductile homeland', which is an 'intermediate category' with 'a more flexible (ductile) use of homeland' (this volume 241); and finally 'liquid homes' with an 'evocation of constant movement and liquidity' of the nomadic kind. Cohen concludes by observing that all three notions of homeland have good arguments to substantiate them, but argues against an entirely indiscriminate use of the concept and in favour of 'insist[ing] on empirical and historical support for any notion of home/homeland' (this volume 242).

Jane Mummery starts out from theorists of Cohen's third category of 'ductile home' concepts, purporting that 'any sense of at-homeness we do feel is actually illusory', but then goes on to differentiate between different forms the desire for at-homeness can take. One is the straightforward at-homeness felt in an ancestral (even if imagined) homeland, while the other, more complex version is, in Mummery's view, to be found in what Vijay Mishra calls 'the hyphen self' (quoted by Mummery, this volume 230). Following this train of argument, she ends up, inspired by the existentialist positions of Heidegger and Sartre, with the insight that such 'hyphenation' and the coexistence of 'not-at-homeness' is inscribed in any construct of home. In that respect, diasporic identities have more in common with 'traditional' or 'native' identities than is usually accepted.

Salman Rushdie's passages from his famous article, 'Imaginary homelands', explore the components at work in creating and using an image of an 'original' home in the diasporic imagination. He brings in the temporal dimension of such imagined homes, as they are usually in the past, or, 'the past is home' (this volume 227). Much like envisaging the past as history, Rushdie pinpoints a strong fictional element in the construction of such desired and remembered homelands, as he memorably puts it: 'we will, in short, create fictions, not actual cities or villages, but invisible ones, imaginary homelands, Indias of the mind' (this volume 227). Quite in keeping with his style, Rushdie celebrates this fuzziness in the concept of home, the fragmentation and fictiveness he finds in it, and the warping distance from which diasporics look at the homeland. For the artist, this standpoint is described as a great boon, and the diasporic Salman Rushdie no doubt has given ample proof of this point, at least for himself.

Note

1 For a succinct summary of the history of the phrase see *The Phrase Finder*, www.phrases.org.uk/meanings/an-englishmans-home-is-his-castle.html, accessed 21 March 2016.

References

Blunt, Alison, and Robyn Dowling. 2006. *Home*. London and New York: Routledge.
Dickens, Charles. [1860–1] 1989. *Great Expectations*. The Oxford Illustrated Dickens. Oxford: Oxford University Press.
Flanders, Judith. 2006. *Inside the Victorian Home. A Portrait of Domestic Life in Victorian England*. New York and London: Norton.
McKeon, Michael. 2005. *The Secret History of Domesticity: Public, Private, and the Division of Knowledge*. Baltimore, MD: Johns Hopkins University Press.
Said, Edward. 2000a. 'An Interview with Edward Said.' *Politics and Culture* 3: n.p. Available at: https://politicsandculture.org/2010/08/10/an-interview-with-edward-said-2/.
Said, Edward. 2000b. 'Reflections on Exile.' In *Reflections on Exile and Other Literary and Cultural Essays*, by Edward Said, 173–186. London: Granta.

31

IMAGINARY HOMELANDS

Salman Rushdie

An old photograph in a cheap frame hangs on a wall of the room where I work. It's a picture dating from 1946 of a house into which, at the time of its taking, I had not yet been born. The house is rather peculiar—a three-storeyed gabled affair with tiled roofs and round towers in two corners, each wearing a pointy tiled hat. 'The past is a foreign country' goes the famous opening sentence of L. P. Hartley's novel *The Go-Between,* 'they do things differently there.' But the photograph tells me to invert this idea; it reminds me that it's my present that is foreign, and that the past is home, albeit a lost home in a lost city in the mists of lost time.

A few years ago I revisited Bombay, which is my lost city, after an absence of something like half my life. Shortly after arriving, acting on an impulse, I opened the telephone directory and looked for my father's name. And, amazingly, there it was; his name, our old address, the unchanged telephone number, as if we had never gone away to the unmentionable country across the border. It was an eerie discovery. I felt as if I were being claimed, or informed that the facts of my faraway life were illusions, and that this continuity was the reality. Then I went to visit the house in the photograph and stood outside it, neither daring nor wishing to announce myself to its new owners. (I didn't want to see how they'd ruined the interior.) I was overwhelmed. The photograph had naturally been taken in black and white; and my memory, feeding on such images as this, had begun to see my childhood in the same way, monochromatically. The colours of my history had seeped out of my mind's eye; now my other two eyes were assaulted by colours, by the vividness of the red tiles, the yellow-edged green of cactus-leaves, the brilliance of bougainvillaea creeper. It is probably not too romantic to say that that was when my novel *Midnight's Children* was really born; when I realized how much I wanted to restore the past to myself, not in the faded greys of old family-album snapshots, but whole, in Cinemascope and glorious Technicolor.

Bombay is a city built by foreigners upon reclaimed land; I, who had been away so long that I almost qualified for the title, was gripped by the conviction that I, too, had a city and a history to reclaim.

It may be that writers in my position, exiles or emigrants or expatriates, are haunted by some sense of loss, some urge to reclaim, to look back, even at the risk of being mutated into pillars of salt. But if we do look back, we must also do so in the knowledge—which gives rise to profound uncertainties—that our physical alienation from India almost inevitably means that we will not be capable of reclaiming precisely the thing that was lost; that we will, in short, create fictions, not actual cities or villages, but invisible ones, imaginary homelands, Indias of the mind.

Writing my book in North London, looking out through my window on to a city scene totally unlike the ones I was imagining on to paper, I was constantly plagued by this problem, until I felt obliged to face it in the text, to make clear that (in spite of my original and I suppose somewhat Proustian ambition to unlock the gates of lost time so that the past reappeared as it actually had been, unaffected by the distortions of memory) what I was actually doing was a novel of memory and about memory, so that my India was just that: 'my' India, a version and no more than one version of all the hundreds of millions of possible versions. I tried to make it as imaginatively true as I could, but imaginative truth is simultaneously honourable and suspect, and I knew that my India may only have been one to which I (who am no longer what I was, and who by quitting Bombay never became what perhaps I was meant to be) was, let us say, willing to admit I belonged.

This is why I made my narrator, Saleem, suspect in his narration; his mistakes are the mistakes of a fallible memory compounded by quirks of character and of circumstance and his vision is fragmentary. It may be that when the Indian writer who writes from outside India tries to reflect that world, he is obliged to deal in broken mirrors, some of whose fragments have been irretrievably lost.

But there is a paradox here. The broken mirror may actually be as valuable as the one which is supposedly unflawed. Let me again try and explain this from my own experience. Before beginning *Midnight's Children,* I spent many months trying simply to recall as much of the Bombay of the 1950s and 1960s as I could; and not only Bombay—Kashmir, too, and Delhi and Aligarh, which, in my book, I've moved to Agra to heighten a certain joke about the Taj Mahal. I was genuinely amazed by how much came back to me. I found myself remembering what clothes people had worn on certain days, and school scenes, and whole passages of Bombay dialogue verbatim, or so it seemed; I even remembered advertisements, film-posters, the neon Jeep sign on Marine Drive, toothpaste ads for Binaca and for Kolynos, and a footbridge over the local railway line which bore, on one side, the legend 'Esso puts a tiger in your tank' and, on the other, the curiously contradictory admonition: 'Drive like Hell and you will get there.' Old songs came back to me from nowhere: a street entertainer's version of 'Good Night, Ladies', and, from the film *Mr 420* (a very appropriate source for my narrator to have used), the hit number 'Mera Joota Hai Japani',[1] which could almost be Saleem's theme song.

I knew that I had tapped a rich seam; but the point I want to make is that of course I'm not gifted with total recall, and it was precisely the partial nature of these memories, their fragmentation, that made them so evocative for me. The shards of memory acquired greater status, greater resonance, because they were *remains*; fragmentation made trivial things seem like symbols, and the mundane acquired numinous qualities. There is an obvious parallel here with archaeology. The broken pots of antiquity, from which the past can sometimes, but always provisionally, be reconstructed, are exciting to discover, even if they are pieces of the most quotidian objects.

It may be argued that the past is a country from which we have all emigrated, that its loss is part of our common humanity. Which seems to me self-evidently true; but I suggest that the writer who is out-of-country and even out-of-language may experience this loss in an intensified form. It is made more concrete for him by the physical fact of discontinuity, of his present being in a different place from his past, of his being 'elsewhere'. This may enable him to speak properly and concretely on a subject of universal significance and appeal.

But let me go further. The broken glass is not merely a mirror of nostalgia. It is also, I believe, a useful tool with which to work in the present.

John Fowles begins *Daniel Martin* with the words: 'Whole sight: or all the rest is desolation.' But human beings do not perceive things whole; we are not gods but wounded creatures, cracked lenses, capable only of fractured perceptions. Partial beings, in all the senses of that phrase. Meaning is a shaky edifice we build out of scraps, dogmas, childhood injuries, newspaper articles, chance remarks, old films, small victories, people hated, people loved; perhaps it is because our sense of what is the case is constructed from such inadequate materials that we defend it so fiercely, even to the death. The Fowles position seems to me a way of succumbing to the guru-illusion. Writers are no longer sages, dispensing the wisdom of the centuries. And those of us who have been forced by cultural displacement to accept the provisional nature of all truths, all certainties, have perhaps had modernism forced upon us. We can't lay claim to Olympus, and are thus released to describe our worlds in the way in which all of us, whether writers or not, perceive it from day to day.

In *Midnight's Children,* my narrator Saleem uses, at one point, the metaphor of a cinema screen to discuss this business of perception: 'Suppose yourself in a large cinema, sitting at first in the back row, and gradually moving up, . . . until your nose is almost pressed against the screen. Gradually the stars' faces dissolve into dancing grain; tiny details assume grotesque proportions; . . . it becomes clear that the illusion itself is reality.' The movement towards the cinema screen is a metaphor for the narrative's movement through time towards the present, and the book itself, as it nears contemporary events, quite deliberately loses deep perspective, becomes more 'partial'. I wasn't trying to write about (for instance) the Emergency in the same way as I wrote about events half a century earlier. I felt it would be dishonest to pretend, when writing about the day before yesterday, that it was possible to see the whole picture. I showed certain blobs and slabs of the scene. [. . .]

Art is a passion of the mind. And the imagination works best when it is most free. Western writers have always felt free to be eclectic in their selection of theme, setting, form; Western visual artists have, in this century, been happily raiding the visual storehouses of Africa, Asia, the Philippines. I am sure that we must grant ourselves an equal freedom.

Let me suggest that Indian writers in England have access to a second tradition, quite apart from their own racial history. It is the culture and political history of the phenomenon of migration, displacement, life in a minority group. We can quite legitimately claim as our ancestors the Huguenots, the Irish, the Jews; the past to which we belong is an English past, the history of immigrant Britain. Swift, Conrad, Marx are as much our literary forebears as Tagore or Ram Mohan Roy. America, a nation of immigrants, has created great literature out of the phenomenon of cultural transplantation, out of examining the ways in which people cope with a new world; it may be that by discovering what we have in common with those who preceded us into this country, we can begin to do the same.

Notes

1 *Mera joota hai Japani*
  Ye patloon Inglistani
  Sar pé lal topi Rusi—
  Phir bhi dil hai Hindustani
  —which translates roughly as:
  O, my shoes are Japanese
  These trousers English, if you please
  On my head, red Russian hat—
  My heart's Indian for all that.
  [This is also the song sung by Gibreel Farishta as he tumbles from the heavens at the beginning of *The Satanic Verses*.]

32

BEING NOT-AT-HOME

A conceptual discussion

Jane Mummery

When we think about diaspora one of our typical starting points is the idea of not quite belonging, of being not-at-home. We think for instance, as Vijay Mishra reminds us, of those 'people who do not feel comfortable [at-home] with their non-hyphenated identities as indicated on their passports' (1996: 67). We think of individuals who are not at-home in any single community or eventuality, and who are therefore constantly remaking themselves. However, I would also suggest that we do think of individuals and communities—uneasy and hyphenated ones perhaps, not certain of really being at-home, but holding onto some sense of identity nonetheless, if by identity we simply mean our way of making sense of ourselves and our world. More specifically, we might want to suggest that the typical diasporic vision of hyphenated identity might in fact represent a new and different way of feeling at-home. Maybe diasporic-style hyphenated identity and its concurrent acceptance of hybridization can represent a new mode of belonging given our inability to sustain older styles of identity in what is fast becoming a postnational or transnational world. However, and as I suggest in this paper, even the most hybridized of these diasporic identities may still be problematic, and this focus on not-at-homeness and hyphenation in terms of a particularly diasporic identity may be a little artificial.

Nonetheless, for now we need to remember that any such desire to find new and different ways of being at-home actually begins with the sense of not belonging, of being not-at-home. And this sense has been explored in a whole range of theoretical spaces, which is where this paper comes in. Indeed, as I will demonstrate, this sense of not-being-at-home can be seen as the imperative driving not only diasporic theorizing but much of the anti-essentialist and anti-subjectivist thinking deriving from the work of Martin Heidegger. More specifically, then, I want to unpack just how this concept has functioned to problematize our ideas firstly about ourselves and secondly about community and our relations within it—ways that stress our practices of being-in-the-world (to use a Heideggerian phrase) rather than any given identities. Further I will argue that diaspora theorizing—and I mean here what Clifford has called 'diaspora discourse' as opposed to 'distinct historical experiences of diaspora' (1994: 302)—whilst it has certainly worked to put forward and affirm problematized notions of identity and at-homeness, does need a reminder concerning these other anti-subjectivist modes of not being at-home.

To achieve this, then, this paper has two main objectives. First I will set out a conceptual analysis of not-at-homeness, focusing on how it has impacted on our ideas of subjectivity and community. This analysis will thus include some preliminary remarks on our idea of the subject itself, and consideration of the anti-essentialist and anti-subjectivist projects of such exemplary thinkers of not-at-homeness as Martin Heidegger, Jean-Paul Sartre, Michel Foucault and Chantal Mouffe. Despite the very real differences between these thinkers, I suggest that their various approaches delineate the primary ways this concept has driven an overall rethinking of our notions of both our communities and our selves. I will also explore how this concept has underpinned diaspora theorizing about subjectivity and community. With this analysis completed, I will then work to support my claim that diaspora theorizing needs to be careful in its quest to affirm hyphenated identities—as I will show, such affirmations are always at risk of rigidifying into closed modes of identity. More specifically I suggest that diaspora discourse might need to explicitly take note of some of the more general implications of the anti-essentialist thinking put forward by the theorists mentioned above. Overall, however, I do contend that these diverse affirmations of not-at-homeness are important in showing us some other fruitful trajectories not just for our notions of subjectivity, but for community. [. . .]

Diaspora: Articulating not-at-homeness

Now it is clear that diaspora discourse in general relies on and articulates many of these reconfigurations of both subjectivity and community that I have delineated above. Diaspora theorizing indeed takes for granted the base points of these disparate theories. These theories, after all, deliver a similar message to that of diaspora discourse in showing us that our subjectivity is never fully at home within itself. They all contend that our subjectivity is unable to fully coincide with itself insofar as its being is inextricable from both its own potentiality and the particular sociopolitical—and of course ethno-cultural—configurations of power and knowledge that converge to produce it. Secondly these theories all contend that we can never be fully at home within the 'they' or, more specifically, that any sense of at-homeness we do feel is actually illusory. Finally, these theories all suggest to us that our focus in retheorizing both subjectivity and community needs to be on our practices rather than on notions of selfness or at-homeness. That is, we need to see subjectivity and community in terms of ongoing actions as opposed to identities.

As I said much of this is basic to diaspora theorizing. First of all we can say in general that diasporic individuals and communities are already seen, by definition, as hyphenated or hybridized individuals and communities. Such individuals and communities are, as such, constituted in terms of practices and actions of not-at-homeness. For instance, and most simply, they are not-at-home in any attempted definitions of them by the 'they,' regardless of whether the 'they' is the host, the homeland, or indeed the wider diasporic community.

However diaspora theorizing also articulates a more complex sense of not-at-homeness whilst simultaneously, as Mishra, Sun, and many others point out, holding on to particular—albeit idealized—senses of at-homeness. Specifically, this desired at-homeness can take two forms. First of all, and most simply it can be the desired at-homeness associated with the ancestral—often idealized or imagined—homeland. At the same time, however it can also be associated with the more complex sense of at-homeness that Mishra, for instance, has discussed in terms of an affirmation of 'the hyphen itself' (1996: 79).

Not-at-homeness for diaspora theorizing thus seems to be indissociable from a desire for at-homeness. However we also need to register that the acceptance of this not-at-homeness drives these desired senses of at-homeness quite differently. As far as the first of these goes, not-at-homeness tends to be seen as characteristic of a feeling of non-acceptance or alienation within the host society. At-homeness, in turn, is tied up with a continued identification with the ancestral society, whether it is through memories of the actual homeland, or through a range of evocative objects, fragments of narratives that [diasporic subjects] keep in their heads or in their suitcases'

(Mishra, 1996: 68). Or, even, through the sort of global diasporic mediasphere that the Chinese scholar Wanning Sun talks about: 'Confronted with endless (Chinese) media choices, my dilemma is not whether I can continue to be Chinese in another country: it is how Chinese or what kind of Chinese I want to be' (2006). Basically, however, it can be claimed that a perceived sense of not-at-homeness leads to the desire to sustain or reclaim some sort of at-homeness with the homeland or home-idea.

In contrast with this, however, and as we have also seen in our discussions of Foucault and Mouffe in particular, not-at-homeness can also underpin a very different sense of—and desire for—at-homeness. In this case, not-at-homeness suggests the possibility of a practice of at-homeness—and identity—in this very not-at-homeness. Such a conjunction has thus been articulated by diaspora theorizing as the affirmation of the hyphen and hybridity, and the feeling of at-homeness in the hyphen and hybridity. We are to affirm, in other words, the complex identity of our hyphenated and diasporic being-in-the-world rather than just that of our illusory subjective being. To borrow Salman Rushdie's words when speaking of his exemplary work of the hyphen, *The Satanic Verses,* such an affirmation would arise from an acceptance and celebration of the practices of 'hybridity, impurity, intermingling, the transformation that comes of new and unexpected combinations of human beings, cultures, ideas, politics, movies, songs' (Rushdie, 1991: 394).

Rethinking diaspora discourse

Now this is all very well, however, I do believe that although this focus on redescribing diasporic identity in terms of hyphenation and practice certainly marks an improvement over subjectivist or essentialist descriptions of identity, it is a practice that not only might have limited its scope unjustifiably but remains irrescuably at risk in a number of ways. Before I consider these issues, however, I should stress that I am in no way claiming that diasporic descriptions do not utilize the notion of identity as practice. Certainly diasporic identities, under any description, are lived out and theorized as performative, strategic, and negotiable practices. Many theorists of diaspora would contend, for instance, that diasporic identity is performed in terms of highly strategic practices of consumption—whether, say, of media or food—along with practices of place and space-making. (For example, with regards to diasporic identity being practiced through the highly specific consumption of media, see the works of Cunningham and Sinclair (2000), Mitra (1996, 1997), Gillespie (1995), Naficy (1999), and Wanning Sun (2006, 2002, 1997-8).

In addition, this redescription is undoubtedly effective if the only aim of diaspora theorizing is simply to better describe the lived identity and practices of particular diasporic groups or, even, of the wider diasporic community. There is no question, after all, that notions of hyphenation and a transnational imaginative practice are far more useful ways of describing diasporic eventuality than are notions of identity fixed in projects of nation-building and national imagination and at-homeness. As Arjun Appadurai reminds us, imagination is a social and political process that is informative of both subjectivity and community:

> It is the imagination, in its collective forms, that creates ideas of neighbourhood and nationhood, of moral economics and unjust rule, of higher wages and foreign labor prospects. The imagination is today a staging ground for action, and not only for escape.
> *(Appadurai. 1996: 7)*

Nevertheless, the problem, as I see it, is that these various notions and practices are still primarily concerned with establishing a highly specific identity and sense of at-homeness

Hyphenated identity, after all, is depicted here as a specifically diasporic identity—despite the fact that this is the very type of delimitation that the work of Heidegger et al. has effectively problematized. Heidegger and Foucault, in fact, would tell us that such a desire risks keeping diaspora discourse in the realm of something like humanism, anthropology or, indeed, ethnography. This would be the realm of simply describing *what is* (i.e. a given identity of community), when what is—its diasporic identity as hyphenated—is already taken as given. Why is this problematic? Simply because if you have already set the limits of what you are describing *before you start,* you tend to forget that these limits are themselves questionable and may not actually exist per se. Further, you tend to stay within these limits. Hence Heidegger and Foucault would contend that intrinsic to this type of description are a set of theoretically dubious assumptions prioritizing certain desired senses of at-homeness and not-at-homeness that simply do not hold up.

This is a tendency that I believe diaspora discourse needs to be cautious of. That is, I would suggest that the manifesto of the journal *Diaspora,* as of 1991, in stating that the aim of the journal—and, by implication, of diaspora discourse—is to describe the 'ways in which nations, real yet imagined communities (Anderson), are fabulated, brought into being, made and unmade, in culture and politics, both on land people call their own and in exile' (Tölölyan 1991: 1), seems to have primarily been construed as the need to describe particular diasporic eventualities. This problem has, I think, been recognized. Kim Butler, for instance, has argued that we need to shift 'the defining element of diasporan studies from the group itself'—what I would see here as the group's actual identity, and concurrent senses of at-homeness and not-at-homeness—'to a methodological and theoretical approach' that starts to consider diaspora 'as a framework for the study of a specific process of community formation' (2001: 193, 194). In other words, we need to look not just at the historical eventuality of diasporic communities and subjectivities, but at the theoretical grounds of the types of assumptions and moves made by diaspora discourses.

A second point to remember, concerning the diasporic affirmation of hyphenation, is that it is a practice that remains at risk. Further it is a practice that *must* remain at risk. Now this is not itself a criticism. Derrida, after all, reminds us that any practice or methodology concerned with thinking relations and borders non-reductively is always at risk of collapsing back into the totalizing horizon of identity (1994: 28). He also stresses that any attempt to elude or surmount this risk marks just such a collapse. And it is with regards to this point that I want to suggest that maybe affirmations of hyphenation that begin with their limitation to—at-homeness within—diasporic eventuality mark such a collapse. Given, then, that it is the risk or not-at-homeness, even in the practices of hyphenation and hybridization—even when we might affirm hyphenation as a practice—that keeps our practices of hyphenation open to hitherto unforeseen articulations, we need to remember that hyphenation articulations, we need to remember that hyphenation is not an identity to be assumed, but a practice to be maintained. We need to remember, in other words, to keep on seeing it as a practice as to *how* we are, given that we can never fully pin down or practice *what* we are.

Conclusions

So what does all this mean? As far as diasporic thinking goes, I would suggest that it needs to remember that hyphenated identity is not simply the domain of diasporic individuals or communities. We need to remember that there already exists a conceptual history of not-at-homeness that suggests that certain practices of hyphenation and articulation—and their various implications—are exemplary of the human condition itself, of our everyday being-in-a-world. That is, Heidegger, Sartre, Foucault and Mouffe all show us that all of our actual being-in-the-world— whether diasporic or not—is inextricably tied up with practices of non-coincidence and not-at-homeness. Consequently, their work suggests that no realizations of either our sub-jectivities or our communities can ever finally be secure or at-home within themselves. It also reminds us that we cannot expect to effectively retheorize or ground any notions of either subjectivity or community on any pre-determined vision of identity, even when that identity is as hyphenated. Finally this means, I think, that in order to achieve Butler's suggestions for con-sidering diaspora as a useful framework for studying practices of community (and I would add, subjectivity) formation, diaspora discourse needs to look much more directly to the articula-tions—and cautions—of hyphenation as set forth by Heidegger et al.

References

Appadurai, Arjun (1996), *Modernity at Large: Cultural Dimensions of Globalisation*, Minneapolis: University of Minnesota Press.
Butler, Kim D. (2001), 'Defining diaspora, refining a discourse,' *Diaspora* 10 (2): 189–219.
Clifford, James (1994), 'Diasporas,' *Cultural Anthropology* 9 (3): 302–38.
Cunningham, Stuart and John Sinclair, ed. (2000), *Floating Lives: The Media and Asian Diasporas*, St. Lucia: University of Queensland Press.
Derrida, Jacques (1994), *Specters of Marx*, trans. Peggy Kamuf, New York and London: Routledge.
Gillespie, Marie (1995), *Television, Ethnicity and Cultural Change*, London: Routledge.
Mishra, Vijay (1996), 'New lamps for old: diasporas. migrancy, border,' in Harish Trivedi and Meenakshi Mukherjee, ed. *Interrogating Post-Colonialism: Theory, Text and Context*, Shimla: Indian Institute of Advanced Study. 67–85.
Mitra, Ananda (1996), '"Nations and the internet": the case of a national newsgroup, "soc.cult.indian",' *Convergence: Journal of Research in New Technologies* 2 (1): 44–75.
——— (1997), 'Disaporic websites: ingroup and outgroup discourse,' *Critical Studies in Mass Communication* 14 (2): 158–81.
Naficy, Hamid, ed. (1999), *Home, Exile, Homeland: Film, Media and the Politics of Place*, New York: Routledge.
Rushdie, Salman (1991), *Imaginary Homelands*, London: Granta/Viking.
Sun, Wanning (1997–8). '"Monster houses," "yacht immigrants," and the politics of being Chinese: media and ethnicity in Canada.' *Australian Canadian Studies* 15 (2) and 16 (1): 143–58.
——— (2002), *Leaving China: Media, Migration and Transnational Imagination*. Lanham: Rowman and Littlefield.
——— (ed.) (2006), *Media and the Chinese Diaspora: Community, Communication and Commerce*, London: Routledge.
Tölölyan, Khachig (1991), 'Nation-state and its others,' *Diaspora* 1 (1): 1–7.

33

CARTOGRAPHIES OF DIASPORA

Avtar Brah

The homing of diaspora, the diasporising of home

As we noted earlier, the concept of diaspora embodies a subtext of 'home'. What are the implications of this subtext? First, it references another – that of the people who are presumed to be indigenous to a territory. The ways in which Indigenous peoples are discursively constituted is, of course, highly variable and context-specific. During imperial conquests the term 'native' came to be associated with pejorative connotations. In the British Empire the transformation of the colonised from native peoples into 'the Native' implicated a variety of structural, political and cultural processes of domination, with the effect that the word Native became a code for sub-ordination. The British diasporas in the colonies were internally differentiated by class, gender, ethnicity (English, Irish, Scottish, Welsh) and so on, but discourses of Britishness subsumed these differences as the term 'British' assumed a positionality of superiority with respect to the Native. The Native became the Other. In the colonies, the Natives were excluded from 'Britishness' by being subjected as natives. But how does this particular nativist discourse reconfigure in present-day Britain? Of course, there is no overt evocation of the term 'native' but it remains an underlying thematic of racialised conceptions of Britishness. According to racialised imagination, the former colonial Natives and their descendants settled in Britain are not British precisely because they are not seen as being native to Britain: they can be 'in' Britain but not 'of' Britain. The term 'native' is now turned on its head. Whereas in the colonies the 'colonial Native' was inferiorised, in Britain the 'metropolitan Native' is constructed as superior. That is, nativist discourse is mobilised in both cases, but with opposite evaluation of the group constructed as the 'native'.

The invocation of native or Indigenous status, however, is not confined to discourses of nationalism. Oppressed peoples such as Native Americans or Native Australians may also mobilise a concept of the positionality of the indigenous, but with quite a different aim. Here, the native positionality becomes the means of struggle against centuries of exploitation, dispossession and marginality. This native subject position articulates a subaltern location. It is important, therefore, to distinguish these claims from those that go into the constitution of structures of dominance. However, it does not always follow that this subaltern location will provide automatic guarantees against essentialist claims of belonging. It cannot be assumed in advance that the hegemonic processes of subordination will invariably be resisted without recourse to the indigene subject position as the privileged space of legitimate claims of belonging. What is at stake here is the way in which the indigene subject position is constructed, represented and mobilised. Oppositional politics from a subaltern location must contend with all manner of contradictions. Can 'first nationhood' be asserted as a 'native' identity while renouncing nativism? How precisely is the 'first nationhood' of subaltern groups to be distinguished from the claims to this status by groups in positions of dominance? How do subaltern indigenous peoples place themselves *vis-à-vis* other subordinate groups in a locale? For instance, how do the claims for social justice by Native Americans articulate with and become 'situated' in relation to those made by black Americans? Are such claims marked by a politics of solidarity or competitive antagonism and tension? In one sense, the problematic can only be fully addressed by studying particular cases. But the answer will depend, at least in part, upon the way that the question of 'origins' is treated – in naturalised and essentialist terms, or as historically constituted (dis)placements?

Where is home? On the one hand, 'home' is a mythic place of desire in the diasporic imagination. In this sense it is a place of no return, even if it is possible to visit the geographical territory that is seen as the place of 'origin'. On the other hand, home is also the lived experience of a locality. Its sounds and smells, its heat and dust, balmy summer evenings, or the excitement of the first snowfall, shivering winter evenings, sombre grey skies in the middle of the day . . . all this, as mediated by the historically specific everyday of social relations. In other words, the varying experience of the pains and pleasures, the terrors and contentments, or the highs and humdrum of everyday lived culture that marks how, for example, a cold winter night might be differently experienced sitting by a crackling fireside in a mansion as compared with standing huddled around a makeshift fire on the streets of nineteenth-century England.

If, as is quite possible, the reader pictured the subjects of this cold winter scenario as white English men and women, it bears reminding that this would not invariably be the case. The group huddled on the street might easily have included men and women brought over to England as servants from Africa and India; the descendants of Africans taken as slaves to the Americas; as well as Irish, Jewish and other immigrants. What effects might this type of intra-class differentiation have in the marking of affinities and antagonisms *amongst* those on the street and *between* the street and the mansion? What range of subjectivities and subject positions would have been produced in this crucible? What are the implications for late twentieth-century Britain of certain ways of imaging 'Englishness' that erases such nineteenth-century, and indeed earlier, 'multiculturalisms'? The question of home, therefore, is intrinsically linked with the way in which processes of inclusion or exclusion operate and are subjectively experienced under given circumstances. It is centrally about our political and personal struggles over the social regulation of 'belonging'. As Gilroy (1993) suggests, it is simultaneously about roots and routes.

The *concept* of diaspora places the discourse of 'home' and 'dispersion' in creative tension, *inscribing a homing desire while simultaneously critiquing discourses of fixed origins.*

The problematic of 'home' and belonging may be integral to the diasporic condition, but how, when, and in what form questions surface, or how they are addressed, is specific to the history of a particular diaspora. Not all diasporas inscribe homing desire through a wish to return to a place of 'origin'. For some, such as the South Asian groups in Trinidad, cultural identification with the Asian sub-continent might be by far the most important element.

We noted earlier that diasporas are not synonymous with casual temporary travel. Nor is diaspora a metaphor for individual exile but, rather, diasporas emerge out of migrations of collectivities, whether or not members of the collectivity travel as individuals, as households or in various other combinations. Diasporas are places of long-term, if not permanent, community formations, even if some households or members move on elsewhere. The word diaspora often invokes the imagery of traumas of separation and dislocation, and this is certainly a very important aspect of the migratory experience. But diasporas are also potentially the sites of hope and new beginnings. They are contested cultural and political terrains where individual and collective memories collide, reassemble and reconfigure.

When does a location *become* home? What is the difference between 'feeling at home' and staking claim to a place as one's own? It is quite possible to feel at home in a place and, yet, the experience of social exclusions may inhibit public proclamations of the place as home (Brah 1979; Cohen 1992; Bhavnani 1991; Tizzard and Phoenix 1993). A black British young woman of Jamaican parentage may well be far more at home in London than in Kingston, Jamaica, but she may insist upon defining herself as Jamaican and/or Caribbean as a way of affirming an identity which she perceives is being denigrated when racism represents black people as being outside 'Britishness'. Alternatively, another young woman with a similar background might seek to repudiate the same process of exclusion by asserting a black British identity. The subjectivity of the two women is inscribed within differing political practices and they occupy different subject positions. They articulate different political positions on the question of 'home', although both are likely to be steeped in the highly mixed diasporic cultures of Britain. On the other hand, each woman may embody both of these positions at different moments, and the circumstances of the moment at which such 'choices' are made by the same person are equally critical.

Clearly, the relationship of the first generation to the place of migration is different from that of subsequent generations, mediated as it is by memories of what was recently left behind, and by the experiences of disruption and displacement as one tries to re-orientate, to form new social networks, and learns to negotiate new economic, political and cultural realities. Within each generation the experiences of men and women will also be differently shaped by gender relations. The reconfigurations of these social relations will not be a matter of direct superimposition of patriarchal forms deriving from the country of emigration over those that obtain in the country to which migration has occurred. Rather, both elements will undergo transformations as they articulate in and through specific policies, institutions and modes of signification.

The *concept* of diaspora signals these processes of *multi-locationality across geographical, cultural and psychic boundaries.*

It bears repeating that the double, triple, or multi-placedness of 'home' in the imaginary of people in the diaspora does not mean that such groups do not feel anchored in the place of settlement. When a British politician such as Norman Tebbit, the former Conservative Cabinet Minister, argues that young British Asians cannot feel allegiance to Britain if they support a visiting cricket team from India or Pakistan, his 'cricket test' is more a reflection of the politics of 'race' in Britain than an indicator of British Asians' subjective sense of their own 'Britishness'. It is unlikely that Tebbit would question the allegiance of populations of European origin in the Americas, Australia, Canada or New Zealand to their countries of adoption. Or that he would consider them less rooted in those places for having ancestors that came there from Europe. It would be interesting to see if Tebbit would describe Irish Americans or Italian Americans as less committed to the USA because they had enthusiastically supported Irish or Italian football teams in the 1994 World Cup. Paradoxically, racialised forms of nationalism which discourses such as that initiated by Tebbit inhabit are precisely the ones which might engender responses whereby to call oneself Bangladeshi, Indian, Pakistani or Sri Lankan becomes a mode of resistance against racist definitions of 'Asian-ness'. But the assertion of such 'identity' cannot be taken as a measure of the processes of 'identification' operating among these collectivities, Norman Tebbit's restricted vision of Britishness is seriously interrogated and called into question by all kinds of old and new diasporic identites in Britain. These identity formations challenge the idea of a continuous, uninterrupted, unchanging, homogeneous and stable British Identity; instead, they highlight the point that identity is always plural and in process, even when it might be construed or represented as fixed.

References

Bhavnani, K. K. (1991) *Talking Politics*, Cambridge: Cambridge University Press.

Brah, A. (1979) 'Inter-generational and Inter-ethnic Perceptions: a comparative study of South Asian and English adolescents and their parents in Southall, West London'. PhD thesis, University of Bristol.

Cohen, P. (1992) *Home Rules: Some Reflections on Racism and Nationalism in Everyday Life*, London: The New Ethnicities Unit, University of East London.

Gilroy, P. (1993) *The Black Atlantic: Double Consciousness and Modernity*, Cambridge: Mass.: Harvard University Press.

Tizzard, B. and Phoenix, A. (1993) *Black, White, or Mixed Race?: Race and Racism in the Lives of Young People of Mixed Parentage*, London and New York: Routledge.

34

SOLID, DUCTILE AND LIQUID

Changing notions of homeland and home in diaspora studies

Robin Cohen

Do we need a homeland in order to conceive of a diaspora? Even asking this question may have seemed absurd to the older generation of scholars and to those who pioneered the growth of diaspora studies in the 1990s. It was, in one sense, logically and etymologically impossible. A diaspora meant 'dispersion' and if people were dispersed, some point of origin – more concretely a homeland – was necessarily implied. One of the most influential statements marking the beginning of contemporary diaspora studies was Safran's article in the opening issue of the then new journal, *Diaspora*.[1] Safran was strongly influenced by the underlying paradigmatic case of the Jewish diaspora, but correctly perceived that many other ethnic groups were experiencing analogous circumstances due perhaps to the difficult circumstances surrounding their departure from their places of origin and as a result their limited acceptance in their places of settlement.

Safran was, of course, not alone in recognizing the expanded use of the concept of diaspora, but he was crucial in seeking to give some social scientific contour to the new claims rather than allow a journalistic free-for-all to develop. The Jewish experience continued to influence Safran's view of the vital importance of homeland in defining one of the essential characteristics of diaspora. For him, members of a diaspora retained a collective memory of 'their original homeland'; they idealized their 'ancestral home', were committed to the restoration of 'the original homeland' and continued in various ways to 'relate to that homeland'. He further maintained that the concept of a diaspora can be applied when members of an 'expatriate minority community' share several of the following features:

- They, or their ancestors, have been dispersed from an original '*centre*' to two or more foreign regions;
- they retain a collective memory, vision or myth about their *original homeland* including its location, history and achievements;
- they believe they are not – and perhaps can never be – fully accepted in their host societies and so remain partly separate;
- their *ancestral home is idealized* and it is thought that, when conditions are favourable, either they, or their descendants should return;
- they believe all members of the diaspora should be committed to the maintenance or restoration of the *original homeland* and to its safety and prosperity; and
- they continue in various ways to *relate to that homeland* and their ethnocommunal consciousness and solidarity are in an important way defined by the existence of such a relationship.[2]

Social constructionist critiques of diaspora

Though the emphasis on an original homeland may have been too strongly stated, a group of critics, who I will describe as 'social constructionists', argued that Safran, this author and others were holding back the full force of the concept.[3] Influenced by post-modernist readings, social constructionists sought to decompose two of the major building blocks previously delimiting and demarcating the diasporic idea, namely 'homeland' and 'ethnic/religious community'. In the post-modern world, it was further argued, identities have become deterritorialized and affirmed in a flexible and situational way; accordingly, concepts of diaspora had to be radically reordered in response to this complexity. Showing scant respect for the etymology, history, limits, meaning and evolution of the concept of diaspora, they sought to deconstruct the two core building blocks of diaspora, home/homeland and ethnic/religious community.[4] The first target of their deconstruction, home/homeland, is considered in this paper.

While a degree of decoupling of diaspora from homeland was signaled in my earlier work,[5] this rupture had taken a more insistent turn in Avtar Brah.[6] 'Home' became increasingly vague, even miasmic. By contrast, her concept of diaspora 'offers a critique of discourses of fixed origins, while taking account of a homing desire, which is not the same thing as a desire for "homeland"'. So, homeland had become a homing desire and soon home itself became transmuted into an essentially placeless, though admittedly lyrical, space. [. . .]

Through this and similar interventions, 'home' became more and more generously interpreted to mean the place of origin, or the place of settlement, or a local, national or transnational place, or an imagined virtual community (linked, for example, through the internet), or a matrix of known experiences and intimate social relations (thus conforming to the popular expression that 'home is where the heart is').

Anthias upped the stakes further by criticizing a number of scholars for using what she described as 'absolutist notions of "origin" and "true belonging".[7] [. . .]

Two years later Soysal amplified the charge. Despite the fact that notions of diaspora were 'venerated', they inappropriately 'privileg[ed] the nation-state model and nationally-defined formations when conversing about a global process such as immigration'.[8] [. . .]

The crucial intent of these appraisals was to force a larger and larger wedge between 'diaspora' on the one hand, and 'homeland', 'place' and 'ethnic community' on the other. Clearly for some authors – of whom Anthias and Soysal are good representatives – diaspora was irredeemably flawed. It simply could not adequately address their own agendas by doing what they wanted – in Anthias's case, it could not produce a platform for a transethnic, gender-sensitive, anti-racist movement while, in Soysal's case, it could not provide a means of understanding post-national citizenship in Europe.

The response

One response to such critiques of diaspora might have been to regard them as inappropriate or misplaced as they reflected political agendas that had little to do with the history and meaning of the term, or the phenomena it sought to, and continues to, explain. Diaspora theorists made no claim to explain the full spectrum of immigrant experiences, did not see their task as creating a progressive anti-racist movement (desirable as that may be), and did not seek to describe patterns of sociality and citizenship unrelated to some degree of prior kinship or religious affiliation. In other words the concept of diaspora is not a magic bullet and cannot be used to slay all enemies. [. . .]

Though the social constructionist position was clearly overstated, the effect of their intervention was to generate a re-questioning and a more sophisticated understanding of shifts in the homeland–diaspora relationship. In so doing three main versions of home/homeland emerged, which I designate *solid* (the unquestioned need for a homeland), *ductile* (an intermediate, more complex, idea of homeland) and *liquid* (a post-modernist rendition of virtual home).

Solid homeland

In general the idea of a homeland is imbued with an expressive charge and a sentimental pathos that seem to be almost universal. Motherland, fatherland, native land, natal land, *Heimat,* the ancestral land, the search for 'roots' – all these similar notions invest homelands with 'an emotional, almost reverential dimension'.[9] Often, there is a complex interplay between the feminine and masculine versions of homeland. In the feminine rendition, the motherland is seen as a warm, cornucopian breast from which the people collectively suck their nourishment. One Kirgiz poet fancifully claimed that the relationship between homeland and human preceded birth itself: 'Remember, even before your mother's milk, you drank the milk of your homeland,' he wrote.[10] Suggesting the same metaphor, the biblical Promised Land was said to be 'flowing with milk and honey'.

In other interpretations, the nurturing white milk of the motherland is replaced by the blood of soldiers gallantly defending their fatherland. Their blood nourishes the soil, the soil defines their ethnogenesis. *Blut und Boden* (blood and soil) was Bismarck's stirring call to the German nation, an evocation that was renewed by Hitler two generations later. Even in the wake of the post-1945 liberal-democratic constitutional settlement, the Germans were unusual in stressing a definition of citizenship and belonging – *jus sanguinis,* the law of blood – that emphasizes descent, rather than place of birth or long residence. Thus, third and fourth generation 'ethnic Germans' from the former Soviet Union, many of whom no longer spoke German, were accorded instant citizenship in preference to second-generation Turks who had been born and educated in Germany. Sometimes the images of motherland and fatherland are conflated. The androgynous British conceptions of homeland evoke the virile John Bull character exemplified in modern times by the indomitable wartime hero, Winston Churchill. They are also derived from the received history of Boudicca, Britannia, Queen Victoria and, perhaps more fancifully, Prime Minister Margaret Thatcher. [. . .]

Ductile homeland

Let me now turn to my intermediate category. Even in a case of the prototypical Jewish diaspora the solid idea of homeland seems to be weakening. Interestingly, William Safran, whose early work on the necessity of homeland has already been discussed, now adopts a more flexible (ductile) use of homeland. Partly on the basis of attitudinal surveys, Safran argues that in the case of Israel on the one hand, and European and American Jews on the other, the links between hostlands and homeland are becoming more tenuous.[11] Those in the Jewish diaspora experiencing a process of 'dezionization' include groups he designates as secularists, socialists, potential investors in Israel, non-orthodox believers, enlightened Western Jews, left-wing ideologues, academics and others disillusioned with the expressions of Israeli state power. The other side of the coin is that (despite intermittent bursts of anti-Semitism) life in the diaspora is sufficiently attractive and sufficiently emotionally and physically secure not to prompt an invariable identification with Israel. [. . .]

Liquid homes

This is a world of 'liquid modernity', says Zygmunt Bauman, where 'we are witnessing the revenge of nomadism over the principles of territoriality and settlement'.[12] The evocation of constant movement and liquidity recalls Marx and Engels's remark in the *Communist Manifesto* that 'All that is solid melts into air, all that is holy is profaned'. The literary scholar, Marshall Berman, echoes this last quote. To be in our world, he says 'is to experience personal and social life as a maelstrom, to find one's world and oneself in perpetual disintegration and renewal, trouble and anguish, ambiguity and contradiction: to be part of a universe in which all that is solid melts into air'.[13] Do we wish to loosen the historical meanings of the notion of a diasporic home even further to encompass new forms of mobility and displacement and the construction of new identities and subjectivities? I propose we adopt the expression 'deterritorialized diaspora' to encompass the lineaments of a number of unusual diasporic experiences.[14] In these instances ethnic groups can be thought of as having lost their conventional territorial reference points, to have become in effect mobile and multi-located cultures with virtual or uncertain homes. [. . .]

Conclusion

If we review the various uses of the idea of home and homeland in diaspora studies we can find good historical and empirical support for all three notions – solid, ductile and liquid. The myths of a common origin are often territorialized, while highly romantic, yet powerful, myths of the 'old country' are avowed. The 'promised land' of the Jews flowed with milk and honey. The aged cedars and scent of mint on Mount Lebanon can be used to brush away the smell of the corpses produced in the recent civil wars and invasions. The impressive buildings of Zimbabwe stand as a testament to the notion that Africans once had superior civilizations and great empires: a direct refutation of their often low social status in the diaspora. The Assyrians in London and Chicago talk of their link to the great civilization in Mesopotamia, while their arch rivals, the Armenians, mount expensive archaeological expeditions to uncover *their* palaces and shrines.

We have also observed that in some cases homeland has given way to a more ductile notion of homeland, which can be displaced, as in the cases of the Sindhis and Parsis of Bombay or somewhat attenuated as in the case of dezionization. We also have noticed that virtual, deter-ritorialized, liquid homes can be constructed through cultural links, as in the Caribbean case, and through the substitution of sacred monuments, rivers, icons and shrines for home, as in the case of diaspora religions. It is perhaps important to stress that Africa does not disappear from the Caribbean imaginary, just as Sind and Persia are still remembered, however distantly, by Hindu Sindhis and Parsis. Rather than a complete process of erasure, the conditions in the natal homeland have become so hostile (and the relatively benign conditions in parts of the diaspora so attractive) that the recovery of homeland has been deferred indefinitely and displaced by newer centres of religious, cultural and economic achievement.

How then do we mediate between the three uses? One possible way of dealing with this escalation is to allow self-declaration to prevail. Home and homeland is what you say it is. Who are we to object? Another strategy is to follow the tactic adopted by the ancient Greek, Procrustes, who offered hospitality in his iron bed to passers-by. So that they would fit the bed precisely, he stretched short people and cut off the limbs of long people. By analogy, we could espouse an utterly rigid set of criteria to which all home/homelands would have to conform before we would allow them to lie on our conceptual bed. Rejecting these two strategies, I have insisted on empirical and historical support for any notion of home/homeland. Largely unsup-ported post-modernist critiques have suggested that there is a one-way movement from solid notions of homeland to liquid notions of home. But, as I have argued, the intermediate category remains important and the solid versions of homeland are gaining increasing support as diasporas become mobilized to play an enhanced role in homeland and international politics and in the economic and social development of their natal territories.

Notes

1 William Safran 'Diasporas in modern societies: myths of homeland and return', *Diaspora*, 1 (1), 1991, pp. 83–99.
2 All phrases in quotation marks from Safran 'Diasporas in modern societies', pp. 83-4. Emphasis added. In response to the normal canons of social scientific debate initiated by this author and others, Safran has amended and extended his list to one that will command considerable consensus among diaspora scholars. See William Safran 'The Jewish diaspora in a comparative and theoretical perspective', *Israel Studies* 10 (1), 2005, p.37.
3 I have used the expression 'social constructionist' to signify a mode of reasoning, closely associated with post-modernism, which suggests that reality is determined by social interaction (or intersubjectivity), rather than by objectivity (the acceptance of a natural or material world) or by subjectivity (a world determined by individual perceptions). The perspective tends to favour voluntarism and collective human agency over structure, history and habituation.
4 It might be worth recalling Marx's crucial insight that 'Men [read 'people'] make their own history, but they do not make it as they please; they do not make it under circumstances chosen by themselves, but under circumstances directly encountered, given and transmitted from the past. The tradition of all the dead generations weighs like a nightmare on the brains of the living'. See Karl Marx 'The Eighteenth Brumaire of Louis Napoleon' in Lewis S. Feuer (ed.) *Marx and Engels: basic writings on politics and philosophy*, New York: Anchor Books, 1959, p. 321 [first published in 1852].
5 Robin Cohen *Global diasporas: an introduction*, London: UCL Press, 1997.
6 Avtar Brah *Cartographies of diaspora: contesting identities*, London: Routledge, 1996.
7 Floya Anthias 'Evaluating "diaspora": beyond ethnicity', *Sociology*, 32 (3), 1998, pp. 557–80. She includes Robin Cohen's *Global diasporas* in her charge, though I thought it was clear that I was arguing for a more complex notion of origin (see Chapters 3 on Africans and 6 on Sikhs). However, I concur that 'belonging' is not a given, but has to be established, mobilized and defended in social, cultural and political practices. My views are clarified at length in Robin Cohen *Frontiers of identity: the British and the Others*, London: Longman, 1994, Chapters 1 and 7.
8 Yasemin Nuhoğlu Soysal 'Citizenship and identity: living in diasporas in post-war Europe?' *Ethnic and Racial Studies*, 23 (1), 2000, pp. 1–2. Nearly all diaspora theorists had in fact pointed out that diaspora was a concept that long pre-dated the nation-state and that diasporic formations were constantly in tension with nation-states. See, for example, Robin Cohen 'Diasporas and the nation-state: from victims to challengers' *International Affairs* 72 (3), July 1996, 507–20.
9 Walker Conner 'The impact of homelands upon diasporas' in Gabriel Sheffer (ed.) *Modern diasporas in international politics*, London: Croom Helm, 1986, p. 16–45. See also André Levy and Alex Weingrod (eds) *Homelands and diasporas: holy lands and other spaces*, Stanford: Stanford University Press, 2004.
10 Walker Conner 'The impact of homelands upon diasporas' in Gabriel Sheffer (ed.) *Modern diasporas in international politics*, London: Croom Helm, 1986, p. 17.
11 William Safran 'The tenuous link between hostlands and homeland: the progressive dezionization of western diasporas' in Lisa Anteby-Yemeni, William Berthomière and Gabriel Sheffer (eds) *Les diasporas: 2000 ans d'histoire*, Rennes: Presse Universitaires de Rennes, 2005, pp. 193–208.
12 Zygmunt Bauman *Liquid modernity*, Cambridge: Polity Press, 2000, p. 13.
13 Marshall Berman *All that is solid melts into air: the experience of modernity*, New York: Simon and Schuster, 1982, pp. 345–6.
14 I have adopted the expression 'deterritorialized diasporas' in the second, revised, edition of *Global diasporas: an introduction* (forthcoming, 2008) to replace 'cultural diasporas' used in the first edition of the book. The latter was insufficiently precise and led to some confusion.

DIGITAL DIASPORAS

Introduction

Although it has not been noted in popular fora such as *Wikipedia* (yet), the 'digital turn' seems set to become, in a series of perceived 'turns' in recent cultural history, the 'turn' en vogue in the scholarship and the wider media landscape of the 2010s. During this decade, an increasing flow of studies on the nature and consequences of digitization has begun to appear, although the implications and issues of technological advance had already been developing for several decades. Thus, Wim Westera (2013) examines 'the role of computers, smartphones, social media, and the Internet at large and how these contribute to our understanding of the world'. He highlights 'the progressive virtualisation of the world and its boundless impact on human existence', which results in 'the fundamentally changing landscape of today's social interactions and our changing perceptions of space and time, knowledge, social relationships, citizenship, power and control, culture, and eventually, life' (6). And with the experience of developments in recent history and today's geopolitical situation in mind, there can be little doubt about the tidal social and political impact of the so-called digital turn. The 'Arab Spring', especially the revolution in Egypt, sometimes referred to as the 'Facebook revolution', has been hugely dependent on the use of smartphones and the new social media. A new way to organize public opinion and to voice dissent has arisen far from and beyond the power of traditional controls; a two-sided develop-ment, no doubt, as much of the recruiting for terrorist organizations and fundamentalist groups happens through these very channels of advanced communication technologies.

With a phenomenon perceived as all-encompassing as this, and the impact of such a broad and epistemic category as the digital turn, it is unsurprising that diasporas and diaspora studies stand to be most affected and to gain significantly from such technological advances, as dispersed communities substantially rely on electronic forms of communication and the new 'social media'. Diasporas are characterized by a double dependency on communication and the media, depending on mediation between diasporic subjects as a group in the host land on the one hand, and on the communication of groups thus defined with their land of 'origin' on the other. With the growing reach and speed, and falling costs, of physical transportation together with increasing growth in communication media, from a speed-up on postal services to affordable and reliable telephone communications and an almost instant news service through official and unofficial channels over the world-wide web, potential spaces for diasporas have undergone massive expansion. Whereas most diasporic group identities would typically be restricted to (often small-sized) geographical areas in antiquity and medieval times, the advent of print cultures and the ensuing development of modern means of mass communication has led to diasporic group formation across nation states, regions and continents. In fact, in view of a global virtual space on the internet diasporas can interact on a global scale, breaking down political boundaries and geographic borders, thus fundamentally transforming diasporic identity formation and putting the entire concept of diaspora under review.

The three texts in this section collectively show how discussion on the digital turn has been introduced into the field of diaspora studies and the directions it has productively begun to take. The text by Victoria Bernal from her book-length study on the world-wide Eritrean diasporic community as a 'digital diaspora' discusses how this medium of communication affects Eritrean politics 'at home', but, on a much more general scale, how it impacts on our understanding of nation formation and national identity. Victoria Bernal in Chapter 37 of this book starts out from the thesis that '[t]here is a synergy between new communications technologies and migration that is changing politics' (this volume 257). One of the effects of the 'growing significance of diasporas' on the one hand and the staggering speed of progress in the digital media on the other is that they have, in combination, 'given rise to the nation as network' (this volume 257). She focuses the new regime of power distribution with the concept of 'infopolitics' as 'the way power is exercised and expressed through communication and through control over media, circulation, censorship, and authorization' (this volume 259). The internet here is not seen as a new or better source of information, but primarily as a platform where everyone can promote their opinion, link up with others who share it and thus question or even subvert 'official' communications in a way that had not been possible before. This ties in with Eickerlman and Anderson's finding, quoted by Bernal, of a 'public space that is discursive, performative, and participative, and not confined to formal institutions recognized by state authorities' (this volume 260). Ultimately, as Bernal concludes, the new digital world is an important factor in that '[d]iasporas are changing the ways states construct citizenship' (this volume 261).

Bernal's central term of 'digital diaspora' is further developed in the text by Alonso and Oiarzabal. Their chapter grapples with the (new) meanings of diaspora in cyberspace, introducing the term 'info-sphere' as a conglomerate for all the communication media. Andoni Alonso and Pedro J. Oiarzabal, in Chapter 35 of this book, describe the growing dominance of the digital media in a Web 2.0 world where the 'info-sphere constitutes a postnational or global media [sic] that transcends national boundaries, creating a deterritorialized space or cyberspace' (this volume 249). In their perception, this new media landscape evokes the idea of the 'republic of letters' from the age of Enlightenment when philosophers and intellectuals communicated (by letter) across the western world irrespective of national borders and physical distances. As 'constraints on synchronicity or locality' thus disappear in the digital world, Alonso and Oiarzabal conclude, 'the Internet offers the possibility to sustain and re-create diasporas as globally imagined communities' (this volume 250). With this 'digital turn' of the diaspora, however, other foundational concepts shift, as well. Life, community and in fact the whole concept of identity become 'virtual', 'digital' or 'online' (this volume 250), so that, in the event, the entire system of coordinates of who is 'native' and who is 'diasporic' may be reshuffled, as everyone entering the internet starts, it is argued, as an immigrant in this cyberspace and new groups are formed following a potentially very different set of social rules and cultural customs.

Angel Adams Parham's contribution, in Chapter 36, further reflects on another discussion started in the text by Bernal, as she follows current research on the changing conceptualization of 'the public' or 'the public sphere' as it is (re-)created on the internet. Comparing in a gesture back to Jürgen Habermas the 'Internet-mediated network-public' with its 'pre-Internet equivalents – the coffee shop, bookstore, or local watering hole' (this volume 254), she finds more similarities with these 'offline cognates' of occasional social exchange than the more formal 'civic groups' whose function it is to collect and pass on local public opinion to decision makers on a higher organizational level in the state. But the latter constitute a channelling of public opinion which also exists in the digital world. Parham calls this, no matter whether it is off- or online, a 'vertical public' – that is, there is a clear hierarchy of leadership, communications and regulation of membership access, and clear (political) goals of the group or platform are set out, while by contrast, the coffee shop or chat forum type of public comprise 'representational and network publics' who have a lower threshold of commitment and much greater flexibility (this volume 254). While the latter type of public thus is characterized as fairly continuous across the digital 'divide', it is the vertical public that has undergone the most striking changes across the digital turn, now easily spreading across national borders and even different languages. Their development, Parham argues, hence calls for a revised 'public-sphere theory that deals well with the special circumstances of communication and action at the transnational, transcultural, and trans-linguistic levels' (this volume 255).

The consolidated readings of the three texts reprinted here leave no doubt that both the social and cultural phenomena of the electronic age and its scholarly study, for better or worse, call for the inauguration of a 'diaspora studies 2.0'.

Reference

Westera, Wim. 2013. *The Digital Turn. How the Internet Transforms Our Existence*. Bloomington, IN: Author-House. Available at: www.thedigitalturn.co.uk/.

35

THE IMMIGRANT WORLDS' DIGITAL HARBORS

An introduction

Andoni Alonso and Pedro J. Oiarzabal

I couldn't take it anymore when we found ourselves alone in that small boardinghouse without love, or any friend to talk to, and release my pain.

—Santiago Ibarra (1954), quoted in *Santiago Ibarra: Historia de un inmigrante vasco,* by Ángeles de Dios de Martina

Santiago Ibarra was born in Bilbao in the Basque province of Bizkaia in 1899, and at the early age of fifteen immigrated to Argentina with his seventeen-year-old brother. The chapter epigraph recounts his first day in Buenos Aires, according to a 1954 autobiography. It addresses his loneliness, nostalgia, and the overall impossibility of communicating with the loved ones who remained at home. In a sense, according to Grinberg and Grinberg,

> migration requires a person to recreate the basic things he thought were already settled; he must recreate another work environment, establish affective relations with other people, reform a circle of friends, set up a new house that will not be an overnight tent but a home, and so on. These activities demand great physic effort, sacrifice, and acceptance of many changes in a short time. But to be able to carry them out gives one a sense of inner strength, an ability to dream, a capacity to build, a capacity for love.
>
> *(1989, 176)*

One can only wonder how different it would have been for Santiago or any pre–information society immigrants, refugees or exiles, if they had had the possibility of connecting to the Internet and establishing not only instantaneous communication with parents, family members, and friends but also a digital network social world shared with others of common affinities.

At the outbreak of the Spanish Civil War in 1936, poet Antonio Machado defined Madrid as "the breakwater of all the Spains"—as the final destination of the incessant waves of refugees seeking protection as well as a solid barrier to repel attacks by Generalisimo Francisco Franco's fascist troops. In contrast to historical points of entry for immigrants, such as the emblematic Ellis Island in the United States, the Internet (along with satellite television and cellular phones and other mobile devices) is becoming the new harbor for contemporary immigrants. For many, the Internet is the first window or point of informational entry into their new destinations, prior to physical arrival, as well as a new interactive link back to their homelands. Even more, cyberspace—the communal space digitally created by the interconnection of millions of computerized machines and people—has become the virtual home for many diverse and dispersed communities across the globe. It is another space to reconnect with fellow natives around the world as well as with those remaining at home. It is a new space of hopes, desires, dreams, frustrations, and beginnings. [. . .]

The creation and development of informal and formal transnational migrant networks among individuals, groups, and organizations from the country of origin and the country of settlement constitute webs of exchange of information and transfers of knowledge in the physical world as well as in the digital world. These networks lead to chain migration, which, in turn, helps to perpetuate migration flows between specific sending and receiving areas and among consecutive generations of immigrants (see Glick-Schiller, Basch, and Szanton 1992; and Vertovec and Cohen 1999).

The United Nations (2006) estimates that in 2005 worldwide international migration involved approximately 191 million people. Contrasted with a world population of more than 6 billion, international migration is not a large proportion of the total and in fact could be considered marginal. Moreover, only a few countries, such as the United States, the United Kingdom, France, and Spain, among others, receive any significant share of international immigrants.

However, over the past few decades immigration has doubled, and socio-economic tensions and political conflict have grown at local, national, and international levels, forcing many to leave their home countries in search of new opportunities. Immigration is a phenomenon that spans time, generations, and geographies; it has a history. According to Appadurai (1996), historical and political changes have reshaped our notion of immigration. As seen, the term *diaspora* conveys different meanings and includes historical phenomena such as globalization, translocalities, and the crisis of the traditional state. Thus, in many circumstances, immigration becomes a question of identity, a diasporic process. A diaspora transcends, though is distinct from, immigration and has a clear political connotation that is reshaped by economy, politics, and technology in the era of globalization.

Statistics show that only 20 percent of the world population uses the Internet, which leaves a large number of people "off-line" (Internet World Stats 2007). Moreover, countries with less Internet usage have larger emigration rates than wealthy countries, which, in turn, become the main destinations of the majority of immigrants. Not all immigrants have equal access to information and communication technologies, even in their new host countries, and consequently there is a potential danger for many to remain behind or become increasingly excluded from their host societies while also becoming detached from the ongoing changes taking place in their homeland.

Historically, there has been a close correlation between technology and migration. Technological advancement of communication and transportation systems and infrastructures has facilitated both population movements and the formation of diasporas. For instance, the use and knowledge of technologies are major forces in motivating scientists and skilled workers to leave their homelands, as can be seen in India, South Korea, China, and Russia. Additionally, the diffusion of awareness of better lifestyles and wealth, as spread by global media and the Internet and by immigrants already settled in "first world countries," is increasingly becoming a stimulator to migration.

Certain aspects of contemporary globalization, such as neoliberal capitalism or the development of so-called global cities and technological advances in information systems, telecommunications, and transportation, are also, according to all the evidence, accelerating diaspora formation, growth, and maintenance. This was also true in past eras. For example, the nineteenth and twentieth centuries witnessed the articulation of national media and systems of communication such as newspaper, radio, and television. For the past two centuries an info-sphere (information environment) has profoundly changed the way national identities are created and reproduced. The speed and the outreach of that info-sphere have exponentially expanded. National media contribute to the imagining of a nation as a shared territorial community of nationals, through the production of homogeneous discourses of identity and culture (Anderson 1991). In this sense, the existence of that info-sphere—first newspapers, later radio and cinema, and, finally, television—helped to articulate and reinforce much of the romantic nationalist discourses. Although there was bitter criticism of such influence, the info-sphere quickly became a very significant and necessary part of everyone's daily life, with both negative and positive effects.

The appearance of new devices such as satellite communications, the Internet, and cell phones has introduced substantial changes within this info-sphere. Now, not only does communication obey a vertical axis like television, radio, and the newspaper, but we are also witnessing an increasing implementation of horizontal communications, which include more active roles by recipients, transforming identity processes into something more complex and diverse. Small communities, isolated individuals, and marginalized groups can use a platform such as the Internet to easily raise their voices and increase their possibility of being heard. For example, cell phones are now used in the effort to change regimes, as happened in the Philippines, where President Joseph Estrada was peacefully overthrown in January 2001, or to alter national opinion, as in Spain after the March 11, 2004, al-Qaeda bombings, or to bypass government control over media and censorship, as happened during the so-called Green Revolution in Iran in June 2009. This mobile technology has become somehow a more affordable and easy-to-use commodity whose ramifications are yet to be fully appreciated.

In addition, the emergence of the so-called Web 2.0 points out that something profound is changing the way that we relate to the Web. New proposals like "cloud computing" open the possibility of a network where users and their knowledge reshape not only content but also economic forces, allowing for the possibility of new business. It is said that 80 percent of the content on the Internet will come from users, from social networks. If this is true, diasporas will play a central role in that process because more and more new generations of immigrants are already embedded in the telecommunication system.

This info-sphere constitutes a postnational or global media that transcends national boundaries, creating a deterritorialized space or cyberspace. The old idea of deterritorialized communities, bounded by common interests and not by space or time, is now real (Licklider and Taylor 1968). This idea echoes the "republic of letters" during the Enlightenment that described the exchange of private correspondence between Western philosophers and other influential intellectuals. Transnational media reach a borderless audience of nationals and nonnationals and disrupt that romantic notion of a single territory for each "race" and one national media for each national culture. Now different nationalisms are confronted with a globalized landscape. Thus, information and communication technologies that were once confined to producing national cultures no longer conform to these fixed territorial boundaries.

At the same time, there is a real political challenge in coping with the new media while making sense of their power to convince, persuade, and recreate the vision of countries and nationalities that might differ from what is posited by existing governments. Part of the effort to develop an information society addresses directly how identity and nation are expressed. For example, in the case of the Basque Country the Basque Autonomous Government in Spain pursues the articulation of a digitally networked nationalist ideology within the Basque diaspora (Oiarzabal 2006). The digital nation could adopt a different, or even contradictory, image to that of the one in the "real" world. That possibility deserves careful attention.

Diasporans map an atlas of identity that occupies multiple geographical locations, construct different ideological discourses, speak different languages and dialects, represent various degrees of assimilation into their countries of residence, and maintain various degrees of transnational connections among themselves and with the homeland. Nationalism becomes a multilayered or multifaceted set of discourses allowing for great diversity. Concepts such as nation, identity, and belonging take on new meanings. Diasporans re-create psychological or emotional communities that "inhibit" an interstitial space between the land of origin and the land of settlement.

In this regard, diasporans have historically utilized a variety of means of communication—from newspapers, newsletters, and radio and television programs to the Internet—as ways to overcome barriers of temporal, spatial, and psychological distance, which exist among diverse codiasporic nodes and their countries of origin. For example, the Internet as a post–geographically bounded global communication system has significantly provided the ability for dispersed groups such as diasporas to connect, maintain, create, and re-create social ties and networks with both their homeland and their codispersed communities. The Internet offers the ability for diasporas to exchange instant factual information regardless of geographical distance and time zones. Again time and space shift meanings; there are no constraints on synchronicity or locality. That is, the Internet offers the possibility to sustain and re-create diasporas as globally imagined communities.

Technology affects human movements in decisive ways as time and space "shrink." Thus, technological devices are continuously reshaping these concepts. In a sense, our own identity is also redefined by information and communication technologies as it is embedded and con-textualized in our perception of time and space. Technologies allow us to re-create our own reality that even employs time that is long gone or space that is far distant, transforming both within an imaginary landscape. *Translocality* is a term closely related to information and communication technologies. Already in the mid-1960s, Joseph C. R. Licklider and Robert Taylor, both of whom worked in the Advanced Research Projects Agency of the Pentagon (head-quarters of the US Department of Defense in Virginia) and were pioneers in promoting the development of the Internet, had begun to conceive of the computer as a communication device more than a calculating machine. That is, Licklider and Taylor (1968) forecast computers as machines able to create communities beyond time and space. The ties among users would be a community of interests and affinities. In a similar vein, these authors referred to identity in an indirect way.

Expansion of new technologies has deepened the question of identity even further. From Haraway's *Cyborg Manifesto* (1985) to Hayles's *How We Became Posthuman* (1999), the question of human identity has produced thousands of scholarly works based on a different array of practical experiences, manifestos, testimonies, and reports floating around the Internet. In addition, Internet phenomena such as Second Life (a virtual-world game created in 2003) evidence how online identity (diasporic or otherwise) is a hot topic for some discourses in our present tech-nological society.

"Virtual life," "virtual community," and "digital diasporas" are concepts that need to be handled with care, as they display an immense range of connotations. We briefly focus on two of those meanings, which we refer to as "weak" or "soft" and "strong" or "hard," depending on the involvement with the real world. Within the first meaning, immigration has been used as a metaphor to explain the passage of an individual from real life into a digital world—that is, new users who acquaint themselves with new technologies. Related terms are *digital nomadism, cyborg identity*, and *virtual community*. At times, questions such as involvement, responsibility, and identity are difficult to resolve in such online communities. Second Life is a good example of this weak, or soft, meaning.

The idea of real people using virtual technologies to interact with the real world relates to the strong, or hard, connotation of the aforementioned concepts. Online activists—people defending the Internet as a way to achieve fair globalization, nongovernmental organizations, independent journalists, and alternative agencies—are an example of such use of the Internet as a way to improve the *real* world. In this category digital diasporans bring to the Internet a sense of identity and community prior to modern technology. So technology either reinforces or transforms their previous meanings and attitudes. [. . .]

We define digital diasporas as the distinct online networks that diasporic people use to re-create identities, share opportunities, spread their culture, influence homeland and host-land policy, or create debate about common-interest issues by means of electronic devices. Digital diasporas differ from virtual communities and nations because in digital diasporas there are strong ties with real nations before creating or re-creating the digital community, thus differing in some ways from Licklider and Taylor's idea of a virtual community. On the Internet, all of us are "immigrants" who simultaneously share a common space called cyberspace. That is to say, cyberspace does not belong to any particular nation, state, or diasporic group. This is essential to the understanding of what we mean by digital diaspora.

There is very little doubt that there exists an increasing interest in the fields of diasporas and information and communication technologies, not only in the academic world but also in society, as reflected by the mass media. It is not a coincidence that *Time* magazine chose the "Internet User" as the "Person of 2006." It is widely common to say that the Internet has completely changed our lives (although the details of those changes are not so well known). If it is true that the Internet has transformed our lives, then the Internet must influence how immigrants (or all people, for that matter) use the new media in relation to different social aspects, including the interrelation with their homelands, identity processes, and roots. Thus, there is a need to understand diaspora communities and their dynamic process of political, cultural, and financial online networking on national, transnational, and global scales. In the near future, the Internet could be a good reflection of what happens with diasporas, their aspirations, rights, and responsibilities.

References

Anderson, Benedict. 1991. *Imagined communities: Reflections on the origin and spread of nationalism*. London: Verso.

Appadurai, Arjun. 1996. *Modernity at large: Cultural dimensions of globalization*. Minneapolis: University of Minnesota Press.

de Martina, Ángeles de Dios. 2004. *Santiago Ibarra: Historia de un inmigrante vasco*. Vitoria-Gasteiz: Servicio Central de Publicaciones del Gobierno Vasco.

Glick-Schiller, Nina, L. Basch, and C. Blanc Szanton. 1992. Transnationalism: A new analysis framework for understanding migration. *Annals of the New York Academy of Sciences* 645: 1–24.

Grinberg, Leon, and Rebecca Grinberg. 1989. *Psychoanalytic perspectives on migration and exile*. New Haven: Yale University Press.

Haraway, Donna. 1985. A cyborg manifesto: Science, technology, and socialist-feminism in the late twentieth century. In *Simians, cyborgs, and women: The reinvention of nature*. New York: Routledge.

Hayles, Kathelyn. 1999. *How we became posthuman: Virtual bodies in cybernetics, literature, and informatics*. Chicago: University of Chicago Press.

Internet World Stats. 2007. World Internet users, December. Available at www.internetworldstats.com/stats.htm.

Licklider, Joseph C. R., and Robert Taylor. 1968. The computer as a communication device. *Science and Technology: For the Men in Management*, no. 76 (April): 21–31.

Oiarzabal, Pedro J. 2006. The Basque diaspora Webscape: Online discourses of Basque diaspora identity, nationhood, and homeland. Ph.D. diss., University of Nevada, Reno.

United Nations, Population Division of the Department of Economic and Social Affairs of the United Nations Secretariat. 2006. Trends in total migrant stock: The 2005 revision. Available at http://esa.un.org/migration/.

Vertovec, Steven, and Robin Cohen. 1999. *Introduction to migration and transnationalism*, ed. Steven Vertovec and Robin Cohen. Aldershot: Edward Elgar.

36

INTERNET, PLACE AND PUBLIC SPHERE IN DIASPORA COMMUNITIES

Angel Adams Parham

This essay considers three types of Internet-mediated publics identified through a review of the literature and through in-depth analysis of the Haitian diaspora's use of online spaces. These Internet-mediated publics are—in order from least to most grounded in geographic place—*representational*; *network*; and *vertical*. Distinguishing among different kinds of Internet-mediated publics allows us to be more precise in our evaluation of how Internet use is shaping public-sphere activity in diaspora communities. [. . .]

Distinguishing varied combinations of Internet and geographic place

As noted by cautious writers who have examined the implications of the Internet for public-sphere activity, we must take care not to assume that online communication can fully, or even largely, substitute for face-to-face interactions. [. . .]

The observations and criticisms of Calhoun, Ong, and others underline the importance of paying careful attention to the strengths and weaknesses of varied combinations of Internet and geographic place among those who wish to organize discussion and action on issues within a given public sphere.

In order to assess the strengths and weaknesses of different kinds of Internet-mediated publics, however, we must first be clear about the kinds of activities actors expect to carry out within public spheres. Public-sphere activity is broadly defined here to include the following: self-expression and group discussion in which participants define or redefine their sense of identity, community, and agency (Fraser 1992; Benhabib 1992); opinion and agenda formation (Habermas 1991, 1996); and the channeling of opinion to public officials and institutions (Habermas 1996).

Each of these public-sphere activities is carried out to some degree within Internet-mediated publics. [. . .]

As the following discussion suggests, because of the different ways in which they combine Internet and cyber terrains, each type is better suited to carry out some public-sphere activities than others.

We begin with the role publics play in forging a sense of identity, community, and agency. While any group—however mainstream or marginalized—can create a public that expresses it identity and interests, our focus here is on subaltern publics. These are publics the majority of whose members stand outside of mainstream or hegemonic social or cultural spaces. Many diaspora communities that consist largely of people of color have made their homes in countries where the majority is largely white and speaks a language other than the language native to the diaspora. In these cases, it is not unusual for members of the diaspora community to see themselves as marginalized and their languages or cultures as embattled. For members of such groups, finding others—whether face to face or online—with whom they can identify is important and empowering.

In her essay on subaltern counter-publics, Nancy Fraser addresses this need for safe spaces within which individuals and groups outside of the mainstream can define their identities and needs. She points to the importance of journals, bookstores, and other "safe" local meeting places within which members of socially marginal groups can meet to discuss their common interests. She writes,

> members of subordinated groups [. . .] have repeatedly found it advantageous to constitute alternative publics. I propose to call these *subaltern counterpublics* in order to signal that they are parallel discursive arenas where members of subordinated social groups invent and circulate counterdiscourses to formulate oppositional interpretations of their identities, interests, and needs.
>
> *(1992, 123)*

Within online settings, *representational publics* provide an ideal venue for participants to engage in these activities.

One of the main goals within the *representational public* is literally to represent the country and/or culture of the diaspora. Within these sites, Web editors and writers strive to create an experience that will welcome ethnic members and/or initiate non-ethnic visitors into the country's history and culture. Daniel Miller and Don Slater found this to be the case with many Trinidadians using the Internet. Members of the Trinidadian diaspora visited online sites to immerse themselves in being "Trini," but they also took pride in creating websites that communicated "Trini" culture to outsiders. Thus, representational publics provide a kind of homecoming for members of an ethnic group as well as an orientation for outsiders (Rai 1995; Sökefeld 2002; Mitra 2005). [. . .]

The technological innovations of the Internet allow *representational publics* [. . .] to be much larger and more dispersed than their pre-Internet equivalents: the newspaper and the magazine. As an added bonus, ideas are disseminated at a much lower cost. Apart from these innovations, however, representational publics largely replicate what was already occurring offline before the appearance of the Internet. It is therefore relatively easy to incorporate the contribution of representational publics into already existing theories of the public sphere. They become just one of many public spaces within the larger configuration of a Haitian or other public sphere.[1]

The second major public-sphere activity—the formation of group opinion and agendas—is more likely to occur within a *network public* than in a representational public. While the relevant terrain is the same—largely or only online—the strength of the network public is its interactivity. There is a good amount of research on forums that are best described as network publics, and much of the theoretical work on the Internet and the public sphere involves an evaluation of the discourse that occurs within these groups (Schneider 1996; Buchstein 1997; Hill and Hughes 1998; Ranerup 2001; Gimmler 2001; Bohman 2004; Bernal 2006; Dahlberg 2007).

The approach to and quality of the discursive analysis in such studies varies considerably, as Davy Janssen and Raphael Kies point out in their review of existing research on *deliberative democracy* online. They note several weaknesses in this literature, including differences between the criteria that studies use for "deliberation" and a rigidly deductive approach in which online deliberation is compared to certain criteria set out by Jürgen Habermas and judged to either fit or not fit the Habermasian ideal. The latter weakness is particularly problematic, Janssen and Kies argue, because there is a real difference between the kinds of forums Habermas has in mind in his writing and those that are established online. They ask,

> to what degree can we apply Habermasian criteria to an online forum that is purely discursive, not tied to any decision making and not part of institutional politics? In this type of forum people discuss politics but are not looking for agreement or consensus, whereas in the Habermasian framework conversations are directed at some outcome, agreement, or consensus.
>
> *(2005, 331)*

This brings us to a consideration of the similarities and differences between the Internet-mediated network public and its closest pre-Internet equivalents—the coffee shop, bookstore, or local watering hole. In practice, online forums *are* more like these offline cognates, than they are like the sites Habermas addresses in his writing. For the most part, online forums have little in common with civic groups that have established reliable, consistent conduits for channeling opinion from local publics to official decision-making bodies.

At the same time, however, it would be too hasty to assume that online forums should be of little or no interest to public-sphere theorists just because they do not conform neatly to the kinds of structure and setting assumed by a theory devised before the rise of the Internet. While deliberation within network publics may not always aim for consensus and the channeling of opinion to official decision makers, participants may decide to come together when there is a problem or crisis in order to circulate petitions, raise money, or engage in other actions designed to address an issue of shared concern.

In addition, [. . .] network publics can facilitate two activities not easily replicated within pre-Internet publics: first, the opportunity for thousands of dispersed others to make sense of and act upon far-away events by engaging in critical discussion and questioning; and, second, the opportunity to communicate, at least indirectly, with representatives of the state who may be actively present or passively "listening in" to the opinions expressed in the forum. [. . .]

Finally, we will consider how Internet-mediated publics facilitate a third kind of public-sphere activity—*the channeling of opinions to public officials and institutions*. While this channeling may occur from time to time within network publics, it is more likely to occur in *vertical publics,* whose participants are drawn together by more than a simple or passing interest in discussing a topic of shared interest. [. . .]

In its structure, the vertical public is characterized by formal leadership and by a formal process for establishing membership. "Leadership" here involves much more than having a designated moderator who sifts through messages, as is often the case in a network public. Likewise, it is not enough simply to sign up with an e-mail address to become a member. [. . .] In contrast to the low commitment and flexibility of the representational and network publics, belonging to a vertical public requires agreeing with the group's goal or mission and supporting that mission with time and, in some cases, financial contributions.

Because of the vertical public's more formal organization, its demand for the time and money of its members, and its often well defined mission, it is here that we are more likely to find that leaders have established channels of communication with public institutions or decision-making bodies. It is also within the vertical public that we would more legitimately look for the kind of Habermasian deliberation whose aim is to carefully evaluate ideas and come to a consensus acceptable to the majority. This is because [. . .] one of the key reasons for establishing a vertical public is the group's desire to achieve a clear goal, or set of goals, to be implemented offline.

With respect to public-sphere theory, the vertical public differs in some significant ways from its closest pre-Internet equivalents. One key difference is that participants may be spread out among different nation-states and may read and write in different languages. The former presents both advantages and disadvantages. One disadvantage is that participants may not be citizens of the state they are trying to influence, which may diminish the power of their voice and effectiveness. On the other hand, the dispersal of the membership may be a strength when the state in question is economically underdeveloped or politically authoritarian. In either case, having access to committed members outside the targeted nation-state may mean access to critically needed material or political resources. Vertical publics, then, require the development of public-sphere theory that deals well with the special circumstances of communication and action at the transnational, transcultural, and trans-linguistic levels. [. . .]

The deliberation and channeling of opinion to non-governmental and state actors makes the vertical public one of the most intriguing Internet-mediated types for public-sphere theorists. In addition to facilitating political discussion, some of these groups raise large sums of money for development projects in their home countries as part of their group mission. [. . .] Their demonstrated capacity to mobilize significant resources and to call forth social and political commitment in members devoted to nation building is proof that we need a great deal of on- and offline research on this and other kinds of vertical publics.[2]

Within the framework of public-sphere theory, these groups are especially intriguing because they provide a new and compelling way to extend the discursive and political space of a country far beyond the borders of the territorial nation-state. Vertical publics are, in this sense, an extension of the kinds of activities common in the "transnational communities" researchers have discussed in the literature on transnational migration (Glick-Schiller et al. 1992; Smith 1993; Glick-Schiller and Fouron 2001; Levitt 2001). At their best, such forums help diaspora or solidarity groups to consolidate and transmit their opinions and concerns to state officials, to receive a response, and to implement specific projects on the ground. We need to identify and study more vertical publics, however, in order to better understand their possibilities and limits.

It is my hope that the delineation of the three types of Internet-mediated publics presented here will help to better focus future research on the Internet and public sphere within diaspora communities. The first step toward this improved focus is to realize that we must pay attention to the varied structures of Internet-mediated publics and be clear about what kinds of public-sphere activity we can reasonably expect to find in those publics. The distinction between types also points to some ways in which public-sphere theory needs to adapt to the reality of the Internet. While the discussion of representational publics suggests that these can easily be integrated into pre-Internet theory on the public sphere, network and vertical publics pose new challenges. Within network publics, we need a better understanding of how participants can responsibly engage with issues and problems at a distance. Within vertical publics, we confront the issue of multiple languages and the difficulty of negotiating differences when politically sensitive issues may make the uncertain identity of users a potential threat to group members. While there is much promising research, we are still in the beginning stages of developing public-sphere theory that deals adequately with the challenges of the new and complex social worlds facilitated by the Internet.

Notes

1 This is true so long as the participants are located in a wealthy country with widespread Internet access, or are able to access some of the few Internet-connected venues in Haiti.

2 I was able to conduct several interviews with Somaliland Forum founders and members, but because one must be a Somalilander in order to join, it was not possible for me to go much further with this line of research. My initial work, however, allowed me to have a fascinating glimpse at the comprehensiveness and complexity of this group.

References

Benhabib, Seyla. 1992. "Models of Public Space: Hannah Arendt, the Liberal Tradition, and Jurgen Habermas." *Habermas and the Public Sphere.* Ed. Craig Calhoun. Cambridge, MA: MITP. 73–98.

Bernal, Victoria. 2006. "Diaspora, Cyberspace, and Political Imagination; the Eritrean Diaspora Online." *Global Networks* 6: 161–79.

Bohman, James. 2004. "Expanding Dialogue: The Internet, the Public Sphere and Prospects for Transnational Democracy." *After Habermas: New Perspectives on the Public Sphere.* Ed. Nick Crossley and John Michael Roberta. Oxford: Blackwell, 131–55.

Buchstein, Hubertus. 1997. "Bytes That Bite: The Internet and Deliberative Democracy." *Constellations* 4: 248–63.

Calhoun, Craig, ed. 1992. *Habermas and the Public Sphere.* Cambridge, MA: MITP.

Dahlberg, Lincoln. 2007. "Rethinking the Fragmentation of the Cyberpublic: From Consensus to Contestation." *New Media and Society* 9: 827–47.

Fraser, Nancy. 1992. "Rethinking the Public Sphere: A Contribution to the Critique of Actually Existing Democracy." *Habermas and the Public Sphere.* Ed. Craig Calhoun. Cambridge, MA: MITP. 109–42.

Gimmler, Antje. 2001. "Deliberative Democracy, the Public Sphere and the Internet." *Philosophy and Social Criticism* 27.4: 21–39.

Glick-Schiller, Nina, and George Fouron. 2001. *Georges Woke Up Laughing: Long-Distance Nationalism and the Search for Home.* Durham, NC: Duke UP.

Glick-Schiller, Nina, Linda Basch, and Cristina Blanc-Szanton. 1992. *Towards a Transnational Perspective on Migration: Race, Class, Ethnicity, and Nationalism Reconsidered.* New York: New York Academy of Sciences.

Habermas, Jürgen. 1991. *The Structural Transformation of the Public Sphere: An Inquiry into a Category of Bourgeois Society.* Trans. Thomas Burger. Cambridge, MA: MITP.

Habermas, Jürgen. 1996. *Between Facts and Norms.* Trans. William Rehg. Cambridge, MA: MITP.

Hill, Kevin, and John Hughes. 1998. *Cyberpolitics: Citizen Activism in the Age of the Internet.* New York: Rowman.

Janssen, Davy, and Raphael Kies. 2005. "Online Forums and Deliberative Democracy." *Acta Politica* 40: 317–36.

Levitt, Peggy. 2001. *The Transnational Villagers.* Berkeley: U of California P.

Mitra, Ananda. 2005. "Creating Immigrant Identities in Cybernetic Space: Examples from a Non-resident Indian Website." *Media, Culture, and Society* 27: 371–90.

Rai, Amit S. 1995. "India Online: Electronic Bulletin Boards and the Construction of a Diasporic Hindu Identity." *Diaspora* 4: 31–57.

Ranerup, Agneta. 2001. "Online Forums as a Tool for People-Centered Governance." *Community Informatics: Shaping Computer-Mediated Social Relations.* Ed. Leigh Keeble and Brian Loader. New York: Routledge, 205–19.

Schneider, Steven M. 1996. "Creating a Democratic Public Sphere Through Political Discussion: A Case Study of Abortion Conversation on the Internet." *Social Science Computer Review* 14: 373–93.

Smith, Robert. 1993. *"Los ausentes siempre presentes:* The Imagining, Making and Politics of a Transnational Community between New York City and Ticuani, Puebla." Papers on Latin America No. 27. New York: Inst. of Latin American and Iberian Studies, Columbia U.

Sökefeld, Martin. 2002. "Alevism Online: Re-imagining a Community in Virtual Space." *Diaspora* 11: 85–123.

37

NATIONS, MIGRATION, AND THE WORLD WIDE WEB OF POLITICS

Victoria Bernal

This book examines Eritrean politics online to reveal the ways that new media and mobilities are transforming sovereignty and citizenship. A focus on diaspora and cyber-space reveals nations as dynamic forms that not only are increasingly difficult to map as bounded communities but also operate through networks in significant ways. There is a synergy between new communications technologies and migration that is changing politics. Relations of citizenship and sovereignty once rooted in national territory increasingly span borders, and the social contracts between citizens and states are being constructed and contested in new political contexts and spaces. There is a profound global shift underway as the mobility of people and the rise of internet communications in the twenty-first century alter the character of nations and the meanings of citizenship and sovereignty (Ong 1999; Al-Ali and Koser 2002; Appadurai 2003). New practices and ideals of citizenship are developing and forms of quasi-citizenship are emerging as industrialized nations grapple with noncitizens within their borders and less industrialized nations deal with diasporic populations that participate in their economies and politics from abroad (Balibar 2005; Glick-Schiller 2005; Coutin 2007). At the same time, the internet is allowing for the creation of an elastic political space that can serve to extend as well as to expose the limits of territorial sovereignty. The growing significance of diasporas coupled with the development of digital media have given rise to the nation as network.

In this book three strands of analysis—politics, media, and diaspora—are woven together to explore the nation as network. I develop the concept "infopolitics" to advance theories of sovereignty and understandings of the internet by foregrounding the management of information as a central aspect of politics. Infopolitics draws attention to the importance of relations of authorization and censorship that govern the ways knowledge is produced, accessed, and disseminated. The heart of this study is an ethnography of the vibrant Eritrean public sphere established on diaspora websites. My analysis of Eritrean politics online explores the significance of violence and conflict for the understanding of citizenship, the public sphere, and new media. Set in the context of Eritrea's turbulent history, the activities of the Eritrean diaspora online reveal the ways that sovereignty and citizenship are being reconfigured and reproduced by means of the internet.

In spring 2011 the Egyptian revolt, which some labeled a "Facebook Revolution," offered a new vision of the significance of the internet for political change. The way Egyptians used new media to circumvent and oppose a repressive regime is revealing. It shows, among other things, that many of our ideas and debates about the nature and potential of digital media are based in Western experience, and particularly, in Western middle-class consumer culture (Ginsburg 2008). Some of the most politically dynamic and innovative engagements with the internet are developed, however, by people in circumstances very different from those of quintessential Western computer users. In fact, by the time Egyptians and others throughout the Arab world drew the world's attention to their online organizing, Eritreans had been engaging in computer-mediated politics for well over a decade. In cyberspace, Eritreans in diaspora have developed a series of websites that continue to serve as an online public sphere where Eritreans around the world debate politics with each other, mobilize actions, and communicate their views to the Eritrean state and wider audiences. This study focuses on three key websites that have been central to this process—Dehai (www.dehai.org), Asmarino (www.asmarino.com), and Awate (www.awate.com).

The design and organization of these websites by their founders and web-managers, the ways they are used by posters, and the social texts, exchanges and activities they have generated offer insights into how political subjectivities are produced, policed, and transformed through the internet. Online Eritreans are engaged in articulating and revising the national narratives that bind Eritreans to each other and to the state as they take part in the construction of Eritrea as a nation and struggle over the dimensions and demands of sovereignty.

Eritrea is a small nation in the Horn of Africa that achieved nationhood in 1991. Eritrea's political culture and institutions, thus, have developed in the context of the growing significance of international migration and digital communications. Eritreans in many countries participate passionately in Eritrean politics, even though they hold citizenship in the countries where they live, work, and raise their children. While physically located outside of Eritrea, the diaspora is not outside Eritrean culture or politics. Moreover, they figure in the national imaginaries of Eritrea's leaders who have been actively cultivating the diaspora's involvement from abroad since before independence (Hepner and Conrad 2005). The resources Eritreans funnel to Eritrea from overseas are vital to the nation, contributing not only to national welfare but also to its resources for warfare (Bernal 2004, 2006; Fessehatzion 2005; Hepner 2009).

Through the web, the diaspora does much more than simply assuage their homesickness or vent their political passions. The websites are compelling for Eritreans in part because something is at stake—the shape and future of Eritrean national society. Online activities have off-line consequences. Eritrean posters shape public opinion, revise national history, mobilize demonstrators, amass funds for national projects, engage in protest, and exert influence and pressure on the government of Eritrea. We cannot understand these online activities simply as a feature of diaspora, but rather as part of the configuration of Eritrean nationhood. These innovative developments in Eritrean politics offer insights into the shifting meanings and experiences of citizenship and sovereignty in the contemporary context of migration, and elucidate the political significance of the internet.

Close readings of the impassioned, humorous, angry, and poetic posts of Eritreans in diaspora reveal their struggle to understand the political conflicts that have shaped their lives, even as they strive to shape Eritrea's future. Posts illuminate the meanings of war, migration, and national belonging in people's lives and illustrate the ways that state power is being reconfigured and reproduced. Websites are sites of conflict that make dominant nationalist discourses and alternative perspectives visible and legible as ordinary people articulate to each other what things mean to them in their own words and collectively construct accounts and analyses of the nation. The websites serve as public, communal space in cyberspace that is a staging ground for ideas and practices that have no off-line counterpart, either inside or outside of Eritrea. [. . .]

Like Eritreans, many populations of migrants and exiles are using the internet to connect with each other and with people and institutions of their homelands (Oiarzbal and Adoni 2010; Panagakos and Horst 2006; Gajjala and Gajjala 2008; Mannur 2003; Ndangam 2008; Ignacio 2005). This phenomenon is sometimes termed "digital diasporas" (Bernal 2005a; Diamandaki 2003; DeHart 2004; Brinkerhoff 2009). The online activities of diasporas are significant, moreover, because the rising influence of diasporas in the twenty-first century is a global trend (Knott and McLoughlin 2010; Clarke 2010; Diouf 2000). Diasporas, of course, have long existed and have been the subject of scholarship (Hall 1990; Clifford 1994; Gilroy 1993). But part of what motivates my study is a belief that contemporary migration and digital media are making a difference in what diaspora means for people and for nations (Piot 2010). Certainly contemporary diaspora populations experience relationships with their homelands that were not possible for the classical diasporas of Jews fleeing persecution and Africans taken overseas as slaves. But developments over the past two decades seem to indicate a disjuncture even with the experiences of more recent twentieth-century migrants and refugees. There is, moreover, a recent proliferation of groups identifying themselves as diasporas (Turner 2008b; Ryang and Lie 2009). Diasporas can be seen as "margins of the state" in Das and Poole's terms, which afford us insight into "the ways in which the conceptual boundaries of the state are extended and remade" (2004, 20).

Diasporas are increasingly being recognized as important players by governments, policy makers, donors, and scholars (Page and Mercer 2012; Lyons 2012). The economic flows of remittances and investment, in particular, attract attention, and much of the interest of official bodies and international agencies is focused rather narrowly on development and the economic activities of diasporas (World Bank 2006; UN 2006). Far less attention has been directed toward what we might think of as the "political remittances" of diasporas and the ways geographic mobility and the internet are facilitating new forms of political agency and giving rise to new transnational public spheres where struggles over meanings, resources, and power are mobilized. [. . .]

Infopolitics and violence

I contend that power, violence, and the politics of knowledge need to be placed at the center of analyses of the internet. I developed the concept of infopolitics to address the way that power is exercised and expressed through communication and through control over media, circulation, censorship, and authorization. Notions like "the information age," "information technologies," and "the digital divide" are misleading in their suggestion that the internet is foremost about access to "information" as if this were a preexisting, neutral, social good. Power relations are embedded in the circulation of knowledge and the management of information constitutes a central aspect of politics and a dimension of sovereignty. State power is constructed not only through control exercised over territory and people, but also through control over the production and communication of knowledge, information, narratives, and symbols. The exercise of infopolitical power by states is both more important and more difficult now that new media are decentralizing communication, opening up alternative avenues of knowledge production and distribution. Attending to infopolitics brings into focus aspects of media that have been undertheorized.

Anderson's (1991) influential conception of nations as imagined communities largely constructs nationalism in terms of a gentle process of belonging and mutual recognition mediated by newspapers and other national forms like the census and the museum, rather than in terms of the kinds of violent struggles over sovereignty, territory, and freedom of expression that have characterized Eritrea's formation as a nation. Michael Warner's (2005) important work on the nature of publics and public spheres also takes for granted the condition of freedom of expression without fear of violent reprisal. Discussions of the networked connectivity offered by the internet, likewise, often downplay or ignore altogether the role the internet might play in situations of violence or war (Castells 2001; Escobar 2000; Ess 2001; Wilson and Peterson 2002). It is only recently that a body of scholarship has emerged that explores questions of violence in relation to the internet (Axel 2004; Whitaker 2007; Turner 2008a, 2008b).

The transformative power of the internet is not that it allows access to information, but rather that it provides a public venue that allows ordinary people to question official discourse, to tell their own stories, to recontextualize existing knowledge and official narratives, and to create their own social networks for sharing ideas and analyzing information, rather than depending on mainstream media and official sources. This has wide-ranging political implications. As Eickelman and Anderson note (2003, 2), "The combination of new media and new contributors . . . feeds into new senses of a public space that is discursive, performative, and participative, and not confined to formal institutions recognized by state authorities."

While questions of access to information and to technology, sometimes framed as "the digital divide," have shaped much thinking about the significance of the internet, for Eritreans it was actually the limited access to the internet in Eritrea that heightened the political importance of the online public sphere at its outset. Access to the internet within Eritrea was largely confined to government elites through the 1990s, so the internet served Eritreans in diaspora, in part, as a special means of communicating their views to the Eritrean state. As the notion of infopolitics is meant to convey, moreover, the internet is not about communication per se any more than it is about information *sui generis*. What makes the internet a powerful and transformative medium is that ordinary people are able to use cyberspace as an arena in which they collectively struggle to narrate history, frame debates, and seek to form shared understandings beyond the control of political authorities or the commercial censorship of mass media. The fact that people can engage in these activities in a virtual space without the same risks of violence present in a physical space is particularly significant for many populations. The new perspectives that are generated in cyberspace reverberate beyond it and can serve as the basis for mobilization and action.

Nations as networks

If nations were once imagined communities as Anderson (1991) famously described them, in the current age of digital communications and migration it is more apt to think of nations as networks. No longer does the image of a nation as a bounded community imagined on a larger scale fit today's world where it is ever less clear what the boundaries of national territories enclose or exclude. National borders are porous, and relations once rooted in national territory—from family to livelihoods to political relationships—increasingly span borders, linking far-flung relatives and fellow nationals to each other and to other people and institutions in complex sociopolitical relationships. Digital media play a significant role by providing easy, cheap, and immediate means of communication across legal and institutional barriers as well as across geographical distances. Transformations of national politics and sovereignty are arising not only from the mobility of populations but also from new modes of communication.

Some of these cross-border relationships were brought into focus by scholarship on transnationalism (Basch, Schiller, and Blanc 1994; Portes, Guarnizo, and Landolt 1999). But attention tended to focus rather narrowly on the migrants who participate in more than one nation, rather than on the transformations of state power and the form of the nation. At the same time, attention to economic globalization and transnational cultural flows led some scholars to argue that the significance of nations was declining (Appadurai 1996; Hannerz 1996; Dahan and Sheffer 2001). In previous work, I drew on the case of Eritrea and its diaspora to argue that transnationalism doe not necessarily work in opposition to nations but can support nations and strengthen nationalism (Bernal 2004). Today much evidence attests to the continued force of nation-states in the world, globalization and transnationalism notwithstanding. The relationships between states and citizens are hardly dissolving, but they are undergoing transformations, operating as networks that connect people and nations in new ways.

In thinking about the international mobility of individuals and populations, I find the concept of diaspora useful because it includes a wider range of political connections and loyalties than terms such as migrant or immigrant typically do. However, migrants, refugees, exiles, immigrants, and diasporas are not distinct populations; they are political forms that overlap and morph into one another. Scholarship on international migration focused on migrants' relations to states often does so through the narrow framework of a binary opposition between legal and illegal status. While legal status certainly has consequences in people's lives, the focus on citizenship as a legal status may obscure from view the growing range of intermediate or hybrid forms of national inclusion and belonging (Coutin 2007; Laguerre 2006; Glick-Schiller 2005). Furthermore, people's sense of belonging and political engagement may not correspond to their legal papers (Baker-Cristales 2008). Increasingly, diasporas are being enfranchised and included in various ways as nationals in their states of origins (Ong 1999; Itzigsohn 2012). We have not yet developed terminology to cover some of these relationships. In the case of Eritreans in diaspora and the Eritrean state, I use the term "diasporic citizenship" to reflect the fact that their membership in the nation is distinct from legal citizenship.

I argue that such relationships between states and diasporas are altering the meanings and practices of citizenship and sovereignty. Therefore, it is not simply the forms of diasporic citizenship that we need to understand, but the changing nature of relationships between people and states around the world. This comes into view more fully when we understand citizenship less as a legal status and more as a relationship of people to the state. As Sieder (2001, 203) writes:

> Citizenship is often conceived of as a fixed and nonnegotiable set of rights and obligations, such as those embodied in a written constitution. However, it is in fact best understood as a dynamic process rather than a static juridical construct. Both in terms of its legal attributes and its social content, citizenship is contested and constantly renegotiated and reinterpreted.

Diasporas are changing the ways states construct citizenship. One reason for this in the global south is the importance of remittances in national economies; vital human resources for the state lie outside its borders. In the case of Eritrea, the citizenship law established after independence defined citizenship through descent from an Eritrean father or mother rather than birthplace, so that Eritreans in diaspora and their children born abroad could be considered citizens. Elsewhere, particularly in the global north, changes in citizenship are designed to exclude certain populations. In Ireland, for example, citizenship was recently redefined around Irish heritage rather than place of birth to exclude the children of migrants from the global south, and from Africa in particular, born in Ireland (Moran 2012). Because so much migration is from the global south to wealthier countries of the global north, diasporas are produced through the combination of exclusionary practices on the part of northern nations toward certain migrants and inclusionary practices on the part of homelands in the global south. Coinciding with the growing significance of diasporas to their nations of origin, the rise of new communications technologies has made migrants' ongoing engagements with the societies they left behind increasingly immediate and continuous.

References

Al-Ali, Nadje, and Khalid Koser, eds. 2002. *New Approaches to Migration?: Transnational Communities and the Transformation of Home*. London: Routledge.

Anderson, Benedict. 1991. *Imagined Communities: Reflections on the Origin and Spread Of Nationalism*. New York: Verso.

Appadurai, Arjun. 1996. *Modernity at Large: Cultural Dimensions of Globalization*. Minneapolis: University of Minnesota Press.

———. 2003. "Sovereignty Without Territoriality: Notes for a Postnational Geography." In *The Anthropology of Space and Place*, edited by Setha Lo and Denise Lawrence-Zuanisa, 337–50. Malden: Blackwell Publications.

Axel, Brian Keith. 2004. "The Context of Diaspora." *Cultural Anthropology* 19 (1): 26–60.

Baker-Cristales, Beth. 2008. "Magical Pursuits: Legitimacy and Representation in a Transnational Political Field." *American Anthropologist* 110 (3): 349–59.

Balibar, Etienne. 2005. "Difference, Otherness, Exclusion." *Parallax* 11 (1): 19–34.

Basch, Linda Green, Nina Glick Schiller, and Cristina Szanton Blanc. 1994. *Nations Unbound: Transnational Projects, Post-colonial Predicaments, and De-territorialized Nation-States*. Langhorne: Gordon and Breach.

Bernal, Victoria. 2004. "Eritrea Goes Global: Reflections on Nationalism in a Transnational Era." *Cultural Anthropology* 19 (1): 1–25.

———. 2005a. "Digital Diaspora: Conflict, Community, and Celebrity in Virtual Eritrea." *Eritrean Studies Review* 4 (2): 185–210.

———. 2006. "Diaspora, Cyberspace, and Political Imagination." *Global Networks: A Journal of Transnational Affairs* 6 (2): 161–80.

Brinkerhoff, Jennifer. 2009. *Digital Diasporas: Identity and Transnational Engagement*. Cambridge University Press: Cambridge.

Castells, Manuel. 2001. *The Internet Galaxy: Reflections on the Internet, Business, and Society*. Oxford: Oxford University Press.

Clarke, Kamari Maxine. 2010. "New Spheres of Transnational Formations: Mobilizations of Humanitarian Diasporas." *Transforming Anthropology* 18 (1): 48–65.

Clifford, James. 1994. "Diasporas." *Cultural Anthropology* 9 (3): 302–38.

Coutin, Susan. 2007. *Nations of Emigrants: Shifting Boundaries of Citizenship in El Salvador and the United States*. Ithaca: Cornell University Press.

Dahan, Michael, and Gabriel Sheffer. 2001. "Ethnic Groups and Distance Shrinking Communication Technologies." *Nationalism & Ethnic Politics* 7 (1): 85–107.

Das, Veena, and Deborah Poole. 2004. "State and Its Margins: Comparative Ethnographies." In *Anthropology in the Margins of the State*, edited by Veena Das and Deborah Poole, 3–34. Sante Fe: School of American Research Press, and Oxford: James Currey.

DeHart, Monica. 2004. "'*Hermano* Entrepreneurs!' Constructing a Latino Diaspora across the Digital Divide." *Diaspora* 13 (2/3): 253–78.

Diamandaki, Katerina. 2003. "Virtual Ethnicity and Digital Diasporas: Identity Construction in Cyberspace." *Global Media Journal* 2 (2): not numbered. American Edition, Graduate section, paper 10. www.academia.edu/5102541/Virtual_ethnicity_and_digital_diasporas_Identity_construction_in_cyberspace_Global_Media_Journal_2_2_Spring_2003. Accessed online April 21, 2011.

Diouf, Mamadou. 2000. "The Senegalese Murid Trade Diaspora and the Making of a Vernacular Cosmopolitanism." *Public Culture* 12 (3): 679–702.

Eickelman, Dale F., and Jon W. Anderson. 2003. "Redefining Muslim Publics." In *New Media in the Muslim World*, edited by Dale E. Eickelman and Jon W. Anderson, 1–18. Bloomington: Indiana University Press.

Escobar, Arturo. 2000. "Welcome to Cyberia." In *The Cybercultures Reader*, edited by David Bell and Barbara M. Kennedy, 56–76. London: Routledge.

Ess, Charles. 2001. "Introduction: What's Culture Got to Do with It? Cultural Collisions in the Electronic Global Village, Creative Interferences, and the Rise of Culturally-Mediated Computing." In *Culture, Technology, Communication: Towards an Intercultural Global Village*, edited by Charles Ess, 1–50. Albany: State University of New York Press.

Fessehatzion, Tekie. 2005. "Eritrea's Remittance-Based Economy: Conjectures and Musings." Special Issue–Eritrea Abroad: Critical Perspectives on the Global Diaspora, edited by Tricia Hepner and Bettina Conrad. *Eritrean Studies Review* 4 (2): 165–84.

Gajjala, Radhika, and Venkataramana Gajjala, eds. 2008. *South Asian Technospaces*. New York: Peter Lang.

Gilroy, Paul. 1993. *The Black Atlantic: Modernity and Double Consciousness*. Cambridge: Harvard University Press.

Ginsburg, Faye. 2008. "Rethinking the Digital Age." In *Media and Social Theory*, edited by D. Hesmond-halgh and J. Toynbee, 127–44. London: Routledge.

Glick-Schiller, Nina. 2005. "Transborder Citizenship: An Outcome of Legal Pluralism within Trans-national Fields." In *Mobile People, Mobile Law*, edited by Franz von Benda-Beckman, Keebot von Benda-Beckman, and Anne Griffiths. London: Ashgate.

Hall, Stuart. 1990. "Cultural Identity and Diaspora." In *Identity, Community, Culture, Difference*, edited by Jonathan Rutherford, 222–37. London: Lawrence and Wishart.

Hannerz, Ulf. 1996. *Transnational Connections: Culture, People, Places*. London: Routledge.

Hepner, Tricia. 2009. *Soldiers, Martyrs, Traitors, and Exiles: Political Conflict in Eritrea and the Diaspora*. Philadelphia: University of Pennsylvania Press.

Hepner, Tricia Redeker, and Bettina Conrad. 2005. "Eritrea Abroad: An Introduction." *Eritrean Studies Review* 4 (2): v–xvii.

Ignacio, Emily. 2005. *Building Diaspora: Filipino Community Formation on the Internet*. New Brunswick: Rutgers University Press.

Itzigsohn, Jose. 2012. "A 'Transnational Nation'?: Migration and the Boundaries of Belonging." In *Politics from Afar: Transnational Diasporas and Networks*, edited by Terence Lyons and Peter Mandaville, 181–96. London: Hurst and Company.

Knott, Kim, and Sean McLoughlin, eds. 2010. *Diasporas: Concepts, Intersections, Identities*. London: Zed.

Laguerre, Michel S. 2006. *Diaspora, Politics, and Globalization*. New York: Palgrave MacMillan.

Lyons, Terrence. 2012. "Transnational Politics in Ethiopia: Diaspora Mobilization and Contentious Politics." In *Politics from Afar: Transnational Diasporas and Networks*, edited by Terrence Lyons and Peter Mandaville, 141–56. London: C. Hurst and Company.

Mannur, Anita. 2003 "Postscript: Cyberscapes and the Interfacing of Diasporas." In *Theorizing Diaspora*, edited by Jana Evans Braziel and Anita Mannur, 283–90. Malden: Blackwell Publishing.

Moran, Erin Joy. 2012. *Geographies of Belonging: Mapping Migrant Imaginaries in Ireland's Ailing Celtic Tiger*. PhD thesis, University of California-Irvine.

Ndangam, Lilian. 2008. "Free Lunch? Cameroon's Diaspora and Online News Publishing." *New Media and Society* 10 (4): 585–604.

Oiarzbal, Pedro, and Alonso Adoni, eds. 2010. *Diasporas in the New Media Age: Identity Politics, and Community*. Reno University of Nevada Press.

Ong, Aihwa. 1999. *Flexible Citizenship: The Cultural Logics of Transnationality*. Durham: Duke University Press.

Page, Ben, and Claire Mercer. 2012. "Why Do People Do Stuff? Reconceptualizing Remittance Behavior in Diaspora-Development Research and Policy." *Progress in Development Studies* 12 (1): 1–18.

Panagakos, Anastasia, and Heather A. Horst. 2006. "Return to Cyberia: Technology and The Social Worlds of Transnational Migrants." *Global Networks: A Journal of Transnational Affairs* 6 (2): 109–24.

Piot, Charles. 2010. *Nostalgia for the Future*. Chicago: University of Chicago Press.

Portes, Alejandro, Luis E. Guarnizo, and Patricia Landolt. 1999. "The Study of Transnationalism: Pitfalls and Promise of an Emergent Research Field." *Ethnic And Racial Studies* 22 (2): 217–37.

Ryang, Sonia, and John Lie, eds. 2009. *Diaspora without Homeland: Being Korean in Japan*. Berkeley: University of California Press.

Sieder, Rachel. 2001. "Rethinking Citizenship: Reforming Law in Postwar Guatemala." In *States of Imagination: Ethnographic Explorations of the Postcolonial State*, edited by Thomas Blom Hansen and Finn Stepputat, 203–20. Durham: Duke University Press.

Turner, Simon. 2008a. "Studying the Tensions of Transnational Engagement: From the Nuclear Family to the World-Wide Web." *Journal of Ethnic and Migration Studies* 34 (7): 1049–56.

———. 2008b. "Cyberwars of Words: Expressing the Unspeakable in Burundi's Diaspora." *Journal of Ethnic and Migration Studies* 34 (7): 1161–80.

United Nations. 2006. "Summary of the High-level Dialogue on International Migration and Develop-ment." UN General Assembly. https://documents-dds-ny.un.org/doc/UNDOC/GEN/N06/571/02/PDF/N0657102.pdf?OpenElement. Accessed 18 July, 2017.

Warner, Michael. 2005. *Publics and Counterpublics*. Zone Books: New York.

Whitaker, Mark P. 2007. *Learning Politics From Sivaram: The Life and Death of a Revolutionary Tamil Journalist in Sri Lanka.* London: Pluto Press.

Wilson, Samuel M., and Leighton C. Peterson. 2002. "The Anthropology of Online Communities." *Annual Review of Anthropology* 31: 449–67.

World Bank. 2006. "Migration, Remittances and Economic Development: The World Bank Program." International Symposium on International Migration and Development, Turin, June 28–30. www.un.org/esa/population/migration/turin/Turin_statements/WORLDBANK.pdf. Accessed May 20, 2011.

INDEX

9/11 20, 51

Abedi, M. 150
Aboulela, L. 187
accented cinema 201; as mode or style 212–13, 215; as offshoot of Third Cinema 214–15; revision of Naficy's definition of 218–19; and the work of Ang Lee 220–1; *see also* Third Cinema
Achebe, C. 190
Adorno, T. 142, 186–7
African Americans 209–10; and the black Atlantic 57–64; estimated number of 52; and literature 190–3, 205
African diaspora 2, 11, 17, 52, 205; and the black Atlantic 57–64, 135; centrality to diasporic debate 187; as created by the slave trade xviii; cyberspace and democracy in 86; and immigration model of diaspora 13–14; as a resource for diasporic writers 191–3; and transnationalism 160, 135; as a 'victim' diaspora 20
Agamben, G. xiv, 69, 80
Agier, M. xiv
Ahmed, A.S. 148
Ahmed, S. 128, 150, 182–3
Aidoo, A.A. 190
Akenson, D. 18
Alevism 30
alienation 114, 131, 127, 231; and citizenship 80; constitutive alienation (Derrida) 122–3; in diasporic cinema 213, 219; in diasporic communities 13; and hybridity 127, 135; and the modern subject 107; in Muslim Britain 150
Aloft 199
Alonso, A. 245, 247–51
Al-Rasheed, M. 30
Althusser, L. 110, 130

Anand, D. 107, 114–18
Anderson, B. 46; imagined communities 42–3, 187, 189, 233, 249, 259
Anderson, J.W. 262
Angé, M.: the 'nonplace' 197
Anthias, F. 18, 171, 225, 240; on concept of hybridity 127–8; evaluating diaspora 157–62; on intersectionality 154, 165; on new hybridities 133–8; translocational positionality 135–7
Anzaldúa, G. 166, 179n17
Appadurai, A. 218, 257; *Modernity at Large* 51, 182, 193, 232, 248, 260
Appiah, A.K. xxi, 57
'Arab Spring' 244
Armenian diaspora 5–9, 32, 85, 110–12, 242; becoming 'less diasporic' in the US 53–4; and cinema 210; estimated size of 52; paradigmatic diaspora experience xx–xxi, 17, 43, 106, 209; and Turkish genocide of 1915 xviii; as a 'victim' diaspora 20
Ashcroft, B. xvi, 3, 106
assimilation 2, 38, 54, 139, 202, 212, 250; assimilationist national ideologies 10, 50–1, 80, 126; resistance to 10–13, 18; 'return of assimilation' (Brubaker) 51; 'soft and 'hard' types of 96
asylum seekers xiv–xv, xix, 51, 163; ethical issues regarding 107; and the law 140
Australia 103, 140; and detention of asylum-seekers xiv; and Hindu immigration 38; indigenous population 83, 235

Bakalian, A.P. 53
Baker, H.A. Jr. 57
Bakhtin, M.M. 136, 152n1, 204–5
Bangladeshi diaspora 211, 237; in the Gulf 140; in the UK 117

Made in the USA
Las Vegas, NV
24 August 2023